The Reception of Learned Law in Fourteenth- and Fifteenth-Century Frisia

Medieval Law and Its Practice

VOLUME 42

The titles published in this series are listed at *brill.com/mlip*

The Reception of Learned Law in Fourteenth- and Fifteenth-Century Frisia

By

Marvin Wiegand

BRILL

LEIDEN | BOSTON

The research project was funded by the Frysk Akademyfûns (FAF).

Cover illustration: Leeuwarden, Tresoar : PBF hs R 6 (image 250, https://db.ecodices.nl/detail/529/overview, last accessed 30 May 2024).

Library of Congress Cataloging-in-Publication Data

Names: Wiegand, Marvin, author.
Title: The reception of learned law in fourteenth- and fifteenth century Frisia / Marvin Wiegand.
Description: Leiden ; Boston : Brill, 2024. | Series: Medieval law and its practice, 1873-8176 ; volume 42 | Includes bibliographical references and index.
Identifiers: LCCN 2024047036 | ISBN 9789004709928 (hardback) | ISBN 9789004712706 (ebook)
Subjects: LCSH: Law, Frisian–History. | Lex Frisionum.
Classification: LCC KJ552 .W54 2024 | DDC 349.43/509023–dc23/eng/20241008
LC record available at https://lccn.loc.gov/2024047036

Typeface for the Latin, Greek, and Cyrillic scripts: "Brill". See and download: brill.com/brill-typeface.

ISSN 1873-8176
ISBN 978-90-04-70992-8 (hardback)
ISBN 978-90-04-71270-6 (e-book)
DOI 10.1163/9789004712706

This book is printed on acid-free paper and produced in a sustainable manner.

Contents

Figures and Tables

Figures

Tables

Abbreviations

Old Frisian Manuscripts and Incunabula

A	*Codex Aysma* (in Buma et al., *Codex Aysma*)
D	Druk (in Nijdam et al., *Frisian Land Law*)
Do	Dousa (in Breuker, *Landrecht der Vriesne*)
F	*Codex Fivelgo* (in Buma, Ebel, *Das Fivelgoer Recht*)
J	*Jus Munincipale Frisionum* (in Buma et al., *Westerlauwerssches Recht* I + II)
P	*Codex Parisiensis* (in Gerbenzon, *Codex Parisiensis*)
Ro	*Codex Roorda* (unpublished)
U	*Codex Unia* (unpublished, partial texts in Brouwer, *Thet Autentica Riocht*)

Old Frisian Law Texts

Aut	*Thet Autentica Riocht*
Dom	*The Eight Provisions*
Exc	*Excerpta Legum*
JF	*Jurisprudentia Frisica*
K^{17}	*The Seventeen Statutes*
L^{24}	*The Twenty-four Land Laws*
Mgn	*The Statutes of Magnus*
PrJ	*Processus Iudicii*
Rud	*The Book of Emperor Rudolf*
RW	*Rechten ende Wilkoeren*
Sel	*The Treatise on the Seven Sealands*
Ska	*On Serious Assaults*
SkRa	*The Older Skelta Law*
SkRb	*The Younger Skelta Law*
SWl	*The Synodical Law of Central Frisia*
We^{17}	*Exceptions to the 17th Statute*
W^5D	*The Statutes of the Five Districts*
WUps	*The Statutes of Opstalsbam*

Roman Law Texts

C./Cod.	*Codex Iustiniani*
D./Dig.	*Digesta*

Inst.	*Institutiones*
Nov.	*Novellae Constitutiones*

Canon Law Texts

D	*Decretum Gratiani: distinctiones*
C. q. c.	*Decretum Gratiani: causae, quaestio,*
X	*Liber Extra*
VI	*Liber Sextus*

Other Abbreviations

FT	*Friese Testamenten tot 1550*
LF	*Liber feudorum*
OF	Old Frisian

Glossary

Asega	The 'law-sayer', a type of judge, legal expert
Bannere	Summoner and sheriff
Erbenlaub	The heir's consent to alienation of property
Ferdban	Proclamation of peace of a sale
Frana	Magistrate and representative of the count
Gretman	Judge, president of the court, replaced the *skelta*
Ius commune	The Medieval common law, Learned law
Mund	A guardian
Mundskip	Guardianship of a *mund*
Niarkap	The right to take over a sale
Skelta	Judge, president of the court
Wergild	'Man compensation'
Wetma	A provision for a woman's widowhood

CHAPTER 1

Introduction

> Keep to laws that are old, but food that is fresh.[1]

∴

These words are attributed to the ancient Greek king of Corinth (died 585 BC), and their meaning can be readily understood. Fresh food, of course, is healthier than the alternative, but a law that stood the test of time, has proven itself to be worthy or, in modern language, "If it ain't broke, don't fix it." This study concerns a period and place where old laws were no longer kept, and the people turned not only to fresh food but to fresh law. In the late Middle Ages, the Frisian people living along the coast of the North Sea began a transformation of their legal system, from their classical, customary law to a new system that incorporated new norms and methods. Why this transformation took place, is the central question of this study.

When old laws and customs are expelled and new, foreign ones received, we can expect that people object to such change. After all, the existing customs stood the test of time, so why abandon them now? An unknown Frisian litigant in the early 15th century, expresses a similar sentiment. When responding to an ecclesiastical rule about priests participating in the making of a last will, the litigant asks: "However, does this also apply according to custom of the fatherland, which is the best interpretation of the laws?"[2] The question is whether the new rule of ecclesiastical law also applies if the custom of Frisia contradicts it. The unknown litigant considered the old customs to be stronger than any new rules, and thus, may have argued for keeping to the old laws.

Despite the above comment, Frisian law changed significantly during the Late Middle Ages and the Early Modern Period. The language of the litigant's

1 Loosely translated into English from German in Snell, *Leben und Meinungen*, p. 103.

2 *A*, I (Exc) 488, p. 340: *Sed numquid eciam et secundum consuetudinem patrie, que est optima legum interpres?* A detailed analysis of this sentence and the entire provision follows in chapter 5.6.4.

 | DOI:10.1163/9789004712706_002

question is indicative of this aspect: the litigant wrote in Latin, the language of learned people in the Middle Ages, rather than the vernacular Old Frisian. However, the transformation of the Frisian legal system did not stop there. Two hundred years later, the Frisian scholar Ulrik Huber (1636–1694) wrote: "[…] that the Roman law is maintained here in a purer and more downright form than in any region, country or state in Christendom."[3] Huber wrote this about his own time, noting a strong presence of Roman law in the Frisian legal system in the 17th century. Frisian law appears to have undergone a remarkable journey from the 15th to the 17th century, experiencing a significant reception of the foreign Roman law.

'Reception' refers to a process in legal theory in which a recipient legal culture takes on ('receives') elements of another legal culture.[4] Some scholars rightfully ask how reception of foreign legal elements could occur in Frisia, considering the rich material of indigenous Frisian law. Scholars sometimes assume that this reception was a development of the late 15th and early 16th centuries.[5] However, Frisians were familiar with both Canon and Roman law (referred to as 'learned laws') before the 15th century. Therefore, one cannot look at that period without considering how Frisians engaged with different legal traditions long before 1500.

Frisia and its inhabitants experienced a long period of self-governance without any form of princely rule or personal servitude.[6] Considering the change in Frisian law in the 14th and 15th centuries, one fact becomes clear: it was the Frisians themselves, locally and communally, who produced this change. In contrast to much of the rest of Europe, there was no authority that introduced legislation or imposed a new legal code. During this time the Frisians themselves reshaped their legal system. Changes after 1500, however, were of a different kind and brought forth by new rulers.

Originally, this research was the first in a two-part project: an examination of the reception of learned law in Frisia until 1500; and a subsequent study of the period after 1500. Although the second part of the project will not be realized in the short term, this should not imply that no further research is required. While the story of reception in Frisia continues into the Early Modern Period,

3 *Dat het roomsche recht hier suiverder en platter onderhouden wort, als in eenig deel, land of staet van de Christene wereld.* Huber, *Heedendaegse*, 1.11.47, p. 9f. English translation in: Huber, *Jurisprudence*, p. 8.

4 More on this in chapter 1.4.

5 Feenstra, "Römisches Recht", pp. 27 and 34.

6 This period is called the 'Frisian freedom'. The concept of what the freedom meant, changed over time, see Vries, "Frisonica libertas", p. 8ff. More on this in chapter 1.2.

this present study is limited to the Middle Ages, when the Frisians—free of central authority—reshaped their own legal system. This unique aspect makes researching reception of law in Frisia especially interesting.

An analysis of primary sources demonstrates that Frisian jurists interacted with various legal traditions, namely their own indigenous law and what were known as 'learned laws' (i.e., Roman and Canon law). Legal sources reveal—as will become clear later—why and how Frisians altered their customary system of law. The interaction between legal traditions sometimes followed non-identical patterns, with the manner of receiving learned law changing over decades and centuries. This study examines the development of the reception and the specific roles that Roman and Canon law played, with the aim of constructing a comprehensive overview of the process.

While Frisia is only one of many cases in the history of reception of law, it may provide additional insight into reception of law in general. The motivations and methods of reception in Frisia may tell us something about the transfer of legal elements under other circumstances, too. This study claims to present only a thorough picture of reception in Frisia. Nonetheless, it also contributes to a wider examination of the transfer of legal elements between legal cultures.

The following sections will outline the methodological approach of this study, provide an overview over Medieval Frisia and the most important primary sources, explain how to interpret the concept of 'reception of law', and discuss the contributions of previous scholars to the question of reception in Frisia.

1 A Legal Historian's Approach to the Past

Considering that this research concerns law of the distant past, the context of that past must be scrutinized. An accurate understanding of reception is impossible without knowing the historical circumstances of Frisian society, polity, economy and so on. Understanding why and how the socio-historical context changed is vital for properly comprehending the evolution of the law and legal system. This is central to any legal historical work.[7] The discipline of legal history has always been in a complicated position: it is often conducted at law faculties but relies on historiographical methods to examine law of the

7 As explained by Husa, *Comparative Law*, p. 34. The reasons for legal change are always rooted in social change.

past. This chapter outlines the relationship between the 'legal' and the 'historical' and the challenges and approaches of this study.

First, legal expertise is indispensable for legal analysis, especially for an understanding of how law is structured and understood. Knowledge of present-day law is not required because surveying Medieval Frisian law calls only for an understanding of past law. However, historians must acquire legal skills for such an endeavor: these skills help in concepts and approaches that are useful for understanding law of the past. Historians must also be aware of and use present-day terminology of law to be comprehensible to an audience of the present day. Legal skills are also necessary for transmitting that understanding to new audiences. More about language and the past later.

Second, this research encompasses multiple legal systems, namely *ius proprium* (law of distinct territories, for example Frisian law) and *ius commune* (Roman and Canon law). These systems interacted with one another and influenced the kind of law that emerged in Frisia in the 15th century. A comparative approach to these historical systems is essential and knowledge of them is consequently required. Such comparisons demand extensive research into multiple systems rather than simply into one system.[8] This, then, is the approach I have chosen to take.

In addition, this research makes limited and sporadic use of comparisons with legal systems outside of Frisia, especially similar legal systems in the Medieval German, Danish, Flemish, Dutch and Norwegian territories. There are several reasons why such comparisons are useful and appropriate. First, because the sources of Frisian history are not extensive, many aspects of Frisian law remain unclear or uncertain even after a reading of the sources. Comparisons can help to clarify customary and undocumented aspects of the law. For example, the primary sources do not explicitly mention whether the Frisian legal system had distinctions of theft based on the value stolen or the time a thief was caught.[9] To investigate such questions, it is helpful to examine similar legal systems. Comparing Frisian and other legal systems may reveal an understanding of the former that is not apparent from the text.

Second, such comparisons can also provide interesting new insights into both legal systems. They may tell us something about Frisian law or Norwegian law that would not otherwise be apparent.[10] The comparisons in this research

8 Husa, *Comparative Law*, pp. 35–36.

9 See for this question, Chapter 4.1.

10 On the merits and complications of comparative legal research, see Husa, *Comparative Law*, p. 34ff.

are limited and serve only to further our understanding of Medieval Frisian law. Further research is needed, and this research is intended to provide an opening for such efforts.

Third, different cities and regions had different, sometimes overlapping legal traditions. And Frisia was no exception. All legal traditions are essentially hybrid creations that include both indigenous and borrowed elements. For example, Canon law borrowed many elements of Roman law. When examining and comparing the legal traditions in Medieval Frisia, the hybridity of law must therefore be kept in mind.[11]

There are various ways to engage in legal history, and research may cover a variety of different subjects of study. This research is primarily interested in law as a self-contained phenomenon. Lesaffer calls this approach the 'history of law'.[12] It focuses on a particular legal system, institution or concept in a particular period. Such an approach is primarily interested in the evolution of law over time. This is the path I am taking in this book. There are, however, other options. A historian's approach to legal history more often resembles what Lesaffer calls 'law in history'.[13] This is more concerned with the position and role of law within a society and the interactions between law and society, culture, politics and economy. Such an approach puts a historical society in the foreground and explores law as an aspect of this society. While a 'law in history' approach results in interesting insights, 'history of law' is more appropriate in the present study. The reception of learned law promoted the evolution of the legal system in Frisia, and in this evolution and in exploring how and why the legal system changed during the Late Middle Ages, lies the focus of this study.

Additionally, 'integral legal history' cannot take all social context into account. In doing so, the work would relegate the law to the sidelines. Instead, the focus must be on all relevant legal branches and systems that were present in a historical region. In this manner, legal history can be integral, while nevertheless remaining 'legal'.[14] Although research into Frisian law cannot encompass all the complex and plentiful facets of Frisian society, it can include all the legal traditions and systems that were present in Frisia. For this reason, and despite the emphasis on the reception of Roman law, the context of other

11 On hybridity in legal traditions, see Donlan, Heirbaut, "A Patchwork", pp. 15 and 21.

12 Lesaffer, "Law and History", p. 136 f.

13 Lesaffer, "Law and History", p. 136. Heirbaut distinguished between 'traditional' and 'contextual' legal history. Broadly, these align with Lesaffer's concepts. Contextual history is often written by social scientists and considers law to be a part and product of society as a whole. See Heirbaut, "Reading Past Legal Texts", pp. 92–93.

14 On 'integral legal history', see Heirbaut, "Reading Past Legal Texts", pp. 109–111.

legal traditions must also be examined. This is especially true for the law of the Medieval Church. Canon law had been in force throughout the Middle Ages and forms part of the background in which elements of Roman law were received. Understanding reception, therefore, also means understanding the context of Canon law. More on this context in chapter 1.3.

1.1 *The Historical Method*

Naturally, the historical context of Medieval Frisia cannot be neglected. The past must be understood before law's place within it can be examined. Moreover, the evolution of law, i.e., changes in the features of a legal system, rely on alterations in the social environment. If the social context changes, law generally changes as well, and thus the legal system evolves.[15] The need to sufficiently understand the historical context and its development consequently requires a historical approach and methodology.

Most importantly, a legal historian must include primary sources of the past. Historical research relies on these sources and their analysis. The selection of primary sources is based on the ambition to answer the question about the reception of learned law in Frisia, a problem-based approach.[16]

The analysis of primary sources follows a chronological order. Starting with the oldest, the texts are appraised in their own historical and legal context. A careful appraisal of each source is crucial.[17] First, it is an examination of the traditional Frisian law texts of the 11th to the 12th centuries. The next step comprises an analysis of the later Frisian texts of the 13th and 14th centuries. This includes a first manuscript tradition that shows how Frisians interacted with learned law. Lastly, a second manuscript tradition is examined. This consists of two editions and was created in the 15th century. Each of these sources is analyzed separately, thus making it possible to see what changed in the decades in between, both regarding structures and contents, as well as singular rules and concepts. Chapter 1.3 introduces the most important sources. Only by appraising each source on its own is it possible to see what changes have occurred. This is the essential work and method of historians wanting to ascertain the past. Understanding the historical context of the primary legal sources is consequently indispensable.

---

15 Husa, *Comparative Law*, p. 245.

16 As opposed to a source-based approach. In that case, a primary source would be examined in regard to all valuable information within it. Since most sources will not have much to say about the central question of this book, it is not the favored approach. For an overview of these two approaches to primary sources, see Tosh, *Pursuit of History*, p. 56.

17 Tosh, *Pursuit of History*, p. 57 ff.

It is impossible at present to conduct the complete and exhaustive analysis that every source deserves: the investigation of the primary sources from the perspective of reception of learned law is a pioneering endeavor and has not previously been undertaken in this manner. Most of the work here is seminal and owes a special debt to recent translations of texts and glosses. The hope is that future historians will be able to assess, expand and build upon this research. Frisian law is a field with great potential for further research, and gaps that remain after this study are worthy of being filled.

1.2 *Distinctions and Understandings of Law*

A significant issue arises when conducting legal historical research: 'law' is an immensely large field and to cover it in its entirety would require Frisian society to be covered in its entirety. Therefore, the field must be reduced to make answers accessible. This study examines a number of distinct topics, corresponding to divergent fields of law, to provide a broad insight into many different aspects of Frisian law.

However, this approach comes with its own problems. The distinction into specific fields of law, such as succession or family law, is foreign to the Medieval Frisian legal system as Frisians did not make such distinctions. For example, there was no formal distinction between private and public law and the different legal rules such distinctions give rise to.[18]

This distinction between a *ius publicum* and a *ius privatum* is supposed to have emerged from the Digest of the *Corpus Iuris Civilis*. Yet, it was not widely utilized, not even among Medieval jurists educated in learned law. Instead, they viewed law as a unitary system and not as being split between private and public law.[19] It was not until the 16th century that these categories became relevant again. Then, in the late 18th and early 19th centuries, the distinction between public and private became fundamental for modern law,[20] with the distinction into separate fields of law having developed out of the natural law doctrines of the 17th century. The codification process of the 19th century, resulting in the promulgation of national codes, and the works of the German Pandectists

18 On applying modern legal terms to Medieval Frisian sources, see Algra, *Oudfries recht*, p. 16. Germanic laws were mostly customary law; see Lesaffer, *Europese Rechtsgeschiedenis*, pp. 143–147. On the evolution of public and private law in the late Roman Republic, see Lesaffer, *Europese Rechtsgeschiedenis*, p. 61 ff.

19 On the emergence of public law, see Sordi, "Public law". The Medieval jurist Azo of Bologna considered law inseparable and not divided into two when commenting on Ulpian's distinction. (Azo, *Summa Institutionum*, Pavia, 1506, anastatic reprint (Officina Erasmiana 1966) ad Inst. 1.1, p. 348.) See Sordi, "Public law", pp. 706–708.

20 Sordi, "Public law", pp. 726–728.

were characterized by a subdivision of the law into fields such as the law of succession, law of property, family law, etc.[21] Consequently, these distinctions into fields of law were foreign to both Frisian and learned law of the Middle Ages.

Nonetheless, scholars have always applied their own paradigms and understandings to legal texts. This is equally true today as it was in the past. Medieval jurists utilized distinctions and categories of learned law when they wrote about or commented on traditional Frisian law. A brief example of this can be seen in the obligations arising following a conviction for theft. A gloss to a Frisian provision identifies such an obligation with the Roman *poena* (penalty). That this is not entirely faithful to the original meaning of the Frisian text is illustrated in the corresponding chapter.[22] What is clear, however, is that jurists of the Late Middle Ages applied their own understanding of obligations to the Frisian text. This means that an analysis of the sources is filtered through many layers: the Old Frisian terminology, the understanding and interpretation of Medieval scholars, the 19th-century distinctions of natural law, and finally present-day usage and comprehension. These filters must be kept in mind when interpreting sources of the past.

Yet, applying a contemporary lens is necessary so that an understanding of the evolution of Frisian law can be created. Contemporary scholars must be able to comprehend the text and its analysis without involving themselves in the same rigorous research. As such, law of the past is inevitably approached with a contemporary lens.[23] However, the presence of that lens should always be kept in mind when Medieval texts are analyzed and interpreted.

A division of this research into five distinct topics provides tangible benefits and compensates for the challenges that arise from applying a present-day understanding to the past. By looking at distinct parts of Frisian law, it is possible to gain insight into reception in general, while also disclosing revelations about specific details and features of the process of reception. Chapter 1.5 provides a brief overview of the five subjects of this study: *niarkap*, proof, theft, testaments and widows.

1.3 *Language and Translation*

A final practical challenge to this analysis is the barrier of languages. Frisian law was recorded in the vernacular; i.e., Old Frisian and, in some areas, Middle

21 On this development, see Stein, *Roman law in European History*, pp. 107–127.

22 Gloss 47 ad *D*, III (SkRa) 67, pp. 156–159. For more, see Chapter 4.

23 See also Heirbaut, "Reading Past Legal Texts", p. 105, who states the benefits of describing past law in contemporary terms, namely that it enables understanding by other scholars, such as jurists and historians.

Low German. The language of learned law was Medieval Latin. Educated people commented on law in the form of Latin glosses, as found in some Frisian sources. Lastly, this study is written in English to make it more accessible to a wider audience. Frisian, Dutch and German are all languages that have some relevance for Frisian studies. However, the aim is to bring Frisian law into a larger context of Medieval Europe: therefore, English is preferred. Each of these languages (Old Frisian, Medieval Latin and English) comes with its own baggage regarding law. Their terms and phrases are defined by their specific context in time and place; providing, for example, specific English terms for specific phenomena in English law. The use of such terms is difficult to avoid; rather, however, than using them in the way they may be applied specifically in English or American common law, I have used them here with a general meaning.

Additionally, the historical context of the languages is considered.[24] The interpretation of phrases and terms is crucial, especially when it comes to Latin terms used for Frisian words. When interpreting, the question is whether the intent was to merely translate; whether a Latin term was intended to provide the Frisian term with an interpretation or whether an equation of Old Frisian and Latin terms occurred.

This is evident in an example in chapter 4 (see below): the private Frisian obligation that resulted from theft is identified in a gloss as *restitutio*. However, the two systems—indigenous Frisian law and Canon law—differed widely. The Frisian obligation was both reipersecutory and penal. Does the presence of the gloss then indicate that this obligation was considered a 'restitution' in the Canon law sense? This is unlikely. Restitution in Canon law meant a return (or compensation) of goods and included no penalties.[25] Two different lines of thought appear to collide here. Is the gloss interpreting the Frisian text as being in conformity with Canon law, or is that phrase merely a translation that does not imply that the Canon law concept of 'restitution' is applied? These questions must be asked when a gloss comments upon Frisian law. Two legal systems, which understand and express their laws in divergent ways, confront each other. Chapter 3 will attempt to provide a possible answer to this question.

Furthermore, interpretation or equation of language can occur later, based on the already translated term. This also applies to the English terms used to describe both Frisian and Latin words. The aim of translating legal texts is gen-

---

24 On language in the interpretation of sources, see Tosh, *Pursuit of History*, p. 60; on the meta language of the historian and the challenges of past and present, see Costa, "In Search", p. 170ff.

25 Kaser, *Das römische Privatrecht* II, p. 434. Penalties were usually separate from and on top of restitution.

erally to convey the text and the legal context as accurately as possible.[26] The goal must be to avoid an interpretation of the text that associates Frisian, Latin and English terms with concepts and ideas they do not imply. Additionally, similarity between terms and words presents a challenge, especially in the case of related languages such as Old Frisian, Dutch, German and English. An equation of terms based on homonymy must be avoided, unless the meaning is similar.[27]

To give an example, consider the Old Frisian *dōm*. Although it is linguistically related to the English word 'doom', their meanings differ. The Old Frisian term denotes a 'sentence' or 'judicial judgment',[28] while in modern English, 'doom' is a negative term expressing damnation or sometimes fate. Therefore, the Old Frisian *dōm* cannot be translated by the modern English 'doom'. Of course, the English term itself also underwent changes. The Old English *dom* and the Old Frisian *dōm* not only have the same origin, but also the same meaning.[29] While comparing Old Frisian and Old English would, therefore, be possible, the present-day understanding of 'doom' is not congruent with either.

To overcome these challenges, I sometimes use terms as they are written in the original language, with the goal being to avoid an interpretation that colors an understanding of the text. Words cannot simply be translated if the translation itself attaches new meanings, even though translation is still required in most places in order to keep this analysis comprehensible and readable. In providing translations, therefore, a balance between accuracy and accessibility has been maintained. Every instance asks for a decision on which connotation to use for Old Frisian and Latin terms. When and how to translate is known only through a thorough analysis of sources.

Employing these methods makes it possible to study sources of the past in order to gain insight into the reception of law. In line with approaching this research on a sound historical basis, I provide a brief overview of the geography, history and legal system of Medieval Frisia.

---

26 Husa, *Comparative Law*, p. 125. A different argument is made in Heirbaut, "Reading Past Legal Texts", pp. 104–106: it can also be fruitful to describe past law in contemporary terms. This allows present-day jurists and historians to understand the past better. Rather than faithfully reproducing law and making it difficult to understand, such an approach would enable further research and discussion. I believe that the two approaches are not mutually exclusive. Accuracy remains significant even when describing in contemporary language. On the other hand, one should always aim to correctly represent the past, even when it is difficult for present-day people to grasp easily.

27 Husa, *Comparative Law*, p. 126.

28 'dōm' Hofmann, Popkema, *Altfriesisches Handwörterbuch*, p. 104.

29 'doom' Hoad, *The Concise Oxford Dictionary of English Etymology*. An explanation of the terms surrounding the Old High German *dôm* is found in Green, *Language and history*, p. 44f.

2 Frisia in the Middle Ages

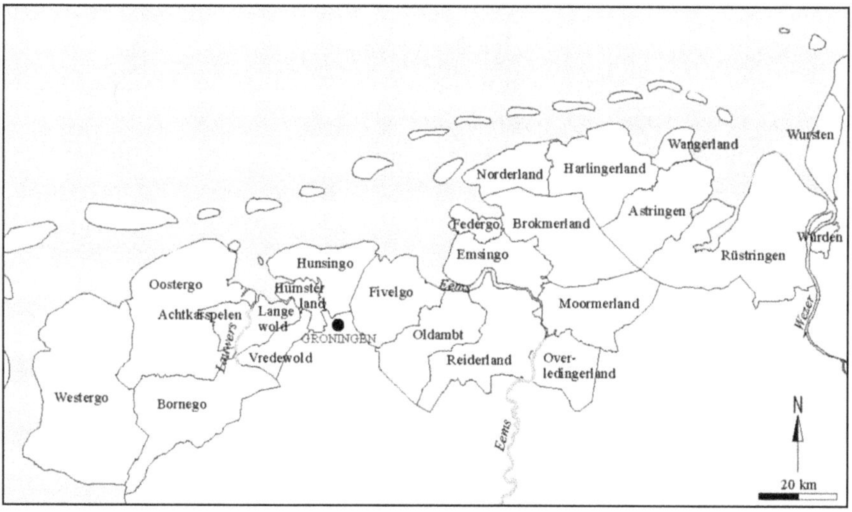

FIGURE 1 The Frisian lands around 1300 from the Vlie to the Weser
AFTER VRIES, *ASEGA, IS HET DINGTIJD?*

Around 1300, the Frisian territories stretched from the Vlie—the estuary of the IJssel before it became the IJsselmeer—to the river Weser. They were divided into many smaller lands (*terrae*). People in these lands spoke variants of Old Frisian, while also being united in a 'textual community' of a common legal canon.[30] They shared some common customary law that distinguished them from their neighbors.

From west to east, this territory can be divided into three larger regions: Westerlauwers Frisia, Oosterlauwers Frisia and East Frisia. Westerlauwers Frisia stretched west from the river Lauwers to the Vlie. The Frisian language is still spoken in these lands to this day. Alternatively, this region is called 'Middle' or 'Central Frisia'. In a German context, the name 'West Frisia' is sometimes used. This region currently makes up the province of Friesland/Fryslân.

Further to the east was Oosterlauwers Frisia. This region was dominated by the non-Frisian city of Groningen and was therefore also called the 'Ommelanden' (surrounding lands). It lay between the Lauwers and the Ems rivers. On the other side of the Ems, and stretching to the river Weser, was East Frisia.

30 For an examination of the Frisian textual community and its specific form, see Bremmer, "More than language", pp. 98–125.

In this book, 'Frisia' is used synonymously with Westerlauwers Frisia. Attention is focused on but not limited to this region. While insights and sources from other regions are occasionally relevant, there is no aspiration to have this research considered transmissible to all Frisian regions. The choice of Westerlauwers Frisia was deliberate: it was the last region that came under princely rule, and this means that it was the place where 'Frisian freedom' persisted the longest. This is keenly relevant for an examination of reception. The questions of how the legal system was arranged and how change came about are critically important. To this end, therefore, a short description of this 'Frisian freedom' is provided.

2.1 *The Freedom of the Frisians*

During the High and Late Middle Ages, the Frisian lands were in a particular social and political situation called the Frisian freedom (Fr. *Fryske Frijheid*). Medieval sources speak of *frisonica libertas* in Latin or *freeska fryheed* in Old Frisian. The understanding of the Frisian freedom to the Frisians changed over the Middle Ages: it originally meant a freedom from personal servitude, but in the 15th century it was understand more as freedom from princely rule. Frisia was part of the Holy Roman Empire, and so a subject of the emperor, but no sovereign or prince ruled over them.[31]

In the eighth century, Frisia was conquered by and became part of the Frankish Kingdom. A mythical origin story of the Frisian freedom at that time is detailed in the *Statutes of Magnus*:

> Listen and hear about the first statutes the Frisians formulated after they had won their freedom in Rome. When the war between the Roman nobility and King Charlemagne began because the Romans had gouged out Pope Leo's eyes, they brought all Frisians into the front line, so that they be slain first. Then the Frisians put their lives at risk and with their own hands fought so valiantly that they conquered the Roman stronghold on the third hour of the day, when the Romans were having their meals. Then Magnus, the standard-bearer of the Frisians, placed his standard on the highest tower in Rome. Charlemagne regretted this very much: before this

31 For literature on the Frisian freedom, see Lengen at al., *Die Friesische Freiheit*; Schuur, "De Middeleeuwse Friese Vrijheid"; Vries, "Frisonica libertas"; Vries, *Het Heilige Rooms Rijk*, pp. 14–27. On the history of Medieval Frisia, I refer to the following literature: Vries, "Geschichte der Friesen"; Vries, *Het Heilige Rooms Rijk*.

> they had been naked Frisians, but now the king had to consider them all lords. [...][32]

For their victory, Charlemagne offered the Frisians many great gifts, such as gold and land.

> [...] All gifts the king offered were declined by Magnus and he chose a better one, and all Frisians agreed with Magnus's choice.

This choice is detailed in the first of the *Statutes of Magnus* as such:

> And he determined that all Frisians were to be free, the born and the unborn, for as long as the wind will blow from the clouds and the world stands firm [...].[33]

This tale about how the Frisians attained their freedom and how it was given to them by Charlemagne himself was of great relevance during the Late Middle Ages, with the Frisians often bringing it up to legitimize their freedom and independence, especially when they were involved in conflicts with external forces. Later historical research revealed the story itself to be a fabrication and to have been written during the Middle Ages to create an argument for autonomy deriving from the semi-mythical figure of Charlemagne. Such an argument was convenient, especially since the Frisians sought to gain support from the Holy Roman emperors for their independence. No such event as the Frisian conquest of the Roman stronghold ever took place.[34]

Under Frankish rule, the Frisian territories became various counties, each nominally led by a count. It was during this time that many of the Old Frisian

---

32 *D*, v (Mgn) pr., pp. 174–175: "Will y harkya ende letet joe sidsa fan da aersta kerren deer da Fresen kerden da hya toe roem den fridoem bicronghen. Ende da dat stryd opheven ward twisscha Romera heren ende den koningh Kaerl om des paeus Leo aeghen deer Romera heren blyndet heden, da brocht ma da nakena Fresen alla fara, ho se aerst foerslayn worden. Da binettent da Fresen mitta live ende efter bifuchten hyaet mitta handen manlike datı hya Romera burich wonnen an dera tredda tyd dis deys, da da Romera heran ur hiara moes weren. Da brochte Magnus, deer di Freesna fanadreger was, syn fana op da alrehagista thoer deer waes binna Roem. Hoe leed dat koningh Kaerl was: eer weren se alle naken Fresen, da heet se di koning alle heren."

33 *D*, v (Mgn) 1, pp. 174–175: "Ende kaes, dat alle Fresen fryheren weren, 2 di berna ende di oenberna, alsoe langh soe di wynd fan da wolkenen wayd ende dyoe wrauld stoede [...]."

34 Janse, "De Waarheid"; Schuur, "De herkomst van het Karelsprivilege"; Vries, *Het Heilige Rooms Rijk*, pp. 21–27.

laws came into being.[35] In the 12th century, however, this configuration into counties disappeared, and the Bishop of Utrecht and the Count of Holland went on to claim the Frisian lands. Their right derived from the earlier counties and the support of the Holy Roman Emperor. Nonetheless, the Frisians rejected these claims. As they were successful in defending their freedom, princely rule was never established in Frisia, and free Frisians never came into personal bondage. Instead, a political system of many small, independent 'lands' (*terrae*) developed, with each land governing itself and appointing its own judges. Occasionally, these lands came together to defend their shared freedom. The location for such assemblies was Opstalsbam, a location near Aurich in East Frisia. It was there that the League of Opstalsbam assembled on 18 September 1323 and pledged to defend the whole of Frisia:

> [...] if any ruler intends to damage or bring shame to any sealand, be it bishop or count, we will all jointly give each other council or assistance and we will fight with our lives and goods in order to uphold our freedom.[36]

The reason for this assembly was an ongoing conflict with the County of Holland. At the end of the 13th century, the Count of Holland had laid claim to Westerlauwers Frisia after having conquered West Frisia in 1289. The Frisians rejected this claim and, when Floris v appointed himself Lord of Frisia, war soon followed. Although Holland's military campaigns in 1345 and 1396 failed, skirmishes and negotiations continued until around 1422. In the end, however, Holland was unsuccessful and Frisia remained free.[37]

A new threat soon arose. After Philip of Burgundy obtained the County of Holland in 1433, he also acquired the title of Lord of Frisia. During the 15th century, negotiations between Frisians and Burgundy took place. As a reaction to the threat of a Burgundian invasion, the Frisians made another pact to defend their lands together. This was mostly confined to Westerlauwers Frisia, which was in danger of open war. However, Philip was busy elsewhere in Europe and never redirected his attention to Frisia. Conflict increased again, however, under his son Charles the Bold, who had demanded loyalty and was rejected by

35 For example the *Older Skelta Law* which mentions the count multiple times. See chapter 1.3.

36 *D*, XX (WuPs) 2, pp. 430–431: "[...] jefter enich landis hera wil enich zeland schaya jefta schanda, hit se biscop jef grewa, dat wi se alle mene in rede ende in dede mit liwe ende mit guede usen fridoem to bihalden."

37 Janse, *Grenzen aan de macht*; Vries, *Het Heilige Rooms Rijk*, pp. 28–36.

a Frisian delegation. Although war then broke out, Charles was also busy elsewhere and so no actual battles were fought. The conflict and the looming threat of Burgundy united the Frisians, strengthening the idea of a Frisian freedom. The death of Charles in 1477 ended the Burgundian threat.[38]

Ultimately, internal conflicts within Frisia led to the end of the Frisian freedom, as influential Frisians called 'headmen' (*haedlingen*) began to dominate politics and society.[39] In the 14th and 15th centuries, these *haedlingen* formed two loosely defined factions, the *Schieringers* and the *Vetkopers*. These factions were made up of *haedlingen* but there was no clear territorial, ideological or social divide between them.[40] The scale of the conflicts between the *Schieringers* and the *Vetkopers* increased over the centuries, and especially after 1480 both factions hired foreign mercenaries to fight against the other. In 1498, the *Schieringers* approached Albert III of Saxony (1443–1500) for support against their rivals. Albert agreed, and defeated both the *Vetkopers* and later also the *Schieringers*, becoming Governor of Frisia in 1499.[41]

In East Frisia, a powerful headman named Ulrich Cirkensa was appointed Count of East Frisia in 1464. This effectively ended the period of Frisian freedom in this region.[42] In the Ommelanden, the non-Frisian city of Groningen began to dominate the Frisian districts, and the autonomy of the latter came to an end.[43] In all three Frisian regions, then, the freedom of the Frisians ended.

2.2 *Political and Legal System*

Before new governmental structures were imposed under Saxon rule, no central authority had imposed law or a legal system on Frisia. The Frisians were organized into local, independent territories or lands (*terrae*), with each *terra* being self-governing. The two big *terrae* of Westerlauwers Frisia were Westergo and Ostergo, but many smaller *terrae* also existed. The inhabitants of each *terra* governed themselves and appointed the members of two communal institutions: the communal assembly and the communal court.[44]

A *terra* was further divided into smaller, judicial districts, where the population democratically elected a judge (the *grietman*) and two co-judges who

---

38 Mol, Smithuis, "De Friezen", pp. 194–198; Vries, *Het Heilige Rooms Rijk*, pp. 72–84.

39 Gosses, "De Friesche hoofdeling"; Schmidt, "Häuptlingsmacht"; Vries, *Het Heilige Rooms Rijk*, pp. 20–21.

40 Noomen, "De Friese vetemaatschappij", p. 56 ff.

41 Vries, *Het Heilige Rooms Rijk*, pp. 162–188; Mol, "Hoofdelingen en huurlingen".

42 Vries, *Het Heilige Rooms Rijk*, pp. 77–80.

43 Vries, *Het Heilige Rooms Rijk*, p. 70.

44 Vries, "Frisonica libertas", p. 3; Vries, *Het Heilige Rooms Rijk*, p. 17 ff.

resided over the district. The judges of all the districts (*grietmannen* and co-judges) formed another, higher court, which was responsible for the entire *terra*. This higher court also had a representative function and could, for example, conclude contracts on behalf of its inhabitants. Later, the abbots of the most important monasteries in Frisia gained a seat on the higher court, and these prelates took leading positions in the court and in governance. In the 15th century, the communal organizations were increasingly influenced by the powerful headmen and the Frisian factions. In East Frisia, the headmen appointed the judges themselves, without any input of the Frisian population, but this development did not occur in Westerlauwers Frisia.[45]

The district courts of Frisia administered but did not legislate. Consequently, there was no legislative authority present. Almost all legal sources were local and regional customs, which were eventually recorded by Frisian jurists. Whenever elements of learned law were received into Frisia, it can be assumed that it was the Frisians themselves that adopted or adapted them. This unique historical situation ceased with the end of the Frisian freedom. Sources tell a similar story when we consider the different manuscript traditions. More on these later in chapter 1.3. For that reason, it is useful to halt the examination of the legal system and its development in 1498 because a completely different historical situation emerged afterwards.

Before this reception can be examined, a brief overview of some aspects of Frisian law and the legal system must be provided.

2.2.1 Honor and Feuds

Frisian society was a society based on honor. The honor of an individual was important, and attaining and retaining honor was crucial. Scholars assert that to gain honor, someone else had to lose it. This means that Frisian society can be typified as an 'economy of honor', in which the resource of 'honor' was limited.[46] Without honor, an individual or a family was excluded from society. Loss of honor was among the greatest fears of individuals and families, who often considered any act that retained or regained honor to be legitimate. The specific acts that led to gaining or losing honor were based on the norms of a society. Damaging a Frisian's honor gave rise to the need for an act of reciprocity. Sometimes, depending on the injury, this included the use of violence, and violent conflicts could escalate.[47]

---

45 Algra, *Ein*, p. 16 ff.; Vries, "Frisonica libertas", p. 3; Vries, *Het Heilige Rooms Rijk*, p. 17 ff.

46 Miller, *Bloodtaking*, p. 30.

47 Nijdam, *Lichaam, eer en recht*, p. 53 ff.

Feuds were the strongest form of these conflicts. Feuding was a possible system for regulating the distribution of honor and has been extensively researched by Medievalists.[48] Feuds were primarily undertaken by wealthy individuals or families as only they had the money, influence and connections needed to organize large groups of people for this purpose. Factions such as the *Schieringers* and *Vetkopers* were influential enough to raise the manpower required to participate in large feuds.[49] Any feuding party had to follow established rules: all feuding activities, for example, had to be performed in the open and not in secret. The feud was a public act and not a crime. The leaders of feuds were also held liable for all damage inflicted by the participants. From these rules it should be evident that feuds were not merely senseless violence, but a meaningful aspect of Frisian society.[50] While reciprocal violence was a feature of feuds, compensation of damages and honor was also possible. In such cases, a feud was ended by the compensation and further violence was prevented.

2.2.2 Courts and Judicial Officials

Every free Frisian had the right to litigate grievances in court. Three times a year, an assembly (*thing*) was held that all Frisians could attend. This was not only for raising claims, but for all political and social matters that were worth discussing. During an assembly, a 'peace' (*ferd*) was proclaimed. Any wrongdoing during this time also invoked a fine for breaching the peace. Frisians initiated legal claims at these assemblies. As no judicial official pursued crimes, scholars speak of an 'accusatory' system.[51] After a claim was raised, the officials would summon the accused to appear in court. How a Frisian legal procedure unfolded is detailed in chapter 3, including the methods of proof and who was allowed to furnish proof.

For brief descriptions of the judicial officials, see the glossary.

---

48 The work of William Ian Miller, *Bloodtaking and Peacemaking*, who examined feuds in Medieval Iceland, is well known. For different definitions of feuds, and their relation to vendettas and *Blutrache*, see Thorlaksson, "Feud and Feuding", p. 94.

49 Feuds were politically calculated undertakings. Revenge was enacted swiftly to present strength and prevent further victimization. On this, see Boehm, "Natural History", p. 191 f.

50 Noomen has written about the role of feuds in Frisian society. He considers them not antithetical to economic success and cautions against thinking of the feuding period of the 15th century as especially violent or chaotic. See Noomen, "De Friese vetemaatschappij", p. 44 ff.

51 Nijdam, *Lichaam, eer en recht*, pp. 149–151; Oosten, *Ambtshalve Vervolging*, pp. 1–3.

2.2.3 The Church and Ecclesiastical Structures in Frisia

In addition to the secular, local organization of government in Frisia, ecclesiastical institutions also played an important role for Medieval Frisian law. Frisia had been slowly Christianized since the 7th century, but organized, ecclesiastical structures were created only later. In the 10th and 11th centuries, the Bishop of Utrecht established a network of churches and parishes in Westerlauwers Frisia. A church synod was also founded, based on three deaneries into which Frisia was divided. This synod dealt with spiritual matters and ecclesiastical matters.[52] This parallel court system was crucial to the Frisian legal system.[53]

Through the network of parishes and the synod, the Church and the bishop of Utrecht gained considerable secular and political influence in Frisia. However, the parishes and the synod relied primarily on the participation and patronage of local, Frisian elites. They had been instrumental in establishing churches in each parish, and wealthy Frisian were involved as laymen in the synod.[54] Although the Frisians rejected the secular rule of the Bishop of Utrecht in the 13th century, ecclesiastical institutions remained present and integral to Frisian society and law.

Much of the intellectual development took place in the Frisian monasteries, where reading and writing of books was a central endeavor. These monasteries were established beginning in the 12th century, and their influence became increasingly important. Monasteries were places of learning, including the study of Roman and Canon law, and chronicles and law texts were written there. The abbots of places like Mariengaarde and Bloemhof often came from wealthy Frisian families and were involved themselves in Frisian politics, often as diplomats or arbitrators.[55]

For the Frisian legal system, therefore, the monasteries and the clergy of the country played an important role, both in arbitration, in the administration of justice and in the creation of new law.

3 Frisian Primary Sources

It is lamentable that few written Medieval sources from Frisia have survived to this day. Most of the sources available are legal sources, which is very fortunate

52 Rules regarding the synod were collected in the text *The Synodical Law of Central Frisia*. More about this later.

53 De Langen, Mol, "Church Foundation"; Nijdam, et al., *Frisian Land Law*, pp. 21–22.

54 Nijdam, et al., *Frisian Land Law*, pp. 21–22.

55 Bremmer, *Hir is eskriven*, p. 85.

for legal historical research.[56] A limited number of documents, such as written contracts and testaments, have also survived. These offer insight in addition to that provided in law books.[57] Frisian sources have periodically attracted scholars' interest. The first significant edition of Frisian sources is the *Friesische Rechtsquellen* by Karl von Richthofen (1811–1888).[58] This collection was published in 1840 and contains legal texts from various regions, including Westerlauwers Frisia. From 1963 to 1977, editions and translations of Frisian sources were published in the series *Altfriesische Rechtsquellen*.[59] These include German translations of many of the regional legal texts, such as the laws of Fivelgo and Rüstringen. Most recently, Frisian sources have translated into English in, for example, the Westerlauwers laws of the *Freeska Landriucht*. More on this source later. All surviving Westerlauwers manuscripts and incunabula were produced in the 15th and 16th centuries. These documents often contain older laws or are based on earlier manuscript traditions. The same is applicable to historical documents: they are almost exclusively from after 1400 and little has survived from earlier centuries.

Legal texts were primarily written in the vernacular. In Westerlauwers Frisia, this was Old Frisian. While few sources have survived, the significance of Old Frisian as a language of law is well established.[60] Under the influence of Groningen, the Ommelanden also produced texts written in Middle Low German.[61] Since we are interested in reception of learned law, the language of learned law is also crucial. Glosses and commentaries on Frisian law texts are often written in Latin. These, therefore, are the languages one encounters when analyzing Frisian primary sources.

To assess the reception of learned law, I have relied on previously completed and ongoing manuscript editions and translations. While many sources pro-

56 For an overview of Frisian sources, see Gerbenzon, *Apparaat II*. See also Vries, "Literatuur" and Johnston, "Old Frisian Law". A bibliography of Frisian studies is provided by Bremmer, *A Bibliographical Guide*. Short summaries on Frisian sources and relevant literature are found in Nijdam, *Lichaam, eer en recht*, pp. 21–25 and Vries, *Asega, is het dingtijd?*, pp. 11–14.

57 Testaments are collected by Verhoeven, Mol, *Friese testamenten*. Frisian documents are collected in Vries, *Ferdban*.

58 Richthofen himself also undertook research into these sources and published his contributions in Richthofen, *Untersuchungen* I–III between 1880 and 1886.

59 For a list of the published editions, see the literature under the name Buma, Wybren Jan and Wilhelm Ebel.

60 For an introduction into the Old Frisian language, see Bremmer, *An introduction to Old Frisian*. On the literacy of the Frisians, see Bremmer, *Hir is eskriven*. Concerning the vernacular language in the Ommelanden, see Bremmer, "Codifying the Law".

61 On the corpus of Frisian law in the Ommelanden, see Meijering, Nijdam, *'Wat is Recht?'*.

vide additional support, such as documents and legal texts from outside Westerlauwers Frisia, the main corpus of interest and the most important primary sources are the *Freeska Landriucht* in the incunable *D*, the *Excerpta Legum* in the manuscript *A*, and the *Jurisprudentia Frisica* in the manuscript *Ro*. All three are extensively detailed below. These three sources are thus the crucial, focal point of analysis. Their survival relied on the constant copying of the text over decades. As such, these copies often included mistakes, which makes transcription and translation precarious.

Most of these manuscripts probably had multiple authors or compilers. In fact, some sources are primarily compilations or collections of existing rules and thus contain no or little authorial intent. Even these collections, too, were made by multiple writers, as is evident in the divisions and handwritings in the manuscripts.[62] Although the identity of these compilers and writers is unknown, a few things can be assumed about them. First, they were Frisians, because they wrote in Old Frisian. Second, they were likely to be educated jurists, learned in the *ius commune*. Many, such as Emo van Huizinge, will have studied law outside Frisia and then returned to Frisia to practice and apply what they had learned.[63] Third, it is plausible that they lived and worked at monasteries such as Mariengaarde and Bloemhof as these were places where people learned and wrote Latin and reproduced older Frisian manuscripts.[64] Lastly, they clearly had access to reference works of the *ius commune* and Frisian texts at these monasteries, as evidenced by the frequent references to and the copying of parts of older manuscripts.[65]

Describing all Frisian sources of the Middle Ages would venture beyond the limits of this book. The following paragraphs therefore provide a brief introduction to some of the more relevant sources, including the three principal objects of analysis.

3.1 *Lex Frisionum*

The *Lex Frisionum* is the oldest known law text for Frisia, dating back to around 800. This legal code incorporates many traditional Frisian elements, such as wergild and compensation tariffs, and categorizes Frisian society into four classes: slaves, serfs, free Frisians, and nobles. While this text was not likely to

62 See, for example, the *Codex Aysma* manuscript, where four handwritings were identified, each corresponding to different parts of the text. Buma, et al., *Codex Aysma*, p. XII.

63 Gerbenzon, *Emo van Huizinge*, p. 6.

64 Apeldoorn, "Romeinsch Recht", p. 405f.

65 For example, the presence of the first part of the *Older Skelta Law* in the late 15th-century manuscript *Codex Roorda*. See Gerbenzon, "Aantekeningen (Eerste Deel)", p. 35.

have been a finished or functioning code, but rather a draft or collection for a future law code, it offers valuable insights into the earliest forms of traditional Frisian law. It was written in Latin, with some vernacular words included.[66] However, this source is of only secondary importance owing to its distance from the 15th century.

3.2 Freeska Landriucht

The first of the three main sources is the incunabulum *Druk* (*D*), which is not a manuscript but a printed document. It contains a compilation of 21 traditional indigenous legal texts, known as the *Freeska Landriucht* (Frisian Land Law).[67] Technically, only the first fourteen texts belong to the Frisian Land Law, and the seven additional texts are explicitly excluded from this canon of classical texts.[68] However, the compilation as a whole is also called the Frisian Land Law. Of the 21 texts, some are specific to Westerlauwers Frisia, and others apply to all Frisian regions in general.[69] Most of these texts can also be found in other manuscripts.[70]

I make extensive use of the recent English translation in *Frisian Land Law. A Critical Edition and Translation of the* Freeska Landriucht.[71] While other editions and earlier translations may differ in some respects, the present translation is the most comprehensive to date and includes all the glosses of the incunabulum *D*, which are not present in any other edition.[72] There are a total of 21 separate texts, from the *Prologue* (I) to *A Treatise on the Seven Sealands* (XXI). A brief description of the most relevant texts follows. As many of the ages of these texts cannot be determined very accurately, approximations are given.

---

66 For literature on the Lex Frisionum, see Siems, *Studien zur Lex Frisionum*.

67 'Land law' refers here to a common set of indigenous legal rules, in contrast to a specific indigenous legal rule, as in the *Twenty-Four Land Laws*. See Vries, "Thet is ac londriucht", p. 585.

68 The phrase is borrowed from Vries, "Thet is ac londriucht", p. 582, who speaks of "eine Art Kanon von verschrifteten Landrechtstexten." The transition between the former fourteen and the latter six is marked in the manuscript by the following quotation after the last provision (15) of the *Currency Conversion and Wergild* (text XV): *Hyr eyndighet dat Landriucht der Fresena ende alhyrnei folged Keiser Rodulphus boeck*. (Translation: *Here ends the land law of the Frisians and after this begins the Book of Emperor Rudolf.*)

69 Vries, "Thet is ac londriucht", p. 585.

70 See the footnotes to the texts on where to find these texts in additional manuscripts.

71 Nijdam, et al., *Frisian Land Law*.

72 The edition of Richthofen, for example, does not include the glosses. He mentions them, but dismisses them as irrelevant for Frisian law. See Richthofen, *Friesische Rechtsquellen*, p. XXV.

From the 11th to the 12th centuries

- *The Seventeen Statutes* (K^{17}) are some of the most important Old Frisian laws. The statutes were universally applied to all Frisians, i.e., they are a pan-Frisian legal text. The seventeenth statute grants the right to sue, to testify, and to swear an oath in court. Later, six exceptions were added to this rule. They are presented as a separate text (We^{17}).[73]
- *The Twenty-Four Land Laws* (L^{24}) probably originated from a collection of land laws, the number of which was later fixed at 24.[74] The contents of these laws concern internal Frisian customs and some elements of criminal law.[75] They are one of the pan-Frisian legal texts and are also found in other Frisian regions.[76]
- *The Older Skelta Law* (SkRa) contains 81 provisions and was specifically designed for Westerlauwers Frisia. Its inclusion of procedural law makes it particularly important for the history of Frisian law.[77] The *skelta* plays a central role in the text.[78]
- *The Younger Skelta Law* (SkRb). Containing 41 provisions, this law is considered to be younger than the *Older Skelta Law*, but probably from about the same time.[79]
- *The Synodical Law of Central Frisia* (SWI) was compiled in the 11th century, but some elements date back to the 10th century. The text contains ecclesiastical law, with 53 provisions governing ecclesiastical jurisprudence. The central figure is the Bishop of Utrecht, to whose diocese and jurisdiction the Frisian lands belonged.[80]

---

73 Meijering, Nijdam, '*Wat is Recht?*', pp. 142 and 194f.

74 Meijering, Nijdam, '*Wat is Recht?*', p. 208.

75 Vries, *Asega, is het dingtijd?*, p. 54. Within Westerlauwers law, the Twenty-four Land Laws are also present in the manuscripts *U* and *J*. Additionally, a number of Ommelander manuscript contain them as well. See Vries, *Asega, is het dingtijd?*, p. 53.

76 For example in Fivelgo. See Buma, Ebel, *Das Fivelgoer Recht*, p. 41. And in Rüstringen, see Buma, Ebel, *Das Rüstringer Recht*, p. 43.

77 Meijering, Nijdam, '*Wat is Recht?*', p. 84. Aside from *D*, SkRa is also present in the manuscripts *U* and *J*. Parts of the beginning are also present in *Ro*. For additional literature, see Vries, *Asega, is het dingtijd?*, p. 62. For an older, English examination, see Fairbanks, *Skeltana Riucht*.

78 Breuker, *Landrecht der Vriesne*, p. 158. On the role and function of the *skelta*, see the glossary.

79 For this particular text, see Klaarbergen, *Das altwestfriesische jüngere Schulzenrecht*. As well as *D*, the law is also found in the manuscripts *U* and *J*.

80 Aside from *D*, it can also be found in *U* and *J*, as well as in the Fivelgoër manuscript (*F*). Bary, Meijering, *Westerlauwers Zeendrecht*, p. 12ff.; Vries, *Asega, is het dingtijd?*, p. 64.

- *The Eight Provisions* (Dom) are closely related to the *Synodical Law* and ecclesiastical matters. They mainly concern minority, guardianship and succession. In the various manuscripts in other compilations, this text is often placed next to the *Synodical Law*.[81]

From the 13th century
- *The Statutes of Magnus* (Mgn) tell the story of Magnus, who helped Charlemagne during the Siege of Rome. He was the leader of the Frisians and requested their freedom as a reward. In seven statutes, the Frisian freedom is established. The statutes are part of the larger myth of an earlier established freedom.[82] In addition to establishing the Frisian freedom, they also formally introduce some of the subsequent laws, including the *Twenty-Four Land Laws* and the *Seventeen Statutes*.[83]
- *The Statutes of the Five Districts* (W^5D) are from and concern the law in the five districts around the city of Franeker. They are therefore not a pan-Frisian legal text, and nor were they written for all of Westerlauwers Frisia.[84]

This is where the additional texts, not belonging to Frisian Land Law, begin.

From the 13th century
- *The Book of Emperor Rudolf* (Rud) contains a pseudo-historical account of the privileges and laws granted to the Frisians by Emperor Rudolf and is, therefore, a central text for the concept of the Frisian freedom. However, it is uncertain who Emperor Rudolf was.[85] Due to the text being dated to the 13th century, it shows influences of Canon law. The version in the *Freeska Landriucht* is the only known version provided with Latin glosses.[86]

From the 14th century
- *On Serious Assaults* (Ska) is one of the later texts. It deals with violent robbery (*schaeckraf*). There are eight provisions in total, but an original manu-

81 For example in the mansucript *J*, as noted in Meijering, Nijdam, '*Wat is Recht?*', p. 355.

82 Buijtenen, *De grondslag van de Friese vrijheid*, p. 20 ff.

83 Vries, *Asega, is het dingtijd?*, p. 68.

84 Although Buma et al. state that they were created in the 14th century. For this source, see Buma, et al., *Westerlauwerssches Recht I*, pp. 24–25.

85 See Bos-Van der Heide, *Rudolfsboek*, p. 11 for the three editions of the book. See Meijering, Nijdam, '*Wat is Recht?*', p. 427 and Nijdam, et al., *Frisian Land Law*, p. 56 f. fort he question of the identity of emperor Rudolf.

86 Gerbenzon, *Apparaat*, p. 59.

script must have contained seven.[87] Influences of Canon law are already visible in this text.[88]
- *The Statutes of Opstalsbam* (WUps) are a relatively recent text, the result of the League of Opstalsbam in the early 14th century. The league was formed by Frisians in response to outside pressure on the Frisian freedom. The text is pan-Frisian and contains 24 clauses.[89]
- This is followed by the last text in the collection, *A Treatise on the Seven Sealands* (Sel), which specifies the various territories of Frisia.

Not only were these legal texts collected in the *Freeska Landriucht*, but the incunabulum *D* also contains a rich gloss that was later added to the collection. There are 188 individual glosses, which are not evenly distributed among the legal texts or the provisions, but rather placed where the author or authors felt that commentary was necessary. These glosses contain references to both Roman and Canon law. A significant number of these glosses might trace back to a manuscript tradition, but no such manuscript has survived.[90]

The incunabulum *D* was printed between 1484 and 1487.[91] The gloss is dated to no later than the late 14th or early 15th century and was probably created in the 13th and 14th centuries since it contains references to learned jurists of that period. Relevant jurists from the 15th century are largely absent, the most recent being Nicolo de Tudeschi (Panormitanus, 1386–1445).[92] Thus, the gloss was written long before the printing date. This indicates that the contents of the Frisian Land Laws and its commentaries continued to have, or to have regained, some relevance in the second half of the 15th century. Of what relevance this was is uncertain. It may have been the intention to display or preserve the outdated law, or to present an updated edition with the help of the glosses. Whatever the case, printing such a book was expensive and there must, therefore, have been good reasons to go to such lengths.

The author of the glosses is unknown. It is possible and indeed probable that the gloss had more than one author. In the 14th century, literate jurists were present in Frisia and had begun to introduce Canon and Roman law into legal

87 Meijering, Nijdam, *'Wat is Recht?'*, p. 402. Aside from *D*, this text is found in *U* and *J*, as well as a version in RW.

88 Gerbenzon, "Kanonisches Recht", p. 41.

89 Vries, *Asega, is het dingtijd?*, p. 64.

90 Hallebeek, "Gloss to the Saunteen Kesta", p. 53. Additional information about the gloss in Nijdam, et al., *Frisian Land Law*, p. 63 ff.

91 Nijdam, et al., *Frisian Land Law*, p. 32.

92 On the dating of the gloss, see Nijdam, et al., *Frisian Land Law*, p. 75 f.

discourse. This influenced a first manuscript tradition that combined Frisian law with elements of Roman law. The *Freeska Landriucht* marks an endpoint in this first tradition, which began well before 1400.[93] As such, it represents a case that can be compared with further developments in reception and interaction in the 15th century.

A copy of the *Freeska Landriucht* can be found in the *Codex Parisiensis* (P) manuscript, which was used as a law manual for clerics in Stellingwerf between 1495 and 1508. Several authors added texts that they thought relevant but that were not present in the original.[94]

3.3 Autentica *Collections*

Another important group of sources are the *Autentica* collections, which were created in Westerlauwers Frisia in the late 14th century. They are of particular significance for the later sources of the 15th century because many of their provisions were copied and reproduced. The Autentica collections include the *Rechten ende Wilkoeren* (*RW*) and *Thet Autentica Riocht* (*Aut*).[95]

The *Rechten ende Wilkoeren* is a law book that was written in Westerlauwers Frisia in the late 14th century.[96] However, all surviving manuscripts are from the 16th century and from the Ommelanden. A total of 27 manuscripts were written in Middle Low German. Gerbenzon nevertheless argues that the origins of the *Rechten ende Wilkoeren* lie in Westerlauwers Frisia. The text contains many paragraphs from older Westerlauwers Frisian sources such as the *Older Skelta Law*. It also formed an essential foundation for *Thet Autentica Riocht*, the *Excerpta Legum* and the *Jurisprudentia Frisica*.[97] It is likely that the 27 editions go back to an Ommelander archetype, which in turn was a translation of a Westerlauwers original.[98] The goal of the *Rechten ende Wilkoeren* may have been to combine traditional Frisian law with the learned laws, because it con-

93 Nijdam, *Lichaam, eer en recht*, p. 23 f.

94 For an examination of the *Codex Parisiensis*, see Gerbenzon, *Codex Parisiensis*. Technically, the *Codex Parisiensis* refers only to the last part of the manuscript, which consists of a copy of the *Freeska Landriucht* and additional texts. For the influence of learned law on this text, see Gerbenzon, "Canon and Roman Law".

95 Gerbenzon examined both, especially in relation to the 15th-century *Excerpta Legum*. See Gerbenzon, *Excerpta Legum*, pp. 428–445.

96 Meijering, Nijdam, *'Wat is Recht?'*, p. 30.

97 Gerbenzon, *Excerpta Legum*, p. 430. Many of the provisions of the *RW* reappear there. For a graphic illustration of the relations between the RW and other sources, see Gerbenzon, *Excerpta Legum*, p. 155. Gerbenzon also created a table where the provisions of the RW can be found in these sources. For this table, see Gerbenzon, *Excerpta Legum*, p. 436 ff.

98 Gerbenzon, *Excerpta Legum*, p. 432.

tains many instances of Roman and Canon rules written in Old Frisian.[99] For this reason, this source is particularly interesting for research on reception.

Thet Autentica Riocht was strongly influenced by the *Rechten ende Wilkoeren*. It contains many of the latter's provisions in the first half.[100] However, the second half contains additional material shaped exclusively by Canon law and including a broad range of moral theological arguments. Provisions of *Thet Autentica Riocht* reappear in later sources, as we will see when we examine the provisions of the *Excerpta Legum*. The birthplace of *Thet Autentica Riocht* was Westerlauwers Frisia. The authors were most likely clerics, given the strong influence of Canon law. Gerbenzon also notes that because the text is written in Old Frisian, it was intended for practical use rather than being just a theoretical endeavor.[101]

Both *Autentica* collections represent an early combination of learned law and traditional Frisian law. The sources of the late 15th century made extensive use of these texts. As such, the *Rechten ende Wilkoeren* and *Thet Autentica Riocht* are relevant for reception. However, other sources remain more important, partly due to the fact that the *Rechten ende Wilkoeren* has survived only in its Ommelander form, and the Westerlauwers original remains inaccessible. Gerbenzon notes that of the 27 editions, RW 1 is closest to the Ommelander archetype and the Westerlauwers original, but there is no certainty as to what the original would have looked like.[102] Thus, there is no clear Westerlauwers form to compare with the other sources.

There is a slightly different problem with *Thet Autentica Riocht*. This source does not exist as a coherent manuscript. Instead, its provisions can be found separately in *Codex Unia*, *Codex Aysma* and *Codex Roorda*. Brouwer compiled these provisions in 1941 in *Thet Autentica Riocht met inleiding, glossen, commentaar en woordenlijst*.[103] Although this provides a coherent and useful overview of the source, a close analysis of the provisions will not provide significant new insights because the content is already available in the *Excerpta Legum* in *Codex Aysma*, as well as in the *Jurisprudentia Frisica* in *Codex Roorda*. The lack of a manuscript of *Thet Autentica Riocht* means that it cannot be utilized in the same way as the other main sources. Nonetheless, examining and considering the content may still be useful, especially if it provides insight into when

99 Meijering, Nijdam, *'Wat is Recht?'*, p. 30.

100 Gerbenzon, *Excerpta Legum*, p. 434.

101 For the material of *Aut* and the influences of Canon law, see Gerbenzon, *Excerpta Legum*, pp. 195–196.

102 Gerbenzon, *Excerpta Legum*, p. 433.

103 Brouwer, *Thet autentica riocht*.

a provision was created. In conclusion, both collections fulfill only an auxiliary role in the analysis of Frisian sources.

3.4 Excerpta Legum *and* Jurisprudentia Frisica

Another, more recent group of sources reveals interactions between Frisian and learned law that emerged later. This second manuscript tradition includes the *Excerpta Legum* and the *Jurisprudentia Frisica*. Gerbenzon conducted extensive research on the entire manuscript tradition in his 1956 work *Excerpta Legum. Onderzoekingen betreffende enkele Friese rechtsboeken uit de vijftiende eeuw*. This work is essential for comprehending the material in the manuscripts and the relationships between the different editions. There are four distinct editions of this manuscript tradition.

3.4.1 First Edition—*Excerpta Legum*

The *Excerpta Legum* (Exc) is a collection of legal rules in Old Frisian and partly in Latin, found in the *Codex Aysma* (A) manuscript, which also includes several other texts such as the *Processus Iudicii* and the *Gesta Fresonum*. The 1993 transcription and translation into German is considered to be the principal edition of the *Excerpta Legum* in this study, including the numbering of provisions.[104] English translations of the texts in the *Codex Aysma* are provided by me.

The aim of this collection was to create a Frisian law book that incorporated learned law. To this end, the compilers included legal rules that they considered valid and relevant, copying them from other sources. Consequently, repetitions and contradictions are common. Their intention was to create a future, systematic law book but the systemization was never finished and the Excerpta Legum, therefore, lacks structure. Rubrics are used on only a few occasions.[105] Four distinct, sometimes alternating, handwritings can be identified.[106]

The *Excerpta Legum* comprises four different types of texts. The first type consists of provisions from *Thet Autentica Riocht*. The compilers evidently had access to that source and copied substantial portions of it—and, by extension, the *Rechten ende Wilkoeren*—into their new collection.

---

104 Buma, et al., *Codex Aysma*.

105 See the chapter "Handschriften en Redacties van de *Excerpta Legum*" in Gerbenzon, *Excerpta Legum*, p. 19 ff., and the conclusion on page 74.

106 For additional information regarding the handwritings, the structure of *Codex Aysma* and the *Excerpta Legum*, see Buma, et al., *Codex Aysma*. It also includes the transcriptions in Old Frisian and Latin, as well as the German translation. The numbering of the provisions and the German translation formed the basis for the analysis of the *Excerpta Legum* in this work.

The second type is a manual on arbitration, written in both Old Frisian and Latin. It shows significant influence from learned law and makes references to the *Decretals*.

The third type is another manual, the *Processus Iudicii*, which provides guidance on how to conduct a learned law procedure. Gerbenzon investigated its origins and found it to be based on a 13th century text, mistakenly attributed to Giovanni d'Andrea: *summula de processu iudicii*.[107] The manual was translated from its original Latin into Old Frisian. However, the version included in the *Excerpta Legum* is incomplete and full of errors. A more complete version of the manual is found in the *Codex Aysma* (A, III) as one of the additional texts.[108]

The fourth and perhaps most important group of provisions collected in the *Excerpta Legum* are those that come from case records. Each fragment comprises an argument or thesis in Old Frisian, along with Latin evidence of the thesis that references Frisian, Canon and Roman law. These fragments, known as *informationes iuris*, were generated during Romano-canonical procedures as defenses (*positiones*) of arguments presented earlier in the proceedings. The parties wrote *positiones* to strengthen their own arguments and weaken those of opposing parties. The fact that they are a key feature in Canonical procedures in the Middle Ages[109] is evidence that litigation in which these *informationes iuris* were written adhered to the rules of Romano-Canonical procedure.[110]

The fragments of the case records do not contain judicial sentences, leaving the actual outcome of the cases unknown. These cases were initiated by the litigating parties, often identified by the letters N and R, the specific meanings of which are unclear. It is likely that these letters stand for *nomen* (name,

---

107 Alternatively, *Ordo iudicarius* (*processus iudicii*). Gerbenzon, Apparaat II, p. 16. Gerbenzon, *Excerpta Legum*, pp. 227–237. Gerbenzon notes that the Frisian translation is based on a manual called *summa antequam* and not the text *Summa super secondo Decretalium*, a later edition of the former. Schulte argues that the *summa antequam* was written in the first decade of the 15th century by Johannes Urbach in Erfurt. Urbach based it primarily upon the *Speculum iudiciale* by Guillaume Durand and commentaries on it by Giovanni d'Andrea; see the *Additiones ad speculum guil. Durantis*. For an overview of Johannes Urbach and the *Processus iudicii*, see Schulte, *Geschichte* II, p. 301f. However, Gerbenzon states that the Frisian text is closer to the original than the German version; therefore it is unlikely that the German version was the origin of the *processus iudicii* in *Codex Aysma*. Gerbenzon, *Excerpta Legum*, p. 229f. in footnote 4.

108 For an analysis of this manual in the *Excerpta Legum*, see Gerbenzon, *Excerpta Legum*, pp. 227–237. Also Buma, et al., *Codex Aysma*, p. xvf. On procedural law, see also chapter 3.

109 For the canonical procedure, see Brundage, *Medieval Canon law*, pp. 129–134.

110 More on these procedures in chapter 3.

i.e., claimant) and *reus* (defendant). The manuscript did not record the names of the people involved in these cases. The fragments of case records also do not contain any evidence of the facts of the cases, but instead simply provide evidence that a particular legal rule existed in Frisian or learned law, thus indicating the validity of the stated argument. The following example illustrates the structure of such a fragment:

> Exc 67. Item. Dit is riucht, dattet riucht is vor den yenne, dar wackat, ende nat vor den yenne, der slept; dat to bywysen mit screwen riucht. Quia uigilantibus et non dormientibus iura subueniunt, ut in c. Inter dilectos, De donacionibus (X 3.24.8).[111]
>
> Exc 67. Item. (1) This is the law that the law helps the one who is awake and not the one who is asleep; (2) this is to be proven by written law. (3) Because the rules of law support the vigilant, not the sleepers, (4) as in X 3.24.8.

This text has a clear structure. First, it presents a thesis in Old Frisian (1). Then, it proposes to support this thesis with written and learned law (2). If a relevant argument is found, it is quoted or paraphrased in Latin (3). Finally, relevant legal texts are referenced (4).

Although the fragments of case records do not contain either the original statements or any results, they are valuable because they provide insight into legal practice. The compilers of the *Excerpta Legum* probably copied only those arguments that they considered important and sound. These fragments were likely to be intended as practical introductions to specific legal rules and arguments.[112]

The dating of the collection is imprecise. Some of the texts, such as *Thet Autentica Riocht*, probably date back to the 14th century, but the *Excerpta Legum* itself was compiled between 1400 and 1480, before the *Jurisprudentia Frisica*, emerged.[113]

111 *A*, I (Exc) 67, p. 56.

112 The components of the *Excerpta Legum* are succinctly summarized in Buma, et al, *Codex Aysma*, pp. XIII–XXI. A more detailed analysis of these texts in the first edition was done by Gerbenzon, *Excerpta Legum*, pp. 93–304.

113 On the dating of the first edition of the *Excerpta Legum*, see Gerbenzon, *Excerpta Legum*, p. 383 ff. Buma et al. place the date for it in the second half of the 15th or the first half of the 16th century; see Buma, et al, *Codex Aysma*, p. XII.

TABLE 1 Structure and sources of the provisions in the Excerpta Legum in A, including the hands

Provisions	Sources	Hand
1–101	Informationes Iuris	A
102–207	Manual of Arbitration	A
208–263	Informationes Iuris	B
264–446	Autentica Riocht	B
447–487	Summa Antequam	A
488–577	Informationes Iuris	A
578–598	Informationes Iuris	C, D

The table above gives a brief overview of the relationships between the sources and the hands. The *Excerpta Legum* in the *Codex Aysma* consists of a total of 598 provisions on 184 pages.

3.4.2 Second Edition

A second edition of the *Excerpta Legum* can be found in the manuscripts *B* and *C*. These two manuscripts are derived from the *Codex Aysma* and contain collections of legal material.[114] However, the language of these manuscripts is Middle Low German, instead of Old Frisian. These manuscripts are not included here as they are more relevant to the Ommelander corpus.

3.4.3 Jurisprudentia Frisica

The *Jurisprudentia Frisica* (JF) is a systematic rearrangement of the material collected in the *Excerpta Legum* and can therefore be considered its third edition. Although the intention of this rearrangement was to create a functional law text, this effort was never entirely finished as the careless rubrics and the space left for later additions indicate.[115] A detailed analysis of the structure and content was made by Gerbenzon in two articles entitled "Aantekeningen over de *Jurisprudentia Frisica*". They provide important information about the manuscript and the text. A Dutch translation was made by Hettema in the 19th century.[116] This translation contains considerable inaccuracies and is

114 For the genealogy of the manuscripts, see Gerbenzon, *Excerpta Legum*, p. 51ff. Also in the same place, pp. 304–378 for an analysis of the second edition.

115 Gerbenzon, "Aantekeningen (Eerste Deel)", pp. 32–34 and 61.

116 Hettema, *Jurisprudentia Frisica*. Published in 1835 in three parts.

no longer suitable or reliable for a proper analysis of the text. It also omits the rich and important gloss.

Fortunately, a new translation of the *Jurisprudentia Frisica* and its gloss is in progress. This is an ongoing project involving several scholars. Han Nijdam and Oebele Vries are translating the Old Frisian provisions, while Jan Hallebeek, Hylkje de Jong and I are translating the Latin gloss. We are following the manuscript title by title, bringing the Frisian and Latin parts together. I can use these translations and include them in my analysis of reception.

The primary manuscript is the *Codex Roorda* (*Ro*). Quires/gatherings and rubrics provide some insight into its structure and how the manuscript was created.[117] For example, titles within a quire were probably added together and may therefore be related to each other. The first quire contains the first texts of the *Freeska Landriucht*: the *Haet is riocht* and parts of the *Older Skelta Law*. After the first 16 provisions, however, the latter is suddenly discontinued. The following quires contain the actual *Jurisprudentia Frisica*, which consists of 87 titled rubrics, beginning with procedural law. The rubrics are written in Latin, the texts of the provisions in Old Frisian. Each title also contains many glosses. The last quire of the manuscript is another traditional Frisian law, the *Statutes of Opstalsbam*. This text was probably added to the manuscript at a later date.[118]

The *Jurisprudentia Frisica* is considered the third edition of the *Excerpta Legum*, because it contains a large part of its provisions, but not the entire text. In the systemization of the material of the Excerpta Legum, the author selected those provisions that were deemed appropriate, and added additional material from other sources. This includes the *Autentica* collections, and the writings of canonists and learned jurists such as Tancredus (1185–1230), Joannes de Imola (1370–1436) and Nicolo de Tudeschi (Panormitanus, 1386–1445). Moreover, some traditional Frisian provisions from the *Freeska Landriucht* are also present in the *Jurisprudentia Frisica*.[119] Evidently, these texts remained relevant even in the late 15th century and were therefore included.

Gerbenzon dates the *Jurisprudentia Frisica* to around 1495; he argues that the content was created after 1481 and the manuscript itself between 1490 and 1504.[120] This places the creation of the *Jurisprudentia Frisica* at the same time as the publication of the *Freeska Landriucht*. A connection between the discontinuation of the *Older Skelta Law* at the beginning of the *Codex Roorda*

117 For a closer analysis of the quires, see Gerbenzon, "Aantekeningen (Eerste Deel)", p. 35 ff.

118 Gerbenzon, "Aantekeningen (Eerste Deel)", p. 30.

119 See Gerbenzon, "Aantekeningen (Tweede Deel)" for a comprehensive analysis of the sources used in the *Jurisprudentia Frisica*.

120 Gerbenzon, "Aantekeningen (Eerste Deel)", p. 32.

and the publication of the *Freeska Landriucht* is a tempting prospect, but one that has not yet been proven.

3.4.4 Fourth Edition

The fourth edition of this manuscript tradition is an excerpt from the material of the second edition. It was compiled in the Ommelanden, in Middle Low German, in the 16th century. This last edition has no value for this current study since it exceeds the temporal and geographical frame.[121]

4 What Is Reception of Law?

In legal theory, reception is a process by which one legal culture adopts elements of another legal culture or tradition, resulting in the transformation of the recipient legal culture. This transformation can range from individual elements to an entire legal system and everything in between. Changes may be temporary and reversible, long-lasting or even permanent.[122] Reception is often not a singular event but should be seen as the result of countless incidents and acts by individuals.[123] This process of human activity is the focus of this study of Medieval Frisian law.

Reception differs from other forms of legal transfer in various significant ways. Two aspects are necessary for genuine legal reception: awareness and voluntariness.[124] First, recipients must be aware that reception is taking or has taken place. In other words, recipients know that an element foreign to their own legal system is being adopted. There are distinctions in this characteristic, namely whether it extends to an entire society, or whether it is limited to the individuals who set it in motion. Does every individual person need to know that their legal culture is changing, or is it sufficient for jurists to be conscious of it? The answers to these questions depend on the recipient legal culture and society, for example on whether societal structures even allow for recipients to become aware of the reception at all. It is therefore difficult to give a precise answer.

---

121 For this edition, see Gerbenzon, "Aantekeningen (Eerste Deel)", p. 25 and Gerbenzon, *Excerpta Legum*, pp. 62–74.

122 'Rezeption' in: Basedow, et al, *Handwörterbuch des europäischen Privatrechts*.

123 Wieacker, "Stand der Rezeptionsforschung", p. 196. There are forms of reception characterized by a single action to receive a foreign law code, for example the reception of the Swiss Civil Code into Turkey. See Atamer, "Rezeption und Weiterentwicklung".

124 For an overview of jurisprudential reception and its requirements, see Luts, "Jurisprudential Reception".

Second, a genuine reception must be voluntary, meaning with the consent of the recipient. If a transfer is involuntary and against the will of the recipient legal culture, an 'imposed reception' takes place. Imposed reception may evolve into a voluntary reception or into a return to the previous legal culture.[125] Examples of imposed reception are often found in colonial societies that were conquered and had law imposed on them by their colonizers. Consider, for example, the French colonial empire, where French civil law was imposed (or partially imposed) on its subjects in the 19th and 20th centuries.[126]

In contrast, sources from the 14th and 15th centuries show a willingness on the part of the Frisians to receive learned law. The sources were recorded in Frisia by Frisian jurists. These jurists facilitated the transfer of legal elements into their own legal culture. The absence of a central authority meant there was no authority that could have imposed a reception. Consequently, changes in the legal culture could come only from the Frisians themselves. There can therefore be said to have been a 'genuine' reception.

Another aspect to consider is the depth of the reception. This depth can range from an eclectic transfer of a small number of legal elements to the adoption of an entire legal system. The latter, a reception *in complexu* or *Totalrezeption*, is rare.[127] In fact, it is generally accepted that there has never been a *Totalrezeption* of Roman law in any territory.[128] An example of reception *in complexu* can be found in the Turkish Republic's adoption of Swiss civil code in 1926, when the entirety of Swiss civil code was adopted and became the basis of Turkish civil law.[129] However, the overwhelming number of reception processes fall somewhere between singular elements and reception *in complexu*.

4.1 *Reception of Norms, Methods and Systems*

In addition to broadly outlining reception and some of its forms, it is necessary to define the 'elements of a legal culture'.[130] Legal rules, institutions and entire systems all fall into this category. Legal rules reflect the norms of a society and are primarily found in normative sources such as laws and statutes. When foreign rules are found in a legal system, it is an indication that reception has

125 Graziadei, "Comparative Law", p. 15; Luts, "Jurisprudential Reception", p. 2.

126 For the colonial laws of European empires and specifically the French empire, see Hooker, *Legal Pluralism*, pp. 190–249.

127 'b) Umfang der Rezeption' in: 'Rezeption' in: Basedow, et al, *Handwörterbuch des europäischen Privatrechts*. See also Daniel, *Gemeines Recht*, p. 132.

128 Coing, *Privatsrechtsgeschichte*, p. 5 ff.; Daniel, *Gemeines Recht*, p. 132.

129 See again Atamer, "Rezeption und Weiterentwicklung", p. 732.

130 Michele Graziadei has also engaged in an answer to that question; see Graziadei, "Comparative Law", pp. 18–19.

occurred. However, the traditional approach of the 19th century, which focused primarily on when and which norms were adopted, is not sufficient because it ignores subtler and equally relevant elements.

An improved approach entails examining the reception of methods, including legal styles, ideas and doctrines finding their way into another legal culture. This approach emphasizes changes in the way people thought about law. The transfer of legal norms often relies on a prior methodological reception; without a methodical approach, norms cannot be applied.[131] The reception of Roman law in the Middle Ages is a good example of how the spread of methods is of great relevance. For example, the spread of legal terminology that originated in Roman law influenced how jurists interacted with and interpreted indigenous European laws.[132] The reception of methods is thus an indispensable part of an examination of reception in its entirety.

Finally, Franz Wieacker strongly emphasizes systematic reception. He argues that in the case of the reception of Roman law, a 'scientification' (*Verwissenschaftlichung*) of law was crucial. Through Roman methods and doctrines, law was approached technically, rationally and reproducibly, resulting in a new foreign system being received—"an internally consistent and systematic approach to law".[133] In the context of both methodological and systematic reception, it is not sufficient just to scrutinize what norms of learned law we can find in Frisia; it is also important to examine the methods Frisians applied and how the Frisian legal system evolved.

However, the Frisian sources present a challenge. An overwhelming number of legal sources from the Middle Ages are normative sources such as records of customary law. This is a limiting factor in this examination since we have less direct evidence of non-normative reception. Nevertheless, the sources are not silent or lacking regarding methods and systems.

4.2 *Motives for Reception*

Reception is a process of countless individual and collective decisions and incidents, motivated by multifaceted and diverse reasons that vary depending on place, person, culture, context and society. Although seeking to identify all these reasons may prove futile, there are some overarching and fundamental reasons for receiving elements of another legal culture.

131 Kunkel, "Das Wesen der Rezeption", p. 2; Luts, "Jurisprudential Reception", p. 3.

132 Wieacker, "Stand der Rezeptionsforschung", p. 198.

133 Wieacker, "Stand der Rezeptionsforschung", p. 198 f. See also Luts, "Jurisprudential Reception", p. 3.

First, there needs to be a requirement to receive foreign norms or methods within a legal culture, particularly where they are otherwise lacking.[134] In such cases, foreign legal elements can be used to fill the gap in the recipient's legal culture, particularly if indigenous law is unable to cover a specific legal field or problem. Reception may also be due to a lack of written sources.[135] Such a motivation was expressed by the Scottish writer Thomas Craig in the early 17th century: "Here there is an extreme scarcity of written laws and naturally we follow the Civil Law (Roman law) in most matters."[136]

Second, a question of choice arises with regard to the willingness to receive new elements, namely which foreign legal culture is best suited for adopting its elements. This leads to the second significant reason for reception: prestige. Prestige is not separate from necessity because when a need arises, the choice of which legal tradition to receive can be motivated by prestige. When a legal culture is perceived as qualitatively superior, the prestige of that culture can motivate its reception. For example, the prestige of Roman law motivated its reception.[137]

4.3 *Reception of Learned Law in the Middle Ages*

This study focuses on the reception of learned law in 15th century Frisia. Learned law refers to the laws studied at Medieval universities, Canon and Roman law.[138] The latter is particularly significant as it was noted to be prevalent in Frisia in the 17th century. In order to explain the circumstances under which reception occurred, it is first necessary to outline how and why this context arose. Fortunately, the reception of Roman law is perhaps the most well-studied example of reception.[139]

Roman law in the context of the Middle Ages consisted of law texts compiled in the 6th century under Emperor Justinian. Prior to the 11th century, Roman law had largely disappeared from Western Europe, with only a few elements found in recorded Germanic laws of the Early Middle Ages, the *leges*

---

134 See Luts, "Jurisprudential Reception", p. 2 on reception motivated by necessity.

135 See Stein, *Roman law in European History*, pp. 88–92 about the example of reception of Roman law in the Medieval German territories.

136 Watson, *Legal transplants*, p. 46f. "*apud nos scriptarum legum maxima inopia, & naturaliter in plerisque negotiis jus Civile sequimur.*" The quotation is extracted from Craig, *Ius feudale*, 1655, lib. 1, tit. 2, p. 11. Alternatively Craig, *Ius feudale*, 1732, lib. 1, tit. 2 § 14, p. 14.

137 Graziadei, "Comparative Law", p. 16; Luts, "Jurisprudential Reception", p. 2.

138 In contrast to local and indigenous laws that were not usually studied. See Brundage, *Medieval Canon Law*, p. 59f.

139 See, for example, Feenstra, *Zur Rezeption in den Niederlanden*; Kunkel, "Reception of Roman law in Germany"; Stein, "Roman law in Medieval Scotland".

barbarorum.[140] The study of Roman law re-emerged in Northern Italy after the rediscovery of the Digest of Justinian's *Corpus Iuris Civilis* in the 11th century. Scholars studied the texts and developed means of comparing and interpreting law, with the University of Bologna at the center of these activities. There, and later at many other universities, scholars learned, taught and commented on legal texts in the form of glosses. The first group of scholars were known as 'glossators' because they wrote explanatory notes, or glosses, to the provisions of Roman law. Their successors, the 'commentators', began writing extensive commentaries on Roman law in the 13th century.[141]

The study of learned law subsequently spread through Western Europe, with universities being established in Paris, Oxford, Salamanca and other cities. At these places, students primarily learned Canon law, with Roman law serving a subsidiary role.[142] Nonetheless, knowledge of Roman law became widespread in European jurists' circles. Canon law was a vehicle for this spreading because wherever the Church was established in Europe, Canon law was applied, and Roman law became known and discussed. However, Roman law was not yet applied in secular courts at the time and was used only in ecclesiastical courts in a supportive manner. The study of Roman law was primarily a scholarly endeavor, influencing methods and systems, as well as Medieval jurists' way of thinking.[143] Additionally, the studying of Roman law attracted great interest because of its use in secular and ecclesiastical administration.

The interaction between Roman and Canon law was crucial, with jurists trained in Canon law adopting elements, techniques and argumentations from Roman law. This changed how Canon law was applied in practice.[144] The combination of Roman and Canon law became general law: *ius commune*. This *ius commune* encompassed concepts and practices of Roman and Canon law that were widely used in Catholic Europe. Additionally, glosses and commentaries of scholars on these laws formed part of the *ius commune*. Divergent legal traditions became comparable by the use of Latin because they were approached within the same framework.[145] Local jurists and courts, for example, turned to the *ius commune* as a supplementary legal system if local indigenous laws

140 One of these laws was the *Lex Frisionum*, the law of the Frisians. A brief overview of this source was given in chapter 1.3.

141 Hallebeek, "Structure of Medieval Roman Law", p. 288 ff.

142 Stein, *Roman law in European History*, p. 89. See also Atzeri, *Roman Law and Reception*, p. 60.

143 Robinson, et al., *European Legal History*, pp. 108–109.

144 Clarke, "Western Canon law", p. 277.

145 Robinson, et al., *European Legal History*, pp. 107–109.

(*ius proprium*) were insufficient.[146] *Ius commune* differed in one significant way from *ius proprium*: both Roman and Canon law emphasized its universality, claiming general validity and, unlike local laws, not being restricted to specific geographical locations.[147]

Despite the absence of universities in Frisia during the Middle Ages, Frisians studied learned law. The first university in the Low Countries was opened in 1425 in Leuven in today's Belgium.[148] Before then, Frisians therefore had to travel far to study in France and Northern Italy and brought their acquired knowledge back home. In Frisia, monasteries became the centers of learned law, with monastic schools becoming places for teaching Canon law and Latin, and for copying manuscripts. By the end of the 15th century, Frisia had around 50 of these monasteries, among them Bloemkamp, Aduard, Mariengaarde and Lidlum. These places were often administered by jurists who had studied at European universities, such as Dirk van Tzummarum (14th century) who became abbot of Lidlum.[149] Another abbot, Emo van Huizinge (1175–1237), had studied in Paris, Orleans and Oxford before returning to Frisia to become head of the monastery of Wittewierum. He was even the first foreign student at Oxford.[150] Abbots such as Emo played a crucial role in the teaching and spreading of Canon and Roman law in Frisia.

4.3.1 The Manners in Which Learned Law Spread

The interactions with local indigenous laws initiated a process of reception. The development and manifestation of this process depended on the circumstances of the societies where the reception took place. In the literature, the process of reception is sometimes categorized into 'early reception' (*Frührezeption*) and 'later or comprehensive reception' (*Spät- oder Vollrezeption*).[151] An 'early reception' of Roman law is considered to have occurred if it took place before the 15th century.[152] Such early reception primarily involved the reception of terminology and legal education, rather than norms. For example, diplo-

146 Atzeri, *Roman Law and Reception*, p. 59; Brundage, *Medieval Canon Law*, p. 60f.

147 Hallebeek, "Structure of Medieval Roman law", p. 303.

148 Lesaffer, *Europese Rechtsgeschiedenis*, p. 225.

149 Apeldoorn, "Romeinsche Recht", pp. 405 and 410–414.

150 Gerbenzon, *Emo van Huizinge*, p. 6.

151 'Rezeption' in: Basedow, et al., *Handwörterbuch des europäischen Privatrechts*. A division in 'Früh- and Vollrezeption' is also noted for the Netherlands in Feenstra, "Zur Rezeption in den Niederlanden", p. 251.

152 This is noted for the Netherlands in Feenstra, "Zur Rezeption in den Niederlanden", p. 251. Atzeri places 'early reception' in central Europe in the late Middle Ages; see Atzeri, *Roman Law and Reception*, p. 59.

matic documents contained influences of Roman law before even jurisprudence did, without any adoption as yet of norms.

According to Wieacker, the early application of Roman law in ecclesiastical courts and documents was an endogenic process, facilitated through internal education and the organization of jurists of the Catholic Church. However, exogenous reception and application of Roman law still occurred without being facilitated through internal ecclesiastical jurists.[153] The *ius commune* and its spread of legal terminology is an example of such an early reception.

Other legal historians have emphasized that the primary difference between early and later reception was quantitative, with the manner of reception not being clearly distinct, but the extent of later reception being much greater.[154]

Reception was often facilitated through a lack of local or regional norms. When indigenous laws were deemed insufficient regarding an area of law, advice from trained jurists was sought. These jurists then turned to the *ius commune* to fill these gaps.

The Romano-canonical procedure is an example of such early reception. Canonists received elements of Roman procedural law that, in combination with existing Canon law, created this new procedure, i.e., Romano-canonical. These new rules were applied in ecclesiastical courts across Europe and were increasingly initiated in secular courts.[155] Indigenous law was not necessarily replaced in a Romano-canonical procedure, but learned law was often referenced to support arguments. When written proof of an assertion was demanded and could not be found in indigenous law, litigants turned to the written *ius commune*. Parties approached university law faculties and their jurists because they perceived them as impartial and preferred their consultation.[156] In this manner, learned law was applied in tandem with local laws. Such an application falls under the category of a reception out of necessity, rather than one out of prestige. Gaps in indigenous law needed to be filled to

153 Wieacker, "Stand der Rezeptionsforschung", pp. 198–201.

154 Feenstra, "Zur Rezeption in den Niederlanden", p. 251.

155 For the canonical procedure, see Brundage, *Medieval Canon Law*, pp. 120–153. See also Helmholz, *The spirit of classical canon law*, p. 89 ff., who examines the *restitutio ad integrum*.

156 Feenstra, "Zur Rezeption in den Niederlanden", p. 264; Robinson, et al., *European Legal History*, pp. 197–199; Stein, *Roman law in European History*, p. 90. A lack of codified local rights was therefore a disadvantage in court procedures and led to increasing Romanization of legal systems; see Atzeri, *Roman Law and Reception*, p. 61. Evidence of such procedures is found in Frisian sources. Especially in the collected arguments from case records in the *Excerpta Legum*, see Buma, et al., *Codex Aysma*, p. XIII f.

resolve ongoing cases. An intent to override indigenous law cannot therefore be attributed to this process.

The Romano-canonical procedure was not received everywhere in the same manner. While examples of this procedure can be found in Scandinavia in the Late Middle Ages, not all aspects of local indigenous procedures were abandoned. Oath-helpers, for example, remained a characteristic feature, and something that was not present in learned law.[157]

Learned law was also consulted and applied even when local laws existed, but where they were not recorded.[158] This was partly a consequence of advisors and jurists demanding proof and evidence in written form. To this end, they consulted written law texts. We can refer to this as 'codification' in the sense that the regional indigenous provisions collected were recorded in a written law text.[159] When local laws were not reliably codified, such evidence could only come from learned law, and jurists were educated in the *ius commune* and could therefore reference it. We find such references to learned law in the case records of Romano-canonical procedures in Frisia, alongside references to recorded and codified indigenous Frisian law.[160]

If the absence of codified laws allowed for the reception of learned law, then the existence of indigenous codified law proved to be an obstacle to such reception. In France and Saxony, for instance, customary law was codified and consulted, resulting in Roman law having considerably less influence than in regions with few or no codifications.[161]

Although Frisia had its own collection of recorded indigenous laws, known as the *Freeska Landriucht*, the presence of such records did not hinder the reception of Roman law. In fact, the application of Roman law was noted as early as the 15th century, and even more so in the 17th century. This challenges the aforementioned theory that recorded indigenous Frisian law would have constituted an obstacle to the reception of Roman law. Part of this study entails examining why the presence of recorded indigenous sources did not constitute a significant hindrance for the reception of Roman law. One possible explanation is that the *Freeska Landriucht* was already outdated by the time it was printed at the end of the Middle Ages, with some texts still making reference to

157 Korpiola, *Medieval Scandinavia*, p. 395. A detailed investigation of the Romano-canonical procedure and oaths follows in chapter 3.

158 Stein, *Roman law in European History*, p. 90.

159 As, for example, with the *Freeska Landriucht* in the incunable *D*. For the later, 19th-century use of codification, see Halpérin, "The Age of Codification".

160 Many case records were collected within the Excerpta Legum. On their nature, see Buma, et al., *Codex Aysma*, p. XIII; Gerbenzon, *Excerpta Legum*, pp. 237–261.

161 Stein, *Roman law in European History*, p. 90.

the *skelta*, an official who had disappeared by the Late Middle Ages.[162] Therefore, the *Freeska Landriucht* did not reflect the 15th-century legal reality.

Another important aspect of reception is the terminology of law. Learned law has its own terms with specific legal meanings, and the challenges and applications of legal terminology were outlined above.[163] Language played a crucial role in facilitating the application and applicability of learned law through translating, describing and interpreting indigenous words.[164] This has crucial relevance for the analysis of Medieval sources.

This linguistic challenge goes beyond loanwords in the Old Frisian language. Loanwords from Latin were introduced through contact between the Roman Empire and the early Germanic societies. With the Christianization of Frisia, Latin loanwords relating to Church and religion, such as *biskop* (from Latin *episcopus*), were introduced.[165] In later centuries, and until the 14th century, Frisians avoided loanwords and translated specific legal terms. For example, the Latin term *legatum* (legacy) was translated as *bisprekma* or *bisprekinge*. Frisians made an effort to find fitting words in their own language. The change from translated terms to loanwords occurred in the 15th century, when such terms were less often translated: *legāt* appears in place of *bisprekma*. The relationship between these loanwords and the reception of learned law has yet to be examined.[166]

A final avenue for the reception of learned law was the motivation of individuals. Kings, emperors and other local and regional authorities were sometimes interested in receiving Roman law.[167] The idea of a continuation between the Roman Empire and the Holy Roman Empire contributed to this willingness. This was expressed by the notion of the *Politische Romidee* or 'political idea of Rome'.[168] The concept of Rome and all its political implications was utilized by kings and emperors for contemporary politics.[169] Reception of this kind was

162 For the offices of the *skelta* and its successor, the *gretman*, see the glossary. See also Algra, *Oudfries Recht*, p. 247; Fairbanks, *Skeltana Riucht*, pp. 16–22; Nijdam, *Lichaam, eer en recht*, p. 150; Vries, *Asega, is het dingtijd?*, p. 15.

163 See chapter 1.1.

164 Hallebeek, "Structure of Medieval Roman law", p. 304.

165 Bremmer, *An introduction*, pp. 94–95.

166 On these terms and the use of translated terms and loanwords, see Gerbenzon, *Friese Rechtstaal*, pp. 14–15.

167 The idea of a '*translatio imperii*' was influential in convincing rulers to favor the study of Roman law. This was especially relevant for the Holy Roman emperors. Hallebeek, "Structure of Medieval Roman law", pp. 290–291; Stein, *Roman law in European History*, p. 91.

168 Koschaker, *Europa und das römische Recht*.

169 Feenstra, "Zur Rezeption in den Niederlanden", p. 251.

consequently influenced more by prestige than by necessity. However, practical purposes also played a role. For one, applying Roman law suggested that rulers and their dominions followed the traditions of Ancient Rome, thus strengthening their legitimacy as successors of Rome. Moreover, application of Roman law served to create internal unity and establish a contrast to other foreign legal systems. The Burgundians aimed to centralize their legal system in the Low Countries in the 15th century and wished to cut any ties with the French and Imperial systems. To this end they supported and influenced reception of Roman law in their territories by establishing their own legal system based on Roman law and separate from the French and Imperial systems.[170] Lastly, reception of Roman law was also beneficial for the many princes in the empire as it increased their authority over their subjects and in particular over local lords.[171]

Regarding Frisia, some differences must be noted. Most importantly, Westerlauwers Frisia was not under princely rule and therefore had no local princes able to actively support receiving Roman law. This lack of central authority appears nonetheless not to have impeded reception as many of the traditional Frisian laws were ascribed to various Frankish or Holy Roman emperors. This was especially true for Charlemagne, who in Frisian myth was responsible not only for the Frisian freedom but for many laws as well.[172] The *Book of Emperor Rudolf* from the 13th century also reflects this sentiment.[173] Frisian law was thus connected to the Medieval emperors who were themselves linked to the Roman Empire, as is clearly apparent in the use of *Keizerrecht*, meaning 'emperor's law', in Frisian sources. *Keizerrecht* referred to imperial law enacted by the Holy Roman emperors, but was also used to refer to Roman law.[174]

Yet, the connection between Frisia and the Holy Roman emperors was nominal at best. Frisians had a long and varied history of connection to the empire. At times they approached various emperors to seek support in their endeavors to stay free.[175] However, the lack of any central structures in Frisia meant that

170 Feenstra, "Zur Rezeption in den Niederlanden", p. 262 ff.

171 Stein, *Roman law in European History*, p. 91.

172 While Frisians of the Middle Ages describe many of their laws and customs to various emperors, these connections were often nothing more than myths and tales. The privileges of Charlemagne that gave the Frisians their freedom were not authentic. Yet, they were used with great pride by Frisians as legitimization. On the inauthenticity of the document, see Von Richthofen, *Untersuchungen* II. See also Vries, *Roomse Rijk*, p. 21 ff.

173 It is unclear as to which emperor is supposed to have given the Frisians this book. See Meijering, Nijdam, '*Wat is Recht?*', p. 427.

174 Feenstra, "Zur Rezeption in den Niederlanden", p. 252 ff.

175 On these relations, see, for example, Vries, *Het Heilige Rooms Rijk*.

neither princely nor imperial authority imposed the reception of Roman law. Consequently, a sovereign's individual motivation was not decisive regarding reception in Frisia.

Let us therefore turn to the reasons and processes that have been identified so far for the reception of learned law in Frisia.

4.4 *Scholarly Endeavors regarding Reception in Frisia*

Although some studies exist, research by historians and legal scholars on reception in Frisia is limited. Early theories attributed the extensive application of Roman law in Frisia to the new Saxon rulers in the early 16th century. Huber claimed that Frisian law had declined in the 15th century, writing that: "for since the new princes found the country almost in a state of anarchy and without any recognized system of law, they at once introduced the Roman law here."[176]

However, recent literature has challenged this view of a 'lawless' 15th century characterized by feuds between the Schieringer and Vetkoper factions. While political and economic decline during this period is debated, it is clear that Frisians had an established legal system that they actively engaged with and modified, as evidenced by sources such as the *Jurisprudentia Frisica*. Therefore, the notion of the 'lawless century' leading to the demise of Frisian law is unconvincing.[177]

Nonetheless, scholars continued to claim until the 20th century that the Saxon dukes brought Roman law to Frisia after the Frisian freedom ended. This idea places reception in the early 16th century, typically in 1504 when George of Saxony supposedly instituted Roman law. According to some scholars, the Frisians had the option to choose between Roman or Saxon law. They decided to follow the former and this was confirmed by George.[178] In the 19th century,

176 "Want alsoo het land schier zonder recht, en onderhout van wetten, by de nieuwe Fursten wierde gevonden, hebben zy het roomsche recht alhier dadelijk ingevoert." Huber, *Heedendaegse*, I.11.46, p. 9. English translation in: Huber, *Jurisprudence*, p. 8. Huber specifically mentions the old Frisians law given by Charlemagne and how they "sunk into oblivion". He also mentions the "barbarity of the times of the Schieringers and Vetkooper" in Huber, *Heedendaegse*, I.11.44, p. 9.

177 On the debate about the crisis of the 15th century, see Noomen, "Friese vetemaatschappij", pp. 48–49, who outlines the role of feuds in Frisian society. Noomen emphasizes that these feuds did not lead to general disorder because they were part of conflict resolution. Other scholars focus on the increasing violence in the late 15th century; see, for example, Mol, "Hoofdelingen en huurlingen" and Gerrits, Mol, "Macht, geweld en monniken".

178 This is stated in Rengers, *Dissertatio*, p. 66. (late 18th century) Others who placed the application of Roman law under the Saxon dukes in the early 16th century are Conring, *De Origine*, p. 206 (17th century) and Hamerster, *Naukeurige*, pr. (18th century), who also mentions a period of common chaos in the 15th century.

Isaac Telting (1831–1895) briefly considered the question of reception, arguing that Frisian law was valid until the end of the 15th century, but that foreign elements of Roman and Canon law had already been incorporated by that time. According to Telting, it was not until the 16th century, with the establishment of the Hof van Friesland high court by the Saxon dukes, that Roman law was consciously accepted and increasingly applied through case law before being formally introduced as subsidiary law in 1524.[179]

4.4.1 Lambertus Johannes van Apeldoorn

The mid-20th century saw renewed scholarly interest in the reception of learned law in Frisia. This resulted in several contributions, the first of which was published in 1940 by Lambertus van Apeldoorn (1886–1979) and entitled "Het Romeinsche Recht in Friesland". Van Apeldoorn's study emphasizes the moment in time when the prevailing legal opinion was that Roman law had validity in Frisia. It de-emphasizes reception through introduction by a legislator or through case law.[180] This makes it possible for reception to have occurred at a very early date. Indeed, Van Apeldoorn argues that Roman law had binding power in Frisia from the 13th century onwards, and thus long before the 15th century.[181] He primarily observes this through references to *keysers riucht*[182] in Frisian sources, which were assumed to refer specifically to Roman law.[183]

However, this interpretation has since been challenged. In "Römisches Recht und Kaiserrecht in den Altfriesischen Rechtsquellen" (1956), Robert Feenstra (1920–2013) details why he disagrees with Van Apeldoorn's assessment. While he contends that rules of Roman law were known and present in Frisian law from the 13th century onwards, he argues that no application of these rules is evident until the late 15th century.[184] Furthermore, he argues that references to *keysers riucht* are not made exclusively to Roman law. Instead, they refer mostly to Frisian law, such as the *Book of Emperor Rudolf*, and other laws connected to various emperors.[185]

Van Apeldoorn further asserts that stagnancy in the 15th century enabled reception of Roman law. A lack of recorded law and case law impeded the development of Frisian law and decreased the use of traditional norms, enabling

179 Telting, "De invoering", pp. 48–49 for Roman law in the 14th and 15th centuries; pp. 56–57 for the introduction by the Saxon dukes.
180 Apeldoorn, "Romeinsche Recht", p. 389.
181 Apeldoorn, "Romeinsche Recht", p. 391.
182 Literally "The law of the emperor". See also Krause, *Kaiserrecht und Rezeption.*
183 Apeldoorn, "Romeinsche Recht", p. 398.
184 Feenstra, "Römisches Recht", p. 34.
185 Feenstra, "Römisches Recht", pp. 31–32.

Frisians to apply Roman law instead of non-functioning Frisian law. Van Apeldoorn deviates from Huber in that he places reception not after the end of the Frisian freedom, but instead in the centuries before. It was the chaos of the 15th century that strengthened application of Roman law.[186] As with Huber, this idea that reception was enabled by a failing Frisian legal system and economic decline is unsatisfying, especially given the many compilations of law texts undertaken in the 15th century. Frisian law was by no means stagnating in this period. As such, Van Apeldoorn's assertion is unsupported.

Van Apeldoorn's final argument concerns the role of ecclesiastical institutions and the clergy. These institutions were not only familiar with Roman law, but also had a widespread presence and considerable wealth.[187] Van Apeldoorn argues that the influence of the clergy in Frisia was especially great when compared to that in the other Low Countries. Clerics were engaged not only in ecclesiastical, but also in secular matters, thus making them influential in local governance.[188] Van Apeldoorn asserts, for example, that ecclesiastical courts took on cases in secular jurisdictions because of the dysfunctionality of secular courts.[189] In conclusion, clerics facilitated the reception of Roman law by studying and applying it in their own legal system. Moreover, this phenomenon appeared wherever the clergy had sufficient influence or participated in government or arbitration.

4.4.2 Pieter Gerbenzon

The final argument made by Van Apeldoorn has been echoed in subsequent literature, particularly in the works of Pieter Gerbenzon (1920–2009), who emphasizes the role of clergy and Canon law in his assessments of reception in Frisia. Gerbenzon was an important scholar for the legal history of Frisia and published extensively in Frisian, Dutch and German from the 1940s onwards. His research on numerous sources is referenced throughout this book. Gerbenzon made two contributions to the question of reception: one in a critique of Van Apeldoorn's arguments in 1956 entitled "Kanonisches Recht in den Friesischen Rechtsquellen" and another in 1959 entitled "Enkele nieuwe gegevens over de receptie van het Romeinse recht in Friesland".

In addition to his work on the question of reception, Gerbenzon's research on Frisian legal sources is invaluable. He published a comprehensive book on

186 Apeldoorn, "Romeinsche Recht", pp. 434–436.
187 Apeldoorn, "Romeinsche Recht", p. 406 ff.
188 Apeldoorn, "Romeinsche Recht", p. 414 ff.
189 Apeldoorn, "Romeinsche Recht", p. 420.

the *Excerpta Legum*, which remains relevant and crucial to this day.[190] This contains examinations of the structure and sources of the text, rather than of the contents of its rules. In 1989, he also published a comprehensive analysis of the structure and sources of the *Jurisprudentia Frisica*, which remains the most significant analysis of this source.[191] Furthermore, in 1993, Gerbenzon, Buma and Tragter-Schubert prepared a complete German translation of the *Codex Aysma*, which includes the *Excerpta Legum*.[192] This book remains the principal translation of the *Excerpta Legum* drawn on in contemporary research.

Despite being written over 60 years ago, Gerbenzon's contributions to this debate remain authoritative. Gerbenzon was a pre-eminent scholar of Frisian law, learned law in Frisia, and their connection in the Frisian sources. The following paragraph explains his response to Van Apeldoorn's assertions and the arguments he put forth. However, this foundation is critically examined and challenged in this study.

Gerbenzon emphasizes how Canon law paved the way for the reception of Roman law in Frisia. According to him, Frisian law was first 'Canonized' before Roman law was adapted and adopted. Canon law entered Frisia early on and had a substantial influence on its secular law through the 13th and 14th centuries. Gerbenzon argues that it was primarily Canon law that was received in Frisia. The rules of learned law were translated into the vernacular, Old Frisian, and customized to suit existing Frisian legal practice.[193] Consequently, a 'Canonized' Frisian law emerged, in which Roman law played only a supporting role. From the second half of the 15th century, both Canon and Roman law were perceived as valid.[194] Gerbenzon sees the prevalence of Roman law as emerging in the 16th century, when the power of the clergy was reduced.[195] In his examination of learned law in the *Codex Parisiensis*, Gerbenzon concludes that these sources provide a link between the "Germanic Frisian law [and] the strongly Romanized Frisian law of the sixteenth and seventeenth centuries".[196] In con-

190 Gerbenzon, *Excerpta legum*. Many of the insights regarding the structure of the source, as well as the origin of its provisions, stem from this analysis.

191 Published in two parts:
Gerbenzon, "Aantekeningen (Eerste Deel)".
Gerbenzon, "Aantekeningen (Tweede Deel)".

192 Buma, et al., *Codex Aysma*.

193 Gerbenzon, "Kanonisches Recht", pp. 38–41.

194 Gerbenzon, "Enkele nieuwe gegevens", p. 137.

195 Gerbenzon, "Enkele nieuwe gegevens", pp. 154–157.

196 Gerbenzon, "Codex Parisiensis", p. 143.

clusion, Gerbenzon argues that Frisian law was initially influenced by Canon law, and that this paved the way for the reception of Roman law. The transition towards a 'Romanized' Frisian law occurred only after the end of the Frisian freedom and the beginning of Saxon rule.

4.4.3 My Own Approach

There has been little significant research about reception since Gerbenzon. Frisian history (especially legal history) is a very small field of study and one that has not attracted large numbers of scholars. Perhaps Gerbenzon's conclusions provide a satisfactory answer to the question of reception. Yet, there are reasons to re-engage with reception in a comprehensive and extensive manner.

First, there has been a lack of focus on the period before 1500. Approaching the question of reception in chronological order, beginning with the Medieval Frisian sources, means placing the emphasis on the preceding centuries. Indeed, this period is crucial for understanding the development of Frisian law, given that the processes of reception began long before 1498.

Second, examination of Frisian law in the Middle Ages has been sparse. Recent research into law has focused primarily on traditional Frisian law, with little interest in the interaction with learned law, thus creating a gap in the research.[197] It is now time, therefore, to fill this gap by re-examining the reception of learned law in 15th century Frisia.

Lastly, Gerbenzon himself supplies a particularly good reason for such re-examination by arguing that only the utilization of new source material can be a valid justification for new research.[198] The source material available has since been greatly improved, with many sources becoming more accessible and understandable through new translations of texts and glosses. Although the latter have so far been neglected by scholars, they will prove to be insightful and revealing. By taking recent translations and findings into account, we can achieve an updated insight into the question of reception of learned law in 15th-century Frisia. Earlier scholars were not able to rely on these qualitative developments, meaning we now have the opportunity to re-examine their assessments through a close analysis of primary sources and to observe the extent to which their findings can be sustained or must be emended.

197 Examples of contemporary research include Bremmer, "The orality of Old Frisian law texts"; Meijering, Nijdam, '*Wat is Recht?*'; Nijdam, *Lichaam, eer en recht*.

198 Gerbenzon, "Enkele nieuwe gegevens", p. 133.

5 The Five Subjects of This Study

This study consists of five topics, covering five distinct fields of law: *niarkap*, proof, theft, testaments and widows.

Chapter 2: *Niarkap*. This chapter delves into the law of contracts and its reception in Frisia. It provides an overview of Medieval contracts, including those in Roman, Frisian and Canon law. The chapter explores how Frisians conceptualized contracts and how the Roman and Canon law of contracts differed. It examines whether the law of contracts was comprehensively received in Frisia because the latter lacked rules regarding contracts. Special consideration is given to *niarkap* (the right of relatives and neighbors to take over a sale), which functionally limited the ability to freely alienate land. The chapter also explores whether the reception of learned law influenced *niarkap* in the context of contract law.

Chapter 3: Proof. The third chapter investigates changes in procedural law, with a focus on the proofs that litigants provided during procedures. The legal procedure in Frisia is described and compared with the procedure of the *ius commune* in the Middle Ages. In traditional Frisian law, the primary ways of providing proof were oaths and ordeals. With the reception of learned law, these proofs were supplemented by proofs of learned law such as witnesses and instruments. This chapter examines the changes in Frisian procedural law and its use of old and new ways of providing proof.

Chapter 4: Theft. This chapter consists of an analysis of theft in Frisian law and the influence that learned law, especially Roman law, had on it. Theft as a criminal act, and representing the field of criminal law in today's understanding of law, was highly relevant in Medieval Frisian society because it was seen as especially reprehensive. The chapter explores the influences of the methods and system of Roman law on Frisian theft, primarily on punishments, as well as house searches, which were traditionally used to investigate theft.

Chapter 5: Testaments. This chapter examines last wills and testaments, which belong to the field of law of succession. They are especially interesting for an analysis of reception because traditional Frisian law lacked any rules regarding testaments. The chapter examines the intestate succession law in Frisia, as well as early forms of wills. The primary emphasis is on the appearance and reception of testament in the 14th and 15th centuries. During the Middle Ages, two distinct forms of testaments existed: those made according to Roman law and those made according to Canon law. As well as analyzing the form that Frisian testators applied and examining the formalities of making a testament, such as the number of witnesses, the institution of heirs, and the requirements of a testator, the chapter explores the relationship between Canon and Roman law and how the reception of elements of the Roman testament occurred in the context of Canon law being present earlier in the Middle Ages.

Chapter 6: Widows and widowhood. This chapter covers the area of family law, which is often assumed to be one of the areas of law least changed by the reception of Roman law.[199] Additionally, widows provide a unique opportunity for insight into the social position of Medieval women. Widows are the most visible of all Medieval women, especially in documents, testaments and other sources. As such, it is possible to examine how the reception of learned law changed their lives, both in theory and in practice. The chapter begins by detailing the financial assets that widows had access to. This relates back to the previous chapter because widows frequently made testaments to distribute their property. The influence of learned law on the life and social status of widows is examined from two perspectives: the ability to be a guardian of their own children and guardianship over widows themselves.

By examining these five topics, I provide an initial insight into the evolution of Frisian law regarding the reception of learned law. This is not a comprehensive overview of reception, as further research and analysis are required. Nonetheless, it serves as a step towards better comprehension of how Frisian law evolved.

199 Floßmann, *Gleichberechtigung der Geschlechter*, p. 129; Wiesner, *Gender, Church and State*, p. 85.

CHAPTER 2

Niarkap and the Law of Contracts

The Old Frisian term *niarkap* (German: *Näherrecht*;[1] Dutch: *naasting*[2]) refers to the right of the 'nearest' to take over a sale. In Medieval Frisia, this right customarily fell to the relatives or neighbors, who could take over a sale and acquire the land for themselves if someone wanted to sell their own land. This prevented land from being sold to someone outside the family or parish.[3]

While *niarkap* was not a contractual right and not part of the law of contracts, it was related to contracts because it limited the persons to whom Frisians could sell their property. A contract of sale preceded every instance of taking over a sale. Therefore, *niarkap* has indirect relevance for contract law. The interest of someone with a right to *niarkap* had to be considered when a contract of sale was agreed upon.

Furthermore, this right to take over a sale contradicted a fundamental principle of the learned law of contracts (in both Roman and Canon law): mutual consent between contracting parties. This consent was necessary for entering into a contract, but it was absent in *niarkap*. No consent was needed in Medieval Frisia for a third party to take over a sale. An examination of *niarkap* in the context of contract law is therefore interesting as it provides insight into the way contracts were concluded in traditional and late Medieval Frisian law.

1 'Näherrecht' in: Erler, at al., *Handwörterbuch zur deutschen Rechtsgeschichte*, p. 828. On the terminology of *niarkap* in Old Frisian, including its many regional and local forms, see Vries, "Nijaer is sijd", pp. 267–273.

2 De Blécourt provides a quick overview of *naasting* in Dutch legal history, see De Blécourt, *Kort Begrip*, pp. 101–102.

3 Vries, "Nijaer is sijd", p. 262 ff. This concept continues to have relevance to this day. In 2022, the Dutch government proposed giving municipalities a right to assign houses and apartments to people already living in the municipality. The intention is to combat the increasing inability of people to pay rent or buy houses where they live. The proposal would allow municipalities to give preference to local inhabitants or crucial professions (teachers, nurses, etc.) when a house is sold. At the end of 2022, the bill was still in preparation and no parliamentary debate has yet occurred. Rijksoverheid. *Gemeenten krijgen meer ruimte om huur- en koopwoningen toe te wijzen aan inwoners met lokale binding*. www.rijksoverheid.nl, 13 September 2022. Accessed: 07 December 2022. This bill is interesting because it relates to the fundamental principle of *niarkap*: relatives and neighbors have a right to acquire land before outsiders. Evidently, communities throughout history have had a vested interest in preserving their communal structures.

 | DOI:10.1163/9789004712706_003

1 Medieval 'Law of Contracts'

Roman law had no general law of contracts. Not all agreements gave rise to enforceable obligations. Moreover, the types of agreement that did were each governed by their own specific rules. The term *conventio* referred to all agreements between parties, while *contractus* referred to agreements that resulted in obligations. *Pactum* or *pactio* originally referred to agreements that were still legally relevant but did not create obligations. Over time, however, *pacta* also included enforceable parts and the distinction from contracts became blurred.[4] The number of different types of *contractus* was limited, and they were a loosely defined category sharing some common characteristics, such as the requirement for mutual consent between parties, given that no contract could exist without such consent. Legal acts resulting in obligations but not requiring mutual consent were called 'quasi-contracts'. Obligations resulting from contracts bound only the two parties and never a third party, and performances had to be both factually and legally possible.[5]

This was a closed system of contracts, whereby the form and content of a contract defined what kind of contract it was. Roman law recognized four categories of contracts: real contracts (*contractus re*), consensual contracts (*contractus consensus*), verbal contracts (*contractus verbis* or *stipulatio*) and literal contracts (*contractus litteris*). For instance, a real contract had to be made in person and involve the transfer of a thing, while a *stipulatio* required a spoken formula (question and answer) that was open-ended in terms of content. This Roman system of contracts was specific to categories of contracts and formulaic in nature.[6]

This system was no longer considered practical during the Middle Ages, when jurists began to modify it to suit the needs of their societies. A new law of contracts, sometimes referred to as the Canon law of contracts, developed from the *ius commune*. Natural law held that all agreements were binding, and canonists interpreted Roman law in the same manner. This led to the fundamental principle that all agreements had to be kept (*pacta sunt servanda*), as expressed in the Decretals of Gregory IX.[7] The salvation of souls was an essential reason for this change because people feared that breaking a contract would lead to suffering in the afterlife.

---

4 Domingo, "The Roman law of contracts", p. 2.

5 Kaser, *Das römische Privatrecht* II, p. 362 ff.; Hallebeek, *Fons*, pp. 173–181.

6 Kaser, *Das römische Privatrecht* II, p. 365 ff.; Hallebeek, *Fons*, pp. 173–181 and Decock, *Theologians*, p. 108.

7 X 1.35.1.pr: "Pacta quantumcumque nuda servanda sunt."

Although the system of contract law remained a closed system, it allowed for more actionability. A 'naked agreement' (*pactum nudum*) was an agreement made with mutual consent between the two parties and had no other formulaic requirements. However, Roman law did not consider naked agreements to be part of the contracts acknowledged by law and prohibited them from being actionable. Medieval jurists began to change this by dressing naked agreements in 'clothes' (*vestimenta*). Such 'clothes' could be specific performances, wording or writing, and they made 'clothed' agreements enforceable. While Medieval contract law did not yet develop a general law of contracts, it succeeded in making naked agreements binding.[8]

2 Contracts in Frisian Law

There is ample evidence of various and distinct agreements between Frisian parties. Frisians sold and purchased land and goods, rented and leased out land and houses, made deposits, and entered into shared partnerships of property, among other things.[9] While it may be argued that Frisian law contained very little on contracts, most of the norms applying to social and legal interactions were not written down. Nonetheless, written sources provide some insight into contracts and contract law in Frisia. A few examples will suffice to provide a brief overview of the topic.

Common terms for a contract or agreement in the Old Frisian language included *ēntele* (agreement, contract),[10] *wed* (pledge, promise, contract)[11] and *forewerde* (agreement, contract).[12]

---

8 Decock, *Theologians*, pp. 108–113.

9 A number of documents from the 14th and 15th centuries concern sales. It can be assumed that earlier sales also took place but were not documented. Indeed, documents of sale are the most frequent types of documents that survived; see Vries, *Ferdban*, p. 14. For some examples of such documents, see the collection of documents in Vries, *Ferdban*, p. 49 ff. Renting and leasing are mentioned in such texts as the *Market Law* (MrWl 3) and the *Eight Provisions* (Dom 3). For more details on these texts, see later in this chapter. For deposits and shared partnerships, see the *Twenty-four Land Laws* (L^{24} 18).

10 'ēntele' Hofmann, Popkema, *Altfriesisches Handwörterbuch*, p. 121.

11 'wed' Hofmann, Popkema, *Altfriesisches Handwörterbuch*, p. 570. This term is often used for a 'pledge'; see Algra, Oudfries recht, p. 349 for promises that are made when a woman is given into marriage.

12 'forewerde' Hofmann, Popkema, *Altfriesisches Handwörterbuch*, p. 160.

2.1 *Contract of Sale*

Frisian written sources do not provide any formal or specific qualifications about how a contract of sale was entered into. However, certain circumstances allowed or prohibited Frisians from selling their property, and these exceptional circumstances were recorded.[13] Some documents detailing purchases (known as a *kaepbreef*) have survived from the Middle Ages. While these documents are not contracts in themselves, they attest to sales that were contracted and the manner in which these sales were contracted. Essentially, a *kaepbreef* is written documentation evidencing that an oral contract has been concluded. For example, a document from 1390 provides details of the land that had been sold and specifies by whom, to whom, the price of the purchase, the manner in which the price was paid (in this particular case, partly in cash and partly in horned cattle) and when the payment had to be made (handed over on three days spread over the entire year); ultimately, the document was sealed by the purchaser.[14]

While this *kaepbreef* provides information on the payment method, it does not specify the form of the contract of sale. Its primary function was to announce and attest to the sale, which was typical for the Frisian legal system. Prior to the late 14th and 15th centuries, sales were announced orally in court. After a contract had been concluded, both parties asked the local court to announce the transfer and proclaim a 'peace' (*ferdban*) over the sale. The *ferdban* was a judicial act that ensured that no-one would harm the buyer and confirmed the buyer's right to the purchased property. In a society that was primarily oral, this served to inform everyone of the purchase and simultaneously created evidence that it had happened. Consequently, the sale was concluded, and the buyer could be certain that their ownership of the sold property could no longer be disputed.[15]

---

13 For example in L[24] 2, which states that a mother was not allowed to alienate her child's goods, except in three circumstances of uttermost need: ransom of the child, famine and homelessness. See *D*, VIII (L[24]) 2, pp. 214–215.

14 The document can be found in Vries, *Ferdban*, p. 49 ff.

15 On the announcement of a sale and the *ferdban*, see Vries, "Also dat wy habbet", p. 244. On the judicial act, see Oosten, "Vredeban", pp. 387 and 396. The term and the concept were likely to have been received from Holland, presumably when the Count of Holland ruled over Friesland in the early 14th century. Vries, "Also dat wy habbet", pp. 246 and 261.

2.2 *Leasing and Renting*

In contrast to learned law, no Frisian law text explains renting and leasing.[16] Rent and lease were likely to have been understood according to customs. However, specific texts arose to deal with particular problems in legal practice, and these provide insight into such contracts, especially those regarding land and houses. Knowledge about Frisian contracts can be gained only by observing specific norms that were written down in legal texts and extrapolating what these norms may tell us about contract law.

How frequently Frisians rented and leased land is unknown. However, land appears to have been the primary object of lease, although people in larger towns also rented houses. Written Frisian law provides neither an explanation of the kind of lease contracts that existed, nor how they should be entered into. The Old Frisian term for a tenant was *landseta*, and the term for landlord was *landhera*. Written law does not define the period of a lease, but at least one lease for an indefinite period is found in the *Older Skelta Law*:

> Van landhera nyer toe witane
> SkRa 50. Dit is riucht: jef di landsata queth dat hi dat land toe aheer ontfensen habbe, dat di hera nyer is toe witane op da helligham hoe langhe dae forwerda se, soe di landsata.

> Concerning the rights of the landlord
> SkRa 50. This is the law: if a tenant says that he holds the land on eternal lease, the landlord has a stronger right to confirm that the period of lease has lapsed by swearing an oath on the holy relics than the tenant (has to deny this).[17]

This provision is believed to have originated from a legal case in which a tenant claimed that the land was leased for eternity, while the landlord denied it. The provision confirms the landlord's stronger right in this matter. According to the provision, the landlord can confirm that the lease period has expired by taking an oath, which was the usual method of proof in a Frisian court.[18] It is likely that this provision was written down to provide guidance for similar disputes in the future.

---

16 The Roman *Digests* explain what leasing and hiring are and how they relate to sale and purchase. See D. 19.2.1.

17 *D*, III (SkRa) 50, pp. 144–145.

18 On the procedural law and proof in Frisia, see the next chapter.

The provision specifically addresses the issue of an "eternal lease," which suggests that Frisians recognized different types of leases of varying lengths, including leases without an end date. It is probable that most leases had a limited period, and that eternal leases were an exception.

The *Freeska Landriucht* mentions leases only one other time, namely in the *Eight Provisions*:

> Dom 3. Di tredda doem is, dat di landsata aegh toe witane mit een ede hwaneer hi da heer urgulden habbe da forma twa jeer. Dat tredde jeer is di landhera nier to witane ho lange hiara eentale se. Als hi him dera heer jecht, soe aegh hi dine ker hor hine urdriwe dan hine sitta leeth.
>
> Dom 3. The third provision is that a tenant has the right to testify under oath whether he has paid the rent during the first two years of the lease. In the third year, the landlord is entitled to further determine the future duration of their agreement. If the landlord acknowledges that the rent has been paid, he may choose to evict the tenant or let him stay (after the third year).[19]

According to this provision, a landlord could reconsider an agreement in the third year and evict the tenant if he wished to do so. It seems that new negotiations were possible regarding lease contracts, as long as the rent had been paid. However, it is also possible that this was a specific legal case in which a dispute arose in the third year of a lease. Two possibilities can be considered: first, that lease contracts allowed landlords to review the lease after two years; second, that this was a particular situation that did not apply to all leases. A definitive answer is impossible due to a lack of additional sources.

An explicit term for a contract is used here: *eentale*. This term refers to an 'agreement' or 'understanding'.[20] *Eentale* is found in another provision concerning rent. The *Market Law of Westerlauwers Frisia* describes a dispute over a house sold in a market town:

> MrWl 2. Hwa so een hus an ene mercket selt ende hi dine steed bihalt ende di caper dine sedel foerd bitinget cortera jefta langera, so sel ma dat bisetta oen da bannena tinge ho lange hiara eental were, jef di seller moet dine caper ofswara hwanneer hi wil mit alle riucht.

19 *D*, IX (Dom) 3, pp. 244–245.

20 'ēntele' Hofmann, Popkema, *Altfriesisches Handwörterbuch*, p. 121.

> MrWl 2. If someone sells a house in a market town but keeps inhabiting the place and the buyer makes a legal agreement over the duration of the occupancy, whether it be for a shorter or a longer period, this is to be settled at court for how long a period they can come to an agreement on, or the buyer may lawfully expel the seller by swearing an oath when he wants.[21]

This provision addresses a specific issue: what happens if someone sells their house but continues to live in it through an arrangement with the buyer. If there is a disagreement about the duration of this agreement, it must be resolved in court. This situation was not common in leases.

All three instances of lease described in the *Freeska Landriucht* contain specific rules regarding the duration of the lease and the relationship between the tenant and landlord. These provisions address particular problems or disputes that arose in legal practice. There were no formal requirements for a standardized lease contract, such as who must be present or what must be said, as written law does not specify any such requirements. It is probable, however, that such contracts did not differ significantly from other contracts.

2.3 *Marriage Contracts*

The marriage contract was a different kind of contract, comprising an agreement made between the heads of the betrothed's families. These contracts determined the goods and properties that each side would bring to the new marriage, but did not concern the betrothal itself. Usually, such contracts were made orally, and the witnesses/brokers (*mekeren*) present during the negotiations attested to the amount of the marriage gifts being exchanged.[22] Documents of written contracts from the Late Middle Ages have survived.[23] One such document details the use of arbitrators when both families were in dispute about what should be included in the marriage gifts. Unable to agree, each side appointed their own arbitrators to reach a consensus.[24]

---

21 *D*, XVII (MrWl) 2, pp. 418–419.

22 On Old Frisian marriage contracts, see Vries, "In een werheyde", p. 347 ff. and pp. 358–362 for the *mekere*. These also appear in other sources such as the *Brokmerbrief* (BrB 97) in Buma, Ebel, *Das Brokmer Recht*, p. 68; and the *Emsinger Pfennigschuldbuch* (PnB 18) in Buma, Ebel, *Das Emsiger Recht*, p. 156. Both sources are from East Frisia and the 13th and early 14th centuries.

23 Called a *mekbreef*. For some examples of marriage contracts, see Vries, *Ferdban*, p. 194 ff.

24 Vries, "In een werheyde", pp. 346–347.

2.4 *General or Specific Frisian Contract Law?*

Owing to the obscurity of the customs during that time, these three examples of Frisian contracts offer limited insight into the practice of concluding contracts. The question arises as to whether the findings thus far suggest that Frisian contract law was general or specific. Written law provides no evidence of general norms for contracts, and the different types of contracts are not clearly linked in terms of approach. In contrast to Roman law, there is no explicit mention of mutual consent as a requirement for contracts. However, it can be presumed that such consent was required. With the exception of *niarkap*, which will be discussed later, the sources do not suggest that contracts could be entered into against a party's will. At the same time, there are no indications that a specific contract law existed. Contracts for sale do not exhibit any specific formal requirements, nor do lease contracts, as far as the sources suggest. All contracts in Frisian law seem to be united by a general approach: an agreement between two parties, presumably with mutual consent.

Moreover, disputes concerning contracts were resolved in court. In the event of a dispute, the parties sought resolution. This can also be observed in the specific circumstances of some of the provisions, which primarily relate to exceptional cases rather than typical and frequent disputes. These exceptional cases were documented to inform future disputants and arbitrators.

Furthermore, all contracts were accompanied by witnesses who attested to what had been agreed upon.[25] The lack of a written culture made this necessary if the contents of an agreement were disputed. The number of witnesses ranged between two and seven. According to the *Statutes of the Five Districts*, two witnesses were required if the assets of the agreement had a value of less than a pound. If the value exceeded a pound, seven witnesses were needed.[26] Seven appears to have been the customary number.[27]

Overall, information regarding Frisian contract law is scarce and it is unclear whether there was such a thing as 'contract law' or merely a few general principles for reaching an agreement. It is likely that a general law of contracts existed, regulated through unwritten customs. Although practices such as the presence of witnesses and public announcement of contracts can be observed in the sources, other details remain unknown.

This lack of concrete information may have contributed to the incorporating of foreign legal elements to supplement indigenous law. The absence of exten-

25 Immink, "Getuigen", p. 447.

26 *D*, XIII (Dom), 31, pp. 324–325.

27 On the witnesses to agreements and documents, see Vries, *Ferdban*, p. 11 f.

sive rules regarding contracts in Frisian law may have allowed for easy adoption of rules from the *ius commune* for regulating and interpreting contracts.[28] In the following chapter, the rules governing contracts in younger Frisian sources will be examined to determine the extent of this adoption.

3 Niarkap in Traditional Frisian Law

3.1 *Property*

To gain an understanding of *niarkap* and contract law in Frisia, it is essential to comprehend the concept of 'property'. Although the aforementioned contracts reveal that Frisians exchanged and transferred goods, they shed little light on how Frisians perceived 'property' or 'proprietary rights'. Unfortunately, there is a lack of scholarly research in this area, and historians have only a tenuous understanding. An insightful overview of property in Medieval Frisia has yet to be provided.

Scholars have examined the concept of property in Frisian law texts in various limited ways. Algra, for instance, provides an analysis of how courts dealt with the transfer of property between individuals. However, he does not offer any definition or outline of the term.[29] Similarly, other researchers who have explored the *ferdban* have provided valuable insights into customs and procedures surrounding transfers of property, without explaining what 'property' entailed and how Frisians understood it.[30]

In Medieval law, property was sometimes classified into allodial and feudal property. Allodial land was land of which the landowner had full ownership. Feudal land was land on which the tenants (feudatories) had only a right to use and were required to perform feudal duties.[31] However, this distinction is not particularly useful in the case of Frisia, as feudalism was not (or almost not) present in the region.[32]

---

28 Peter Stein argues that Roman law became very seminal in the law of contracts in the German territories. The reason for this was that indigenous laws allegedly contained little in this regard. See Stein, *Roman law in European History*, p. 90.

29 Algra, Nikolaas Egbert. *Ein: enkele rechtshistorische aspecten van de grondeigendom in Westerlauwers Friesland.* Groningen: P. Noordhoff, 1966.

30 For example, Oosten, "Vredeban", and Vries, "Also dat wy habbet".

31 On allodial property (*allod*), see 'Allod' in: Erler, at al., *Handwörterbuch zur deutschen Rechtsgeschichte*, pp. 120–122.

32 While noble families remained powerful, and hierarchies a part of Frisian society, feudal property had almost entirely disappeared by the late Middle Ages. On the counts of Frisia and feudal property, see Noomen, *De stinzen*, pp. 81–90.

Comparisons with Medieval law in German territories can provide helpful insights into the concept of property in Frisian law. The legal history of the German territories demonstrates that property (*Eigentum*) had diverse definitions and meanings, which depended largely on the context in which they were used. Many distinctions existed between different types of property, such as alienable and unalienable property, hereditary and lifelong property, and encumbered and unencumbered property. However, the Medieval law of the German territories did not differentiate between *Eigentum* and *beschränkten, dinglichen Rechten* (limited, proprietary rights), thus making the property system both unified and internally varied.[33]

Similarly, the concept of property in Frisian law may not be clearly outlined, but rather context-dependent. The Old Frisian common term *ein/ain* was often used to refer to property,[34] whereas the term *were* denoted the power of a free Frisian over his wife, children, servants and household, and this power was relevant to the ownership of land, house, and even slaves.[35]

Scholars have previously argued that a shift from family-owned to individual private property occurred during the Middle Ages. According to this traditional view, land initially belonged to a clan or family, and alienation to outsiders was not possible. During the Middle Ages, however, individuals gained the ability to own property, although the family retained rights to it and could determine how and when it could be sold to another party.[36]

This traditional view has been challenged by more recent research. Previously, understanding of property in these societies was primarily derived from ancient sources such as Tacitus and Caesar, but their writings are no longer seen as sufficiently authoritative.

Evidence from early Medieval sources has shown that individuals in Germanic societies did, in fact, own property. Inheritance of property was not limited to the father's side, but also included the mother's side and was passed down both to sons and daughters. Property was not held by a fixed entity like a clan, but was instead always in individual hands, making it unlikely that a development from family-owned property to private property occurred in Frisia.[37]

---

33 'Eigentum' in: Erler, at al., *Handwörterbuch zur deutschen Rechtsgeschichte*, pp. 883–884.

34 'ain' Hofmann, Popkema, *Altfriesisches Handwörterbuch*, p. 6.

35 The term *were* had various definitions. On the term and its meanings, see Vries, *Asega, is het dingtijd?*, p. 27.

36 On this view of property during the Middle Ages in Frisia, see Algra, Oudfries recht, p. 358; Meijering, *De Willekeuren*, pp. 142–143; De Blécourt, *Kort Begrip*, p. 98.

37 Noomen, *Stinzen*, p. 22 ff.

However, it is worth noting that an individual's family still held rights to and influence over their property, as exemplified in the case of *Erbenlaub*.

3.2 *The Predecessor to* Niarkap—Erbenlaub

> Van graetheit des forkapa guedis
> SkRa 38. Dit it is riucht, dat neen man syn eerwe foercapia moet, hit ne se bi syn eerfnama moede, him ne dere hongher jefta heer need, jef dat hy also sondich se dat hi dat land rema wil ende syn sonda bettria: soe aech hyt syn erfnama toe bieden dae fyaerda penningh lichtera dan hit wird se. Jef hit aeck ymmen capet buta dis eerfnama mode, als di odera man sterft deer dat eerwe seld haet, so aech di eerfnama een ferd oen da gued ende eerwe ende di odera nene fyafellingha.

> Concerning the dimensions of sold land
> SkRa 38. This is the law, that no man may sell his inheritance, save by consent of his heir, unless he is constrained by hunger or military necessity, or if he is so sinful that he wishes to give up the land in order to make atonement for his sins: he must then offer it to his heir for the fourth penny less than it is worth. If anyone buys it without the consent of the heir, then, when the man who sold it dies, the heir shall have a right to undisturbed possession of the goods and the land, and the other will not be compensated.[38]

This provision stipulates that the consent of an heir (*eerfnama moede*) is essential for the sale of an inheritance. An inheritance refers to property that was acquired through the transfer of assets from a family member. Typically, familial property consisted of immovable assets such as land and houses, but could also encompass movable assets. The rationale behind obtaining consent from heirs is rooted in the fact that an inheritance was typically viewed as the future property of the heirs. Although the property may have been privately owned, the family retained a sense of entitlement to it. This concept is referred to in German as *Erbenlaub*, which mandates the consent of heirs when property is transferred to someone else.[39] The practice of *Erbenlaub* was a prevalent custom in the Medieval laws of the German territories and is documented in the *Sachsenspiegel*, a legal text dating back to the 13th century:[40]

38 *D*, III (SkRa) 38, pp. 136–137.

39 'Erbenlaub' in: Erler, at al., *Handwörterbuch zur deutschen Rechtsgeschichte*, p. 956.

40 Köbler, *Deutsche Rechtsgeschichte*, p. 142.

> I 52 § 1. Gift he it weder rechte sunder erven gelof, de erve underwinde't sek ordelen, alse of he dot si, jene de it dar gaf, so he is nicht geven ne mochte.
>
> I 52 § 1. If he gives it away unlawfully without consent of the heir, the heir recovers it on the basis of a judicial decree, as if he who gave it away is dead, because he should not have given it away.[41]

The High Middle Ages witnessed a development towards greater freedom to sell property, which first emerged in the cities and later in rural areas. *Erbenlaub* thus became less prevalent and exceptions to it increased.[42]

The provision of the *Older Skelta Law* above (SkRa 38) contains some of these exceptions. An heir's consent was not required if the owner of the land was facing hunger or military necessity. In addition, individuals could donate land freely as a form of atonement for their sins, without needing the consent of an heir. The latter exception demonstrates the influence of the Church on the practice of *Erbenlaub* in Frisia, as the Church was interested in enabling people to donate land and goods freely to the Church. As a result, the Church preferred privately owned property over family-owned property, and over time this led to an increase in the exceptions to *Erbenlaub*.[43]

The *Older Skelta Law* is among the oldest Medieval Frisian sources and the only place where *Erbenlaub* is found in the *Freeska Landriucht*, dating back to between the 11th and 13th centuries.[44] Over time, *Erbenlaub* disappeared and was replaced by *niarkap*, a custom that allowed families to retain influence over an individual's land.[45] *Niarkap* permitted alienation but enabled relatives and others to intervene and prevent land from being sold to individuals outside the family or parish by taking over the sale.[46]

3.3 Niarkap *in the Frisian Sources*

Two groups of people held the primary entitlement to claim *niarkap*, namely relatives and neighbors. Vries has identified various terms for these two groups: *nestbloed unde nestleger* ("nearest blood or nearest location") and *niaer in da sib* [...] *ende in da legere dis landis* ("nearer in kin and nearer in the location of

41 For a German translation of this text, see Kaller, *Sachsenspiegel*, p. 45.
42 Köbler, *Deutsche Rechtsgeschichte*, p. 142 f.
43 De Blécourt, *Kort Begrip*, p. 99.
44 Meijering, Nijdam, '*Wat is Recht?*', p. 84.
45 Meijering, *De Willekeuren*, p. 142 ff. See also Köbler, *Deutsche Rechtsgeschichte*, pp. 142–143.
46 Vries, "Nijaer is sijd", p. 262 ff.

the land").[47] There are two instances concerning *niarkap* in the *Freeska Landriucht*. The first of these is in the Statutes of the Five Districts:

> W^{5}D 33. Hwa so een land sella wil, dat hyt ur sine ghaekerka biede alle dam deer nest wessa willet tree dagen. Jef hit nimmen capet om dat bod, soe aegh hy to da waer toe commen ende aldeer to bieden tree dagen, alle dam deer nest wessa wil. Jef hit dis tredda deis nimmen capet deer nest is, soe aghen da riuchteren hine to ferdien, deer hit oen hiara andert caped, dat him nimmen wald jefta onriucht dwe deeroen.

> W^{5}D 33. If someone wants to sell a piece of land, he must offer it for sale for three days to those individuals in his parish who think they are entitled to purchase it. If no-one wants to buy it, he has to come to the district court and offer it for sale there for three days to those who think they are entitled to purchase it. If none of these persons has purchased it on the third day, then the judges have to proclaim a peace over the person who buys it in their presence, so that no-one does him any harm or injustice as a consequence of this purchase.[48]

This provision clearly pertains to the entitlement of certain individuals to take over a sale. Notably, a spatial distinction is made, with those living closer to the land having a stronger claim than those living further away. This rule was likely to have been intended to keep land within the local community, as selling it to outsiders could result in neglect or disinterest. The growth of cities may have also contributed to this trend, as urban residents sought to acquire rural land. In Frisia, the right of neighbors to take over a sale was likely to have been established to prevent the disintegration of rural communities.[49]

A similar distinction is found in Medieval German law, namely the *Marklosung* and *Nachbarlosung*, which gave communities and neighbors the right to purchase land offered for sale. These provisions prevented outsiders from buying land and allowed neighbors to retain or create larger tracts of land.[50] While not explicitly stated in the provision above (W^{5}D 33), it appears that individuals living closer to the land, i.e., in the same parish or district, were more entitled to purchase it than others.

---

47 On these terms, see Vries, "Nijaer is sijd", pp. 277–279.

48 *D*, XIII (W^{5}D) 33, pp. 326–327.

49 Meijering, *De Willekeuren*, p. 143.

50 'Näherrecht' in: Erler, at al., *Handwörterbuch zur deutschen Rechtsgeschichte*, p. 828. Both for the *Marklosung* and the *Nachbarlosung* as distinctions of *Näherrecht*.

Comparisons could also be made with other legal systems, where concepts similar to niarkap existed. The *odelsrett* in Norway and the *bördsrätt* in Sweden come to mind, both of which aimed to keep property within the family.[51] However useful such comparisons may be, they are beyond the scope of this research. For this reason, comparisons are limited to the more accessible and closely related concepts of *naasting* and *Näherrecht* in Dutch and German law. Further research and comparisons between *niarkap* and similar practices are needed.

However, the above provision mentions only "those individuals in his parish who think they are entitled to purchase it" (*alle dam deer nest wessa willet*), without specifying who these individuals are. While these individuals are likely to have included parishioners and members of the district, *niarkap* was primarily a way for families to retain familial land, as demonstrated in the *Statutes of Opstalsbam*:

> WUps 16. Dio xv seec is fan lande deer ma kapet jefta selt jefta wandelet, dat di nest se ti winnane ist hera jefta frowe deer fan da fedriem jef fan da swirdsida ut kommen se, hit ne se dat dio der niaer in da sib se ende in da legere dis landis. Ende sint hia lika sib dio swirdsida ende dio spindelsida, so is nier dio swirdsida.
>
> WUps 16. The 15th clause is about buying, selling or exchanging land. A man or woman descending from the paternal line or 'sword side' is more entitled to take over the land, unless descendants from the maternal line are of closer descent or their estates lie closer to the land. And if they are equally close in descent, the paternal line takes priority over the maternal line.[52]

This provision concerns the prioritization of relatives, which will be discussed shortly. Most importantly, it is evident that relatives, in general, enjoyed the right to take over a sale, with the primary intention being to keep the land within the family. If the land was to be sold, the seller was obliged to offer it to their family members first. This practice is also found in *Näherrecht*, where external parties were prevented from obtaining land in favor of family members purchasing it.[53]

---

51 See Dackling, "Traditional", p. 64 and Gelting, "Odelsrett".

52 *D*, XX (WUps) 16, pp. 432–433.

53 'Näherrecht' in: Erler, at al., *Handwörterbuch zur deutschen Rechtsgeschichte*, p. 827.

Distinctions within the category of relatives are apparent, with those closest in degree being the most entitled.[54] Additionally, individuals living closer to an estate had a greater right. This corresponds closely to the *Statutes of the Five Districts* (W^5D 33), where spatial proximity was a significant factor in determining who was entitled to land. Relatives who lived closer were preferred, presumably for the same reasons why individuals who lived in the same parish or district were preferred: to ensure that land remained within the local community.

Lastly, in cases where there were multiple relatives of equal degree and proximity, agnates were given preference over cognates. This was not a common aspect of *naasting*, but it was unique to Frisia.[55] The preference for relatives from the 'sword side' (agnates) also existed in inheritance and when determining guardianship over orphaned or half-orphaned children. According to the *Book of Emperor Rudolf*, an agnate, usually the brother of the deceased, became the guardian of the children.[56]

Summarizing, legal sources provide information on how Frisians could be entitled to *niarkap*, either as neighbors or relatives. Some additional considerations can be made. So far, *niarkap* has been connected only to land. This was also a common feature of *Näherrecht*, which primarily concerned immovable property. However, it was sometimes also used for movable goods.[57] As the Frisian sources do not make any direct mention of this, it cannot be determined whether this was also possible in Frisia.

Another aspect to consider is the method of announcing a sale to those who may be entitled to take over the sale. The *Statutes of the Five Districts* (W^5D 33) state that the land must be offered for sale for three days (*tree dagen*), although the location is not specified. Three days appears to be a rather short period for all individuals to be notified, but these days were not in fact consecutive. The city law of Bolsward from 1455 specifies that sellers had to proclaim their

---

54 This corresponds with succession in Frisian law: the nearest relatives succeed. On the Frisian law of inheritance, see Meyers, "Het Friese Erfrecht", p. 54. See also L^{24} 16 for the inheritance of the closest relatives, the so-called 'six-hands'. These included the mother, father, brother, sister, children and grandchildren. For more on intestate succession, see Chapter 4.

55 Meijering, *De Willekeuren*, p. 144.

56 On agnates in Frisian inheritance, see Meyers, "Het Friese Erfrecht", pp. 54–56 and below in Chapter 5. On the preference of agnates in guardianship, see *D*, XVI (Rud) 21, pp. 396–397. Glosses to this provision show that this preference of agnates was abandoned in the late Middle Ages; the subsequent aligning more closely with learned law allowed all relatives to fulfil that role. Chapter 6 analyzes guardianship in detail.

57 'Näherrecht' in: Erler, at al., *Handwörterbuch zur deutschen Rechtsgeschichte*, p. 829.

intention to sell on three consecutive Sundays in the local church.[58] This effectively gave entitled individuals two weeks to respond.[59] For relatives who lived outside of Bolsward, the period was extended to a month.[60] It can be assumed that in the Five Districts, too, a sale had to be announced on three consecutive Sundays, rather than on three days in general.

Many variations of the length of time that *niarkap* could be claimed existed. *Näherrecht* often granted a year and a day for claiming the right of the nearest, but it was also common to have a period of three days (or Sundays), seven days, several weeks or even three years.[61] It is likely that different time limits existed in different Frisian regions and cities, and that these changed over time. Rules pertaining to *niarkap*, *Näherrecht* or *naasting* were primarily local customs that varied from region to region and community to community.[62] Consequently, providing a definitive answer for the whole of Frisia is not feasible. However, it can be stated that in the Five Districts, the time for announcing a sale was set at three days (or Sundays).

Vries succinctly summarizes a typical procedure involving the announcement of a sale, claiming *niarkap* and arbitration.[63] Initially, a sale was publicly proclaimed in three court sessions.[64] The *Statutes of the Five Districts* (W⁵D 33) specify that a seller had to approach the "district court" (*to da waer toe commen*), while in other instances, such as the city law of Bolsward, the sale was announced in a church and then again at the court.[65] The place of proclamation was determined by local custom and differed from region to region. In East

58 "*Wie land off huysinghe vercofft heeft, die salse laeten bieden drie Sondaeghen by en over dye kerck* [...]" Bolsward (1455) 64 in: Telting, *De Friesche Stadrechten*, p. 28. On this provision, see also Robijn, *Het recht*, p. 76. For a more detailed analysis, see later in this chapter.

59 From Sunday to the Sunday after the next, two weeks would pass. Traditionally, if no-one objected to the sale on the third day, a peace over the sale was proclaimed. See Oosten, "Vredeban", p. 387 and Vries, "Also dat wy habbet", p. 244. Thus, two weeks elapsed between the first and third Sunday.

60 Bolsward (1455) 64 in: Telting, *De Friesche Stadrechten*, p. 28. On this provision, see also Robijn, *Het recht*, p. 76.

61 'Näherrecht' in: Erler, at al., *Handwörterbuch zur deutschen Rechtsgeschichte*, p. 829 f.

62 For example, also regarding to *naasting* in the rest of the Netherlands. There are mentions of a year and a day, as well as six weeks. Some regions did not have *naasting* at all. See De Blécourt, *Kort Begrip*, p. 101.

63 Vries, "Nijaer is sijd", p. 263.

64 The person proclaiming the sale varied. Usually, it was the buyer, but in some cases it was the seller. This is evident in the above provision from the Statutes of the Five Districts and was also the case in the cities of Bolsward and Sneek. On the proclamation of a sale in the context of the *ferdban*, see Vries, "Also dat wy habbet", p. 244 ff.

65 *D*, XIII (W⁵D) 33, pp. 326–327. And Telting, *Friesche Stadrechten*, p. 162 f. respectively. On this, see also Vries, "Also dat wy habbet", p. 245.

Frisia and the Ommelanden, courts were not usually involved.[66] If no objection arose, the sale was approved, and a peace was proclaimed (*ferdban*).

Someone with the right to *niarkap* could object orally during the last of the three sessions. Those claiming such right had to provide information about their relationship to the seller, such as whether they were a relative, neighbor or parishioner. A guarantee for the purchase price was then given to ensure that the buyer and the court were satisfied that the individual seeking to take over the sale had sufficient funds. As *niarkap* entailed a right to take over a sale, the guarantee only needed to be for the price agreed upon by the seller and the buyer. If the buyer rejected the objection, a court procedure was initiated. If the court upheld the right to *niarkap*, the more entitled party repaid the buyer the sale price, and the property was transferred to the person entitled to *niarkap*. Finally, the judge proclaimed a peace on behalf of that individual to prevent others from claiming to be more entitled.[67]

The right of *niarkap* is thought to have emerged in the 13th century, according to Meijering, who asserts that it is no older than that.[68] This argument appears sound, considering the available sources. The *Statutes of the Five Districts* and the *Statutes of Opstalbam* date back to the 14th century, while the city law of Bolsward was written in the 15th century. Although the *Older Skelta Law* is an earlier text, it refers to *Erbenlaub* rather than *niarkap*, which supports Meijering's assertion that *niarkap* arose in the 13th century.

From the 14th century onwards, *niarkap* faced challenges due to the increasing presence and influence of learned law. It is worth, therefore, examining how learned law interacted with Frisian contract law and with *niarkap* specifically.

4 Did Frisians Receive the Law of Contracts Comprehensively?

Frisian sources from the 15th century indicate that a shift occurred in how contracts were approached. The *Excerpta Legum* and *Jurisprudentia Frisica*, the two main sources from this period, offer insight into this change.

4.1 *In the* Excerpta Legum

The *Excerpta Legum* does not contain a specific rubric concerning contracts. However, it does feature a rubric entitled "de fide manuali", which was copied

---

66 Vries, "Nijaer is sijd", p. 264. And Vries, "Also dat wy habbet", p. 245 f.

67 Vries, "Nijaer is sijd", p. 263 f.

68 Meijering, *De Willekeuren*, p. 143. See also Algra, *Oudfries Recht*, p. 361.

from an unidentified manual on arbitration. This rubric includes a single provision (Exc 179), which presents three arguments. Firstly, it asserts that the first party should not disturb the second party in the latter's possession after the contract has been concluded. Secondly, it emphasizes the importance of observing contractual promises:

> Exc 179. Item. Dit is riucht om dat gued ende forwerth. Int arste, dat sy dat gued op forwerth on heten ende louweth hath ende her nat to behindryane in da guede. Hoc cum proprio iuramento, jtem mit ij orkenen, dar disse lowyinga an syon habbeth.
> Item. Ney dam dat hy dit onheten ende lowat hath, dat hy dath al schildich is to halden. Dit to biwisen mit iiij, der hem man riucht vorstaet. [...][69]

> Exc 179. Item. This is the law concerning an agreement about an asset. First, that they (the first party) promised and pledged the asset by agreement and that they should not disturb them (the other party) in the possession of the asset. This (is to be proven) with my own oath and also with two witnesses who were present at (pronouncing) this promise.
> Item, after he has promised and pledged this, then he is wholly obligated to keep to it. This is to be proven with four (persons) who understand the law. [...]

The mention of two witnesses is significant because it highlights the continued importance of witnesses in the creating of contracts. In the absence of written documents, the presence of witnesses was necessary.

The third argument that the provision makes is that an agreement has to be observed even if it was made only in simple words:

> Exc 179. [...] Item. Weer so een man en forwerth makat ende biswerth ende bi loweth, dat hy da forwerth ende swerringha ende lowingha al scildich is to halden, al hede hijt nat mer dan mit ene **sliuchta werde** spritzen, ut patet infra. [...][70]

> Exc 179. [...] If someone enters into an agreement, and afterwards confirms it by taking an oath, then he is wholly obligated to keep that agree-

69 *A*, I (Exc) 179, p. 128. This part of the provision was also copied into the *Jurisprudentia Frisica* as *Ro*, III (JF) 22, no. 7.

70 *A*, I (Exc) 179, p. 128. This part of the provision was also copied into the *Jurisprudentia Frisica* as *Ro*, III (JF) 22, no. 8.

> ment, oath, and promise, even if he had spoken with but a **simple word**, as is shown below. [...]

The Old Frisian words used here, *sliuchta werde*, may be a reference to a naked agreement (*pactum nudum*), though this is uncertain. Regardless, a "simple word" was a much simpler formality than even the Roman *stipulatio*, which required parties to pronounce questions and answers. Therefore, nude agreements also had to be honored. This position is supported by Canon law, rather than Roman law, indicating that the former is followed here.

Naked agreements are also mentioned in other provisions. One case recorded in the *Excerpta Legum* concerns the return of goods given to a monastery (Exc 226–234). The litigant claimed that the monastery should return his goods since he had left the monastery within the first year. While this case has little relevance to this present study, one argument in it (Exc 231) relates to naked agreements:

> Exc 231. Item. Hweerso en man in ener sliuchter spreke ende mit vorwerde vr en wert, dat ma da vorwerth al scildich is to halden, als da monken my of geen sint, ende alder to vorbonden sint. Dit to biwisen mit scrioun riucht. Probatur, quia ex solo nudo pacto oritur obligatio et per consequens nudum pactum est seruandum, quia obligat hominem: Extra, De pactis, c. I (X 1.35.1) et iii (X 1.35.3); xviii q. ii Eleutherius (C. 18 q.2 c.30).[71]

> Exc 231. Item. If someone agrees to something with simple words and agreement, then he is wholly obligated to observe that agreement, even if the monks have renounced me when they were still bound to it. This is to be proven with written law. It is proven, because from a single nude agreement an obligation arises and, consequently, a nude agreement is to be observed, because it obligates a human. See X 1.35.1 and X 1.35.3; C. 18 q.2 c.30.

In the Old Frisian section, the term "simple words" (*sliuchter spreke*) is used, which refers to naked agreements. The Latin section of the text explicitly mentions *nudum pactum* and cites the relevant provisions of Canon law, specifically X 1.35.1.

These provisions indicate that all agreements, including naked agreements, had to be observed. This reflects the Canon law of contracts, as confirmed by

71 *A*, I (Exc) 231, p. 188.

the reference to X 1.35.1. Unlike Roman law, which did not recognize naked agreements as actionable, Frisians followed Canon law.

We need to revisit the first provision (Exc 179) and clarify its scope. The rule on observing an agreement comes with an important exception: if keeping the agreement would result in the loss of eternal salvation:

> Exc 179. […] Nota quod fides manualis siue iuramentum ibi est seruandum, vbi non vergit in interitum salutis eterne: Extra, De jurejurando, c. Si vero (X 2.24.8) vbi dicitur: "Non est tutum quemlibet contra iuramentum suum venire"—siue fidem manualem, que equiparantur in c. Ad aures, De hiis que vi metusue, etcetera (X 1.40.3)—"nisi sit tale iuramentum, quod seruatum vergat in interitum salutis eterne", ut dicit papa: "Alicui non volumus dare materiam veniendi contra proprium iuramentum, ne autores periurii videamur." Similiter dicitur in l.i, C. Si aduersus vendicionem (*Cod.* 2.27.1): "Ymmo si negligenter ea que male vsurpentur omittimus excessus viam aliis aperimus":[72] ff. De pactis, I. vnus, § Pacta (*Dig.* 2.14.27.4); De restitutione spoliatorum, Accepta (X 2.13.3). […][73]

> Exc 179. […] Note that a handshake or oath is to be observed when it does not lead to a loss of eternal salvation, see X 2.24.8, where is written: "It is not prudent for anyone to act against their own oath"—or a handshake, which is equated (with the oath) in X 1.40.3—"unless the observation of such an oath leads to a loss of eternal salvation", as the Pope says: "We do not want to bring anyone in the situation to go against their own oath, so that we are not viewed as supporters of perjury." A similar thing is said in C. 2.27.1: "Indeed, if we negligently omit things which could be used badly, we open the way for digressions to others." D. 2.14.27.4; X 2.13.3. […]

While the references to the *Liber Extra* are unsurprising, there are also two references to Roman law and a quotation. Let's take a look at the quotation first. The text implies that the quotation may be from the *Codex* or *Digest*, but neither text actually contains this quotation. In fact, it comes from Canon law, namely from the end of D. 93 c. 21: *Nam si negligenter ea, quae male usurpantur, omittimus; excessus viam aliis aperimus.*[74]

The first allegation to Roman law (C. 2.27.1) concerns restitution in the case of a minor and is unrelated to the preceding arguments. The second allegation,

72 D. 93 c. 21.

73 *A*, I (Exc) 179, p. 128.

74 D. 93 c. 21.

however, is relevant because it concerns agreements that are immoral: *Pacta, quae turpem causam continent, non sunt observanda.* (Translation: "Agreements which contain an immoral provision should not be observed.") The inclusion of a reference to Roman law indicates that Roman law was not entirely ignored on the matter of contracts.

However, Frisians were not ignorant of the contradictions between Canon and Roman law regarding naked agreements. To illustrate this, we can consider another extensive case record collected in the *Excerpta Legum* (Exc 218–223). In this case, a Frisian named Sibrand claims that a dowry was promised to him but never delivered. He argues that lawful agreements have to be observed:

> Exc 221. [...] Et patet quod legitima pacta, que neque dolo malo neque aduersus leges facta sunt, seruari debent, ut in proposito probatur et in c. i De pactis (X 1.35.1), et in c. Qualiter (X 1.35.3), vbi dicitur: "Studiose agendum est vt ea que promittuntur ore etcetera." [...][75]

> Exc 221. [...] It is apparent that a lawful agreement, which was neither made fraudulently or illegally, should be observed, as is proven in the beginning and in X 1.35.1 and X 1.35.3, where is written: "One should studiously endeavor that what is promised orally etc." [...]

In addition, Sibrand addresses a potential counterargument, namely that Roman law prohibited naked agreements from being actionable:

> Exc 221. [...] Sed si obiceret pars aduersa de l. iuris gentium, ff. De pactis (*Dig.* 2.14.7.4), vbi innuitur quod ex nudo pacto non oritur actio, ex De prescripcionibus, c. finali (X 2.26.20), respondeo: Quando lex non potest seruari sine peccato statuitur canoni indistincte, quia ut est in proposito, quia quis recedendo a pacto uel simplici promisso peccat mortaliter, ut habetur allegatis. Vel posset responderi aliter ad contrarium, sic quod contrarium sit regulare, sed illud est speciale in dote sicud et multa alia, scilicet ex nudo pacto uel promisso oritur actio, quod probatur per l. Ad exactionem (*Cod.* 5.11.6), vbi sic legitur: "Ad exactionem dotis, quam semel prestari placuit, qualiacumque uerba sufficere censemus, siue scripta fuerint siue non." [...][76]

75 *A*, I (Exc) 221, p. 178.

76 *A*, I (Exc) 221, p. 178.

> Exc 221. […] However, if the opposing party uses D. 2.14.7.4 as a defense, where it is hinted that no action arises from a nude agreement, I respond with X 2.26.20: whenever (Roman) law cannot be observed without sin, Canon law is followed indistinctly, because, as is mentioned at the beginning, someone sins mortally who retreats from an agreement or a simple promise, as is held in the allegations. Alternatively, the response to the opposing party could be another, namely that the contrary may be the rule but that it is a special case for the dowry and in many other cases, namely that an action arises from a nude agreement or promise, which is proven in C. 5.11.6, where this is written: "Regarding the exaction of a dowry, which someone once agreed to hand over, we decree that simple words suffice no matter what kind, whether they were written or not." […]

It appears that Sibrand was aware of the contradiction between Roman law and Canon law in this matter. The opposing party may have argued that, according to Roman law, a promise of a dowry made as a naked agreement was not enforceable. Sibrand, on the other hand, provided two reasons why the promise had to be fulfilled.

Firstly, he argued that not fulfilling the promise would be a mortal sin, as Canon law required all agreements to be upheld, and breaking an agreement was considered a serious offense. Sibrand believed that Canon law took precedence over Roman law in this regard.

Secondly, Sibrand referred to a specific provision in Roman law (C. 5.11.6) that allowed a simple agreement to be enforceable in the case of a dowry. He argued that this provision applied generally, whereas Roman law considered it to be specific to a dowry. Therefore, Sibrand did not entirely disregard Roman law, but instead found common ground by (mis)interpreting a specific rule.

In conclusion, it is clear that Canon law superseded Roman law in this aspect of contract law for Frisians: all agreements were actionable. However, Sibrand sought to support his argument with a provision in Roman law, despite the latter's subsidiary role. Therefore, Roman law remained to some extent relevant in this regard.

4.2 *In the* Jurisprudentia Frisica

A significant portion of the titles in the *Jurisprudentia Frisica* are related to various contracts in Canon law. Although the *Codex*, *Digesta* and *Institutiones* also cover similar topics, their arrangement differs. The *Codex Roorda* manuscript's sixth gathering includes several titles related to contracts, beginning with "de

TABLE 2 Comparison of the structure of the Canon law Liber Extra and the Frisian law Codex Roorda manuscript

Liber Extra	*Codex Roorda*
X 3.15 De commodato	JF 32 De emptione et venditione
X 3.16 De deposito	JF 33 De causa possessionis
X 3.17 De emptione et	JF 34 De rebus relictis
venditione	JF 36 De praescriptionibus
X 3.18 De locato et conducto	JF 37 De locato et conducto
X 3.19 De rerum permutatione	JF 38 De iure emphyteotico
X 3.20 De feudis	JF 39 De commodato
X 3.21 De pignoribus et aliis	JF 40 De deposito
cautionibus	JF 41 De pignoribus
X 3.22 De fidejussoribus	JF 42 De fidejussoribus
X 3.23 De solutionibus	JF 43 De solutionibus
X 3.24 De donationibus	JF 44 De donationibus

emptione et venditione".[77] The table above provides a comparison of the titles related to contracts in Liber 3 of the *Liber Extra* and the titles in gathering six of the *Codex Roorda*.

Upon closer examination of the titles, a significant number of references to both Roman and Canon law are visible in the *Jurisprudentia Frisica*. In many instances, the corresponding title of the *Liber Extra* is referenced in the title of the *Jurisprudentia Frisica*. For instance, 'de deposito' (X 3.16) is heavily referenced in JF 40:1, 'de deposito'.[78]

Table 2 shows substantial concordance between the *Liber Extra* and the *Jurisprudentia Frisica*. However, the two structures are not entirely identical. Not every title in the *Liber Extra* has an equivalent title in the *Jurisprudentia Frisica*. For instance, the title on fiefs ('de feudis') is missing, presumably because it was deemed unnecessary owing to the lack of feudalism in Frisia. Conversely, some titles in the Frisian text have no equivalent in the *Liber Extra*, such as 'de rebus relictis.' Moreover, the sequence of titles is slightly different. Thus, the *Liber Extra* was not the direct example from which the sequence

77 Titles included in one gathering imply that they were added together or in short succession, given how manuscripts were compiled. For an analysis of the gathering, see Gerbenzon, "Aantekeningen (Tweede Deel)", pp. 38–39.

78 Gloss 1 ad *Ro*, III (JF), tit. 40, no. 1.

of titles was transferred into the *Jurisprudentia Frisica*. Instead, an intermediate compilation of Canon law was used, although the specific compilation is unknown.

Titles JF 33 to JF 44 are included in one gathering in the manuscript, indicating that they were likely to have been added together. This suggests that these different contracts were perceived as a common concept, i.e., a 'general contract law.' This is supported by the inclusion in the *Jurisprudentia Frisica* of a title named 'de pactis' (JF 22). The name of the title was likely to have been taken from the equivalent title X 1.35 ('de pactis'). Within the title, the Old Frisian term for an agreement is *forwirda*, denoting all kinds of agreements. This very general term, denoting all kinds of agreements, corresponds to the Latin term *pactum*.

Title 22 shares the core principles of the Canon law of contracts. The system of contracts is open instead of closed, allowing all contracts to be binding, including naked agreements. This was one of the core developments in the Medieval Canon law of contracts (*pacta sunt servanda*), as clearly expressed in the fifth provision:

> JF 22:5. HWaso een man onthaet jn eenre tingh ter spreek myt forwirden wreen kompt datma da forwirda al schildich is to halden.
>
> Glossa 6. *Haetso een man onthaet* Probatur quod ex solo nudo pacto oritur obligacio et ergo per consequens nudum pactum omnino est seruandum, quia obligat hominem, extra de pactis c.i (X 1.35.1) et xviii q.ii Eleutherius (C. 18 q.2 c.30).[79]
>
> 22:5. If someone promises (something) in a matter and orally agrees something, then one is wholly obligated to keep to the agreement.
>
> Gloss 6. *Haetso een man onthaet*. It is accepted that a mere nude agreement results in an obligation and hence, as a consequence, a nude agreement should be completely observed, because it obligates man, see X 1.35.1 and C. 18 q.2 c.30.

This gloss explicitly mentions the Canon law principle of *nudum pactum omnino est seruandum*. This argument is supported by two provisions of Canon law: X 1.35.1 contains the phrase *Pacta quantumcumque nuda servanda sunt*. No

79 *Ro*, III (JF), tit. 22, no. 5.

reference is made to Roman law because Roman law did not allow for naked agreements to be actionable. Therefore, there can be no doubt that Frisian law received the Canon law of contracts.

Another principle of the law of contracts in the *Jurisprudentia Frisica* was that anyone could independently enter into an agreement concerning his own goods.

> JF 22:15 Item ellick menscha mey wr syn vry ayn gwed meckkia redelick forwirda dy van da riucht naet foerbaden se.[80]

> JF 22:15 Item. Anyone may enter into reasonable agreements, which are not prohibited by law, about his free personal assets.

These two provisions indicate that the law of contracts in the *Jurisprudentia Frisica* was influenced by Canon law rather than by Roman law. Nevertheless, Title JF 22 of the *Jurisprudentia Frisica* still refers to Roman law. These references are often unsatisfactory because they suggest that something is similar according to Roman law even when that is not entirely true or only true to a certain extent. For example, let us examine the gloss attached to the previous provision (gloss 16 to JF 22:15):

> Glossa 16. *Item ellick menscha mey*. Cum in re propria unusquisque moderator sit et arbiter potest quo[d]libet pactum componere in re sua legibus non reprobatum, C. comm. de successione l. Iure (*Cod.* 6.59.7). Preterea, cum huiusmodi pactum sit nulla lege prohibitum, immo uerius lege permissum est, ut superius allegatum Inst. de pupillari substitucione § i et ii (*Inst.* 2.16.1–2) et quasi per totum titulum extra de testamentis (X 3.26), Reynaldus presbyter (X 3.26.1) in glosa. Ergo firmum est et ualidum.[81]

> Gloss 16. *Item ellick menscha mey* (Item. Anyone may). Since everyone is the manager of his own asset, he can also decide to enter into whatever agreement concerning his asset that is not prohibited by the law, see C. 6.59.7. Furthermore, since such an agreement is not prohibited by any law whatsoever, it is sooner permitted by the law, as adduced above, in Inst. 2.16.1–2, in almost the entire title X 3.26 and in the gloss to X 3.26.18. Hence it is firm and valid.

80 *Ro*, III (JF), tit. 22, no. 15.

81 Gloss 16 ad *Ro*, III (JF), tit. 22, no. 15.

The gloss states that anyone can enter into any agreement concerning their assets, as long as that agreement is lawful. Two allegations to Roman law are provided, but these are not directly related to the first sentence of the gloss and do not mention agreements at all. The first reference (C. 6.59.7) concerns succession: *Adfinitatis iure nulla successio promittitur* (Translation: "No succession is permitted by the law of relationship by marriage"). The second reference (Inst. 2.16) also concerns succession, specifically the substitution of minors.[82] Although neither reference contains anything regarding agreements, both emphasize the freedom of a person to manage his own property. The references to Canon law also concern succession. It is likely that the glossator attempted to find a principle in Roman law that allowed for anyone to determine the future destination of his assets, but found only the principle that anyone can make substitutions for minor children.

These findings suggest a systematic reception of contract law in Frisia, where there was a 'general' concept of contracts connecting various kinds of contracts and principles governing contracts in general. However, the individual contracts are still very specific and largely derived from the *Liber Extra*, which in turn derived these contracts from Roman law. The structure of the titles in the *Jurisprudentia Frisica* also suggests that the influence of Canon law on the Frisian law of contracts was likely to have been very direct.

5 Interaction between Learned Law and *niarkap*

Given the circumstance of the reception of contract law, it is interesting to examine how *niarkap* evolved. In this regard, it is worth exploring how jurists engaged with the concept of indigenous customary law in the sources of the 14th and 15th centuries.

5.1 Niarkap *in the Gloss to the* Freeska Landriucht

None of the various law texts compiled in the *Freeska Landriucht* contains glosses on *niarkap*. In the *Older Skelta Law*, however, there is one gloss that relates to *Erbenlaub* (SkRa 38). This states:

82 Inst. 2.16: *Liberis suis impuberibus, quos in potestate quis habet, non solum ita, ut supra diximus, substituere potest.*

> Glossa 33. Hoc ius habet textum pro se Leuitici xxv., ubi dicitur 'Si attenuatus fuerit, uendiderit possessionem, potest redimere propinquus'.[83] Sed lex contradicit C. de contrahen. emp. l. Dudum proximis consortibus concessum erat ut extraneos ab emptione remouerint (*Cod.* 4.38.14). Primum tenetur in Frisia et utentium moribus approbatur iiii di. Leges dicunt, sic secundum Cinum super Codice,[84] quod quilibet potest emptorem querere et uendere. Sed lex non prohibit, quando proximiores et uiciniores possunt emptores expellere et redimere, ad hoc ff. de contrahen. emp. l. Qui offi. (*Dig.* 18.1.62), ff. de mino. xxv an. l. Si ⟨in⟩ emptione (*Dig.* 4.4.35). Pro uicinioribus facit ff. de lega. ii, Libertus (*Dig.* 31.77.27) et in constitutione Fredrici imperatoris de feudis Per quos fiat inuestitura post principium (*LF* 2.3) et ibi in glossa.[85]

> Gloss 33. This provision is supported by Leviticus 25, where it is said "when someone became impoverished and sold his possession, his relative may redeem it." However, Roman law contradicts this in C. 4.38.14. The former is observed in Frisia and customs of those who observe these are approved of in the fourth distinction. The Roman law provisions say, at least according to Cinus in his commentary on the Codex, that anyone can look for a buyer and sell. But Roman law does not prevent close relatives and next-door neighbors from expelling the buyers and redeeming what was sold. See for this D. 18.1.62 and D. 4.4.35. An argument for the neighbors can be found in D. 31.77.27 and in the constitution lf 2.3 of Emperor Frederick and the gloss to the latter.[86]

Note that while the main text discusses the need to obtain the consent of an heir (*Erbenlaub*), the gloss addresses the ability of heirs to regain property sold without their consent. The basis for this right is found in Leviticus 25, although there are some discrepancies between Leviticus 25 and the *Older Skelta Law* (SkRa 38). Leviticus 25 states that a relative can redeem land that was sold on the grounds of poverty, whereas in the *Older Skelta Law* consent was not required if the property was sold out of necessity, such as for reasons of hunger. If, therefore, a Frisian sold land without an heir's consent out of necessity, such land could not be recovered. According to Leviticus, however, it could be redeemed. Thus, these two rules do not entirely align. The reference

83 Leviticus 25.25.
84 Cinus de Pistoia, *Commentaria in Codicem*, *Cod.* 4.38.14, n. 1–2.
85 The gloss *proximiori* ad *LF* 2.3.
86 Glosa ad *D*, III (SkRa) 38, pp. 136–137.

to Leviticus is likely to have been intended to support the general argument that a relative has the right to recover or redeem familial property under certain circumstances, thus highlighting the relative's right to the land or goods. Moreover, Frisian and Biblical law are linked.

However, a counterpoint is immediately raised in a reference to Roman law (C. 4.38.14), which states:

> Dudum proximis et consortibus concessum erat ut extraneos ab empcione remouerent neque homines suo arbitratu distraherent. […][87]
>
> Formerly it was permissible for the nearest and those in an undivided community of goods that they excluded extraneous persons from a purchase and that persons did not alienate anything by their own free will. […]

Roman law mentions the exclusion of extraneous persons, which bears some similarities to *niarkap*, as the nearest relative could take over the sale from the extraneous person. However, the use of the term "formerly" indicates that this rule had been abolished. It is evident that Roman law valued the freedom of alienation more than familial rights to property, which is also mentioned in the commentary of Cinus to the *Codex*.[88] Meanwhile, the gloss notes that Leviticus was observed in Frisia: *primo tenetur in Frisia*, suggesting that Roman law was not. The gloss takes a sympathetic stance towards the ability of relatives to recover or redeem property.

However, this does not mean that Roman law did not have significant authority. Instead of rejecting it entirely, the gloss provides reasons why Roman law allowed for the right to recovery to exist. What is especially interesting here is that it is stated that "Roman law does not prevent close relatives and next-door neighbors from expelling the buyers and redeeming what was sold," which is proven by two references to the *Digest*. There is no mention of next-door neighbors in the Frisian provision, Leviticus 25 or Roman law. *Erbenlaub* only concerned heirs, while *niarkap* allowed both relatives and neighbors to take over a sale. This suggests that while gloss 33 is attached to a provision about *Erbenlaub*, it actually provides commentary on the principle of *niarkap*. This is especially plausible since the former was considered to have been replaced by the latter from the 13th century onwards.[89] An examination of

87 *Cod.* 4.38.14.
88 Cinus de Pistoia, *Commentaria in Codicem*, *Cod.* 4.38.14, n. 1–2.
89 Meijering, *De Willekeuren*, p. 142 ff.

the glosses places their creation no later than the end of the 14th century.[90] For this reason, this gloss is relevant to *niarkap*.

It appears that two contradicting sets of rules were aligned: Roman law did not allow relatives to have a say in alienation and prioritized the freedom to sell, while Frisian law emphasized the right of relatives and neighbors to take over a sale. However, the gloss attempts to harmonize the two positions by deriving from the Roman sources an argument to support the Frisian concept of *niarkap*. Multiple allegations are provided to support the thesis that Roman law allows for similar arrangements as in Frisian law. In this attempt at reconciliation, it is evident that the glossator did not want to dismiss Roman law, but instead brought it into concordance with Frisian law, albeit by misinterpreting Roman law. This goes beyond a mere comparison between two legal systems.

The first two references in the Digest concern land held by ancestors. D. 18.1.62pr states that a public official or soldier could not own land in the province in which they served, unless it was ancestral land. In D. 4.4.35, a minor can claim complete restitution in a bidding process if it is ancestral land. Although this is not the same as a right to take over a sale, a similar principle is apparent: ancestral land, i.e., land of the family, was connected to that family, and descendants were more entitled to it than others. Although this does not demonstrate that Roman law supported *niarkap*, it shows distinct but similar connections between land and family in Frisian and Roman law.

While the first two allegations concern the interest of relatives, the other two support an interest of neighbors in adjacent land. However, the first (D. 31.77.27) makes no mention of neighbors. Instead, it concerns a shared tract of land that had been left to freedmen with the request not to alienate it. Therefore, this text has some relevance to the topic, as it forbade alienation. The reason for this was: [...] *utque in familia libertorum retinerent*. (Translation: "[...] so that they would retain it in the family of the freedmen.")[91] This shares some similarities with *niarkap*, namely the intention to keep property within a family. Neighbors are mentioned at another instance in the same title of the Digest, with D. 31.1.54 stating: [...] *saepe enim confines fundos etiam supra iustam aestimationem interest nostra adquirere*. (Translation: "for it is often in our interest to acquire neighboring land even above its just price.")[92] Yet, this provision does not state whether neighbors can expel a buyer. It merely confirms the principle that neighbors had an interest in lands bordering their own.

90 Nijdam, et al., *Frisian Land Law*, p. 75f.
91 D. 31.77.27.
92 D. 31.1.54.

The last allegation in the gloss is to the constitution of Emperor Frederick (*Libri Feudorum*). This text was a collection of feudal customs written in Lombardy in the 12th and 13th centuries.[93] It makes reference to a custom that appears very similar to *niarkap*. *LF* 2.3 concerns who can receive and distribute investiture:

> LF 2.3.1. Sed etiam res, cuius alienatio prohibetur, nec per beneficium dari conceditur, nisi in casibus; ut ecce si quis ex agnatis tuis rem, quae a communi parente per successionem ad eum pervenerit, alienari voluerit, non permittitur ei, etiam secundum antiquam consuetudinem, alii eam vendere, nisi tibi vel alii proximiori, pro aequali pretio accipere volenti.[94]

> LF 2.3.1 But it is also not permissible for a property, the alienation of which is prohibited, to be issued as a benefice, except in certain cases. For example, if one of your agnates wants to alienate property, which has been left to him through inheritance from a common relative, he is not allowed to sell it to a third party according to ancient custom, except to you or another near relative, who want to accept it [the property] for the same price [as the third party had offered].

This rule has some striking similarities to *niarkap*. While the source dates from the 12th and 13th centuries and *niarkap* is recorded from the 13th century onwards, the custom in the *Libri Feudorum* is called an "ancient custom" (*antiqua consuetudo*), indicating that it had existed for quite some time. It is therefore uncertain as to whether these concepts truly are the same, i.e., whether the *Libri Feudorum* contains some form of *niarkap*, *Näherrecht* or *naasting*. The glossator does not draw any parallels between the two customs, and reference is made to a gloss *proximiori*, which does not mention neighbors in either the main text or the gloss. Therefore, it is unclear why this text was referred to as proof for a right of neighbors.

The arguments and references in this gloss demonstrate that the glossator was aware of the incompatibility of Frisian law and Roman law regarding *niarkap*. At the same time, they could not simply disregard Roman law. Instead, they acknowledged that Roman law prohibited this custom while also argu-

93 Hallebeek, "Structure of medieval Roman Law", p. 293. 'Liber feudorum' in: Weimar, *Lexikon des Mittelalters*, cols 1943–1944.

94 LF 2.3.1. For a Dutch translation, see Spruit, Chorus, *Corpus Iuris Civilis*, XII Addendum, p. 35f. See also Lehmann, *Das Langobardische Lehnrecht*, p. 118.

ing that it remained valid. This argumentation was based on similarities in the ideas underlying the concepts, namely that relatives had a special interest in familial property. There is no application of Roman law. On the contrary, Frisian law is supported by finding arguments in Roman law in its favor. This demonstrates three things: first, that Frisian law was intended to be maintained regarding *niarkap*; second, that Roman law had authority in the thinking of jurists; and, third, that there was a willingness to express Frisian rules in the language of Roman law.

5.2 Niarkap *in the* Excerpta Legum

Niarkap is mentioned several times in the *Excerpta Legum*, with all of these occasions being in copies of case records. This indicates that *niarkap* was still in use in legal practice at the time. The absence of any instance other than case records suggests that manuals and texts such as *Thet Authentica Riocht* probably did not cover this topic. Alternatively, the compilers may have not deemed engagement regarding *niarkap* to be worthwhile. Traditional Frisian legal texts were also not included, although there are references to these texts:

> Exc 244. Item. Hweerso datter land falt to kaeph, to wixla ief to panda, dat dy sibbiste nyar is dan di land leger ief oers emma; dat to biwisen mit Opstallis bames wilkeren. Item. Dat het onder set is, dat toe biwisen mit iiij, der da wirde witen.[95]

> Exc 244. Item. If (a plot of) land is bought, exchanged or pledged, the nearest relative has a stronger right to it than the neighbor or anyone else; this I will prove with the Statutes of Opstalsbam. Item. The fact that it was pledged, I will prove with four witnesses, who know the truth.

Undoubtedly, this text refers to the *Statutes of Opstalsbam* (WUps 16), which was analyzed earlier. It was still considered authoritative, and while it spoke of buying and exchanging land, the above provision (Exc 244) also mentions pledging (*to panda*) of land. It is possible that this was a deliberate addition by the person making the argument in the case. The final sentence indicates that the case concerned a pledge. Additionally, the text mentions that relatives have a stronger right than neighbors, which was not explicit in the *Statutes of Opstalsbam* (WUps 16).

---

95 *A*, I (Exc) 244, p. 198.

It is evident that the right to take over a sale was still widely used in 15th-century Frisia, as various documents attest. They demonstrate the ongoing legal practice of claiming *niarkap*. At times, however, this right was also questioned, as recorded in the *Excerpta Legum* (Exc 556). The following two texts (Exc 557 and Exc 558) then provide arguments in favor of the custom. It is possible that all three consecutive provisions came from a single court case and perhaps represented the arguments of both sides: contra and pro. Alternatively, they may have been arranged in this way by the compilers.

> Exc 556. Jtem. Dit is riucht, dat en man moet syn land sella ende capia sonder nyar, want nyar is een syda allenna in Fryeslant ende geet to yens dat riucht; dit to biwysen in screwen riucht: **Quia quilibet libere uti potest suis bonis.**[96]

> Exc 556. Item. This is law, that one may sell and purchase land without consideration of the right to take over a sale, because the right to take over a sale is only a custom in Frisia and contradicts (Roman) law. This I will prove with written law: **Because anyone can freely make use of their own goods.**

The right to take over a sale is rejected, based on its contradiction to law (*riucht*). This can refer only to learned law, and most likely to Roman law in particular. The argument is that *niarkap* was only a custom and was set aside for that reason. Roman law prohibited similar rules and preferred the freedom to use and alienate property as one pleases.

The quotation underlined at the end of the passage, which is written in Latin, has an uncertain origin. It may have originated from the works of Aulus Gellius, a Roman writer living between 125–180 CE.[97] Alternatively, it may have come from Bartolus de Saxoferrato (1313–1357), a 14th-century commentator and a widely known and respected jurist. It is plausible that Bartolus was known in Frisia.[98] He expressed a well-known and frequently quoted description of ownership (*dominium*), which is similar to the sentence in the preceding provision: *Quid ergo est dominium? Responde: est ius de re corporali perfecte disponendi,*

96 *A*, I (Exc) 556, p. 386.

97 Gell. 13, 24, 1. This concerns the frugality of Marcus Cato the Elder: "*Suum cuique per me uti atque frui licet.*"

98 Although he is not mentioned in the gloss to the *Freeska Landriucht*, see Nijdam, et al., *Frisian Land Law*, p. 76. However, Bartolus is quoted in the *Jurisprudentia Frisica*; see Gerbenzon, "Aantekeningen (Tweede Deel)", pp. 357–358.

nisi lege prohibeatur. (Translation: "What then is dominium? Answer: it is the right of having a physical thing completely at one's disposal, unless it is prohibited by law.")[99]

The notion of *libere uti* bears some resemblance to *perfecte disponere*. Without further texts, however, it is impossible to determine the exact origins of this sentence. It remains unclear, for example, whether the author of this argument regarded learned law as more authoritative than Frisian law. Such a view would suggest a particularly strong reception of Roman law. The following provisions present counterarguments to this view:

> Exc 557. Item. Dit is riucht, dat dy sibbesta nest is ty da land cape ief panden, der dy sibba nat lechya wol; dit noechlijc to bywisen in screwen riucht. Nota quod quis habet ius proximitatis contra alienos habemus tam ex consuetudine patrie eciam iure canonico approbato iure ciuili ac municipali: Extra, de restitutione in integrum, Constitutus (X 1.41.8), cum ibi allegatis in glosa ordinaria,[100] et eciam consuetudo rationabilis iure ciuili approbatur, ut C. Que sit longa consuetudo, l. Leges (*Cod.* 8.52.3).[101]

> Exc 558. Item. Zo is hit zyde ende pliga vr gastland ende by waldem ende in Weynbritzera deel ende in Woldenzera deel, dat dy sibbesta nest ka ep is, wanneer dat syn bloed syn land vorcapia wol, bupta fremda, ende disse zyde ende pliga scelma halda to riuchta, ut C. Que sit longa consuetudo; quia est rationabilis et prescripta ergo ualet, ut in l. Leges, tytulo iam allegato.[102]

> Exc 557. Item. This is law that the nearest relative has the strongest right in the sale or pledging of land which his kinsman wishes to part with; this I will prove definitively with written law. Notice that we owe the fact that one has the right to take over a sale (*ius proximitatis*)[103] against others to the custom of the territory, also confirmed by Canon law, Roman law and municipal law; see X 1.41.8 with the allegations there in the gloss *consuetudinem*, and also on the ground that a reasonable custom is approved by Roman law; see C. 8.52.3.

---

99 Bartolus de Saxoferrato, *Commentaria*, ad. D. 41.2.17, § 4.
100 Gloss *consuetudinem* ad X 1.41.8.
101 *A*, 1 (Exc) 557, p. 386.
102 *A*, 1 (Exc) 558, p. 386.
103 This term is identified as a Latin term that refers to *niarkap*. See Vries, "Nijaer is sijd", p. 270.

> Exc 558. Item. It is custom and usage in Gaasterland and Zevenwouden and in Wymbritseradeel and in Wonseradeel that the nearest relative has the strongest right to buy when his relative sells his land to a stranger. This custom and usage shall be legally maintained, as in C. 8.52; because it is rational and prescribed, it is valid, as in C. 8.52.3.

Both provisions recognize *niarkap* as a custom in Frisia (*consuetudo patrie* and *zyde ende pliga*). Instead, however, of being an argument against it, this is presented as a reason for its validity. Both texts refer to the same rule in Roman law, namely C. 8.52.3, which asserts that a long-standing custom that is observed gains the force of law.[104] This principle can be applied to the custom of *niarkap*, which serves as a counterargument to the previous provision (Exc 556). The same argument is made in Canon law: X 1.41.8 stipulates that an observed custom is valid law. The custom in question pertains to the city of Perugia, and a gloss specifies that such a custom is approved.[105] As such, and while a right to take over a sale was not found in learned law, there was support for the observing of customs.

These three consecutive provisions are intriguing. Did the compilers of the *Excerpta Legum* doubt whether *niarkap* was enforceable in Frisia? Arguments both for and against the custom were included, which could suggest uncertainty. However, the alternative seems more probable, based on the arrangement of the provisions. It appears that an argument against the custom was initially raised, and then refuted by other more convincing arguments. Furthermore, their inclusion generally implies approval of the custom. At the same time, an argument against the custom was presented in legal practice, i.e., in a court case (Exc 556). Thus, the custom was not undisputed, with some individuals considering it invalid law that should not be followed.

Possible explanations for this rejection can be gleaned from the sources. First, it is evident that the argument against *niarkap* (Exc 556) is based on the limitations on the freedom to dispose of property. People were not free to transfer their own property to whomever they wished, or to purchase from anyone they wanted, without taking into account the rights of relatives. This may have led to conflicts between relatives and buyers and sellers of property. Additionally, there were concerns about the abuse of this custom. Another case record indicates that the right to take over a sale was lost if it was used fraudulently.

104 C. 8.52.3: "*Leges quoque ipsas antiquitus probata et servata tenaciter consuetudo imitatur et retinet.*"

105 "*Consuetudo erat approbata illius loci* [...]" Gloss *consuetudinem* ad X 1.41.8.

> Exc 546. Item. Dit js riucht: Jef en man den kap wel wiste ende hy van byhindicheit swigat ende thochte, hy capye dat nu, als ick dat yeld habbe of reda mey, zo scel jc hem wel weder of driwa mit niare, dit is en onnutte bihindicheit ende scel hym scaya ende nat helpa in syn riuchte. Ende hy vr sumat syn nyar, want der screwen steet: Maliciam et dolum nulli patrocinari debere: De dolo et contumacia, Ex litteris (X 2.14.2).[106]

> Exc 546. Item. This is law: If someone knows of the sale and stays silent out of malice and thinks: "He buys it now, when I have the money or can obtain it, I will expel him with the right to take over the sale." This is useless malice and shall harm him and not help his right. And he loses his right to take over the sale, because it is written: Malice and deceit should not protect anyone, X 2.14.2.

This text describes a situation in which a person hears about the sale of property by a relative but lacks the funds to claim their own right to take over the sale. Consequently, the person waits until the sale has been completed and they have gathered enough money to pay the price, and only then come forward to claim their right. Such behavior would be highly disadvantageous for the buyer. Entitled relatives and neighbors may also intentionally have chosen to wait and see the sale price before deciding to claim their right.[107] However, this is less likely because previous sources indicate that the sale price was announced after the agreement between the seller and buyer, and thus entitled persons would have known the price. But if entitled persons declined to exercise their right, it would lapse.[108]

Interestingly, the reason for the deceitfulness of such behavior is grounded in Canon law, specifically the ecclesiastical norm that "malice and deceit should not protect anyone." The argument is that those who wait to claim their right act unlawfully and should not profit from deceit. It is noteworthy that the reason for the deceitfulness of this behavior is sought in learned law. In Frisian legal practice, if no-one came forward to claim their right, a peace (*ferdban*) was declared over the sale, which meant that no person could subsequently disturb the property. This mechanism prevented entitled persons from waiting until a later point to claim their right to *niarkap*. However, this is not mentioned here; instead, Canon law is referenced. This may be due to the authority of learned

106 *A*, I (Exc) 546, p. 380.
107 This is argued by Vries, *Ferdban*, p. 284 f.
108 This is also stated in a document of 1499. See Vries, *Ferdban*, p. 283.

law, as a reference to Canon law may have been a stronger argument, especially within a Romano-canonical procedure.[109]

It is possible that, at the time and location in question, the involvement of a court and the proclamation of peace over a sale was not a common practice. For instance, Frisians east of the Lauwers did not involve courts in *niarkap*.[110] This seems less likely, however, since the account in question is contained in *Excerpta Legum*, a text compiled in Westerlauwers Frisia.

Another issue that may have caused confusion is the regional variation in the time limits for claiming *niarkap*. The *Excerpta Legum* mentions widely differing time limits. For example, Exc 552 states that *niarkap* is lost if the land sold had been lawfully owned by the buyer for a year.[111] In Wymbritseradeel, the time limit is given as two years instead of one.[112] The *Excerpta Legum* (Exc 553) also states that after ten years have passed, a buyer of land cannot be expelled through the use of *niarkap*.[113] This is an extremely long duration compared with Exc 552 and Exc 555, and even more so when compared with W⁵D 33. It is possible that this refers to the period during which *niarkap* could be claimed if a sale had not been announced. When no *ferdban* had been proclaimed over the property, the sale could be disputed. Conflicts may have arisen frequently about the period during which one could claim *niarkap*, and this may explain why some people opposed such a right. No buyer wanted to be surprised by a claimant of *niarkap* after they thought that peace had been proclaimed on the sale.

5.3 Niarkap *in City Laws*

The city laws of Bolsward, Sneek and Leeuwarden also include mentions of *niarkap*.[114] The law of Bolsward of 1479 states:

> 74. Van land of huusinghe te vercopen.
> Item, die landt of huusinghe vercoeft heeft, die salsie laten beden drie Sonnendaghen byeen ouer die kercke, ende als die boeden omghecomen sijn, soe sal dat Recht eenen dach daertoe legghen den coop ghaer te wysen, ende wort dan die coop niet verseth, soe salmen ghaer wysen;

109 Of which these case records were part. On that, see the introduction on the *Excerpta Legum*. On the procedure in Frisian law, see Chapter 2.

110 Vries, "Nijaer is sijd", p. 264.

111 *A*, I (Exc) 552, p. 384: *Jtem. Dit is riucht: Als en caper bysit en land rechtelike sonder weerspreke **een jeer lang**, efter dam so hath dy sibbesta syn nyar, darhy der on hath, vrleren.*

112 *A*, I (Exc) 555, p. 386.

113 *A*, I (Exc) 553, p. 384.

114 Telting, *Friesche Stadrechten*, p. 28 f., 86 f., 162 f. and 261 f.

ende dairnae mach nyemant nyaer dairaen hebben, ten waer saeke dat hi buten landes waer, die daer dat nyaer aen hebben mach, ende als die to huus compt salment hem nowelike kondighen, ende sprect hi dan niet binnen der maent, soe is hi sijn nyaer quit.[115]

74. On the sale of land or houses.
Item, if someone has sold land or a house, they shall announce the sale over three consecutive Sundays at the church and if the announcements are done, then the court shall determine a day when the sale is proclaimed and if no-one opposes the sale, then it should be proclaimed effectual; afterwards, no-one may make use of the right to take over the sale, unless he was outside of the country and when he comes home, one should inform him sufficiently of it and if he then does not act within a month, then his right to take over the sale is lost.

An almost identical text is found in Bolsward (1455) 64 and Sneek (1456) 72.[116] It is likely that all three instances derive from the same, albeit unknown, source. However, it is clear that *niarkap* was firmly anchored in local city laws during this period. Therefore, the 15th century did not show a decline in legal practice or in the existence of written laws regarding *niarkap*.

The provision mentioned above reflects many of the central aspects of *niarkap* that were present before the 15th century. These include the requirement to announce a sale on three consecutive Sundays, as well as the practice of announcing the sale at the church (in the case of Bolsward) rather than the court. If no-one opposes the sale, it is deemed effectual (*ghaer wysen*). There is no evidence that these norms were influenced by learned law.

5.4 Niarkap *in the* Jurisprudentia Frisica

The *Jurisprudentia Frisica* contains an entire title on *niarkap* (JF 30). It consists of many provisions from the *Excerpta Legum* (13 out of 30, or 43%), but also additional texts. The table below shows this relationship. Title 30 appears in the manuscript just before gathering six, which contains most of the titles on contracts. It is in gathering five, which contains other specific Frisian laws.[117] These are the last four titles in gathering five (titles 28–31) and include titles such as

115 Telting, *Friesche Stadrechten*, p. 162 f. For a recent edition of the city laws of Bolsward from 1455 and 1456, see Robijn, *Het recht*, pp. 124 and 145, respectively.
116 Telting, *Friesche Stadrechten*, p. 28 f. and 86 f., respectively.
117 Gerbenzon, "Aantekeningen (Tweede Deel)", p. 49.

TABLE 3 Provisions of title JF 30, with corresponding provisions and an overview of their content

Jurisprudentia Frisica	Corresp. Provisions	Content
JF 30:1		Land of the clergy
JF 30:2		*Niarkap* only for immovable land
JF 30:3 JF 30:4	Exc 545 Exc 546	Deceit in the use of *niarkap*
JF 30:5	WUps 16, Exc 244	Agnates are preferred
JF 30:6 JF 30:7 JF 30:8 JF 30:9		Women have equal access to *niarkap*
JF 30:10 JF 30:11 JF 30:12 JF 30:13 JF 30:14 JF 30:15	 Exc 552 Exc 553 Exc 554 Exc 555	When *niarkap* may not be claimed: unborn children, duration of claim
JF 30:16 JF 30:17 JF 30:18 JF 30:19 JF 30:20 JF 30:21	Exc 556	Arguments against *niarkap*
JF 30:22	Exc 243, Exc 557	Closest relative has the most right
JF 30:23 JF 30:24 JF 30:25 JF 30:26	Exc 558 Exc 559 Exc 560 Exc 561	Customs as valid law

TABLE 3 Provisions of title JF 30, with corresponding provisions and an overview of their content (*cont.*)

Jurisprudentia Frisica	Corresp. Provisions	Content
JF 30:27	W^5D 33	
JF 30:28		The procedure of claiming *niarkap* in Frisian law
JF 30:29		
JF 30:30		

niarkap and *ferdban*.[118] The title on *niarkap* consists of 30 provisions and 34 glosses in total. Although it is not clearly structured internally, an examination of the provisions reveals some degree of organization, as shown in table 3.

5.4.1 Object of *Niarkap*

Let us look at what is new, what is recurrent and what is unusual in this title. The first provision concerns a case where the right to take over a sale is not allowed:

> JF 30:1 Dat is riucht datma oen gastlicke lyodena gued ende der helliger tzercke gued off land ende pronda land mey nymmen nyaer oen habbe.

> JF 30:1 This is law, that no-one should use the right of taking over the sale concerning the good of clerics and the good or land of the holy church and prebend land.[119]

The placing of this provision at the beginning suggests something about the authors of the Frisian law text. Educated jurists from the clergy collected, compiled and edited the text during the Late Middle Ages. It is very likely that the authors themselves were affiliated to the Church, given their interest in emphasizing the exception for ecclesiastical property when considering *niarkap*.[120] This is supported by two allegations in the first gloss:

118 Gerbenzon, "Aantekeningen (Tweede Deel)", pp. 37–38.
119 *Ro*, III (JF) 30, no. 1.
120 For the authors and compilers of Frisian sources, see the introduction.

> Glossa 1. Dat is riucht datma De in integrum restitucionibus, super uerbo 'municipii', C. de sacro sanctis ecclesiis et rebus et preuilegiis earum l. i (*Cod.* 1.2.1).

> Gloss 1. Dat is riucht datma See the gloss municipii to X 1.41.8, C. 1.2.1.[121]

We previously encountered the first reference (X 1.41.8) in the *Excerpta Legum* (Exc 557), which pertains to the validity of customs but does not mention ecclesiastical property. It is unclear, therefore, why this part of the *Liber Extra* is cited in this context. However, the second allegation is more noteworthy: C. 1.2.1 states that individuals can freely donate land to the Church or charitable organizations through their will.[122] Although this pertains to testaments rather than *niarkap*, the underlying principle remains the same: land given to the clergy and Church should be protected.[123]

The second provision establishes the right to take over a sale, but it contains a few peculiarities that are worth noting.

> JF 30:2 Dat is landriucht ende keysers riucht dat inda kaep dy sibste ende dy nest leger nyaer habbe mey fan lidzen land ende eerff ende is nyaer inda kaep ende mey dyn kaper oeff drywe.

> JF 30:2 This is land law and imperial law, that in case of a purchase the nearest relative and the adjacent are allowed to use the right of taking over the sale concerning immovable property ['land and yard'] and they are more entitled to the purchase and may expel the (principal) buyer.[124]

This section outlines the most significant features of *niarkap*, including the ability of the nearest relative and neighbors to take over a sale. Notably, this provision applies only to immovable property (*land ende eerff*), which suggests that *niarkap* could not be applied to movables, as was the case for *Näherrecht*.[125]

The text establishes at the outset that this right is a form of land law (*landriucht*). However, this term does not necessarily refer to the *Twenty-four Land*

121 Gloss 1 ad *Ro*, III (JF) 30, no. 1.

122 C. 1.2.1: "*Habeat unusquisque licentiam sanctissimo catholicae venerabilique concilio decedens bonorum quod optavit relinquere.*"

123 For further information on testaments in Frisia, see chapter 4.

124 *Ro*, III (JF) 30, no. 2.

125 'Näherrecht' in: Erler, at al., *Handwörterbuch zur deutschen Rechtsgeschichte*, p. 829.

Laws specifically.[126] Although the specific *landriucht* in question is not identified, the first gloss provides some indication.

> Glossa 2. De ista materia eciam in landriucht de predio priuati uendendo.

> Gloss 2. See about this also in the Land Law on the tenement of a private person to be sold.[127]

It is possible that *landriucht* refers to the *Statutes of the Five Districts* (W^5D 33), which clearly establish how *niarkap* can be claimed when a person wants to sell land. The second place where one can find such a rule on taking over a sale is in imperial law (*keysers riucht*). However, Roman law did not allow for a right to take over a sale. It is also possible that "imperial law" refers not to Roman law, but to the law related to the emperors of the Holy Roman Empire or the *Libri feudorum*. Once again, a gloss provides references to the laws in which we can find this information.

> Glossa 3. *Dat is landriucht ende key* Iuxta consuetudinem patrie et iura municipalia melioris condicionis est consagwineus ad predia emenda uel ad alia non mobilia; ad hoc de consuetudine c. Cum dilectus (X 1.4.8), quia consuetudo approbata est optima legum interpres; facit ad hoc de in integrum restitucionibus c. Constitutus (X 1.41.8), ubi dicitur "Proximiores et uiciniores possunt emptores repellere et redimere", ff. de contrahenda empcione l. Qui officii (*Dig.* 18.1.62), ff. de minoribus xxv annis l. Si empcionem pro uicinioribus (*Dig.* 4.4.35), ff. de legatis et fidei commissis ii l. Si cui fundus (*Dig.* 31.1.54).

> Gloss 3. *Dat is landriucht ende key*. According to the custom of the territory and the Land Law (*iura municipalia*) the blood relative has a better position to purchase the tenements and other immoveable things; about this see X 1.4.8, because an approved custom is the best interpreter of the law; this is furthermore said in X 1.41.8, where it is written: "The persons more close or nearby can expel and redeem the buyers", see D. 18.1.62, D. 4.4.35 and D. 31.1.54.[128]

126 On this term, see Vries, "Thet is ac londriucht", p. 585.

127 Gloss 2 ad *Ro*, III (JF) 30, no. 2.

128 Gloss 3 ad *Ro*, III (JF) 30, no. 2.

Further analysis of this gloss is unnecessary since its arguments and references provide few new insights, as they have all been previously discussed. The first half of the gloss concerns customs, with *niarkap* being confirmed through customs (*consuetudo patrie*) and the Land Law (*iura municipalia*). The references are generally the same as those in the *Excerpta Legum* (Exc 557 and Exc 558).[129] The latter three allegations are the same as in the *Freeska Landriucht* (gloss 33 to SkRa 38) and generally acknowledge the interest of neighbors in adjacent land. This indicates that the author of this title had access to the *Freeska Landriucht*. Furthermore, *keysers riucht* must refer to Roman law, as references to it can be found here.

5.4.2 Arguments against *niarkap*

A significant portion of the title (JF 30:16 to JF 30:21) presents arguments against *niarkap*. There are two possible reasons for this inclusion. Firstly, the authors may have disagreed with the custom. While the compilers were learned jurists, they were also Frisians for whom *niarkap* was an "ancient custom". Nevertheless, they could have omitted the title altogether or included only the counterarguments if they disapproved of *niarkap*. The fact that they included the title in its current form suggests that the first explanation is unlikely.

Secondly, the inclusion of counterarguments was a common scholarly practice. Jurists often presented arguments both pro and con before arriving at a conclusion. The authors may have followed this convention in this title by listing the counterarguments and then disproving them. This practice is similar to the arguments presented in the *Excerpta Legum*, which also listed arguments against *niarkap* and subsequently refuted them (Exc 556 to Exc 558). These provisions indicate that *niarkap* was disputed in Frisian courts, which may explain why the authors included arguments both for and against *niarkap* in their compilation of provisions.

Let us examine the arguments presented against *niarkap*. One recurring argument is that *niarkap* was only a custom and, therefore, not valid law. This same argument was made in the *Excerpta Legum*, and JF 30:16 is indeed a copy of Exc 556.[130] The counterargument in the *Excerpta Legum* was that customs were also valid law. These same arguments are present in JF 30:22 to JF 30:26,

---

129 There is a reference to X 1.4.8: "[...] *quam etiam contra consuetudinem approbatam, quae optima est legum interpres, minus canonice attentat* [...]." Here it is stated that an approved custom is valid. Additionally, X 1.41.8 is mentioned, as in Exc 557 and gloss 1 to JF 30:1. It also concerns customary law.

130 See the table above.

which correspond to the same texts in the *Excerpta Legum*.[131] See the above table for the corresponding provisions in both texts. Consequently, arguments both for and against *niarkap* are provided. This may have been the purpose of this section of the title (JF 30:16–26): to include arguments to the contrary, which are then rebutted.

This section also presents new arguments against *niarkap*, such as the claim that it is forbidden by imperial law (*keysers riucht*) because the Emperor Justinian disallowed it.

> JF 30:17 Dat keysers riucht seyt datma neen nyaer mey habba hor om sib ner om nest leger, hwant dy keyser justinianus deer dat riucht haet maket seyt aldus in syn riucht jn lex dudum Codice de contrahenda empcione [*Cod.* 4.38.14]: jn foertiden wast riucht, datma nyaer habbe mocht om sib ende om nest leger. Mer nu saegh dy keyser justinianus dat dy seller jeffta wrbringer meer ward in lien brocht dat hy syn gued naet most wrbringa ney syn ayna willa. Aldeer om so haet hy dat nyaer wrbaeden.

> JF 30:17 Imperial law says that one should not use the right to take over a sale, neither on the basis of kinship nor on the basis of adjacency, for Emperor Justinian, who codified the law, thus says in his law [reference to C. 4.38.14]: in the past it was law that one could use the right to take over a sale on the basis of kinship and of adjacency, but then Emperor Justinian saw that the seller or alienator was (even) further disadvantaged, because he was not allowed to alienate his property according to his own will. That is why he forbade the right to take over a sale.[132]

This Roman rule (C. 4.38.14) was previously cited in a gloss to the *Older Skelta Law* (gloss 33 to SkRa 38) and used as evidence that Roman law does not permit the right to take over a sale. The latter part of the text is an Old Frisian translation of the original Latin text of C. 4.38.14. However, there is one significant difference: the Frisian text refers to the right to take over a sale (*datma nyaer habbe mocht*), which is a Frisian concept not found in the Latin original. The Latin text states that the nearest person has the right to exclude outsiders from a sale (*ut extraneos ab emptione remouerent*). The Frisian text also mentions a right for neighbors ("on the basis of adjacency"), which is not present in the

131 Exc 557 to Exc 561.

132 *Ro*, III (JF) 30, no. 17.

Codex. The Frisian translation implies that the Roman rule specifically concerns *niarkap*, although this was not the case. The original Latin text is quoted in a gloss:

> Glossa 21. *Dat keysers riucht se* in lege Dudum, C. de contrahenda empcione et uendicione (*Cod.* 4.38.14), ubi dicet lex: "Dudum proximis et consortibus concessum erat ut extraneos ab empcione remouerent neque homines suo arbitratu distraherent."

> Gloss 21. *Dat keysers riucht se* (*Imperial law says*) in C. 4.38.14, where the provision states: "Formerly it was permissible for the nearest and those in an undivided community of goods, that they excluded extraneous persons from a purchase and that persons did not alienate anything by their own free will."[133]

The concept of excluding extraneous persons may seem similar to *niarkap*, but the two are not congruent. *Niarkap* developed out of the Frisian tradition of family property rights, and it is unlikely to be related to the subject written about in C. 4.38.14. However, Roman and Frisian customs are sometimes equated. The main text (JF 30:17) confirms that Emperor Justinian forbade *niarkap*, not just the exclusion of strangers from a sale, and this is reiterated in another provision.

> JF 30:20 Jtem nu ist to fara bewyd dat dy keyser dat nyaer wrbeden haet ende ist seeck dat een man hyr to buppa enich nyaer wirth to wysd so is dat nyaer naet ende dy doem is onmachtich als justinianus dy keyser seyt.

> Glossa 26. *Jtem nu ist to fara bewysd* C. de legibus et constitucionibus principum l. Non dubium (*Cod.* 1.14.5), ubi dicit lex "Non dubium est in legem committere eum ...". Concordat regula iuris in vi (VI 5.12.5, reg. 64): "Que contra ius fiunt, pro infectis debent haberi", eodem in vi "Qui contra iura mercatur, bonam fidem non presumitur habere" (VI 5.12.5, reg. 82).

> JF 30:20 Item. Now it has been proved before this that the emperor has forbidden the right to take over a sale, and if contrary to this taking over a sale is assigned to a person, then the taking over of the sale is null and void, and the judgment is powerless, as Emperor Justinian says.

133 Gloss 21 ad *Ro*, III (JF) 30, no. 17.

> Gloss 26. *Jtem nu ist to fara bewysd* (*Item, now it has been proved before*) See C. 1.14.5, which provision reads: "There is no doubt that one acts against the law …". This is confirmed by the rule of law in the *Liber Sextus* "Whatever is done against the law, should be considered not done" (VI 5.12.5, reg. 64) and in the same *Liber Sextus* "Who acts against the law, is presumed not to be in good faith" (VI 5.12.5, reg. 82).[134]

To make the statement, as in the gloss, that acting against the law renders an action null and void presupposes the validity of Roman law in Frisia. The gloss further supports this argument, suggesting that *niarkap* is considered null and void because it goes against the law. However, the question of which law is referred to is crucial if one wants to claim that any consideration of *niarkap* is void because it contravenes the law. Frisian law did not forbid *niarkap*, and so it must be Roman law that is being referenced. This implies that Roman law was valid in Frisia, and that acting against it would prevent one from claiming *niarkap*. If Roman law was not seen as valid, Frisian rules such as *niarkap* would not be in violation of any law. Despite the debate around *niarkap*, it is clear that the author of this text and gloss considered Roman law to be effective in Frisia. However, this did not mean that all Roman rules were applied or that Frisian rules were not enforced at all. Although *niarkap* remained lawful and practiced, some jurists clearly viewed Roman law as authoritative and even applicable in Frisia.

The final argument against *niarkap* emphasizes the right to alienate property freely.

> JF 30:21 Jtem Soe haet dy keyser to jown da joden dat hya mogen hyare gued wrcapia hwam dat hya willet ende om dyn haegste penninck. Alzo fule meer schillet da cristena dat riucht halde deer dy keyser da joden haet jown.

> JF 30:21 Item. The emperor has allowed the Jews to sell their assets to whomever they please and for the highest price. The more so must the Christians have the right which the emperor gave to the Jews.[135]

The argument presented is one of principle: if Jews were allowed to sell their own goods, then Christians should also be allowed to do so. This principle is

134 *Ro*, III (JF) 30, no. 20.

135 *Ro*, III (JF) 30, no. 21.

explained in C. 1.9.9.[136] The issue of *niarkap* is not directly related to the original question of Jews selling their goods in the Roman Empire. However, the argument against *niarkap* rests on the principle of free alienation. Similar points are made in two other instances, where it is stated that someone could sell their share of communally held land without the consent of the partners.[137] These examples also emphasize the right to alienate freely.

To summarize the arguments against *niarkap*: it was not valid because it was only a custom; it was against Roman law and therefore had no legal effect; and one could freely alienate one's own assets, thus making *niarkap* unlawful. The latter two arguments depend on the relationship between the right to take over a sale and Roman law. Roman law prohibited the exclusion of extraneous persons from a sale and emphasized the ability to freely alienate. The first argument is later disproved in the text, which shows that a long-standing custom can be considered valid law, as supported in learned law.

5.4.3 Subjects of *Niarkap*

Additional aspects of *niarkap* are discussed in the *Jurisprudentia Frisica*. These are specifications of certain persons—women, unborn children, multiple claimants and in-laws—who could or could not claim the right to take over a sale.

5.4.3.1 *Women*

The *Jurisprudentia Frisica* contains four provisions: JF 30:6 to JF 30:9, which pertain to the ability of women to take over a sale. It is evident from classical sources, such as the *Statutes of Opstalsbam* (WUps 16), that Frisian women were granted this right.[138] Nonetheless, it is notable that this fact is specified in four separate provisions, which may suggest that it was not clear to educated individuals whether such rights were applicable to women in the context of learned law. The possible theoretical or practical arguments that existed are not discernible from these provisions. However, it is clear that the author sought to establish that women did indeed possess the right to take over a sale.

According to Roman law, all persons gained legal capacity at the age of majority (25 years). This also included women since gender-based tutelage

136 It is also briefly quoted in gloss 30 ad JF 30:21, showing where this argument came from.

137 Found in both JF 30:18 and JF 30:19.

138 *D*, XX (WUps) 16, pp. 432–433: "A man or woman (*hera jefta frowe*) descending from the paternal line or 'sword side' is more entitled to take over the land […]."

(*tutor mulieris*) had been abandoned.[139] Women with legal capacity could enter into contracts, unless specifically prohibited by law.

The legal capacity of women in Frisian law, by contrast, is more complex to define. Some women were under the guardianship of their relatives or spouses and required their guardian's approval for certain legal actions. It is not entirely clear whether these actions included entering into a contract. During a marriage, women had their own property and were permitted to alienate it, thereby allowing them to enter into contracts for sale.[140]

The *Jurisprudentia Frisica* offers two reasons why women were entitled to *niarkap*. Firstly, women were entitled to inherit and thus also had the right to take over a sale. Secondly, *niarkap* is a right provided to "children," which includes both sons and daughters. Concerning the first argument, which is found in JF 30:6, JF 30:7 and JF 30:9, it should be noted that we do not know for certain how intestate succession was organized. It has been argued that the son's share of an inheritance was twice that of a daughter's, with the former inheriting two thirds and the latter one third of the estate.[141] However, the sources on succession are not entirely clear and so the exact distribution of shares is uncertain. Nonetheless, sons and daughters both inherited, albeit potentially unequally. Therefore, the provisions specify that sons and daughters were equal in kinship regarding inheritance, meaning that a daughter was not excluded if a son existed.

> JF 30:7 Jtem neydam dat dochter ende zoen sint lyck sib to dat eerffscip hyare faders ende moders sisters ende broders meghis ende niftis dyr dat maer ende principael is, soe agens aeck lyck sib to wessen to dat nyaer hyare fryondes deer dat minre is.

> JF 30:7 Item, since daughter and son are equal in kinship concerning the inheritance of their father and mother, sister and brother, nephew and niece, which is the greater and the foremost, therefore they must also be equal in kinship concerning the right to take over the sale in relation to their kinsman, which is the lesser.[142]

139 Kaser, *Das römische Privatrecht* II, pp. 116–120.

140 Fockema Andreae, "De onzelfstandigheid der vrouwen", p. 41. For further information on guardianship over women, see chapter 6.

141 Algra, *Oudfries Recht*, pp. 355–356; Noomen, "Consolidatie", p. 77. For more on Frisian succession law, see chapter 4.

142 *Ro*, III (JF) 30, no. 7.

It is evident from the text that the principle of equality in kinship was used as an argument for entitling women to *niarkap*, and this argument is also present in another provision (JF 30:6). The nature of this argument derives its strength from a more fundamental principle, as indicated by the terms *principael* and *minre* in the text. This same argument is repeated in a third provision (JF 30:9), making it unnecessary to analyze that provision further. The type of reasoning employed in this argument, which draws from a stronger principle, was transmitted through learned law, as detailed in this gloss:

> Glossa 10. *Jtem neydam dat da dochter* Per arg. a maiori quod est in iure ualidum, in auth. Multo magis C. de sacrosanctis ecclesiis (auth. post *Cod.* 1.2.14 [ex Nov. 7.11, Nov. 120.7]). Et dicitur arg. a maiori illa racione, quia in eo quod probatur, habet in se maiorem racionem, etc. Et est arg. a simili, "propter quod unumquodque tale facit, ipsum magis tale", quod ponit Aristoteles primo Posterioris[143] et in l. Ex diuerso § i ff. de soluto matrimonio (*Dig.* 24.3.17.1).

> Gloss 10. *Jtem neydam dat da dochter*. Through the 'argument drawn from the stronger', which is valid in legal reasoning, see the authentica *Multo magis* (post C. 1.2.14). And it is termed 'argument drawn from the stronger' for this reason, that it contains a stronger ground for what is proven, etc. And it is an 'argument drawn from something similar', "in virtue of which something is as it is, it is itself more so", which Aristotle points out in the first book in his *Posterior Analytics*, and in D. 24.3.17.1.[144]

There are two ways of reasoning that support the provision granting women the right to take over a sale. The first reasoning is known as "an argument drawn from the stronger", which originates from learned law. This argument states that since both sons and daughters inherit property, which is a stronger and more important custom, they should also both be allowed to take over a sale. The second reasoning is referred to as "an argument drawn from something similar", which is attributed to Aristotle and references a text of the Digest.[145] Both of these methods of argumentation were introduced into Frisian law through learned law and logic.

143 Aristoteles, Posteriorum analyticorum Libri. Medieval Latin text in Thomas Aquinas, Posteriorum analyticorum, Liber I, lectio 6.

144 Gloss 10 ad *Ro*, III (JF) 30, no. 7.

145 In the latter, a connection between such reasoning and the contents of the Digest or its glosses is not apparent to me. As such, it remains unclear why this allegation appears here.

Another argument in support of women's right to take over a sale is that they also fall under the term 'children'. This is stated as follows:

> 30:8 Lettera tyd so mogen da dochtera alz wel nyaer habbe als da sonen, hwant dat riucht seyt ful claerlick dat da kynden mogen nyaer oen hyare moderlycke gueden habba, ende onder dy nama dis kyndes wirth naet allynna foerstinzen dy soen mer alzo wel da dochtera.

> 30:8 Secondly, the daughters have as much right to take over the sale as the sons, because the law says quite plainly that the children may use the right to take over the sale concerning their maternal goods, and (that) by the term 'child' not only the son is meant, but also the daughters.[146]

Which legal text or legal system that "says quite plainly" can only be speculated. Earlier texts often mention only next of kin (*sibste*).[147] They do not mention only children (*kynden*) in respect to *niarkap* since this includes all close relatives. It is therefore unclear which law is meant, and a gloss sheds no more light:

> Glossa 12. *Ende onder dy nama des* ut in l. Congnoscere § Liberorum (*Dig.* 50.16.56.1) et l. Filii appellacione ff. de uerborum significacione (*Dig.* 50.16.84), ubi dicitur "Liberorum appellacione continentur non tantum qui sunt in potestate, sed omnes qui sunt sui iuris, siue uirilis siue feminini sexus sunt exue feminini sexu descendentes".

> Gloss 12. *Ende onder dy nama des* as in D. 50.16.56.1 and D. 50.16.84, which states: "The term 'children' includes not only those under paternal control, but (also) all who are of their own right, no matter whether they are of the male or female gender or whether they are descendants from the (male or) female line."[148]

The term 'children' (*liberi*) is stated to include both male and female descendants. However, apart from the fact that the Frisian provision reproduces this text, little of interest is contained here. One must wonder why these arguments

146 *Ro*, III (JF) 30, no. 8.

147 As, for example, in JF 30:2 or in Exc 244, Exc 557 and Exc 558. On the term 'sibste', see Vries, "Nijaer is sijd", pp. 276–277.

148 Gloss 12 *Ro*, III (JF) 30, no. 8.

are included. As far as we have seen, Frisian law never defined those entitled to *niarkap* as children, whether minors or adults. Rather, it always included all close relatives (*sibste*), regardless of whether they were direct descendants. There may have been disputes or doubts about whether women had a right to *niarkap* at all, but unfortunately no other sources confirm this. However, it seems unlikely that such disputes arose from Frisian law since the latter made no distinction between women and men in terms of who could take over a sale.

What can be asserted at the very least is that the addition of these arguments indicates a greater influence of learned law on the law of contracts and *niarkap*. Specifically, it demonstrates that this influence led to the reception of more specific rules and arguments than were previously present in written Frisian law. The latter evidently allowed women to claim *niarkap* since they also owned property in their own right. Therefore, there was no need to state this separately and specifically. The appearance of such written norms in the *Jurisprudentia Frisica* shows precisely what kind of reception occurred, i.e., it was the method, system and approach of learned law that was received. When arguments in favor of women claiming *niarkap* were written down, they were not argued through Frisian traditions or customs, but derived instead from learned law. Therefore, it is learned law that provides the basis for women having the right to take over a sale. That this was already the case in Frisian law is neither mentioned nor apparent.

5.4.3.2 *Unborn Children*

Something similar can be observed in another context, with a further addition and clarification being found in JF 30:10, which states that an unborn child cannot inherit or use *niarkap*.

> JF 30:10 Een kynd dat nae lyff ontfinzen haet dat mey neen eerua wessa ner nyaer habba fanda gueden deer fader ende moder off syn sibba fryonden habbet foerbrocht.

> JF 30:10 A child which has not received life must not inherit and not use the right to take over the sale concerning the assets that his father and mother or his near relatives have accumulated.[149]

This provision appears to be similar to the previous ones in that it probably would not have been included in traditional Frisian law. Nonetheless, it

149 *Ro*, III (JF) 30, no. 10.

is explicitly stated here and supported by justification found in Canon law. Gloss 14 references Canon law to argue that an unborn child cannot suffer a loss and is not legally relevant, and thus had no right to take over a sale. Similarly, as with women being allowed to claim *niarkap*, the disallowing of unborn children is justified in context and with reference to Canon law.

5.4.3.3 *Multiple Claimants*

A third example of such references to learned law is found in relation to the number of claims of *niarkap* that could be made on a sale. This is stated in the following provision and gloss:

> JF 30:13 Dat is riucht datma op een land joff een seeck naet meer dan een hlest jeffta nyaer jeff een pina lidza mey.
>
> Glossa 18. Quia nemo duplici pena punitur, in c. Ac si clerici, de iudiciis (X 2.1.4).
>
> JF 30:13 This is law that one may not place more than one burden or right to take over the sale or encumbrance on (a plot of) land or an asset.
>
> Gloss 18. Because no-one is punished by a double penalty, see X 2.1.4.[150]

This text suggests that only one person could claim *niarkap* over a piece of land, which implies distinctions between those entitled to do so. Some of these distinctions are known in Frisian law, such as giving preference to those living in the parish over those living in the district (W^{5}D 33) and to agnates over cognates when considering equally close relatives (WUps 16). These distinctions suggest that two people could not take over a sale at the same time, as one would expect. There were also differences between those entitled to determine who could provide a guarantee and take over a sale.

A reader of these Frisian provisions might not have even considered the possibility of two people taking over a sale at the same time, given that there is only one sale to take over. Yet, the provision above (JF 30:13) codifies this rule explicitly. The act of writing down this rule has one significant consequence: to legitimize this argument, learned law is referenced. Specifically, it is stated that no-one should be punished by double penalty, which is a common maxim of learned law. In the case of *niarkap*, therefore, the buyer should

150 *Ro*, III (JF) 30, no. 13.

not be expelled from the purchase twice. While this may be obvious to modern readers, it may also have been obvious to Medieval Frisians. However, the use of learned law's reasoning to legitimize this norm makes it seem as though learned law is responsible for it.

5.4.3.4 *In-Laws*

The last case of a similar note concerns another group of people who were not entitled to claim *niarkap*: in-laws. Apart from unborn children, sisters-in-law (*snoerscip*) and brothers-in-law (*swagerscip*) were also not entitled. This rule was added in two glosses (Gloss 27 and Gloss 28, written in Old Frisian) and is not included in the main text.[151] Furthermore, it is not mentioned anywhere else in Frisian law.

> Glossa 27. Jtem. Swagerscip ende snoerscip mogen neen nyaer habbe neyda riucht hwant swagerscip ende snoerscip agen neen lawa ner nen mondscip deer mara is deer om agens neen nyaer deer mynra is, quia "id si quod magis uidetur inesse non inest, [nec] id quod minus".[152]

> Glossa 28. Jtem dat riucht seyt datti sib mey habbe deer heten is consanguinitas nyaer hit seyt naet swagerscip off snoerscip deer heten is affinitas mogen nyaer habba dat dit weer is schelma beuisa myt gastlike riuchten, in c. Cum dilecti, per ordinem consuetudinis, de in integrum restitucione (X 1.41.4). Ende om dattet riucht to jowt dattet sib nyaer aegh so ist to foerstaen dat swagerscip ende snoerscip neen nyaer agen, arg. ad hoc quia intelligit prohibitum quod non inuenitur expresse concessum.

> Gloss 27. Item. Brothers-in-law and sisters-in-law are not legally allowed to use the right to take over a sale because brothers-in-law and sisters-in-law are not entitled to inheritance nor to tutorship, which is the more important; therefore they are not entitled to take over the sale, which is the lesser, because "if that which much more seems to be the content, is lacking, also that which less seems to be the content will be."

151 The two glosses follow JF 30:20, which states that *niarkap* is null and void. It is curious that they are arranged like this since both glosses recognize a right to take over a sale, just not for in-laws. It is more probable that these glosses are connected to JF 30:22, which concerns the right of the closest relatives and is on the same page in the manuscript (Page 140 of *Codex Roorda*).

152 Aristotle, Topica 2.10.

> Gloss 28. Item, the law says that relatives—which is called consanguinity—are entitled to take over the sale. It does not say that brothers-in-law and sisters-in-law—which is called affinity—are entitled to take over the sale. That this is true is to be proved with ecclesiastical law, see X 1.41.4, according to the rule of customary law. And because the law agrees that relatives are entitled to take over the sale, it is to be understood that brothers-in-law and sisters-in-law are not entitled to take over the sale. An argument is that what is not explicitly found to be permissible is understood to be prohibited.[153]

Two distinct arguments are made here. First, it is argued that sisters-in-law and brothers-in-law do not inherit or gain guardianship over children. What does traditional Frisian law say about this? The contrary argument is found in the Book of Emperor Rudolf, where it is precisely the brother of a deceased husband who gains guardianship over the widow and her children.[154] Regarding inheritance, however, in-laws did not inherit as they were not among the close relatives (*sib*).[155] Nevertheless, this gloss argues that, in both cases, in-laws are not considered, and therefore are also not able to take over a sale. The reasoning comes from learned law and is based on the principle of "an argument drawn from the stronger". Succession is deemed stronger and, consequently, the lesser *niarkap* follows the same principle.

The second argument mirrors what has been argued previously about the term 'children'. Since relatives (*sib*) include only blood relatives and not in-laws, the latter have no right to *niarkap* because *niarkap* is the right of relatives to take over a sale. As such, and in contrast to the term 'children', relatives do not include sisters-in-law or brothers-in-law. Yet, it is the same reasoning, albeit flipped. This is made particularly clear by mentioning the corresponding Latin terms. *Sib* is equated with *consanguinitas*, and the in-laws are referred to as *affinitas*. It may very well have been that in-laws were also not considered 'relatives' in Frisian law. The gloss seems to think that they were, and that relatives were entitled to take over a sale, which is *riucht*; i.e., not Roman or Canon law, but Frisian law. The allegation to Canon law confirms that customs are valid law. Therefore, the glossator clearly argues that this norm originates in Frisian

153 Gloss 27 and gloss 28 ad *Ro*, III (JF) 30, no. 20.

154 Rud 21. For more on guardianship, see Chapter 5.

155 Succession is detailed in L^{24} 16. Firstly, to the 'six-hands' (mother, father, sister, brother, children and grandchildren) and then to all other relatives according to degree. See also Meyers, "Het Friese Erfrecht", p. 54.

law. However, the reasoning for why this was the case is taken from logic deriving from norms of learned law, i.e., "an argument drawn from the stronger" and "what is not explicitly found to be permissible is understood to be prohibited." This is most obvious in these two glosses because this reasoning is expressed in Latin and not in Old Frisian.

In all four examples—women, unborn children, the placing of two burdens of *niarkap* on a sale, and in-laws—it is either evident or very likely that these norms already existed in Frisian law or customs. What makes their addition so significant is that they are reasoned and legitimized through learned law. On the one hand, this strengthens the validity of *niarkap*. On the other hand, it also means that norms and methods of learned law were influential on and authoritative regarding this Frisian custom. *Niarkap* was not only approached by means of the Frisian legal system, but also through the lenses of Roman and Canon law. This, therefore, was a systematic and methodological reception without any actual reception of new major norms.

Title 30 of the *Jurisprudentia Frisica* concludes with a group of provisions that outline part of the *niarkap* procedure, all of which are included in Frisian law without any explanatory notes. Several details can be gleaned from these four provisions. If, for instance, someone wished to claim the right to take over a sale, they had to do so within three days or before the fourth day, as specified in all the provisions. Additionally, the other party had to confirm under oath that the claimant was entitled to *niarkap*. Furthermore, the claimant was required to provide a pledge for the price of the sale before the fourth day, and failure to do so, withdrawal of the claim or being proven wrong in court resulted in the claimant losing the right to take over the sale, and in the sale becoming legally binding.[156]

None of these texts appears to be influenced by learned law, as each is unmistakably Frisian law. Although their origins are largely unknown, one provision (JF 30:27) references the Five Districts. Various traditional legal texts, including the *Statutes of the Five Districts*, are presumed to comprise the foundation of *niarkap* in the *Jurisprudentia Frisica*.

156 *Ro*, III (JF) 30, no. 27–30. On this procedure, see also Vries, "Nijaer is sijd", p. 262ff., who cites these as sources.

6 Conclusion

6.1 *Law of Contracts*

Overall, we have observed a systematic and methodological adoption of the contract law of the *ius commune* in Frisian law. In traditional Frisian law, various contracts were regulated by custom, and little is known about how these contracts were established. Contracts in primary sources share Old Frisian terms and the principle of mutual consent, but were written as detached and separate provisions. Consequently, they form a 'general law of contracts', where singular forms of contracts are loosely connected as general agreements.

This circumstance, where much information about contracts is hidden in unwritten customs, facilitated the adoption of learned law. The sources reveal that Frisians adopted the Canon law of contracts. The system of contracts applied is general instead of specific, and it is open instead of restricted. In court cases collected in the *Excerpta Legum*, Frisians argued that all agreements had to be observed, including naked agreements (*pactum nudum*). In this, they followed the principles of Canon law, even though they were aware that Roman law prohibited naked agreements from being actionable.

The adoption of Canon law is even more apparent in the *Jurisprudentia Frisica*. Again, the system of contracts is general rather than specific and open rather than restricted. Various contracts are placed together in the manuscript, indicating that they were all seen as being governed by a general law of contracts. The names of these contracts' titles are taken from the *Liber Extra*. Moreover, one title concerns agreements in general (*de pactis*) and includes the principles of the Canon law of contracts, and most importantly the principles that all contracts had to be observed, including nude agreements.

In conclusion, Frisian law received the contractual system of Canon law both in the principles (observation of nude agreements) and the structure (titles concerning contracts). It cannot be said that the Roman law of contracts, with its formalities and limited number of obligatory contracts, was adopted in any form in the late 15th century.

6.2 *Niarkap*

The practice of *niarkap*, which involved taking over a sale of property, was prohibited by learned law, which preferred property to be alienated autonomously. However, the custom continued as a deeply entrenched practice in Frisian society. While traditional Frisian sources on *niarkap* remained relevant and valid in the late 15th century, newly included provisions indicated doubt about the custom, and disputes about its misuse and general validity were apparent.

Arguments against the right to take over a sale were brought forth from norms of learned law, but arguments were also mentioned in support of the custom. It was emphasized that *niarkap* was valid according to learned law because it was a long-standing custom. In this manner, a harmonization of *niarkap* and learned law took place, with specific elements of learned law being added into the framework of Frisian *niarkap*.

These included provisions exempting the goods of the Church and clergy from being claimed, and specific legally relevant groups—such as women, unborn children and in-laws—were also deliberated upon. A reception of legal reasoning can be observed in these provisions, and the maxims of Roman and Canon law were especially visible.

The reception of learned law in 15th century Frisia was not primarily normative. Rather, it involved incorporating the system, its approach to contracts and its reasoning into individual norms of Frisian law. While this cannot therefore be considered a comprehensive reception of the law of contracts during this period, it did not harm the practice of *niarkap*. Instead, Frisian jurists aimed to harmonize learned law and Frisian law by applying the system, methods and norms of learned law to Frisian rules. This helped to legitimize and provide reasoning for Frisian law in accordance with learned law.

There were several reasons why Frisians maintained their custom of taking over a sale. First, it was an old custom and deeply entrenched in their society. Second, families, neighbors and the local community all had an interest in taking over a sale to ensure that land stayed in the hands of the family or a parishioner, and extraneous persons consequently could not take over land.

Niarkap continued to be practiced long into the Early Modern Period and was still mentioned in the written law of the 16th and 17th centuries, with the Frisian *Landsordonantie* of 1602 and 1723 both dedicating a title to *niarkap*.[157] *Naasting*, the Dutch variation of *niarkap*, remained valid law in the 17th and 18th centuries due to the economic and social advantages it gave families and local communities, but was officially abolished in the Netherlands in 1809.[158]

157 L.O. (1602), liber 1, tit. 12, art. 1: "Dat het niar alleenich plaetse heeft in contracten van coope." And the same in L.O. (1723), liber 1, tit. 12, art. 1.

158 Bezemer, "Romeins recht", pp. 122–124; De Blécourt, "Heerlijkheden", pp. 504 and 512f.; Vries, "Nijaer is sijd", p. 265.

In conclusion, the survival of *niarkap* is not surprising, given its deep roots in Frisian society and the powerful tool it provided those who were entitled to enforce their interests. As such, *niarkap* and its regional variations remained relevant in Medieval society and also during the subsequent centuries.[159]

159 And arguably even until today, considering the recent attempts to allow local communities to determine who can buy a house in their community. On this, see the footnote at the beginning. Throughout time, communities have had and still have a vested interest in ensuring that their internal structures are not disturbed.

CHAPTER 3

Proof and Procedure: Oaths, Ordeals and the Emergence of Other Evidence

This chapter analyzes the procedural law of Medieval Frisia and its roots in Medieval learned law. Several primary sources are of great importance for this purpose, including the *Processus Iudicii*, a manual on procedural law. This manual contains the procedure of learned law and was translated into Old Frisian from another manual (the *summa antequam*). It was based on the *summula de processu iudicii*, which is attributed to the famous canonist Giovanni d'Andrea (1270–1348). The *Codex Aysma* manuscript contains fragments of the *Processus Iudicii* manual within the text *Excerpta Legum*, and the *Processus Iudicii* is included in its entirety in *A*, III.[1] The *Processus Iudicii* is consequently of great importance for the reception of procedural law in 15th century Frisia.

Additionally, sources of the *ius commune* are also important. Frisian sources sometimes copied and quoted the works of canonists. This is especially relevant for procedural law: an example of this is the aforementioned *summula de processus iudicii*, which appears in its earliest edition in the *Jurisprudentia Frisica*.

1 Frisian Legal Procedures in the High Middle Ages

Medieval Frisian law did not formally distinguish between civil and criminal procedures. It did, however, distinguish between procedures initiated by an accuser ('accusatory procedures') and procedures initiated by a court ('public procedures'). This chapter describes both procedures, but deals primarily with the accusatory procedure.

1.1 *Accusatory Procedure*

The accusatory procedure was the most common and predominant form of legal procedures in Medieval Frisia. In such a procedure, a private accuser brought a claim against someone who had disadvantaged them. It was not a public institution or court that initiated such procedures or pursued wrong-

1 For more on this manual and the manuscript, see chapter 1.3.

 | DOI:10.1163/9789004712706_004

doings that disadvantaged a claimant. Instead, the victim (as the claimant) and the perpetrator (as the defendant) negotiated procedures between themselves. The goal of such a procedure was not to establish the facts of what happened, but rather to formally convince one party of the other party's truth. The claimant sought punishment of the defendant and compensation, while the defendant's aim was to persuade the claimant of his or her innocence. This should not be seen as private reconciliation, but rather as a public cessation of the dispute. A secondary aim was to normalize relations between the two parties and thereby restore the social peace that had been disturbed.

If a wrongdoing was evidenced with sufficient proof, the statement of the claimant became true. If a defendant provided proof of innocence or the claimant failed to prove the opposite, the statement of the defendant prevailed. The success of either the claimant's or defendant's proof had the character of a judicial sentence.[2]

The role of officials in this procedure was passive, with their main function being to attest to the procedure and supervise its proper implementation. The *asega* announced the outcome of a trial but did not determine the sentence imposed on a guilty party. Instead, the sentence depended on the wrongdoing: killing someone, for example, always warranted paying the victim's wergild. More on the appropriate penalties for crimes and delicts later.

After a sentence had been pronounced, it was also up to the claimant to implement it. If, for example, someone was sentenced to death, the victorious claimant carried out the execution or paid someone else to do it.[3] The *asega* or another official were not usually involved in implementing a sentence, unless someone was unwilling to abide by the law. If a guilty person refused to accept a sentence, the local community got involved. The *bannere* and members of the district went to the unwilling person's house and destroyed it as punishment. This process was called the *brond ande breke* in Old Frisian (German: *Wüstung*) and involved burning down (*brond*) and breaking (*breke*) the house.[4]

---

2 Immink, "Getuigen", pp. 433–435. Already by the time of the *Lex Frisionum*, this was the way procedures were conducted; see Oosten, "Inleidende Beschouwingen", p. 443.

3 As detailed in *D*, XII (SkRb) 29, pp. 310–311: "This is the law, if a thief has been caught and brought before the *skelta*, and if he is sentenced to death, then the *skelta* is not obligated to either hang the thief or blind him. Then the *bannere* has to bind him and lead him to the gallows. Then the claimant has the choice between hanging him himself and paying someone to do it for him."

4 As is evident in *D*, XII (SkRb) 3, pp. 294–295, where, after not appearing in court, "[…] The *asega* then decrees that since the defendant has been summoned nine times to appear before court and this has been testified by twenty-one persons, each *skelta* now has to light the beacon at night and make the official announcement within his own district. On the next

This lack of public prosecution in favor of accusatory procedures was characteristic of other Medieval legal systems, too, specifically the Norwegian, Danish and other Germanic systems of law. In Norwegian law, for example, judges also did not weigh the evidence or pronounce a sentence. Instead, the central questions were which party had the advantage in proving their statement, what kind of proof had to be furnished, and when was that proof regarded as successful?[5] The same questions defining the procedure in Frisia were characteristic of Medieval Norwegian laws. We can therefore gain insights by comparing how other indigenous traditions changed during the Late Middle Ages and what happened in Frisia.

It would also be interesting to compare the Frisian procedure with medieval Dutch and German procedures, which may have had many similarities. However, further comparisons are beyond the scope of this book, but additional research is encouraged. Norwegian procedural law offers a unique opportunity because of a recent English treatment and is therefore preferred here.[6]

1.1.1 Procedural Sequence

A comprehensive account of the procedural progression in the High Middle Ages can be found in the *Younger Skelta Law* (SkRb 3), which is too lengthy to quote in full here.[7] This procedure was a complex exchange between the claimant and defendant, with each repeatedly raising the stakes. Initially, the claimant would raise a claim by specifying the wrongdoing committed and the atonement required. Committing a wrongdoing meant breaching the public peace, and this breach required compensation. The presiding judge[8] would then order the defendant to either confess or deny the accusation, with the defendant stating that there was no requirement to do so; this, however, was only a formality with no influence on the procedure.

---

morning, a militia shall go to his estate in the same way one would march against an enemy of the king. His house and goods are then to be burnt down and laid to waste [...]."

See also Vries, "Seka mit brande", p. 284ff. and Nijdam, "Compensation", p. 52.

5 For the procedure in Medieval Norwegian law, see Nordby, *Judicial Oath*, p. 51; and for a brief overview of the procedure in Medieval Danish law, see Andersen, *Legal Procedure*, p. 188ff.; Tamm, *Danish Medieval Laws*, p. 22.

6 See Nordby, *Judicial Oath*.

7 *D*, XII (SkRb) 3, pp. 290–295. See also Nijdam, *Lichaam, eer en recht*, p. 154ff. for a summary of the procedure.

8 *The Younger Skelta Law* speaks of the 'count' ordering. This is likely to refer to the count's representative, the *frana*. In later centuries, this order was given by whoever replaced the *frana* as the presiding judge.

The presiding judge would then refer to the *asega*, who possessed knowledge of the relevant law and confirmed that the defendant was indeed obligated to confess or deny. The *asega* would then ask the defendant again to confess or deny. If the defendant confessed, the trial ended. If the defendant denied the accusation, the procedure advanced towards the furnishing of proof. This involved a formulaic back-and-forth exchange between the accuser and the accused. First, the defendant offered to prove innocence by means of an oath. Then the accuser did the same, offering to prove the claim by means of an oath. Lastly, the defendant escalated again and offered to make an oath of innocence with the help of compurgators. More on these oaths and compurgation later.

The procedure was an escalating exchange of claims and denials, with each step leading to a more serious stage. For instance, the defendant could raise the stakes by offering a more serious oath, such as one with compurgators, after the claimant and defendant had both offered their respective, less serious oaths. Before the parties furnished proof, the *asega* gave a judgment concerning who had the right to make an oath. This 'right to prove' is detailed later in this chapter.

The two primary kinds of proof were the oath and the ordeal. Proofs by oath and ordeal are sometimes considered 'irrational' proofs when compared to the 'rational' proofs of learned law, such as witnesses and instruments. Medieval Frisians did not use written instruments because their society was primarily oral. However, the increase, over time, in written instruments and documentation marked an important shift in procedural law in Frisia.[9]

1.2 *Public Procedure*

Initially, in the High Middle Ages, crimes were not typically pursued by public institutions or courts.[10] However, an exception to this general rule is found in the *Synodical Law of Central Frisia*, where a jury of the synod (known as *ēthswera* in Old Frisian) assumed the role of the accuser. This was not a jury in the sense of a tribunal, but rather a group of witnesses appointed and sworn in by local authorities and who acted as claimants instead of the person who had been disadvantaged by the wrongdoing. This procedure appears to have been restricted to wrongdoings falling under ecclesiastical jurisdiction.[11]

9 More on this later.

10 This changed somewhat in the Late Middle Ages, when, in some cases, public officials could also raise claims. See Oosten, *Ambtshalve Vervolging*, p. 36 ff. and 43.

11 For example, altar robbery, adultery and theft of corpses. See in *D*, XI (SWl) 20–25, pp. 264–267. Such procedures could also be inquisitory rather than accusatory. For an overview of this procedure in the Synodical Law, see Hallebeek, *Layci Erant Coiudices*, p. 12 ff.

A similar concept is found in the Medieval law of the German territories, known as the *Rügegericht*, where reputable men of a district were sworn in and acted as public accusers. Membership of the jury was mandatory and not voluntary. Individuals often sought to avoid being a member of the jury because a false accusation could lead to the accusers themselves being punished, and failing to accuse someone made the members of the jury liable. The *Rügegericht* was an alternative to the usual accusatory procedure when an official approach was needed or desired. It originated in the Frankish period and spread in the 9th century.[12] This procedure was called *wrōginge* in Frisia.[13]

The ecclesiastical institutions adopted the *Rügegericht/wrōginge* as the *Sendgericht* (known as *sineth* in Old Frisian[14]). This procedure functioned similarly, with seven jury members (*Sendschöffen, iurati*), and concerned itself primarily with heresy, murder, adultery and perjury. This is the procedure mentioned in the *Synodical Law of Central Frisia*. The *Sendgericht* became more widespread during the 13th and 14th centuries, and its use disappeared only with the Reformation and the Council of Trent in the 16th century. Traditionally, the *Sendgericht* also used oaths and ordeals as forms of proof.[15]

1.3 *Oaths of Innocence and Compurgation*

An oath (OF: *ēth*) was the primary means of providing proof in the Frisian legal system, and a common practice in Germanic legal systems.[16] Generally assertory, oaths confirmed the truth of a statement made by the claimant or defendant.[17] These oaths were considered sacred acts, and their power was tied to divine supervision. Oaths were often taken with the hand placed on sacred objects, such as holy relics, the church altar or the gospel, which were thought to be imbued with spiritual power. By swearing upon these objects, it was believed that God bore witness to the oath-taking event.

In Frisia, the existence of an oath taken on holy relics, along with the right to be claimant or defendant, was legitimized by connecting it to a supposed priv-

12 Eisenhardt, *Deutsche Rechtsgeschichte*, p. 731; 'Rügegericht, Rügeverfahren' in: Erler, et al, *Handwörterbuch zur deutschen Rechtsgeschichte*, pp. 1201–1205.

13 '*wrōginge*' Hofmann, Popkema, *Altfriesisches Handwörterbuch*, p. 602.

14 '*sineth*' Hofmann, Popkema, *Altfriesisches Handwörterbuch*, p. 428.

15 Eisenhardt, *Deutsche Rechtsgeschichte*, p. 731. See also: 'Send, Sendgericht' in: Erler, et al, *Handwörterbuch zur deutschen Rechtsgeschichte*, pp. 1630–1631.

16 For Norway, for example, see Nordby, *Judicial Oath*; for Denmark, see Tamm, *Danish Medieval Laws*, p. 22; for Flanders, see Caenegem, *Geschiedenis*, p. 147 ff.

17 Dirks, "Der Eid", p. 169. The other form was a promissory oath, where something was promised for the future. This was more common in the making of contracts, which also involved the swearing of oaths.

ilege of Charlemagne, as explained in the *Seventeen Statutes*. Similar, however, to the mythical origins of the Frisian freedom, it is unlikely that this privilege was actually granted by Charlemagne.

> K^{17} 17. Dioe saunteende kest is, ende dis koningh Kaerlis jeften ende aller Fresena riucht, dat alle Fresen tingie bi twira tale ende bi aesga dome ende aller manick wyte him self haet hi deen habbe oen da wyteden, [...].

> K^{17} 17. The seventeenth statute is, and this was a privilege given to us by King Charles (Charlemagne) and it is the law of all Frisians, that all Frisians have the right to bring a claim before court and defend themselves in court according to the judgment of the *asega* and each has a right to testify of his own actions before court with an oath on the holy relics, [...].[18]

In the Middle Ages, the breaking of an oath was understood to invoke divine retribution. It was considered a mortal sin and to lead to the loss of eternal salvation.[19] Perjury also had social consequences. It meant the loss of honor in a society governed by honor. As taking a false oath could lead to social ostracism or expulsion, oaths were not taken lightly. The formula of an oath had to be followed very precisely; otherwise, the oath could fail.[20] The *Jurisprudentia Frisica* contains such a formula for an oath to tell the truth:

> JF 56:12 DJt is dy maneer fan een eed to stowien
> "Jck zwer op den libbende godes zoen dy om mynra willa is steern oenda crywse op alda waldeda dyr mey fen hym comme mey. Ende op al dat quaed dyr him oen siel ende lijff bore mey sonder argelist dat dyo riuchte wird godis aldus is. Also help my god ende al syn helligen to enen riuchten eed ende on meens."[21]

> JF 56:12 This is the way to corroborate a statement with an oath.
> "I swear on the son of the living God, who died on the cross for me, on all the mercies that may come to me from him, and on all the evil that

18 *D*, VI (K^{17}) 17, pp. 202–203.
19 The breaking of an oath is, for example, discouraged in Matthew 5:33.
20 Nijdam, *Lichaam, eer en recht*, pp. 165–167. Losing a case could similarly influence the honor of the loser, Nijdam, "Compensating", p. 53.
21 *Ro*, III (JF), tit. 56, no. 12.

> may come to his body and soul, without guile, that the just truth of God is thus. So help me God and all his saints to perform a rightful oath, and not a perjury."

Certain accusations required specific oaths and the touching of specific objects. A provision in the *Statutes of the Five Districts* (W^{5}D 38) details some distinctions:

> W^{5}D 38. Hiir sint lada scrioun. Herdefanges ende duustslekis, duuststowes ende duustswenges, so schil di man an sine nates hand faen ende swara dat him God alsoe helpe ende riuchte hand trowa, so hi dera deda onschieldich se. Om faxfang so schil hi faen oen synre gara ende swara so him siinre schette fia ti frome wirde so hi onschieldich se. Item bloedresene: twirasum onswara. Metedulgh: fiowerasum onswara. Faxfangh, weedscreed, fliueswerp, bloedresene, duiststeet, duistsleeck, dis is di fria Fresa nier op da helligem to witane dan hi aegh enich tiugh to ontfaen.

> W^{5}D 38. Here the oaths of innocence are written down. In case of grabbing someone by the shoulders, hard blows or pushes or swings, the defendant must grab the hand of his relative and swear that God may help him and judge over this hand-oath that he is innocent of this act. In case of hair grabbing he must take his own clothes in his hand and swear on the loss of his cattle that he is innocent. Also, for a bleeding wound: two oaths, for a measure wound: four oaths. Hair grabbing, cutting someone's clothes, pushing someone into the water, bleeding wounds, hard push, hard blow; in case of all these offences, a free Frisian may testify of his innocence by swearing an oath on the holy relics rather than having to listen to any testimony to the contrary.[22]

Evidently, it was customary to grab relevant body parts or objects when taking an oath. For instance, pushing someone required the hand of a relative to be held. Grabbing hair entailed the placing of a hand on a piece of cloth during the oath. There is also mention of two or four oaths, depending on the wound inflicted. This indicates that oath-taking was not always singular but could be magnified by taking multiple oaths. Therefore, perjury meant breaking not one but two or four oaths.

---

22 *D*, XIII (W^{5}D) 38, pp. 328–329.

Each of these oaths was also taken "on the holy relics". There seems to have been a distinction in the kinds of oaths a defendant took. During a procedure the defendant took multiple oaths: one to state innocence, and another to prove it. The provision above (W^5D 38) is not entirely clear on this, but it is possible that the first oath (the one to proclaim innocence, *onschieldich se*) involved placing the hand on a relevant object or body part. However, it is not certain whether there were two distinct oaths. Alternatively, an oath could be taken on a relevant or sacred object. Frisian law distinguished between the oaths used for various general and specific situations. If, for example, the accusation concerned movable goods, a defendant swore a *fiāēth*.[23]

The oath relevant for proof was the oath of innocence (OF: *lāda, wīthēth, riucht*). Defendants could exonerate themselves (OF: *undswera*) through such an oath.[24] An accused who denied an accusation could offer to confirm the statement of denial and thereby confirm their innocence. This practice was very old and is attested to from at least the 8th century.[25] As well as being sworn by the defendant, such an oath required the help of additional participants, the 'oath-helpers' or 'compurgators'. These individuals were typically recruited from among the family of the person taking an oath of innocence.[26] A compurgator's role was to confirm the defendant's statement by swearing a separate, assertory oath. This was not intended to establish or confirm facts, but instead served as validation of the accused's statement.[27] A compurgator's attesting to the character of the defendant was a crucial building block in the system of honor that existed in Frisia. Both the defendant and oath-helper put their honor in jeopardy by taking this oath.[28]

1.3.1 'Right' to Prove

The above leads to the question of which party was required to provide proof. According to learned law, as well as in our present-day legal systems, the burden of proof commonly rests on the person raising the claim. The claimant had to provide evidence to prove statements, as clearly stated, for example, in the Digest:

---

23 On the terminology of oaths in Old Frisian, see Popkema, "Die altfriesischen Eidesbezeichnungen" and p. 333 f. for the *fiāēth*. See also Nijdam, *Lichaam, eer en recht*, pp. 178–181.

24 *Wīthēth* specifically refers to an oath on holy relics, see Popkema, "Die altfriesischen Eidesbezeichnungen", p. 344.

25 On manslaughter, see the entire title I in the *Lex Frisionum*.

26 Dirks, "Der Eid", p. 169; Immink, "Getuigen", p. 434.

27 Immink, "Getuigen", p. 434.

28 Nijdam, *Lichaam, eer en recht*, p. 167.

Dig. 22.3.2. Ei incumbit probatio qui dicit, non qui negat.

D. 22.3.2. Proof is incumbent on the one who makes a claim, not the one who denies it.

Frisians conceptualized this in a different manner. I call this the 'right to prove', although it can be more accurately described as having the 'benefit to be allowed to provide proof that supersedes proof by the other party'. Sometimes the term *niar* was used to indicate that someone was 'closer', i.e., to a greater extent entitled to such proof:[29]

SkRb 33. Jeff een frowe her des foermeth dat hio oen her manne voercoft habbe half be ende half bodel ende trymene syn ain, lawiged ende onlawiged, jeff di eerfnama des bisecka wil, soe is hio **nier** hyne to jechten mit saun orkenen [...]

SkRb 33. If a woman declares that she transferred to her deceased husband half of the profit the estate yielded during their matrimony and half of the movables and (she can therefore claim a right to) one third of the entire property, both acquired through inheritance and otherwise, and if the heir wants to deny this, then she has a **stronger right to prove** her case with the help of seven witnesses [...]

It is essential to understand the difference between the civilian tradition and Frisian law. The person who was allowed to provide proof was at an advantage. Unlike in learned law, however, this was not always the claimant. If defendants had the 'stronger right' (to prove), they could exonerate themselves. If claimants had the stronger right (to prove), they were allowed to produce evidence. Proof by the party with the stronger right excluded proof by the other side. Consequently, Frisian law did not observe a principle comparable to *audi et alteram partem* (i.e., listen also to the other party).

Which party had that advantage varied over the centuries. In earliest Frisian law, the defendant had a stronger right to present proof than the claimant. If someone raised a claim against another, the accused was entitled to swear an oath of innocence to exonerate themselves of the accusation. The *Lex Frisionum* mentions these circumstances multiple times, for example in this provision:

29 In German *näher berechtigt*; see '[2]*niār*' Hofmann, Popkema, *Altfriesisches Handwörterbuch*, p. 352.

> Lex Frisionum 3.1. Si nobilis furtum quodlibet dicitur perpetrasse, et negare voluerit, cum quinque sacramentalibus iuret.[30]

> Lex Frisionum 3.1. If a nobleman is accused of having committed any theft and he wants to deny this, then he swears with five oath-helpers.

As is apparent, only the defendant took an oath with the help of compurgators. There is no mention of an oath of accusation (with oath-helpers). The procedure may have advanced in this manner: a claimant accused someone in court of a wrongdoing, and the defendant could subsequently swear an oath and exonerate themselves of the accusation. We can clearly see that such a 'right to prove' was an advantage rather than a burden. The claimant could not win the dispute by providing proof if the defendant was allowed to swear an oath of innocence. For this reason, it is more appropriate to speak of a 'right' instead of a 'burden' of proof. Whether this means that claimants took no oaths at all is not quite clear from the sources. The *Lex Frisionum* makes no mentions of oaths of accusation except where a defendant wanted to designate another person as the culprit, as is stated here:

> Lex Frisionum 9.5. Producat hominem quem voluerit, et iuret: "Quod ille homicidii, de quo ego interpellatus sum, reus est," [...][31]

> Lex Frisionum 9.5. He produces the person whom he wants (to be accused) and swears: "That he is the culprit of the homicide, of which I am accused," [...]

It is plausible that every claim involved swearing an oath, as demonstrated in the *Younger Skelta Law*.[32] Oath-helpers, on the other hand, are mentioned only for defendants. This then can be reconstructed: a claim was raised by a claimant, swearing an oath that accused another person. That person then had the 'right' to swear an oath with the help of compurgators to exonerate themselves. If the oath succeeded, the defendant was found not liable. The claimant had no opportunity to prove their own accusation. This constellation was to the advantage of a defendant able to find compurgators. Because of the sanctity of oaths and the potential social consequences of perjury, an oath was believed to

30 *Lex Frisionum* 3.1.

31 *Lex Frisionum* 9.5.

32 See above for the sequence of a procedure in the *Younger Skelta Law* and in *D*, XII (SkRb) 3, pp. 290–295 where the claimant offers an oath.

suffice and to sufficiently prove the truth. I therefore call this a 'right to prove' as opposed to a 'burden of proof'.[33]

A very similar idea existed in Medieval Norwegian law. The central question was which party had the right to prove its claim. Compurgation was used only by the defendant.[34] As with Frisian law, this concept of 'right to prove' differs from the one in the learned laws. In Romano-canonical procedure, the claimant had to prove the claim, and if the claimant brought evidence, the defendant was equally entitled to bring evidence to the contrary. In Frisia, however, the 'right to prove' was of a different nature: although in the earliest sources this was granted to the defendant, it changed over time.

According to the sources of the 11th to 13th centuries the claimant, instead of the defendant, now had the 'right to prove'. Something, apparently, had changed. There are no sources that attest to this change in the centuries between the *Lex Frisionum* (8th century) and the High Middle Ages (11th to 13th centuries), and we do not know why it came about and how. The oath of accusation now superseded the oath of innocence in certain instances, as explained in this provision of the *Younger Skelta Law*:

> SkRb 3. [...] Nu deelt dy aesgha dat hy nyaer se mitta oenbring him schieldich toe winnane dan hy se mitta edem deer hy byoeth oenschieldich toe wirdane. [...]

> SkRb 3. [...] Now the *asega* declares that the claimant is entitled to accuse the defendant under oath and thus get him convicted, rather than that the defendant is allowed to produce oaths of innocence and thus be found innocent. [...][35]

The claimant's 'right to prove' the accusation thus prevailed over any right of the defendant to prove innocence. The 'right to prove' had switched from defendants to claimants in general. There was yet another difference. Now claimants had to swear to the charges with the help of their own oath-helpers or the support of the *tolva* (see below). If a claimant succeeded in finding sufficient oath-helpers or obtaining the support of the *tolva*, the defendant was no longer allowed to swear an oath of innocence. If a claimant failed to do so—because,

33 This may be the most archaic form of oaths as proof. See Oosten, "Inleidende Beschouwingen", p. 443.

34 Nordby, *Judicial Oath*, p. 51f. Nordby also calls this "Which party has the right to prove its claim [...]?"

35 *D*, XII (SkRb) 3, pp. 290–291.

for example, of a lack of sufficient compurgators—the defendant was allowed to swear an oath of innocence. If this was successful, the defendant was then exonerated.

The primary method of proof remained the oath. We can compare this system to that applying in Norway in the 13th century. Norwegian procedures unfolded similarly. If a claimant provided proof, the defendant was excluded from taking an oath of innocence. Only if the claimant failed to provide proof was exoneration by oath possible. The major difference was that Norwegian law already relied on witness evidence: the claimant provided proof in the form of eyewitnesses, instead of an oath with oath-helpers.[36]

The reason for this switch from the defendant providing proof to the claimant providing proof is unclear. It is possible that an oath of innocence by the defendant was no longer considered trustworthy. Fear of perjury may have persuaded people no longer to allow defendants to exonerate themselves with oath-helpers. In 13th-century Norway, fear of perjury resulted in compurgators no longer being selected by the oath-taker, but instead being chosen by the court.[37]

Classical Frisian law also indicates that not all oaths could be considered trustworthy. Certain defendants were excluded from the possibility of taking an oath of innocence.[38] Servants, for example, were considered insufficiently trustworthy to be allowed to administer oaths. Consequently, they were not able to swear an oath of innocence at all. Instead, their masters were required to swear in their place.[39] The same applied to unfree Frisians and all women.[40] It is possible that the fear of perjury led to the changes regarding who had the 'right to prove'. However, a lack of any primary sources for the period before the 11th century leaves uncertainty in this regard.

---

36 Nordby, *Judicial Oath*, p. 51f.

37 Nordby, *Judicial Oath*, p. 247.

38 Oosten, *Ambtshalve Vervolging*, pp. 21–23. See also Oosten, "Inleidende Beschouwingen", pp. 454–458 and 466–467.

39 For example in *D*, VIII (L^{24}) 10, pp. 228–229: *Dat xde landriucht is: hweer so ma een daedbante werpt op enis mannes schalck, soe moet di hera ontswara mit ene wytede*, [...] (Translation: "The 10th land law is: if a charge of homicide is brought against someone's servant, then the servant's master has the right to exonerate his servant of the claim by swearing an oath on the holy relics [...].")

40 As is evident in *D*, VIII (L^{24}) 10, pp. 228–229. And in *Lex Frisionum* 3.5–6. Slaves and foreigners were also unable to swear oaths and therefore underwent ordeals instead. These were persons who did not have the trust and reputation needed for an oath. See Bartlett, *Trial*, pp. 31–32.

1.3.2 Effects of Notoriety and Doubt on Oath-Taking

The circumstances of a wrongdoing influenced who could prove their statement in court. There were several exceptions that prohibited defendants from swearing an oath of innocence even if the claimant did not have sufficient evidence. The first exception is mentioned at the end of the last of the *Seventeen Statutes*:

> K^{17} 17. [...] hit ne se dat hi een wed deen habbe aen een worpena were jefta an kedena tinghe jefta an da banda synde, soe ne mey ma dera deda nene wyteed byeda.

> K^{17} 17. [...] unless someone has given a statement before a normal court, a special court or a synodical court; in that case he can no longer deny his acts by swearing an oath on the holy relics.[41]

This refers to making a prior statement to a court of law about the accusation. Such a statement could not simply be ignored or denied. Other situations are described in the *Exceptions to the Seventeenth Statute*.

> We^{17} pr. Dae Fresen tinghaden toejeens dyne koningh Kaerl hor se mosten alle secken mitta wythedem fan wisa. Da noem hy em sex weer off deer alle Fresem froem ende fere was.

> We^{17} pr. The Frisians petitioned King Charles to grant them the privilege to exonerate themselves before court against all types of charges by swearing innocent on the holy relics. He then set apart six types of cases in which they could not swear innocence, which all Frisians considered just and good.[42]

The six types are: 1) what is done in public during a feud; 2) when a counterfeiter is caught with counterfeit money on his body; 3) when a commitment has been previously made in court;[43] 4) when a woman is rescued from her attacker's house by the people and the *frana*; 5) when a thief is caught at night with stolen goods in his hands; 6) when someone openly attacks another and

---

41 *D*, VI (K^{17}) 17, pp. 202–203.

42 *D*, X (We^{17}) pr., pp. 254–255.

43 This is in fact the same exception as in K^{17} 17. Normal, special and ecclesiastical courts are mentioned.

wounds or kills the other.[44] Two of these types (the first and the sixth) deal with wrongdoings committed in public.[45] See, for example, the first exception:

> We^{17} 1. Dat aerste is: hweer so ma bi liachta dei ende bi schinende sonna tweer heerfanen opriucht ende tween heerkedden mit ofledena togara laet: haet so ma deer fiucht oen dulgen jefta oen daden dat dis al jechta se.

> We^{17} 1. The first exception is: if two leaders raise their banners and bring together two armies, accepting all responsibility, in broad daylight and while the sun is shining: whatever is perpetrated there, be it wounds or homicides cannot be denied in court.[46]

The defendant was not able to deny involvement in public acts during a feud in court. This highlights the exceptional circumstances surrounding such acts, as they excluded exoneration through an oath. As a result, the accusation made by the claimant alone was sufficient to secure a conviction.[47]

In cases of doubt, by contrast, defendants had a stronger right to prove their innocence and exclude the claimant from providing proof. While the claimant still made an accusation, it was the defendant who could exonerate themselves by providing proof through oaths. This is exemplified in the *Twenty-four Land Laws*, which state that, in cases of homicide without any bodily wounds, defendants had the right to exonerate themselves through an oath:

> L^{24} 8. Dat viiide landriucht is dat ellic eerwe mei leda siin tredknia mit twam dededem toe dade ende to dulge om dat hi is mei fan sine blode commen. Hweer so ma een bannethe werpt op een man deer nen dulg ne haet endma queth dat hi se slain mit bamem jefta huinsen so moet hi tolwasum onswara ende nen meer onbringh daia. [...]

> L^{24} 8. The 8th land law is that each estate holder may rightfully call to court his relatives up to the third degree to act as compurgators in a case of homicide or severe injury by means of swearing two assertory oaths because they are related by blood. If a case of homicide is brought before

44 *D*, X (We^{17}) 1–6, pp. 254–257.

45 This is also arguably true for the exception in K^{17} 17 and for W^{17} 3, where a prior statement or commitment was made publicly at court.

46 *D*, X (We^{17}) 1, pp. 254–255.

47 Presumably with oath-helpers. Oosten, "Inleidende Beschouwingen", pp. 448–453.

> court but the body shows no wound and the claimant states that the victim has been hit by a bludgeon or hanged, the defendant has the right to exonerate himself by swearing an oath on the holy relics, together with eleven compurgators and after that is not compelled to answer to any more claims brought against him. [...][48]

The logic was that if a body showed no wounds, but the claim stated a case of death by bludgeoning or hanging, it was not sufficiently proven that the victim died in that manner. Because the facts of the case remained unclear, the defendant could swear an oath of innocence and preclude the claimant from swearing their own oath. The defendant's right to provide proof was stronger than the claimant's right.

A similar example concerns the theft of goods and a subsequent search of the suspect's house:

> SkRa 67. Jef ma een gued binna enis mannes huse in synre camer bifaert ende deer een reeckhol in is ende hit soedeen gued se dat ma hit deerin werpa moge, so is hi nyer sexasum op da helligem to witen ende schaedloes dat gued wer to jaen dan hi tief aegh to wessen. Jef hit binna sine huse bidulven se, jefta dat ma hit fynt binna sine tredda slette, soe schil hi schieldich wessa jefta een schieldigraı winna. [...]

> SkRa 67. If a good is found in a man's room, and there is a chimney in it, and the good is so small it could have been thrown in, then the owner of the house has more rights to exonerate himself with five compurgators and return the good without having to compensate for it rather than be proclaimed a thief. If it is found buried in his house or locked behind three locks, then he shall be found guilty of theft or produce a guiltier person. [...][49]

The question of who was allowed to provide proof hinged on the presence or absence of doubt. If there was doubt about whether an object was thrown into a house, exoneration was possible. However, if the object was buried or locked away, it could not have been thrown in, thus leaving no doubt of guilt and making exoneration by oath forbidden. Both examples are drawn from relatively

48 *D*, VIII (L^{24}) 8, pp. 226–227.

49 *D*, III (SkRa) 67, pp. 156–157. This provision and the house search are discussed in detail in chapter 3 on theft.

old Frisian texts (L^{24} 8 and SkRa 67). It is assumed that these specifications regarding notoriety and doubt were firmly established by the 11th and 12th centuries.[50]

The ability to swear an oath of innocence was at least partly dependent on the specific circumstances of the claim. In cases of a publicly known act of violence, it was impossible to deny an accusation, and exoneration by oath was therefore excluded. In cases of doubt, however, it was possible for a defendant to exonerate themselves through an oath of innocence, thereby excluding the claimant's capacity to furnish proof.

1.3.3 The tolva and the koninges orkenen

Having been excluded from an oath of innocence, defendants could prove their innocence by referring to 'official testimony', as explained in the *Younger Skelta Law*:

> SkRb 3. [...] Nu deelt di aesgha dat neidam deer hi an dat seckwird bitinget wirth, dat hi ti da sikeringha habba schil dine schelta deer him dae ban ur lath ende **dera tolwa saun.** [...]

> SkRb 3. [...] Then the *asega* declares that the defendant, since he was allowed to bring a defense, he shall produce the testimonies of the *skelta* under whose authority he falls and **seven of the twelve district witnesses.** [...][51]

The twelve district witnesses (*tolva*) mentioned in this text were twelve trusted men of a district who were chosen and had taken oaths to testify the truth. The *tolva* were knowledgeable of the goings-on in a district. They were not witnesses of facts, but witnesses of character and context. As such, like the compurgators, they attested to the character of a defendant and could support and confirm the defendant's statement. Moreover, they actively attempted to ascertain the truth about an issue in court. Claimants utilized the *tolva* by referring to them and seeking confirmation of their statement and claim. The support of seven of the twelve district witnesses was necessary for success. If the claimant was successful, the defendant was excluded from taking an oath of innocence, and the initial claim was confirmed. Only if a claimant failed to

50 This is also what Van Oosten claims; see Oosten, "Inleidende Beschouwingen", pp. 454–455.

51 *D*, XII (SkRb) 3, pp. 293–294.

obtain the support of the *tolva* was the defendant able to exonerate themselves through an oath.[52]

The 'king's witnesses' (*koninges orkenen*), on the other hand, fulfilled a different function. These witnesses, usually seven, were representatives of the Frankish king. Their origin lies in the Frankish period, but they survived in some form during the comital period of Frisia. They are mentioned, for example, in the *Older Skelta Law* of the 11th to 12th centuries.[53] A defendant could refer to such testimony if the object of a claim had been part of a preceding court procedure. The *koninges orkenen* attested to what had previously been decided in that procedure. In this manner, these witnesses could be brought up as proof that a claim had been resolved earlier and should now be dismissed.[54] 'King's witnesses' were therefore not witnesses of facts, but of something that had been decided in court.

One may question whether this system of oaths should be considered 'proof'. No evidence of facts was presented, but rather the character and honor of the parties were attested to. There were no other means of evidence for or against a claim. Although this may be vastly different from present-day notions of evidence, it is consistent with the Medieval approach to proving a statement. Therefore, it is appropriate to call these oaths 'proof'.[55] This understanding of proof differed from that in learned law. The Frisians clearly considered this system of oaths and witnesses as evidence, as seen in a later addition to the *Younger Skelta Law* that referred to the necessity of producing the testimonies of the *skelta* and seven of the twelve *tolva*:

> SkRb 3. […] Dat is alle riucht, jef him dera utha breckt—dat is biwiis—deer him di aesgha wiisd haet, […]

> SkRb 3. […] This is the law, if he is unable to produce the required evidence—that means proof—which the *asega* ordered him to, […][56]

52 On this official testimony, see Nijdam, et al., *Frisian Land Law*, p. 30; Immink, "Getuigen", pp. 447–450; Oosten, *Ambtshalve Vervolging*, p. 40 and Oosten, "Inleidende Beschouwingen", pp. 459–470.

53 *D*, III (SkRa) 42, pp. 138–139.

54 Oosten, "Inleidende Beschouwingen", p. 459f.

55 This is also the opinion of Immink, "Getuigen", pp. 434–435.

56 *D*, XII (SkRb) 3, pp. 292–293. Here, the archaic *uta* is clarified with the 15th century *biwiis*. See Nijdam, et al., *Frisian Land Law*, p. 33.

1.4 *Ordeals*

An ordeal was a trial in which defendants had to undergo specific tasks to establish their innocence. Defendants could also name a 'champion' to undergo the trial in their stead. Originally from pre-Christian times, Medieval procedures continued to use ordeals, based on a belief that magical or divine power influenced the trial in favor of the righteous person. After Christianization, people expected God to act as a judge and to intervene on behalf of those who were truly innocent. As such, and not unlike oaths, ordeals were sacred instruments of providing proof. They were ubiquitous throughout Frisia and much of Western Europe.[57] Ordeals are sometimes considered 'irrational' proof as opposed to the 'rational proofs' of learned law.

In Frisia, ordeals could be initiated only if all other options had failed, i.e., when no-one could provide proof in any other way.[58] Consequently, they were subsidiary to other kinds of evidence, especially oaths. Yet, when doubt remained and truth could not be established, ordeals helped to find resolution. This occurred under various circumstances. If, for example, the proof provided by both parties was equally weighted (e.g., neither succeeded in their oath), an ordeal could be used to resolve that stalemate. A lack of oath-helpers or their lacking in quality were reasons for considering there to be insufficient proof. Additionally, people who could not provide the usual proofs at all—like slaves, unfree Frisians and women—instead underwent ordeals.[59]

An ordeal also required a dispute to be sufficiently serious: an ordeal of water had to involve a claim of at least "four ounces and thirteen and a third pennies",[60] while an ordeal of combat required "no less than three pounds and eight ounces".[61] Consequently, parties initiated ordeals in only very serious cases. These included manslaughter, arson, theft, rape and counterfeiting, but also when paternity was in doubt, in disputes about inherited land and in cases of false tariffs.[62] In most other cases, ordeals were not permissible. And even in cases of serious crimes, they were not the norm, but rather the exception.

When an ordeal was initiated, a committee made up of local officials exercised oversight and organization.[63] In classical Frisian law, the *skelta* and *asega*

---

57 Buma, *Godsoordeel*, p. 5ff. On the importance of ordeals in conflict resolution, see Auer, "Konfliktlösung durch Ordalien", pp. 161–162.

58 Bartlett, *Trial*, p. 26.

59 On using ordeals as proof, see Auer, "Konfliktlösung durch Ordalien", pp. 161–163; Bartlett, *Trial*, p. 26; Buma, *Godsoordeel*, pp. 7–8.

60 *D*, III (SkRa) 39, pp. 138–139.

61 *D*, III (SkRa) 44, pp. 140–141.

62 See Hettema, "Godsoordeelen", pp. 277–282 on which ordeals were used in what cases.

63 Auer, "Konfliktlösung durch Ordalien", p. 163.

played a particularly important role. Cases were tried at the *skelta's* court, and the *asega* acted as the judge in these procedures.[64] They decided on the place in which an ordeal was held and ensured that it proceeded fairly. In the case of duels, they examined the weapons of the dueling parties.[65] Detailed descriptions of some trials are present in the *Older Skelta Law*.[66]

Additionally, ordeals were also part of ecclesiastical practice and for this reason were often held at churches. Local priests acted as witnesses and assessors of the outcomes of such trials.[67] There were usually also additional witnesses, such as 'king's witnesses', who assessed the body parts involved.[68] However, despite ordeals taking place at churches, they were not mentioned or regulated in the *ordines iudicarii*,[69] which were various treatises written from the 12th to 16th centuries and dealing with procedural law.

Some scholars assert that ordeals were part of the negotiation strategy between conflicting parties. A litigating party initiated an ordeal—and especially an ordeal by combat—to make a statement of how far the claimant or defendant would go in resolving the dispute in their favor. Neither party wanted to participate in a painful ordeal or risk their lives in combat. The hope was that the opposing party would relinquish rather than pursue a potentially unfavorable outcome.[70] Frisian sources make no mention of ordeals being used in an insincere way, but the lack of sources means that this question cannot be answered satisfactorily. Other scholars have emphasized the role of ordeals as tools to eliminate ambiguity in a procedure.[71] Through the appeal to divine intervention, any uncertainties deriving from the procedure at court were resolved.

Different types of ordeals existed in Frisia, as mentioned in the *Synodical Law of Central Frisia*:

64 A 'sort-of-judge'. On the role of the *asega*, see the introduction.

65 *D*, III (SkRa) 46, pp. 142–143.

66 *D*, III (SkRa) 39–49, pp. 138–145.

67 *D*, III (SkRa) 42, pp. 138–139.

68 See in *D*, III (SkRa) 42, pp. 138–139. In this case, the 'king's witnesses' acted as witnesses of the ordeal. They could attest to the outcome if it was questioned.

69 Litewski, *Der römisch-kanonische Zivilprozeß*, p. 371. The opposite is stated by Auer, "Konfliktlösung durch Ordalien", p. 162.

70 Auer, "Konfliktlösung durch Ordalien", p. 162 f.

71 To produce moral comfort for those making the decisions. Whitman, *The Origins*, pp. 10–25. In the accusatory procedures of Frisia, it would be the comfort of the accuser. As judges rarely pronounced sentences themselves, it may be questioned whether moral comfort was of particular importance in Frisian procedures.

> SWl 53. […] di camp is dera fyf ordela Godes een, dera trina heta ende dera twira caldera.

> SWl 53. […] the trial by combat is one of the five ordeals instituted by God; the three hot ordeals and the two cold ordeals.[72]

1.4.1 'Hot' Ordeals

Let us first have a look at the group known as 'hot ordeals' or 'ordeals by fire'. These ordeals involved exposing the defendant to some form of heat that would leave marks on his body; these marks were later examined to determine the defendant's guilt or innocence. Hot ordeals were typically one-sided, as only defendants or their champions could prove their innocence by undergoing them. All hot ordeals involved the infliction of wounds on the body, which were later examined. If a wound had healed, the defendant was innocent; if the wound had not healed sufficiently, guilt was proven.

The first hot ordeal was the ordeal of hot water (OF: *ketel*, *tzetelfeng*; Latin: *aqua fervens*), also called the ordeal of the kettle (*ketel*). In this, defendants or their champions had to reach into a kettle of boiling water, sometimes to retrieve a stone or ring. This ordeal is described in the *Older Skelta Law*.

> SkRa 42. Dit is riucht, dat di ketel oen dae kerckwalle hingia schil buta dis widelis werp on da walle ende di prester op da hofwal staen ende dat ordel wya with ane schillingh penninga. Soe aegh di kempa buta hofwal toe staen ende al stede in to faen, als di strydeed swerren is. So aegh di schelta ende di aesga ende di prester ende fyower dis koninges orkenen, hya saun, dis tredda deis da hand to schoyen binna dae kerka; dae tre mitta prester ende di ena mitta schelta ende mitta aesga. Jof se aet sanet, soe is di prester nyer ende dae tree mit him dae hand toe helane, so dae tre to urbaernene. Wirt hi schowet to heelre hand, so schil di ora den meeneed festia ende da grewa twa pond jaen. Ende wirth hy baernd, soe schil hi ja da grewa twa pond dis strydferda ende twa pond dis raefferda ende syn decken ja heer ende heed, jefta mit sine fia laesta ende den meneed festia.

> SkRa 42. This is the law, that the kettle shall hang on the church wall outside the holy ground on the outside of the wall and the priest shall stand on the churchyard wall and consecrate the ordeal and receive one

72 *D*, XI (SWl) 53, pp. 280–281.

> shilling for this. The champion has to stand outside the churchyard and reach into the kettle right after the ordeal oath has been sworn. On the third day the *skelta* and the *asega* and the priest and four of the king's witnesses, seven in total, shall inspect the hand inside the church; three of the king's witnesses shall form a group together with the priest, and the remaining one with the *skelta* and the *asega*. If they disagree to any extent, then the priest and the three king's witnesses have more rights to declare the hand to be healed than the other three to declare it to be burnt. And if his hand is declared healed, then the claimant shall compensate for his false oath by means of a fast and pay two pounds to the *frana*. And if his hand is declared burnt, the defendant shall pay the *frana* two pounds for breaking the peace by holding an ordeal and another two pounds for robbing someone's goods and he shall offer his hair and hide to his dean or pay for it with his goods and fast as compensation for the false oath.[73]

The ordeal of hot water is also found in the *Lex Frisionum*, and in law texts of other Frisian lands such as Rüstringen, Brokmerland and Emsingo.[74]

The ordeal of the hot iron involved the defendant carrying a heated piece of iron over a specific distance, often the distance between the baptismal font and altar in the local church.[75] Afterwards, the hand carrying the iron was bandaged and inspected after three days. As with the ordeal of hot water, the healing of the wound was taken to mean the defendant was innocent.[76]

The ordeal of fire, or the ordeal of walking over ploughshares, was another hot ordeal. In it, a defendant had to walk over nine or twelve heated ploughshares, the number of which depended on the source. The walker often had to be barefoot, although Frisian law allowed both for socks and wax to prevent greater injury. As in the case of the previous ordeals, the defendant's feet were subsequently bandaged and examined after three days.[77]

There was also a fourth ordeal involving heat; this is not found in the Westerlauwers version of the *Twenty-four Land Laws*, but is present in the Emsingo and Hunsingo versions. It involved the wearing of a robe soaked in wax, which

73 *D*, III (SkRa) 42, pp. 138–139.

74 *Lex Frisionum* 3.6 and 3.8. Buma, Ebel, *Brokmer Recht*, pp. 66–67; Buma, Ebel, *Emsiger Recht*, pp. 92–93; Buma, Ebel, *Rüstringer Recht*, pp. 80–81.

75 As in *D*, VIII (L^{24}) 10, pp. 228–229.

76 Buma, *Godsoordeel*, p. 17. Auer, "Konfliktlösung durch Ordalien", p. 164.

77 This ordeal is mentioned in L^{24} 23. It is also mentioned in SWl 35 and 37 in the case of establishing parentage. On this ordeal, see also Buma, *Godsoordeel*, p. 18 and Hettema, "Godsoordeelen", p. 280.

was then set on fire. If the defendant sustained no injuries during the burning, innocence was proven. In the Westerlauwers version, this ordeal is replaced by an ordeal of hot water.[78]

1.4.2 'Cold' Ordeals

In addition to the ordeal of hot water, there was also an 'ordeal of cold water', which was frequently used in ecclesiastical procedures before ordeals were prohibited in 1215. This ordeal, also called *aqua frigida*, involved binding the defendant's hands and feet before throwing them into a body of blessed water, such as a lake or river. The belief was that the blessed water would reject the guilty; if the defendant sank, their innocence was proven. Contrary to what modern horror stories may tell us about Medieval trials, defendants were retrieved before they could drown. Although not clearly mentioned in Frisian sources, it is possible that the *Twenty-four Land Laws* (L^{24} 10) refer to such an ordeal. The same is true for the *Synodical Law of Central Frisia*, which also mentions an ordeal by water.[79] As no other ordeals using cold water are described elsewhere, it is plausible that the *aqua frigida* ordeal is the ordeal referred to in these Frisian texts.

The second cold ordeal was the ordeal by combat, trial by combat or judicial duel (OF: *camp*; Latin: *iudicium pugnae/duelli*). This has been the most studied of all ordeals because of its controversy in Medieval legal and theological thought. It was rejected by Church authorities. The participants of such trials were free men, who were often substituted by champions fighting the duel in place of the parties. These champions could not claim damages from injuries sustained during the trial. Judicial duels are described in the *Older Skelta Law*.[80] A surety for the claim first had to be provided by the defendant. Both parties then swore a duel oath, which was a back-and-forth of affirmation and denial that culminated in:

> SkRa 45. [...] Nu schil hi swigia ende di ora swara: "So ic mit riuchta dat raef tojeens him naet beta thoer". Nu schil hi swigia ende di ora swara: "So y nu mit riuchte tojens mi beta schillet".

---

78 This ordeal is absent in *D*, VIII (L^{24}) 10, pp. 228–229. On this, see also Buma, *Godsoordeel*, p. 16. For the other versions, see Buma, Ebel, *Emsiger Recht*, p. 34 and Buma, Ebel, *Hunsingoer Recht*, p. 36.

79 *D*, XI (SWl) 54, pp. 280–281. See also Buma, *Godsoordeel*, p. 15 and Auer, "Konfliktlösung durch Ordalien", p. 164 on this particular ordeal.

80 *D*, III (SkRa) 44–49, pp. 140–145.

> SkRa 45. [...] Now he shall be silent and the other shall swear: "That I am lawfully not obligated to compensate the robbery performed on him". Now he shall be silent and the other shall swear: "That you shall now lawfully compensate me".[81]

In the next step, the *skelta* specified when the ordeal should take place, and the *asega* named the place. They also inspected the parties' weapons. Each champion received two swords. A group of umpires (*greetwirderen*) was also present to oversee the trial. The two champions fought each other on three occasions over three days, with one of them then emerging as the winner.[82]

Third, another ordeal in the Frisian sources was the 'ordeal by ingestion' (OF: *wyder corbita*) or the 'ordeal of the cheese' (OF: *tzīsordēl*; Latin: *iudicium panis et casei*). No detailed description of this ordeal is present in the sources, but it is known from surrounding regions that a defendant would have to ingest a piece of food (*iudicium offae*), either blessed by a priest or a poisoned drink. In other cases, dry bread and cheese were used, hence the name 'ordeal of the cheese'. If the defendant failed to swallow the food, i.e., because the food got stuck in the throat, their guilt was proven. Some argue that this ordeal was primarily psychological. A guilty person swallowing food may have been unable to swallow it quickly due to guilt and nervousness.[83]

Finally, there is a single mention of an ordeal of the cross. This involved both parties standing with their arms stretched out, either horizontally like a cross or vertically in front of a cross. Whoever lowered their arms first lost the ordeal. An ordeal of the cross is mentioned in *Of the Two Kings Charles and Radbod*, which tells the story of how Charlemagne and Radbod competed over Frisia. In the end, Charlemagne won the ordeal and Radbod retreated.[84] An ordeal of the cross is not mentioned in respect of Frisian procedural law.[85]

---

81 *D*, III (SkRa) 45, pp. 140–143.

82 On this ordeal, see Auer, "Konfliktlösung durch Ordalien", p. 164; for an old assessment, see Kuyk, "Bijdrage", pp. 312–342. The ordeal of combat in Frisia is examined in Buma, *Godsoordeel*, pp. 22–23 and in Hettema, "Godsoordeelen".

83 Buma, *Godsoordeel*, pp. 20–21. Mentions of this ordeal are found in *D*, VIII (L^{24}) 10, pp. 228–229. and *D*, XI (SWl) 54, pp. 280–281. In Anglo-Saxon England this ordeal was called the *corsnæd*. It was an ordeal intended only for the clergy. See Keefer, "Ut in omnibus", pp. 237–254.

84 *D*, IV (KaR), pp. 170–171.

85 Buma, *Godsoordeel*, pp. 23–24; Nijdam, et al., *Frisian Land Law*, pp. 45–46.

1.5 *Judicial Punishments*

After establishing guilt, by either oath or ordeal, the *asega* proclaimed a sentence. The *asega* did not decide what the sentence obligated the guilty party to do: obligations were specific to the issue in dispute and the claimant's claim. They were of both a private and public nature.[86] Obligations were primarily monetary; physical punishments were rarely imposed. The reason for this was a privilege of the Frisians in the *Seventeen Statutes*:

> K[17] 16. Dio xvi kest is dat alle Fresen aghen hyara ferd mit hiara fia to beten. Om dat schillet alle Fresen wessa an Saxena merkum utoer stock ende utoer stupa, utoer scheran ende utoer filan ende utoer ander pinen. [...]

> K[17] 16. The sixteenth statute is that all Frisians have the right to compensate their wrongdoings with valuables. Because of this, all Frisians will not have to be subjected to punishment by stick or pillory, hot scissors, flagellation or any other corporal punishment in the Saxon territory. [...][87]

This circumvention of corporal punishment also applied to the death penalty. Someone sentenced to death could pay off the pending execution. This was called *hāvedlēsene* (German: *Halslösung*; Dutch *hoofdlossing*), literally 'salvation of the neck or head'.[88] For this reason, corporal punishment is rarely mentioned in Frisian law texts and was applied only when someone was unwilling or unable to compensate their wrongdoings.[89]

Each wrongdoing required a specific compensation, which was listed in compensation tariffs such as *The Calculated Tariffs*. If, for example, a man grabbed another man's beard, he was obliged to compensate him with 16 groats.[90] A claimant's claim also stated what was required as compensation for the wrongdoing. Claimants demanded justice not only for themselves but also for the general public. In this way, they litigated for both private 'compensation' as well as a public 'fine':[91]

---

86 Oosten, *Ambtshalve Vervolging*, pp. 12–15.

87 *D*, VI (K[17]) 16, pp. 200–203.

88 'hāvedlēsene' in: Hofman, Popkema, *Altfriesisches Handwörterbuch*, p. 205; 'Halslösung' in: Lieberwirth, Rolf. *Handwörterbuch zur deutschen Rechtsgeschichte*. https://www.hrgdigital.de/id/halsloesung/stichwort.html Accessed: 24.08.2022. See also His, *Strafrecht*, p. 346.

89 There are some exceptions to this rule, which I will not further elaborate upon. On performing sexual acts with cattle, see, for example, *D*, XI (SWl) 11, pp. 280–283.

90 *D*, XIV (BBr) 11, pp. 332–333. More on these later.

91 For more on these specific terms, see below.

> SkRb 4. Jef ma greta schil om een lamthe, so queth ma aldus: "Jo sprect di man to dat y him habbe deen een dullich, dine middel ende bede da einden ende oen da dullich een lamthe also onriucht ur riucht, soe y nu mit riuchta aghen toejenst him to beten ende dine ferd deer mit riuchta deerto heert." [...]
>
> SkRb 4. If someone wants to bring a case before court concerning a paralysis, one shall speak thus: "This man accuses you that you have done him an injury; a wound consisting of a middle part and two ends, and that because of this injury you have caused a paralysis, in such an illegal way, that you now lawfully will have to compensate the claimant and pay the corresponding fine for the breach of the peace." [...][92]

The claimant demanded both compensation (*him te beten*) and a fine for disturbing the peace (*dine ferd*). Neither the judge nor the prosecutor pursued the breach of the public peace, but the private claimant did.[93] If a defendant was found guilty, the sentence obligated him to pay both compensation and a fine. This can be clearly seen in the example of obligations arising from theft:

> SkRa 67. [...] Jef hy aeck neen schieldigra wint so schil hy dat gued eenschet ende dat oder wederjae ende da frana deer dat gued binna sine banne nimmen is dat wederjeld jaen ur al sine hinden deer jerich sint ende hi binna sine dorem haet. So is dat wederjeld iiii einsa ende fyoerteensta trimene penningh.
>
> SkRa 67. [...] If he is unable to do so, he shall return the good and give its value on top of that, and he will pay a wergild for all adult members of his household to the *frana* within whose jurisdiction the good was stolen. And the wergild is 4 ounces and thirteen and a third pence.[94]

Two distinct obligations are evident in the above provision: to pay 'compensation' and to pay a 'fine'. The meaning of these terms in the context of Frisian law needs to be explained.

92 *D*, XII (SkRb) 4, pp. 294–297.
93 Oosten, *Ambtshalve Vervolging*, p. 21.
94 *D*, III (SkRa) 67, pp. 156–157.

1.5.1 The Private 'Penalty'—Compensation

The first obligation was not only payment of compensation, but also had the characteristics of a penalty: *schil hy dat gued eenschet ende dat oder wederjae* ("He shall return the property and give its value on top of that"). Therefore, we must not confuse this 'compensation' with the present-day term or even with the terminology of the *ius commune*. Rather, it consisted of two parts: a reipersecutory part ("return the property") and a penal part ("give its value on top of that"). This was not just compensation or restitution, but neither was it just a punitive action, i.e., a twofold penalty. Apart from these obligations (in SkRa 67), it is not mentioned anywhere else in this provision or in the *Older Skelta Law* that stolen property had to be returned. That the *eenschet ende dat oder wederjae* is congruent with *him te beten* from the previous example (SkRb 4) is evident from another provision concerning theft:

> SkRb 35. Dat is riucht, jef een huusnata syn hera offstelt ende hi des jechtich urwonnen wirt, **soe schil hy beta toejenst syn hera dat een schet ende dat oder.** So ist riucht dat di hera foer syne huusnaet da schelta dat weerjeld jouwa schil om syn ayn gued om dat hine taegh mit met ende mit mele.

> SkRb 35. This is the law, if a servant steals from his master and he is found guilty of this before court, **he shall compensate his master once and a second time (twofold).** Then it is the law that the master shall pay the *skelta* his servant's wergild in view of the theft of his own property because the master fed and nourished the servant.[95]

Both *beta* and *wederjaen* (in SkRa 67) describe the same act, which consists of two parts: returning the goods once and paying the value on top of that. The etymology of *bēta*—derived from the noun *bōte*—is 'to make better'.[96] In other words, literally making better (compensating) what has been made worse by a wrongdoing. *Wederjaen* translates as 'giving back'. Since both terms describe the same thing, there was obviously no single legal term in Frisian law. This must be taken into account when considering obligations arising from a judicial sentence.

95 *D*, XII (SkRb) 35, pp. 314–315.

96 'bēta' Hofmann, Popkema, *Altfriesisches Handwörterbuch*, p. 36. On this, see Nijdam, *Lichaam, eer en recht*, p. 60f. and Nijdam, et al., *Frisian Land Law*, p. 29. Compare also to German *Büße* and Dutch *boete*.

Additionally, there was a third way to describe 'compensation', as can be seen by comparing two other provisions of the *Younger Skelta Law*:

SkRb 10. Dat is riucht. Elkerlyck deer een kase deth binna da huse jefta een raef, jef hi bitiuged wirt ende jechtich biradet, so **ist twybeet** ende dae schelta tweer schillenghen ende dae grewa twae pond.	SkRb 11. "Ick bitigie jo des dat y dissen man een huisraef deen habbet binna da huse alsoe onriucht buppa riucht als y nu mit riuchta tojenst him beta schillet dat raef dat **eenschet ende dat oer** ende da schelta tweer schillingen ende dae grewa twae pond to ferd."
SkRb 10. This is the law. If someone fights inside a house or commits a robbery there and if testimony is brought against him and he is found guilty, he must compensate twofold and pay a fine of two shillings to the *skelta* and two pounds to the count.[97]	SkRb 11. "I accuse you that you have performed a robbery on this man inside his house, so illegally and in breach of the law, that you shall now compensate him once and a second time for what you have robbed and you will pay two shillings to the *skelta* and two pounds to the count for breaking the peace."[98]

Both provisions are written almost identically and concern the same topic: obligations resulting from robbery. Therefore, it can be assumed that *twybeet* and *beta eenschet ende dat oder* are also analogous. *Twybeet* is a combination of the words *twīa* (two) and *bete*, meaning 'twofold compensation'.

In conclusion, these examples demonstrate that Frisians used unspecific terms for the first obligation resulting from theft/robbery. However, *eenschet ende dat oder wederjae*, *beta eenschet ende dat oder* and *twybeet* all clearly describe the same thing. While this could be described as a reipersecutory obligation plus a penal obligation, Frisians perceived the obligation as a single entity. The examination of the Frisian law of delict by His refers to this as "*doppelten Ersatz*", a twofold replacement.[99] In the above translations, the word 'compensation' has been used. Although this word will be continued to be used, it should be noted that this obligation is not compensation in the sense that it is understood today or in Medieval learned law. No term can fully cover

97 *D*, XII (SkRb) 10, pp. 300–301.

98 *D*, XII (SkRb) 11, pp. 300–301.

99 His, *Strafrecht*, p. 346.

this Frisian construct, which was both reipersecutory and penal.[100] Nevertheless, Frisians would not have used these distinctions in the Medieval period as they perceived this as a single construct. For the sake, therefore, of simplicity and accessibility, the obligation to the victim is referred to here as 'compensation'.

1.5.2 The Public Penalty—A Fine

The second obligation resulting from a judicial sentence was a penalty for disturbing the public peace (OF: *ferdia*). This had to be paid to the local authorities and can therefore be classified as a 'fine'. Symbolically, the public received compensation for the breach of the peace.[101]

1.5.3 Amount of Compensation and Fine

The amount to be paid for both the private compensation and public penalty was fixed and dependent on the wrongdoing. Homicide, for example, had to be compensated by paying a wergild to the victim's family. A wergild was a standard unit of compensation, equivalent to the worth of a person (a 'man compensation'), and aimed to prevent ongoing chains of blood feuds. In effect, to prevent revenge on the perpetrator and the latter's family, the victim's family was compensated for the loss through monetary means.[102]

Wergilds were paid not only for manslaughter but also for other serious crimes such as rape, while smaller wergilds and fractions could be required in the case of bodily injuries.[103] The wergild was the standard for certain punishments, with the amount of a wergild often being fixed in lists of compensation tariffs. In Wymbritseradeel, for example, a wergild was set at 30 *marks*, while in the Five Districts it was 22 *marks*.[104] Any serious crime requiring a wergild to be paid obligated the perpetrator to pay a specific amount, depending on the territory.

The amount of a wergild also depended on who was killed. A higher wergild was owed for a nobleman than for a freeman, for example. This was an old practice, seen from the 8th century onwards.[105] Indeed, the wergild was a central aspect of the Frisian legal system and, because of its importance, survived the

100 It is perhaps most comparable to the term 'punitive damages' in common law legal systems.

101 Oosten, *Ambtshalve Vervolging*, p. 14.

102 Nijdam, "Compensation", p. 26 ff.; Nijdam, "Wat was een menseleven waard?", p. 196 ff.

103 See, for example, in *D*, VI (K^{17}) 15, pp. 198–201.

104 *D*, XV (Pay) 12, pp. 380–381 and *D*, XV (Pay) 11, pp. 380–381 respectively.

105 See, for example, in *Lex Frisionum* 1.10 and in the entire title on homicide.

Middle Ages.[106] In cases of theft, robbery, or other property delicts, the compensation due by the perpetrator was based on multiples of the property stolen or damaged.[107]

A public penalty could also require the guilty to pay a wergild, thus avoiding corporal punishment such as the death penalty. This is evident in the *Older Skelta Law* (SkRa 67), which even required every member of the household to pay for the "salvation of their neck". In other cases, the fine was fixed in a legal provision, such as in the *Younger Skelta Law* mentioned above (SkRb 10): "He must [...] pay a fine of two shillings to the *skelta* and two pounds to the count."[108]

These compensations and penalties play a crucial role in the next chapter on theft.

2 Romano-Canonical Legal Procedure

Having outlined the Frisian legal procedure, it is necessary to also explain the procedure according to learned law. The procedural law of the *ius commune* was developed in the 12th century. Influenced by Roman law, Church jurists created an ecclesiastical procedure, sometimes called the Canonical procedure or the Romano-canonical procedure, which differed significantly from the Frisian one.

The Romano-canonical procedure was conducted in written form, with statements, testimonies and the positions of the parties recorded. Frisian procedures, by contrast, were primarily oral owing to the society being predominantly oral. Additionally, every Romano-canonical procedure was presided over by a judge who was an educated professional and an expert in (learned) law. These judges pronounced a sentence based on the evidence presented rather than on their own conscience. Both litigating parties had equal rights in any Romano-canonical procedure, meaning there was no distinction in what the claimant or defendant could do.[109]

106 On the topic of *wergild* in Frisia, see Nijdam, *Lichaam, eer en recht*, p. 135.

107 See again *D*, III (SkRa) 67, pp. 156–157: "He shall return the property and give its value on top of that". Also: Oosten, *Ambtshalve Vervolging*, pp. 12–15.

108 *D*, XII (SkRb) 10, pp. 300–301.

109 The entirety of the procedure and additional aspects are excellently described in Brundage, *Medieval Canon Law*, pp. 129–150. For a comprehensive analysis of the entire Romano-canonical civil procedure, see Litewski, *Der römisch-kanonische Zivilprozeß* I and II; Nörr, *Romanisch-kanonisches Prozessrecht*.

The distinct parts of the Romano-canonical procedure are detailed in the corresponding titles of the Decretals (Liber Extra 2). The various Medieval *ordines iudicarii* (treatises from the 12th to 16th century and dealing with procedural law), the *Speculum iudiciale* by the canonist Guillaume Durand (1230–1296) and the *Summula de processu judicii* by Giovanni d'Andrea (ca. 1270–1348) also describe such procedures. The relevant parts are summarized briefly here.

The Canonical procedure (*ordo iudiciarius*) was originally accusatory, similar to the Frisian procedure. A litigant initiated a procedure by submitting a petition, a written statement of claim. If this was accepted, the judge would then cite the defendant. The defendant had 30 days to appear in court, with failure to do so resulting in a declaration of contumacy.[110] In court, the claimant raised a claim (*libellus*), naming the claimant, defendant and judge by name, as well as the reason for the lawsuit and the remedy demanded. The defendant then had 20 days to make a formal reply or raise an exception. There were two forms of exception: peremptory, which questioned a legal or factual aspect of the claim; and dilatory, which pointed out a procedural error. These exceptions were adjudicated before the trial began; if they were rejected, the procedure advanced to the next stage.[111]

In the delineation of the trial (*litis contestatio*), the claimant and defendant restated their claim and denial, respectively, and swore an oath of calumny, i.e., an oath that they were speaking the truth. The burden of proof rested on the claimant; while the defendant did not have to provide positive proof of their innocence.[112] However, the defendant had to prove the defenses brought, other than denying the claims made by the claimant. In bringing defenses the defendant acted 'as a claimant' (*reus in exceptione actor est*). The proofs required in Romano-canonical procedures are sometimes called 'rational' proofs because they relied less on the 'irrational' methods of oaths and divine intervention (ordeals), but instead on the establishment of facts.

The primary method of providing evidence was testimony by witnesses. Both parties listed the persons they intended to call on to give testimony, and the judge summoned these persons, placed them under oath and separately questioned them. The litigating parties prepared the questions for the witnesses. The standard for full proof was high: only a confession or two credible

---

110 For the citation and *contumacia*, see Nörr, *Romanisch-kanonisches Prozessrecht*, pp. 68–77.

111 Brundage, *Medieval Canon Law*, pp. 129–130. On the *exceptiones*, see Litewski, *Der römisch-kanonische Zivilprozeß* I, p. 299 ff. and specifically p. 305 f. for the peremptory and dilatory exceptions.

112 Brundage, *Medieval Canon Law*, p. 131; Nörr, *Romanisch-kanonisches Prozessrecht*, p. 127 ff.

witnesses who saw and heard the event were sufficient. The rule that two witnesses were needed originated from the Old Testament (Deut. 19:15).[113]

Written documents (*instrumenta*) were a second method of proof. These could include signatures of witnesses, notaries and seals for authentication.[114] While other kinds of proof also existed, these were classified as 'partial proofs' (*semiplena probatio*) and included, for example, presumptions and inferences (*indicia*).[115] Canonical law and literature contained further forms of proof, such as those mentioned by Giovanni d'Andrea (ca. 1270–1348) in his *Summula de processu judicii*: "obviousness of a fact, inspection of the body, rumor, taking an oath within the prescribed period of time, presumption, witnesses and instruments."[116] The work of d'Andrea is cited multiple times in Frisian sources and the proofs he mentions are quoted in full in the *Jurisprudentia Frisica*. We will return to these later.

Canonical procedures were recorded by clerks and, once all the evidence had been collected, their records were published. The parties then wrote answers, called *positiones*, to substantiate their own arguments or weaken the other party's arguments. The parties also provided references to legal provisions that supported or opposed certain arguments made in the trial or in the *positiones*. These were called the *allegationes*.[117]

The final stage involved the judge announcing a day for pronouncing a decision, when the outcome would be pronounced orally in a brief statement, without reasons for the decision being given. This marked the conclusion of the procedure. However, most procedures ended prematurely, with the litigating parties resolving their dispute out of court, or the claimant abandoning the action if the outcome seemed likely to be unfavorable.[118]

---

113 Deutoronomy 19:15 (NIV): *One witness is not enough to convict anyone accused of any crime or offense they may have committed. A matter must be established by the testimony of two or three witnesses.* See also Nörr, *Romanisch-kanonisches Prozessrecht*, p. 153.

114 There was also a distinction between documents. An *instrumentum publicum* provided full proof, while an *instrumentum privatum* did not. Nörr, *Romanisch-kanonisches Prozessrecht*, p. 154. According to Brundage, there was debate over whether they were less trustworthy because of fears of forgery, Brundage, *Medieval Canon Law*, p. 132 f.

115 Brundage, *Medieval Canon Law*, p. 95. On the status of presumptions as partial proof, see Litewski, *Der römisch-kanonische Zivilprozeß* II, p. 442 f. On distinctions of *praesumptio*, see Nörr, *Romanisch-kanonisches Prozessrecht*, p. 169 f.

116 Which is attributed to d'Andrea, who mentions seven kinds of proof. Giovanni d'Andrea, *Summula de processu judicii* (ed. A. Wunderlich), Basel 1840, Cap. VIII § 1 (p. 37).

117 Brundage, *Medieval Canon Law*, p. 133. On the *positiones*, see also Litewski, *Der römisch-kanonische Zivilprozeß* II, pp. 358–359.

118 Brundage, *Medieval Canon Law*, p. 134. On the sentence and preliminary sentence, see Nörr, *Romanisch-kanonisches Prozessrecht*, p. 193 ff.

2.1 *Procedure* per notorium

In the early 13th century, another form of procedure arose, the procedure *per notorium*. Many people were dissatisfied with the *ordo iudiciarius* because the high standard for full proof meant that many crimes went unpunished if they were committed without being publicly known. An accusatory procedure also always required a person to initiate the action; this placed a significant burden on that individual because if they were unsuccessful, they would be liable for damages.[119]

To remedy these deficiencies, the rules of procedure were simplified, such that where a crime was publicly known, a judge could proceed against a criminal *ex officio* without requiring an accuser, and many of the formal procedural rules of the *ordo iudiciarius* were waived. Partial proof (one witness) was sufficient to establish guilt and impose a sentence. This severely restricted the rights of the defendant.[120]

2.2 *Procedure* per inquisitionem

A third form of procedure, *per inquisitionem*, combined certain elements of the previous two forms. This was initiated by a judge acting *ex officio* as both investigator and prosecutor. To begin this type of procedure, there needed to be a widespread and public belief in the guilt of the accused. In this case, however, the strict requirements of the *ordo iudiciarius* remained in place, meaning that all steps from complaint to sentence had to be followed. Medieval jurists debated whether this required full or only partial proof. If such procedures were too detrimental to the accused, judges often applied them only partially.[121]

2.3 *The* purgatio canonica

To address the relatively weak role of defendants in the two previously mentioned procedures, a suppletory oath, known as the *purgatio canonica*, was established. This oath, which differed from the oath of calumny taken by both the claimant and defendant at the beginning of a procedure, was taken by the defendant. If a claimant provided only partial proof, the judge could assign either side to supplement their arguments with an oath. The person who administered the oath was dependent on the judge, who also acted as the prosecutor. In a case of *per notorium*, the judge could require someone whose crime was publicly known to take an oath with the help of compurgators. The judge

119 Brundage, *Medieval Canon Law*, pp. 142–144.
120 Brundage, *Medieval Canon Law*, pp. 144–145.
121 Brundage, *Medieval Canon Law*, pp. 148–150.

then announced several oath-helpers, chosen from among the defendant's relatives. Subsequently, the defendant swore an oath of purgation, and the compurgators confirmed this oath by swearing an oath of their own. If these oaths were successful, the claimant's proof failed, and the defendant's innocence was confirmed.[122]

This aspect of Canonical procedural law was remarkably similar to the Frisian oath of innocence. In both cases, oath-helpers supported the suppletory oath by taking an assertory oath. This, too, was allowed only when the claimant failed to provide full proof. The same is seen in Frisian law in, for example, the *Younger Skelta Law*, with Frisian procedure allowing an oath of innocence only when a claimant failed to provide proof of the accusation or a crime was not publicly known. A significant difference was that oaths were the central proof in Frisian law, while they were only suppletory in certain forms of Canonical procedure. Despite this difference, it is fruitful to investigate how Frisian jurists connected both the Frisian oath of innocence and the *purgatio canonica*.

3 Legal Procedure in 15th-Century Frisian Sources

The structure of Frisian courts underwent a significant change in the 13th century. Following the comital period, the old judges appointed by the count (known as *skelta*) were replaced by judges appointed by local Frisians. These new judges were called *gretman*, and *gretman* courts were made up of a body of two or three co-judges led by a *gretman*.[123]

When examining later Frisian sources on legal procedures, we can see the influence of Canonical procedure on Frisian law in the *Codex Aysma* manuscript. This is particularly evident in a procedural manual called the *Processus Iudicii*, which describes a procedure that is clearly Romano-canonical in nature. Although an error-prone version is found in the *Excerpta Legum*, a full Frisian translation can also be found in the third part of *Codex Aysma* (A, III).[124] This version contains rubrics in Latin, as outlined in the table below.

Looking at the structure of procedural law in the Decretals, we can see that many of the titles in the *Processus Iudicii* deal with the same procedural issues.

---

122 Brundage, *Medieval Canon Law*, p. 147; Helmholz, *The spirit of classical canon law*, pp. 156–159.

123 Nijdam, *Lichaam, eer en recht*, p. 150; Vries, Hempenius-van Dijk, *Asega, is het dingtijd?*, p. 15; Vries, *Het Heilige Rooms Rijk*, p. 17.

124 Buma et al., *Codex Aysma*, pp. 442–481.

TABLE 4 Titles in the Liber Extra, Processus Iudicii and Jurisprudentia Frisica concerning procedural law. Titles in brackets are not in the manuscripts

Liber Extra	*Processus Iudicii* (*A*)	*Jurisprudentia Frisica* (*Ro*)
X 2.1	1 (de iudiciis) →	JF 1 De iudiciis
	2 (de iudicibus) →	JF 2 De iudicibus et officio iudicis
	3 Qui non possunt esse testes	JF 3 De citatione
X 1.38	4 De procuratore (JF 25)	JF 4 De dolo et contumatia
	5 De auditore	JF 5 De feriis
	6 Recapitulatio ordinis iudiciarii	JF 6 De exceptionibus
X 2.5	7 De litis contestatione	JF 7 De libelli oblatione
	8 Recapitulatio	JF 8 De dilationibus
	9 De citatione	JF 9 De litis contestatione
X 2.9	10 De feriis	JF 10 De mutuis petitionibus
X 2.14	11 De contumatia rei	JF 11 De iuramento calumpnie
X 2.25	12 (de exceptionibus)	JF 12 De confessis
X 2.3	13 De libelli oblatione	JF 13 De probationibus
X 2.7	14 De iuramento calumpnie	JF 14 De presumptionibus
X 2.18	15 De confessis	JF 15 De testibus et eorum attestationibus
X 2.19	16 (de probationibus)	JF 16 De testibus cogendis
X 2.23	17 De presumptionibus	JF 17 De fide instrumentorum
X 2.20	18 De testibus	JF 18 De sententia et re iudicata
	19 De pluralitate testium	JF 19 De appellationibus
X 2.22	20 De fide instrumentorum	JF 20 De foro competenti
	21 (de sententia)	JF 21 De arbitris
X 2.28	22 (de appellationibus)	JF 22 De pactis
		JF 23 De voto et voti redemptione
		JF 24 De iure iurando
		JF 25 De procuratoribus

However, the sequence of the titles is not identical as they have been rearranged. Some rubrics, such as "de citatione", are absent in the *Liber Extra*. The *Processus Iudicii* contains many titles of the Liber Extra, but is not congruent with it and, instead, comprises a rearrangement into its own manual.

Processus Iudicii therefore had a significant influence on the structure of procedural law in 15th-century Frisian law.

The *Processus Iudicii* was the foundation of procedural law in the *Jurisprudentia Frisica*. The latter begins with a section on procedural law, starting with "de iudiciis" (JF 1) and ending with "de procuratoribus" (JF 25). While its titles are not congruent with those in the *Processus Iudicii*, the order and structure clearly follow it in parts.[125]

Some rubrics in the *Processus Iudicii*, such as "de auditore", do not appear at all in the *Jurisprudentia Frisica*, while others, such as "de litis contestatione", appear in a different place. Interestingly, the latter example restores the sequence of the Romano-canonical procedure. The *litis contestatio* occurred after the exceptions ("de dilationibus") and before the oath of calumny ("de iuramento calumpnie"). This may have been intentional.

The *Processus Iudicii* is a manual written for ecclesiastical procedure: *Alhyr is bigripen di foerdgungh van dae gaestlika riochte*. (Translation: "Here the procedure of an ecclesiastical court is described.")[126] Since, however, the compilators of the *Excerpta Legum* intended to turn the text into a secular law book,[127] it makes sense to assume that the Romano-canonical procedure must have been intended—or already existed—as a blueprint for secular procedures as well.

Additionally, the *Excerpta Legum* contains material from another Canonical legal manual, namely one on arbitration. The original manual was written in Latin but not handed down. The fragments of this manual in the *Excerpta Legum* were translated into Old Frisian. Frisians in the 15th century commonly used arbitration; as often, indeed, as they used the *gretman* courts. That this other manual was translated into Old Frisian indicates that it was used in legal practice.[128]

The fragments of case records in the *Excerpta Legum* also provide insight into the use of learned law and Romano-canonical procedure in legal practice. These records were written both in Old Frisian and Latin and contain cases from Romano-canonical procedures.[129] Consequently, it is evident that such procedures were present in Frisia in the 15th century. The compilers of the *Excerpta Legum* included fragments of these case records in their compilation.

The question remains as to where and how Frisians applied these manuals. Gerbenzon provides a convincing answer to these questions. In his examination of the case records in his *Excerpta Legum*, he concludes that both ecclesi-

125 Gerbenzon, "Aantekeningen", p. 43ff.

126 *A*, III (PrJ) 33f., p. 480.

127 Buma et al., *Codex Aysma*, p. XIV

128 On this manual, see Gerbenzon, *Excerpta Legum*, pp. 133–135.

129 For an overview, see the introduction to the Frisian primary sources (chapter 1.3) and specifically the *Excerpta Legum*.

astical and secular courts proceeded in this manner. First, the subjects of these records are diverse. They include topics that clearly could have fallen under ecclesiastical jurisdiction, such as testaments, although this was not necessarily the case. While other issues fit more into the secular domain, this did not necessarily mean that people brought them before a secular court. Gerbenzon asserts that ecclesiastical courts would sometimes judge cases when a secular court was not available (jurisdiction *ex defectu justitiae*).[130] As such, it is possible, albeit not likely, that the cases in question are exclusively from ecclesiastical courts.

The second edition of the *Excerpta Legum* (found in the manuscripts *B* and *C*) contains clear instances of parties addressing secular judges.[131] While this edition is more recent than that in *Codex Aysma*, it is an indication that secular courts also proceeded in this manner. That the case records were in part from ecclesiastical courts is easier to prove: in *Codex Aysma*, we find a text addressing a dean and so it is likely that the litigant in this case was addressing an ecclesiastical court: *Ergo, domine iudex et decane, sentenciam ferre dignemini* [...] (Translation: "Therefore, lord judge and dean, it behooves you to pass the sentence [...].")[132]

Gerbenzon concludes that the fragments came from both ecclesiastical and secular courts, as well as arbitration, due to the variety of topics covered.[133] There are cases concerning testaments, dowries, loans, deposits, guardianship and more that are not exclusive to a secular or ecclesiastical jurisdiction.[134] While Canon law often regulated testaments and dowries, ecclesiastical courts did not have exclusive jurisdiction in these matters. The diversity of cases suggests, therefore, that issues from both secular and ecclesiastical jurisdiction were adjudicated.

We have observed that Frisians in the 15th century adopted procedural law through manuals and followed learned law in their legal practice. This indicates a strong reception of procedural law in Frisia. However, Gerbenzon claims that

130 For Gerbenzon's examination of the origins of these fragments of case records, see Gerbenzon, *Excerpta Legum*, pp. 240–243.

131 Gerbenzon, *Excerpta Legum*, p. 371f.

132 *A*, I (Exc) 55, p. 46.

133 Gerbenzon, *Excerpta Legum*, p. 243. Gerbenzon provides further analysis of the case records and their origins and argues that Romano-canonical procedures were undertaken at secular courts, such as the courts of the cities and the grietmans. Gerbenzon, *Excerpta Legum*, p. 371ff.

134 *A*, I (Exc): 208–217, pp. 152–172 (testaments, donations); 218–223, pp. 172–182 (dowry); 235–238, pp. 190–194 (loans); 243–251, pp. 196–202 (deposits); 260–263, pp. 210–216 (guardianship).

the Frisians did not adopt Romano-canonical procedural law in its entirety.[135] There are two aspects in the case records that demonstrate this.

First, the case records in the *Excerpta Legum* are written both in Old Frisian and in Latin: a thesis in Frisian and the arguments in Latin. This was quite unusual for the time. Romano-canonical procedures in neighboring Utrecht, by contrast, were conducted exclusively in Latin, as were the *positiones* and other records, while only a few German cities proceeded in both the local language and Latin.[136] The use of the vernacular in proceedings must have made them more accessible to a larger portion of the population than if they had been litigated solely in Latin. Although the use of the vernacular was uncommon, it did not necessarily contradict the *ius commune*, and shows the value that Frisian courts placed on litigating in Old Frisian.

The second aspect is the significance of oaths and oath-helpers in these Romano-canonical procedures. Although learned law did not prohibit their use, it discouraged oaths in favor of material evidence (witnesses and instruments). The presence of oaths is evident in the *informationes iuris*.[137] One example is this fragment:

> Exc 239. Hoc cum proprio iuramento, jtem mit vi sibben ende mit xij fremden op din punth.

> Exc 239. This [he will prove] with his own oath, and also with six relatives and with twelve non-relatives.[138]

This is a typical example of proof through an oath according to Frisian law. The Romano-canonical procedure in Frisia also differed from that of the *ius commune* in a third way. Full records of arbitration cases in Frisia demonstrate that they were abbreviated, although it is unclear whether procedures in ecclesiastical and secular courts were also shortened.[139] The *Processus Iudicii* presents

---

135 Gerbenzon, *Excerpta Legum*, p. 251. An interesting and similar finding was made by Donahue, "Proof by Witnesses", concerning the reception of witnesses as proof in Medieval English Church Courts. While witnesses were received, local circumstances inhibited a full application of proof by witnesses. This included the intentions of powerful elites and the social expectations of court procedures.

136 Gerbenzon, *Excerpta Legum*, p. 230 f.

137 Gerbenzon, *Excerpta Legum*, p. 251.

138 *A*, I (Exc): 239, p. 194.

139 Gerbenzon examined these full, extended records of arbitration procedures and compared them with the arbitration procedures in learned law. See Gerbenzon, *Excerpta Legum*, pp. 259–261.

a complete procedural manual, albeit not as detailed as the *ordines iudiciarii*. Thus, it is plausible that Frisians also initiated complete Romano-canonical procedures.

In the 15th century, Frisians litigated in a Romano-canonical manner, but did not strictly adhere to the instructions and manuals of learned law. This is most apparent in their use of oaths as proof. A similar trend occurred in the use of proof by witnesses in Medieval Church courts in England; this use of proof was widely accepted, but not fully and accurately implemented due to local circumstances.[140] To evaluate how closely Frisians followed Romano-canonical procedures, we have to investigate how oaths were utilized alongside other methods of proof. This will help determine whether Frisians adapted learned law to their own procedural needs or altered the practice of oath-taking to fit the new procedural law.

4 Room for New Means of Proof?

Immink states there to have been no place in the Frisian legal system for any means of proof other than oaths and ordeals.[141] The reception of the Romano-canonical procedure clearly shows that this statement is not true for the 15th century. The changes in the Late Middle Ages mean, instead, that we can observe how and when other means of proof appeared. At the same time, we can ask whether there was still a place for oaths and ordeals as forms of proof in a new, changed legal system of procedural law.

The earliest mention of new forms of proofs is found in the *Freeska Landriucht*, where the gloss to the *Seventeen Statutes* and *Twenty-four Land Laws* mentions proofs of learned law. A gloss (93) to the last of the *Seventeen Statutes* (K^{17} 17), as described above, reads as follows:

> Glossa 93. *Uued deen* Hoc est notorium iuris, extra de coha. clerico. et mulierum c. Vestra (X 3.2.7). Quatuor modis conuincitur aliquis, scilicet per euidentiam facti, secundo per testes, de testibus per totum (X 2.20), tercio per instrumenta, de fide instrumentorum per totum (X 2.22), quarto per confessionem in iudicio factam, extra de resti. spoli. Cum ad sede. (X 2.13.15) et de cohabitione c. fi. (X 3.2.10), si quinto potest addi, scilicet uiolenta presumptio xxxii q.i Dicit Dominus (C. 32 q.1 c.2).

140 Donahue, "Proof by Witnesses", p. 158.
141 Immink, "Getuigen", p. 435.

> Gloss 93. *Uued deen* (*given a statement*) That is, judicial notoriety, see X 3.2.7. In four ways someone can be convinced, namely by the obviousness of the fact; secondly through witnesses, see the entire title X 2.20; in the third place through instruments, see the entire title X 2.22; in the fourth place through confession in court, see X 2.13.15 and X 3.2.10; if a fifth way can be added, that is, 'strong presumption', see C. 32 q.1 c.2.[142]

The lemma *Uued deen* refers to the exception, where an oath of innocence was no longer possible if someone had already given a statement in court. This is referred to as "judicial notoriety" (*notorium iuris*) in X 3.2.7, which describes a case where a priest's fornication was widely known. While I have doubts about equating the two (confession in court and notorious fornication), the glossator clearly thought they were connected. The intention was to identify *Uued deen* as "judicial notoriety" in Romano-canonical procedures and to connect Frisian law with Canon law.

The gloss may be attempting to harmonize Frisian and learned law by equating the statement given in court with *notorium iuris* in the *Liber Extra*. This could imply that Frisian law was congruent with that part of Canon law and therefore in harmony with it. Alternatively, the gloss may simply have sought to explain the Frisian rule in the terms of Canon law without implying that the function was the same.

Another possibility is that the lemma refers only to statements given in a synodical court (*banda synde*). However, the choice of words for the lemma suggests that this is not the case, given that it refers to the oath in general rather than specifically to the synodical court.

Equally interesting are the other ways in which one could supply proof. All of them—notoriety, witnesses, instruments, confession and presumptions—were common means to provide evidence in Canonical procedures. It is evident that 15th-century Frisian law (the oath) was categorized within the terminological framework of Canon law. However, this does not necessarily mean that Canon law was directly applied in Frisian procedures. The categorization is merely a classification of Frisian law in terms of the Canon law tradition, without necessarily asserting the validity of these other means of proof.

The second instance mentioning a new kind of proof is a gloss to the *Twenty-four Land Laws*. As the text has been presented earlier, let us now consider only the part referred to in the lemma of the gloss (*endma queth*: "and the claimant states"). The claimant states that the victim was hit by a bludgeon. If the body

142 Gloss 93 ad *D*, VI (K[17]) 17, 202–203.

showed no wounds, i.e., if there was doubt about the facts of the claim, the defendant was allowed to swear an oath of innocence.

> L^{24} 8. [...] Hweer so ma een bannethe werpt op een man deer nen dulg ne haet endma queth dat hi se slain mit bamem jefta huinsen so moet hi tolwasum onswara ende nen meer onbringh daia. [...]
>
> Glossa 120. *Endma queth* Nec hoc idoneis testibus nec apertissimis documentis approbari possit, C. de proba. l. Sciant cuncti (*Cod.* 4.19.25), ff. de pe. Absen. (*Dig.* 48.19.5), extra de homi. Ex litteris (X 5.12.14).
>
> L^{24} 8. [...] If a case of homicide is brought before court but the body shows no wound and the claimant states that the victim has been hit by a bludgeon or hanged, the defendant has the right to exonerate himself by swearing an oath on the holy relics, together with eleven compurgators and after that is not compelled to answer to any more claims brought against him. [...][143]
>
> Gloss 120. *Endma queth* (*and the claimant states*) And this can neither be proved by appropriate witnesses nor by the clearest documents, see C. 4.19.25, D. 48.19.5 and X 5.12.14.[144]

The gloss refers to the two primary kinds of proof in learned law: witnesses and instruments. If the claimant's statement cannot be proved by witnesses or instruments, the defendant has the right of exoneration. However, the Frisian text makes no mention of any proof by the claimant. Instead, it describes a situation where a statement by the claimant is doubted owing to a lack of visible wounds. In such cases, the claimant has no right to furnish proof and the defendant is able to exonerate himself.

Romano-canonical procedures, by contrast, required the claimant to fail in providing sufficient proof before the defendant could take an oath of innocence.[145] This highlights the different approaches of traditional Frisian and learned law to who is responsible for providing proof. The gloss adds something to the text by stating that the Frisian claimant must first fail in providing proof before the defendant can take an oath of innocence, which was not a requirement in traditional Frisian law.

143 *D*, VIII (L^{24}) 8, pp. 226–227.

144 Gloss 120 ad *D*, VIII (L^{24}) 8, pp. 226–227.

145 Helmholz, *The spirit of classical canon law*, p. 158.

The kinds of proof mentioned in the gloss (witnesses and instruments) are typical for Canonical procedures, although interestingly there are no references to X 2.19, the title of the *Decretals* concerning proofs. Instead, the allegations in the gloss refer mostly to Roman law; this is not surprising, given that the procedural law of the *ius commune* contained elements of Roman law. Owing to the limited number of references, however, it is not possible to draw any conclusions as to whether the glossator preferred Roman law over Canon law. The allegations indicate nevertheless that the glossator was familiar with more kinds of proof than those mentioned in the gloss. For example, C. 4.19.25 mentions dependable witnesses and instruments, while D. 48.19.5 rules out suspicion as sufficient proof, and X 5.12.14 concerns scandal and rumor in connection with homicide, as well as mentioning the *purgatio canonica*.

5 Oaths in the Jurisprudentia Frisica

Among the titles of the *Jurisprudentia Frisica* is "de probationibus" (title 13, *on proofs*), which deals with the various ways in which proof can be provided. At the beginning of the title, seven different types are mentioned:

> JF 13:2 Haet is prowinghe. prowinge is een bywisinge der wird in twyflicke tingen. Dyo bywisinghe is sander handa wys. Als dyo openbeericheed der deda. Dyo oensyoen dis lichama. Dat hluud. Dyo rossche weninge. Dyo weninge. Dyo bywisinge myt orkenscip. Ende dyo prowinge iefta bywisinge deerma deth myt breuen deer hetet jnstrumenta.

> Glossa 2. *Haet is prowinge* "Notandum quid sit probacio et quot sunt species eius. Sciendum est, quod probacio sic diffinitur: Probacio est tractus rei dubie, faciens fidem per argumentum probacionis et dicitur probacio ab aduerbio 'probe' et non a uerbo, quia qui probat quod dicit, probe agit."[146]

> Glossa 3. *Dyo biwisinghe is* "Sunt autem septem species probacionis, scilicet per euidenciam facti, per aspectum corporis, per famam, per iuramenti dilacionem, per presumptionem, per testes, per instrumenta."[147]

146 Giovanni d'Andrea, *Summula de processu judicii*, Cap. VIII § 1 (p. 37).
147 Giovanni d'Andrea, *Summula de processu judicii*, Cap. VIII, § 2 (pp. 37–38).

> JF 13:2 What is evidence? Evidence is proof of the truth in questionable things. There are seven kinds of evidence, namely, publicity of the act, inspection of the body, rumor, immediate suspicion, presumption, witness evidence, and the evidence or proof that is furnished with charters called *instrumenta*.

> Gloss 2. *Haet is prowinge* (What is evidence?). "It should be noted what proof is and how many kinds there are. One should know that proof is defined as follows: proof is the clarification of a doubtful case, showing the truth by furnishing proof. And proof (*probatio*) is said to be derived from the adverb 'properly' (*probe*) and not from the verb, because the one who proves what he says acts properly."

> Gloss 3. *Dyo biwisinghe is* (There are ... evidence) "There are seven kinds of proof, namely through obviousness of a fact, inspection of the body, rumor, assigning an oath (to the other party), presumption, witnesses and instruments."[148]

As indicated in the notes above the Latin text, JF 13:2 was copied from a Latin source and then translated into Old Frisian. In this case, it is almost an exact quotation from Giovanni d'Andrea's *Summula de processu iudicii*. However, there is a puzzling difference in the translation of *Dyo rossche weninge Dyo weninge* for what should be *per famam, per iuramenti dilacionem*. These words appear to be superfluous as *weninge* means rumor and is congruent with *fama*. Therefore, the second *weninge* cannot mean "assigning an oath (to the other party)" (*per iuramenti dilacionem*). It seems as if the translator made an error and wrote rumor (*weninge*) twice, whereas on the second occasion it should have been translated differently.

When considering the rest of the title, however, it becomes less likely that the translator or copyist made an error. Some of the seven kinds of proof are elaborated upon in the following provisions: notorious acts (JF 13:3); inspection of the body (JF 13:4); rumor (JF 13:5); and suspicion (JF 13:6). Each of the remaining three proofs has its own title: presumptions (JF 14), witnesses (JF 15 and JF 16) and instruments (JF 17). These are also the only proofs that have their own title in both the *Processus Iudicii* and the *Liber Extra*.[149]

---

148 *Ro*, III (JF) 13, no. 2.

149 There is no title concerning *per iuramenti dilacionem* but there is a mention in the title on presumptions (*Ro*, III (JF), tit. 14, no. 3 and in gloss 4 attached). However, this is not deliberated upon. This proof appears not to have been deemed relevant by Frisian jurists. Possibly, it came into conflict with Frisian judicial oaths.

There is no title elaborating on oaths as a means of proof, and neither do the seven proofs include an oath. There is more elaboration about judicial oaths in title 24, "de iure iurando". However, this primarily concerns promissory oaths, while Frisian judicial oaths were assertory. The oath does not play a prominent role in the part of the *Jurisprudentia Frisica* concerning legal procedure. At the same time, however, it is not absent: in title 13, "de probationibus", we find rules regarding the oath of innocence.

> JF 13:33. Hwaso orem oen spreckt my edem so is dy sitter nyaer riuchtis.

> JF 13:34. Hweerso een man een tingh wil oenprowya myt riucht byseckt dy ora so schil dy ora myt also dene riucht ontgaen ende nel hy naet myt alsodena ponten ontgaen so schelma dat riucht prowia ende dat better foerd fynda. Autentica.

> JF 13:33. When someone complains against another with oaths, then the defendant has the stronger right (to exonerate himself).

> JF 13:34. If someone wants to prove his case against another with evidence (and) if the other (then) denies, then the other [the defendant] shall exonerate himself by such remedy, and if he will not exonerate himself on such points, then the claim shall be examined and the case shall be decided in favor of the stronger (evidence). Autentica.[150]

Two points are evident from these provisions. Firstly, JF 13:33 suggests that, in the late 15th century, a claimant could still use an oath to support a claim, following the procedure outlined in the *Older Skelta Law* (SkRb 3), i.e., a claimant took an oath when accusing another. This shows that traditional procedural methods still had a place in Frisian law at that time. Secondly, JF 13:34 implies that a defendant had a stronger right (*nyaer*) to prove innocence through an oath than a claimant. This arrangement, however, is archaic and goes against the usual procedure, where the claimant had the right to prove a claim from the 11th century onwards. It seems outdated for the 15th century and, while it may have been an exception, there is no indication to suggest it was used.

JF 13:34 is also present in the *Excerpta Legum*.[151] However, its origins date back even earlier, as signified by the word *Autentica* at the end. It is not present

---

150 *Ro*, III (JF), tit. 13, nos. 33 and 34.

151 *A*, I (Exc) 405, p. 284.

in *Thet Autentica Riocht*, but in the *Rechten ende Wilkoeren*.[152] This indicates that it was a product of the late 14th century and not the late 15th century. This provision is also likely already to have been significantly influenced by learned law, even though it pertains to the Frisian oath of innocence. Therefore, the reference to "stronger evidence" (*better*) may be a reference to the procedure and proof of learned law.

It is crucial to understand how much influence learned procedural law had on the *Rechten ende Wilkoeren*. Many of the provisions following JF 13:34 also originate from this source. By examining oaths of innocence in the rest of title JF 13, we can see when influences of learned law surfaced.

5.1 *Right to Prove and Burden of Proof*

The above two provisions (JF 13:33–34) seem to say that defendants had a stronger right to prove their statement than claimants. This contradicts classical legal texts such as the *Younger Skelta Law* (SkRb 3). Who had the right to prove in the *Jurisprudentia Frisica*, and how was this related to the 'burden of proof' in learned law? Let us examine other provisions concerning who furnished evidence.

> JF 13:17. Hweerso een man een lada weddeth ende haet hy dera ladena breck, so is hy inder wird naet wrwonnen. So schillet da oen prowinge foerd soe fyr so hit se een meet ryck man. Autentica.[153]

> JF 13:17. If a man offers an oath of innocence and he has too few compurgators, then he is found not guilty according to the truth. Then the claimant's evidence prevails if he is a moderately rich man. Autentica.

This puzzling text needs further explanation. The first sentence can be understood as meaning that the defendant has the right to prove and thereby to exclude the claimant's evidence. The defendant can take an oath of innocence before the other party even has a chance to present any evidence. Failure to take the oath of innocence does not mean that the defendant is guilty, but that the plaintiff can furnish proof. This is the most archaic form of proof by oath, but had been altered by the time of the 11th century. As with JF 13:33 and JF 13:34, it is unclear, therefore, why this appears in this 15th century text.

---

152 RW 27.

153 *Ro*, III (JF), tit. 13, no. 17.

The final part of JF 13:17 seems to be completely out of place: "if he is a moderately rich man" (*so hit se een meet ryck man*). What did a person's wealth have to do with the evidence? It is likely that this was an error in the transmitting of this text over many decades. For a better understanding, another version of this text must consequently be consulted, namely the *Rechten ende Wilkoeren*:

> RW 108. Van ener ladinghe to beghynnen.
> Soe waer een man ene ladynghe beghynnet, ende heft he gebreck der ladynghe, soe en is he inder ladynghe nyet verwonnen. Soe sal de anclagher daer voer ghelden, alsoe veer als dat een mate ryck man is, syne kosst ende terynghe.
>
> RW 108. About the offering of an oath of innocence
> If a man offers an oath of innocence and he lacks oath-helpers, then in (not being able to offer) the oath of innocence he has not lost his case. The complaining party must then pay for it, insofar as the defending party has limited monetary resources, i.e., his own expenses and digestibles.[154]

The wealth of an individual is relevant here because if the defendant is too poor, the claimant may have to cover the expenses. However, it is unclear what exactly the "complaining party must then pay for" (*daer voer ghelden*) and what the relationship is between the failed oath and the payment of expenses. Additionally, it is not mentioned who would succeed in the proof if the defendant were to fail. The first text indicates that the term "moderately rich man" does not refer to the strength of someone's proof, but rather to the expenses of a poor defendant. However, there are no answers to the questions raised. Both texts have common origins in a Westerlauwers, Old Frisian edition of the *Rechten ende Wilkoeren*, with the Old Frisian text in the *Jurisprudentia Frisica* and the later Middle Low German text in the Ommelander *Rechten ende Wilkoeren* both being corrupted transmissions of that original. Without any other older examples to consult, this question will remain unanswered.

The previous provisions suggest that the defendant, rather than the claimant, had a right to prove their statement . However, this was an archaic rule because, by the 11th century and certainly by the 15th century, the claimant should have had the right to prove their claim, rather than the defendant. This should not be confused with the burden of proof in learned law.

154 RW 108. The text is also present in *A*, I (Exc) 444, p. 305, but that instance is congruent to the one in the *Jurisprudentia Frisica*.

Another instance in the *Jurisprudentia Frisica* states the correct rule, namely that a claimant had a "stronger right" (*nyar*):

> JF 13:44. Di oensprekir is nyar syn secken to witen also langh als hyt noeglick oenbringhe mey dan dy sitter hem to ontgaen.

> Glossa 37. *Dy oensprekir is nyaer* Nam dicenti et non neganti incumbit probacio, ut in l. ii ff. de probationibus et ff. de testi. l. Eii (*Dig.* 22.3.2), quia negantis factum per rerum natura nulla est directa probacio, ut supra.[155]

> JF 13:44. The claimant, as long as he can sufficiently swear to the complaint, has a stronger right to prove his case satisfactorily than the defendant has to exonerate himself.

> Gloss 37. *Dy oensprekir is nyaer.* Because the burden of proof rests upon the one who asserts not the one who denies, as in D. 22.3.2, because by the nature of things there is no direct proof of the one who denies a fact, as stated above.

This text (JF 13:44) is congruent with classical Frisian law from the 11th century onwards, but the situation is different in the case of the gloss (gloss 37). Note the connection between the "stronger right" (*nyar*) and the "burden of proof" (*incumbit probatio*) in the gloss. The claimant has the burden of proving the defendant's guilt, as also clearly stated in JF 13:30:

> JF 13:30 Hweerso een seeck to waer comnt jeffta ee*n* spreeck brinckt, so aegh hy da oenprowing*e* deer spreckt en*de* dy naet dyr byseckt.[156]

> JF 13:30 When someone brings a case to court or makes a complaint, the one who complains should provide the evidence and not the one who denies.

In this provision, there is no mention of the right to prove (*niar*). Instead, it appears that the claimant is obligated (*aegh hy*) to provide evidence rather than having an advantage in doing so. It is important to recall that this was the fundamental difference between the Frisian 'right to prove' and the 'burden of proof'

155 Gloss 37 ad *Ro*, III (JF), tit. 13, no. 44.
156 *Ro*, III (JF), tit. 13, no. 30.

in learned law. The right to prove allowed the exclusion of the other party's proof. If a defendant had this right, the defendant could take an oath of innocence without the claimant being able to furnish proof. If a claimant had this right, the claimant could furnish proof without the defendant being able to do so. Only if the proof failed, was the other party able to provide their own proof. In learned law, the claimant was burdened with presenting the proof; if this failed, the defendant was presumed innocent. These two concepts are not the same.

Despite this difference, the "stronger right (to prove)" (*niar*) in JF 13:44 is connected to the "burden of proof" (*incumbit probatio*) in gloss 37. Similarly, the text of JF 13:30 concerns a burden rather than a right. A gloss to JF 13:30 (gloss 29) supports this because it contains the same sentences and references as gloss 37.[157] The two glosses quote and refer to D. 22.3.2: *Ei incumbit probatio qui dicit, non qui negat.* (Translation: "The burden of proof rests upon the one who asserts, not the one who denies.")[158]

The texts and glosses interpret the right of the claimant to prove (classical Frisian law) as the burden of proof (learned law). They connect the two different understandings of who was able or had to furnish proof. The consequences for procedural law are uncertain. Frisians may have still considered providing proof an advantage, or their thinking may have shifted to seeing proof as a burden.

5.2 *Notoriety and Doubt*

Previously, I outlined how public notoriety and doubt influenced the oath of innocence in classical Frisian law. On the one hand, if a wrongdoing was publicly known, the claimant had the right to prove their statement. On the other hand, doubt reversed the 'right to prove' from the claimant to the defendant. This is also clearly stated in the *Jurisprudentia Frisica*:

> JF 13:35. Alle tingh dyr openbeer sint neyder byhodinghe da oenprowinge sint nyaer dan da lada Ende al tingh dyr twiuel in is dyr sint da lada nyaer dan da oenprowinge. Autentica.

> JF 13:36. Dit is riucht dat da lada sint set weder leyna ende weder nene wird weder twyuelicka thingh ende weder neen opera tingh want dyo leyna schamet her selnn. Autentica.

157 Gloss 29 ad *Ro*, III (JF), tit. 13, no. 30.

158 D. 22.3.2.

> JF 13:35. (In) all matters which are publicly known, on the basis of the law, the evidence of the claimant has a stronger right than the oaths of innocence (of the defendant). And (in) all cases where there is doubt, the oaths of innocence have a stronger right than the evidence. Autentica.

> JF 13:36. This is law, that the oaths of innocence have been instituted against lies and against untruth, against doubtful things and against things not publicly known, for the lie falsifies itself. Autentica.[159]

What is said here is essentially no different from Frisian law in the *Older Skelta Law* and the Twenty-four Land Laws. However, the effect of notoriety and doubt is now explicitly stated. In the older Frisian sources, by contrast, various texts implied this but never stated it as clearly as in the above provisions. Both provisions are also found in the *Rechten ende Wilkoeren*.[160] It is clear, therefore, that this was Frisian law, written down and made explicit in the *Rechten ende Wilkoeren* sometime in the 14th century. If, then, there was an influence of learned law, it is not immediately apparent.

There is also a third mention, which is of particular interest.

> JF 13:38. Hweerso een bantha een man op seyt ende dy man habbe neen dulligh ende hit quede hit se mit stock deen so sint nyaer da lada dan dyo oenbringh. Autentica.

> JF 13:38. If someone states a complaint for wergild, and the man [the victim] would have no wound, and he [the claimant] would say that it had been done with a stick, then the oaths of innocence have a stronger right than the adjuration of the complaint. Autentica.[161]

The mention of *Autentica* confirms that this fragment derives from the *Rechten ende Wilkoeren*.[162] Indeed, it is even older: JF 13:38 is a shortened version of a traditional text from the Twenty-four Land Laws (L^{24} 8).[163] This version makes no mention of oath-helpers or holy relics, but the text is otherwise the same.[164]

---

159 *Ro*, III (JF), tit. 13, nos. 35 and 36.

160 JF 13:35 is present in *A*, I (Exc) 406, p. 286, and in RW 28. A shortened version of JF 13:36 is found in RW 93. This states only that oaths are instituted against doubtful things and things not publicly known.

161 *Ro*, III (JF), tit. 13, no. 38.

162 From RW 121 to be precise.

163 *D*, VIII (L^{24}) 8, pp. 226–227.

164 It is important not to read too much into the lack of mentions of oath-helpers and holy

Evidently, the rules about who had the right to prove in the *Jurisprudentia Frisica* were reproductions of older, traditional Frisian law. These reproductions were recorded by jurists in the 14th century and remained unchanged until the end of the 15th century. The *Jurisprudentia Frisica* thus contains the classical Frisian rules on the effects of doubt and notoriety on who had the right to prove their statement.

5.3 *Purgation among Other Proofs*

What happened when other proofs, i.e., non-oaths, entered the procedure? Since these are detailed at the beginning of title 13, we may expect an interaction between the seven proofs of Giovanni d'Andrea and the judicial oaths. At least in ecclesiastical matters, the oath of innocence was subordinate to other proofs:

> JF 13:37. Dit is riucht dat in alle gastlicke tingen sint nyar da oenprowinge dan da lada. Autentica.

> JF 13:37. This is law, that in all ecclesiastical matters the evidence supplies more justice than the oaths of innocence. Autentica.[165]

The term "evidence" mentioned in this context refers to the proofs, such as witnesses and instruments, typically used in Canonical procedures.[166] The provision clearly states that these proofs were given priority over the judicial oath in all ecclesiastical matters litigated in Canonical procedures. This provision is also found in the *Rechten ende Wilkoeren*.[167] Hence, it is evident that, in the 14th century and possibly even earlier, the Frisian judicial oath was subordinated to witness testimony and instruments in Church procedures. Frisians had been using the oath of innocence for centuries to prove their innocence and resolve cases. Therefore, Medieval jurists had an incentive to clarify its role in the context of ecclesiastical procedures. Additionally, the above provision (JF 13:37) demonstrates that the oath of innocence was used in such procedures.

---

relics. It is plausible that they disappeared when the text was shortened or adapted to other local circumstances. The RW 121 version contains no mention of holy relics, but does mention compurgators.

165 *Ro*, III (JF), tit. 13, no. 37.

166 See previously in the section on the Romano-canonical procedure and Brundage, *Medieval Canon Law*, p. 132.

167 In RW 118. Another part of RW 118 is present in *A*, I (Exc) 445, p. 308, but this concerns jurisdiction and not proof.

Implicit in this provision (JF 13:37) is that secular matters had different priorities regarding proofs. However, there are also indications to the contrary, namely that the rules concerning evidence were likely to have been the same. Firstly, the above provision was included in the *Jurisprudentia Frisica*, which was undoubtedly intended as secular law. It is plausible that the provision is merely a point of comparison with ecclesiastical law, but it may also have been applied in (some) secular courts despite its saying "in all ecclesiastical matters" (*alle gastlicke tingen*).

Another provision in title 13 provides insight into this question:

> JF 13:10. Hwerso een man een tingh noeglick by wyst myt andert orkenscip deer heten is affirmatiua. So mey hym dy ora naet sykeria ner ontgong habba ner wedriucht byeda.

> JF 13:10. When one sufficiently proves a case with witnesses present, which (proof) is called *affirmativa*, then the other may not purify himself or exonerate himself or offer proof to the contrary.[168]

No limitation to ecclesiastical courts is implied in this text. The term *sykeria* refers to purgation through an oath of innocence and was used frequently in Old Frisian Medieval law texts.[169] It is more plausible, therefore, that it refers to the Frisian oath rather than to the *purgatio canonica*. The meaning of this provision is also clear: if a claimant provides sufficient evidence, the defendant can no longer swear an oath of innocence or "offer proof to the contrary" (*wedriucht*; German: *Gegenbeweis*).[170]

One may attempt to read this text as establishing a hierarchy, where witness testimony supersedes the oath of innocence (*sykeria*) and *wedriucht*. However, I believe this to be improbable. The term *wedriucht* emerges only in the sources of the late 15th century. It appears twice in the *Medieval Register of the Jus Municipale Frisonum* (RgJ), where it summarizes the 17th provision of the *Seventeen Statutes*.[171] Compare these two texts from the *Freeska Landriucht* and the *Jus Municipale Frisonum* (*J*) manuscript:

---

168 *Ro*, III (JF), tit. 13, no. 10.

169 'sikeria' in: Hofman, Popkema, *Altfriesisches Handwörterbuch*, p. 426.

170 'wedriucht' in: Hofman, Popkema, *Altfriesisches Handwörterbuch*, p. 571.

171 On the *Jus Municipale Frisonum*, see Buma et al., *Westerlauwerssches Recht I*.

> K^{17} 17. [...] hit ne se dat hi een wed deen habbe aen een worpena were jefta an kedena tinghe jefta an da banda synde, soe ne mey ma dera deda nene wyteed byeda.[172]
>
> RgJ 39. En wed deen on standen waer, deer aech ma nen wedriucht tojenst.[173]
>
> K^{17} 17. [...] unless someone has given a statement before a normal court, a special court or a synodical court; in that case he can no longer deny his acts by swearing an oath on the holy relics.
>
> RgJ 39. (If) a statement was made during the court session, one may not provide proof to the contrary.

In the *Seventeen Statutes*, the term is *wyteed*, literally meaning oath to the contrary (German: *Gegeneid*). In the *Jus Municipale Frisonum* manuscript, it is *wedriucht*. Two possibilities are plausible. First, both terms have the exact same meaning: denying an act by swearing an oath of innocence. Consequently, JF 13:10 should state that witness testimony excludes an oath of innocence and denying an act by swearing an oath of innocence. I find this unlikely. In the *Jus Municipale Frisonum* version of the *Seventeen Statutes*, *wedriucht* is not used.[174] Instead, the term *withedan*, which is related to *wyteed*, appears.[175] Only the register at the beginning uses a different term.

The second possibility is more plausible. *Wedriucht* is a relatively young term describing not just an "oath to the contrary" (*Gegeneid*) but any proof to the contrary (*Gegenbeweis*). This would also include proof by instruments and witnesses. Reading the text (JF 13:10) under this assumption implies that it does not indicate a hierarchy between various kinds of proof, but instead pertains to the order of proof: if a claimant provided sufficient proof, no oath of innocence or any other proof of innocence could be furnished by the defendant. This is the less interesting option of the two. The provision (JF 13:37) does not indicate that Frisians considered witness testimony to be superior to proof by oath.

What is remarkable is that the provision contains learned law, namely a mention of witness testimony and proof *affirmativa*. Yet, the provision is writ-

172 *D*, VI (K^{17}) 17, pp. 202–203.

173 *J*, I (RgJ), 39, in Buma et al., *Westerlauwerssches Recht I*, p. 36.

174 Buma et al., *Westerlauwerssches Recht I*, pp. 135–146.

175 'wīthēd' in: Hofman, Popkema, *Altfriesisches Handwörterbuch*, p. 592.

ten in Old Frisian. This may be a good example of a harmonization of Frisian and learned law: the procedure is Frisian, meaning that the claimant had a right to prove, and success in this regard prohibited the defendant from providing proof; at the same time, witness testimony was the primary kind of proof in Romano-canonical procedures. What is missing is any indication of proof through instruments. Moreover, the procedure is not reciprocal: proof by the claimant excludes proof by the defendant, whereas in Romano-canonical procedures both parties had equal rights to furnish proof (*audi et alteram partem*). Consequently, this is not so much procedural learned law, but rather Frisian procedural law that includes a few elements of learned law (namely witness testimony).

Lastly, a few words on the proof called *affirmativa*. For a better understanding, consider the gloss attached:

> Glossa 11. *Hweerso een man een tingh* Contra negantem factum per rerum natura nulla est directa probacio, ut de probationibus c. Quoniam (X 2.19.11) et de electione c. Bone, in textu (X 1.6.23) et in glosa super uerbo 'per rerum natura'.[176] Item in c. Ad nostram de probationibus (X 2.19.12) in fine ubi dicitur "Mandamus quatenus in huiusmodi probacione negatiuae (dum tamen possit ex aduerso affirmatiua probari), neminem audiatis" et supra eodem c. Volentes (X 1.30.8), igitur ut hec pestis contraria omni iure penitus exstirpetur in glosa, eodem super uerbo 'affirmatiua': "Illa enim primo probari debet, quia ei qui dicit, incumbit probacio, ergo etcetera"[177] et in c. dicto Ad nostram, in glosa super uerbo 'contraria omni iure': "Negantis factum nulla est directa probacio".[178] Et dicit Bernardus in glosa super uerbo 'contraria omni iure' quod purgacio tamen admitti debet, quia ei qui dicit, non ei qui negat, incumbit probacio,[179] ff de probationibus l.ii (*Dig.* 22.3.2), ff. de publicis iudiciis l. Quicumque (*Dig.* 48.1.?[180]), "sed contra probacionem testium non admittitur purgacio", ut in glosa dicti c. Ad nostram.[181]

> Gloss 11. *Hweerso een man een tingh.* According to the nature of things there is no direct proof against the one who denies a fact, as in X 2.19.11,

176 Glossa *per rerum natura* ad X 1.6.23.
177 Glossa *affirmatiua* ad X 2.19.12.
178 Glossa *contraria omni iure* ad X 2.19.12.
179 Glossa *contraria omni iure* ad X 2.19.12.
180 This allegation remains unresolved.
181 Glossa *affirmatiua* ad X 2.19.12.

> X 1.6.23 and the gloss *per rerum natura* ad X 1.6.23. We find the same in X 2.19.12 at the end which reads "We order that in the case of such a proof of the negative, although the positive can be proven from the opposite, you will hear no-one" and see X 1.30.8. So that this plague, contrary to all law, is entirely eradicated in the gloss *affirmatiua* ad X 2.19.12: "This should first be proven, because the burden of proof rests with the one who states something, and thus etc." and in the gloss *contraria omni iure* ad X 2.19.12: "By the nature of things there is no direct proof of the one who denies a fact." And Bernardus says in the gloss *contraria omni iure* ad X 2.19.12 that purgation should nevertheless be allowed, because the burden of proof rests with the one who states something, not with the one who denies it, see D. 22.3.2 and D. 48.1.?, "but purgation is not allowed against proof by witnesses", as in the gloss *affirmatiua* ad X 2.19.12.[182]

The gloss pertains to the burden of proof and is similar to arguments presented in gloss 37: "The burden of proof rests upon the one who asserts, not the one who denies."[183] Proof that is *affirmativa* refers to proof of a positive fact, meaning that a claimant had to provide positive proof, while a defendant could not prove the opposite. If the claimant's proof (*probatio affirmativa*) failed, the defendant was not required to prove the negative (*probatio negativa*).[184]

Regarding the claim that proof by witnesses excludes purgation, the focus should be on the last line of the gloss and the reference to the gloss *affirmativa* to X 2.19.12. References to this are also found in gloss 29 ad JF 13:30 and gloss 31 ad JF 13:35. 'Purgation' refers to the *purgatio canonica*, the purgatory oath that could be taken in Canonical procedures. This was only possible if the claimant's proof had failed; for example, if there were not enough witnesses to testify. It is worth noting that this mention of purgation is not a reference to the Frisian oath. At the same time, *purgatio canonica* is not mentioned elsewhere in the title in *Jurisprudentia Frisica* on proofs, suggesting that it was not relevant to Frisian procedural law as presented in this source. Lastly, mentions of *purgatio* are too few and incidental to conclude that it was compared with or equated to the Frisian oath of innocence.

---

182 Gloss 11 ad *Ro*, III (JF), tit. 13, no. 10.

183 Gloss 37 ad *Ro*, III (JF), tit. 13, no. 44.

184 Brundage, *Medieval Canon Law*, p. 131. For the affirmatio and negatio, see Litewski, *Der römisch-kanonische Zivilprozeß* II, pp. 362–363.

5.4 *Comparing Frisian and Norwegian Developments*

The presence of the judicial oath in late 15th century Frisian law is a topic of interest. It has been claimed that witness evidence replaced oaths during this period, but this is not entirely true.[185] Oaths and witnesses coexisted in Frisian law texts from the 14th century onwards, as evidenced by the core finding of this chapter. Despite the reception of the procedural system of learned law, Frisians retained the oath as the primary proof and developed a legal tradition that included new kinds of proof such as witnesses.

Immink argues that this retaining of the oath as a means of judicial proof was linked to the idea of Frisian freedom.[186] It was an important aspect of Frisians' rights in court, giving them the ability to exonerate themselves with their own words. While it is unclear whether the capacity to take an oath was truly seen as a sign of freedom, oaths were maintained within procedural law even under the influence of learned procedure.

Moreover, the core aspects of Frisian procedure remained unchanged. Claimants' right to prove their claim was stronger than defendants' right to prove their innocence by means of an oath and with the help of compurgators, a principle that applied in High Medieval Frisian law and continued to apply in the late 15th century. In conclusion, the judicial oath remained a viable option in the new Canonized Frisian law.

However, the introduction of many other kinds of proofs represented a significant change. Witness testimony, in particular, became a crucial aspect of Canonical procedures and an impediment for taking purgatory oaths: while oaths were retained in the new procedural law and did not disappear as a means of proof, they were no longer the primary means to furnish evidence.

Comparisons can be made with the history of the judicial oath in Medieval Norway, which also underwent changes in its procedural law under the influence of learned law. Although the judicial oath remained the central proof in Norwegian law throughout the Middle Ages and was not replaced by witnesses or lost its significance,[187] the nature of oath-helpers in Norwegian law changed, with the court increasingly selecting them from outside the defendant's support system because of concerns about perjury.[188]

In classical Frisian law texts, persons taking an oath could select the compurgators from among their relatives.[189] Only in the *Statutes of the Five Districts*

185 As claimed by Oosten, "Inleidende Beschouwingen", p. 470.
186 Immink, "Getuigen", p. 457.
187 Nordby, *Judicial Oath*, pp. 245–249.
188 Nordby, *Judicial Oath*, p. 247.
189 As written, for example, in the Twenty-four Land Laws (L^{24} 8): "The 8th land law is that

(W^5D 24) is there a mention of other people, namely having nine *atthas* (jurors) as compurgators.[190] The sources of the 14th and 15th centuries contain no further information on selecting oath-helpers.

However, concerns about perjury were also present in Frisian law, as evidenced by the condemnation of perjury in the title "de iure iurando" (JF 24).[191] This shows that Frisians were concerned about perjury violating the social trust needed in a society based on oaths and honor. The capacity to be a witness also fell into this category, requiring people to believe the testimony of a witness.

In conclusion, Frisian and Norwegian law both underwent distinct changes regarding judicial oaths. Both kept oaths as a means of proof, but in Frisian law they became one of many proofs permitted, at least in theory. If Immink is correct in stating that Frisians valued their oaths so much, it is curious that Norwegian law retained them as the central proof, while Frisian law did not. This difference can be attributed to the strength of the reception of learned law. Procedural law of the *ius commune* was strongly received in Frisia, while the reception of learned law in Norway was less extensive. The Frisian judicial oath nevertheless remained prominent in the 15th century, which is remarkable given the influence of learned law on Frisian legal traditions.

6 End of Ordeals

Ordeals underwent almost the opposite historical development as judicial oaths in Frisia. The *Synodical Law of Central Frisia* describes how someone who was not burned after an ordeal with hot water succeeded in proving their case. As a result, the synod could not put him on trial.[192] A gloss to this was written in the 14th century:

---

each estate holder may rightfully call to court his relatives up to the third degree to act as compurgators […]" *D*, VIII (L^{24}) 8, pp. 226–227.

190 *D*, XIII (W^5D) 24, pp. 322–323: "[…] if the defendant wants to swear innocence and have nine *atthas* as compurgators […]".

191 *Ro*, III (JF), tit. 24, no. 1.

JF 24:1 *HWaso swert een eed dy is falsck ende onriucht so is dy man meenedich ende haet syn guede namme wrlerren Ende wyrt heten een meenedich hond Ende dyr alzo falsck swert dy is jnfames ende mey neen tywgh dwaen jeffta nen orkena wessa.* (Translation: "JF 24:1. If someone swears an oath that is false and unjust, then this person is perjured and has lost his reputation and is called a perjured dog, and he who thus swears falsely is infamous, and is not allowed to testify or to be a witness.")

192 *D*, XI (SWl) 55, pp. 280–281.

> Glossa 160. Duella et purgaciones wlgares, scilicet ferri candentis uel aque bulientis, sunt hodie prohibite, quia Deus temptatur et innocens frequenter condemnatur, extra de pur. wlga. per totum (X 5.35). Et si clericus duellum susceperit uel optulerit, deponatur, de cle. pug. in du. c. i et ii (X 5.14.1–2).

> Gloss 160. The duel and public purgations, namely (the ordeals) of red-hot iron or boiling water, are nowadays prohibited, because God is put to the test and often an innocent man is sentenced; see the entire title of X 5.35. And if a cleric accepts or offers a duel, he will be removed from office; see X 5.14.1–2.[193]

It is apparent from the gloss that the author believed ordeals to be unlawful, which was a later development. The purpose of this gloss was to update the Old Frisian text, without adding a comparative analysis and thus making the statement declarative and leaving no room for alternative interpretation. The gloss provides two arguments against ordeals: firstly, that they put God to the test (*Deus temptatur*) and, secondly, that innocent people can be wrongfully convicted (*innocens frequenter condemnatur*). These arguments, along with other reasoning against ordeals, are derived from Canon law and are a replication of the rubric to X 5.35, which states: *Duella et aliae purgationes vulgares prohibite sunt; quia per eas multotiens condemnatur absolvendus, et Deus temtari videtur.*[194]

The above gloss adds a specific detail, namely, which ordeals are forbidden. This adaptation to the local context is important since both the ordeal of hot water and the ordeal of hot iron are mentioned in the text that the gloss is attached to. The last sentence of the gloss replicates Canon law: *Clericus iniens duellum sive obtulerit sive susceperit, deponendus est.*[195]

The prohibition of ordeals in Canon law came about from the Fourth Lateran Council in 1215. The Church and canonists had already rejected them from the late 12th century onwards. This rejection was based on two core arguments: firstly, Augustine's argument that God should not be tempted and, secondly, the theologians' argument that there was no common dimension between fire and water and the human conscience.[196] The first argument is reiterated in the above gloss. At the Fourth Lateran Council, attended by two hundred repre-

193 Gloss 160 ad *D*, XI (SWl) 55, pp. 280–281.

194 DG post X 5.35.

195 DG post X 5.14.

196 Foreville, *Lateran I–IV*, p. 362.

sentatives of Christian nations, the ordeals were prohibited. Specifically, the clergy's participation in ordeals was forbidden, thus effectively reducing their viability.[197]

As a result of this prohibition, ordeals were outlawed all over Europe, and this marked their decline as instruments of proof in procedural law.[198] In Denmark, for example, the king banned the use of ordeals not long after the council of 1215.[199] In Frisia, however, there was no institution to enforce a ban, and this may have hindered any attempts to prohibit their use in practice. For this reason, ordeals may have persisted for a long time in Frisia.[200] However, as we have seen in gloss 160, Frisian learned jurists also considered them unlawful, as is evident from a second gloss written alongside the *Older Skelta Law*.

> Glossa 35. Nota. Hec est ratio quare ⟨usus⟩ aque bulientis uel frigide sit prohibitum scilicet ne sors cadit super innocentem, ii q.v Consuluisti (C. 2 q.5 c.20), de purgatione uulgari per totum (X 5.35). Item nota. Vulgaris purgatio dicitur quia sibi uulgus inuenit scilicet per duellum, aquam et ignem, ut extra de purgatione uulgari per totum (X 5.35). Triplex est ratio quare huiusmodi purgatio prohibetur: prima quia facta fuit inuidia fabricante, ut in c. Mennam ii q.v. (C. 2 q.5 c.7) et c. Consuluisti (C. 2 q.5 c.20), secunda quia Deus in ea temptari uidetur, ut e. ti. c. ult. (X 5.35.3), tertia quia plurimus innocens condempnatur, ut e. ti. Significantibus (X 5.35.2) et officium etiam atletarum hodie reprobatur, et secundum leges ut C. de gladiatis l.i lib. xi (*Cod.* 11.44.1).

> Gloss 35. Note that this is the reason why the use of boiling or cold water is prohibited, viz. to avoid fate indicating someone innocent, see C. 2 q.5 c.20 and the entire title X 5.35. Also, note that the ordeal is called a 'public purge', because the public becomes aware of it through duel, water and fire, as in the entire title X 5.35. There is a threefold reason why such a purge is prohibited. In the first place because performing it arouses disgust, see C. 2 q.5 c.7 and C. 2 q.5 c.20, secondly because it seems to put God to the test, see X 5.35.3, and in the third place because many an innocent is

197 On the Fourth Lateran Council, see Baldwin, "The Intellectual Preparation"; Foreville, *Lateran I–IV*, p. 289 ff.; Pennington, "Due Process".

198 Auer, "Konfliktlösung durch Ordalien", p. 164.

199 Tamm, Vogt, *Danish Medieval Laws*, p. 23.

200 As suggested by Bartlett, *Trial*, p. 133, who makes the remote location of Frisia responsible for the persistence of judicial ordeals.

> condemned, see X 5.35.2, and even the profession of athletes is nowadays disapproved of, also according to Roman law, as in C. 11.44.1.[201]

We have discussed most of the arguments presented in this gloss before. However, a curious reference to Roman law appears at the end. Until now, only references to Canon law were made since it was Canon law that prohibited ordeals. This particular provision, however, prohibits all gladiatorial contests.[202] A parallel between public ordeals and public gladiatorial contests is established. This passage is a replication from the end of the gloss *aliquatenus tolerare* to X 5.35.1, which is the origin of the contents of the gloss above. It also refers, for instance, to C. 2 q.5 c.7 and C. 2 q.5 c.20, as well as X 5.35.3.[203] As it is probable that the writers of gloss 35 largely reproduced this particular gloss (*aliquatenus tolerare* to X 5.35.1), we are unlikely to be able to attribute a deeper meaning to the reference to Roman law here.[204] However, we can note that the gloss mentions specific ordeals, namely "boiling and cold water" (*aque bulientis uel frigide*), adapting them to the Frisian context.

The *Jurisprudentia Frisica* specifically mentions the ordeal by combat, which was often criticized by the Church and sometimes forbidden outright.[205] Anyone who forced another into such a trial committed a deadly sin:

> JF 2:31. Hweerso een man een kamp op gript so ne thoerma hyne naet wrwerpa hit ne se dat hyne da riuchteren deer tho twinga ende datze hyne thingie oen lyf jefta oen gued, so dwase een folle haudsonde. So were hit bettera dat hy dine daed oen tingh dan hy hym werworpe, want dy paws haet alle falscha ordel ende alla falscha prowinghe wrbeden. Autentica.[206]

> JF 2:31 If a man challenges another to a judicial duel, the other may not accept that challenge unless the judges compel him to do so and cause him to do so on pain of loss of limb or assets. Then, however, they com-

201 Gloss 35 ad *D*, III (SkRa) 42, pp. 138–141. This gloss refers to a provision detailing the ordeal of hot water or ordeal of the kettle and use of a champion.

202 *Cod.* 11.44.1: […] *Quapropter omnino gladiatores esse prohibemus.* (Translation: "For that reason we prohibit all gladiatorial contests.") The reason being that bloody contests are not appropriate for peace.

203 Gloss *aliquatenus tolerare* ad X 5.35.1 i.m.

204 Possibly a connection between professional fighters (gladiators) and someone who fights for another (champion) is made. The prohibition of gladiatorial fights may have been brought up as an argument against judicial duels.

205 Auer, "Konfliktlösung durch Ordalien", p. 163; Buma, *Godsoordeel*, p. 24.

206 *Ro*, III (JF) 2, no. 31.

> mit an absolute mortal sin. Then it would be better for him to suffer death than to accept the challenge to the duel, because the Pope has forbidden all false ordeals and all false forms of evidence. Autentica.

Although the first instance of this provision derives from *Thet Autentica Riocht*, its original source is not Frisian.[207] Similarly, it is also not a reproduction of X 5.35.3, which makes no mention of clergy being forced to participate. However, it is possible that the original source of this provision is a commentary by a canonist, with this provision (JF 2:31) being a clear example of a reception of Canon law.

From the glosses and Frisian sources of the 14th and 15th centuries, it is apparent that ordeals were prohibited or at least reduced, indicating that they should have ceased to exist as a means of proof in legal procedures. However, other instances suggest that this prohibition was not fully enforced or that practice lagged behind norms. The *Rechten ende Wilkoeren*, for example, includes a provision about ordeals relating specifically to the amount of money needing to be in dispute to initiate a trial by combat.[208] This is in fact a copy of a provision from the *Older Skelta Law* (SkRa 44), and its inclusion in the *Rechten ende Wilkoeren* suggests that it was still relevant in the late 14th century. During that time, some Frisian jurists strongly favored the prohibition of such ordeals (as seen in gloss 35 to the *Older Skelta Law*), but this opinion may not always have been followed.

Moreover, even the late 15th century *Jurisprudentia Frisica* contains a reference to ordeals in JF 60:22, where the champion of a thief is mentioned.[209] The contents of this provision appear outdated and are likely to be a remnant rather than an indication of the validity of ordeals.[210]

Due to a lack of case records and other primary sources, it is difficult to assess whether legal practice continued to involve ordeals in the 14th and 15th centuries. It is possible that some ordeals continued to be undertaken, particularly those not involving combat or fire. The ingestion of bread and cheese, for

207 See Brouwer, *Thet Autentica Riocht*, pp. 62–63. The older *Rechten ende Wilkoeren* contains no such text. It is also found in *A*, I (Exc) 354, p. 260, from where it was copied into the *Jurisprudentia Frisica*.

208 RW 57.

209 *Ro*, III (JF) 60, no. 22.

210 For example it references the *skelta*. This may have been an addition to the provisions about house searches and theft in the *Older Skelta Law*, specifically *D*, III (SkRa) 67, pp. 156–157. See also Gerbenzon, "Aantekeningen (Tweede Deel)", p. 348, who dates this text to the early 13th century at the latest. For other archaic paragraphs in the *Jurisprudentia Frisica*, see Gerbenzon, "Aantekeningen (Tweede Deel)", pp. 342–350.

instance, did not involve violence or injury and was not specifically forbidden. However, there is no clear evidence to suggest whether these ordeals continued or ceased.

7 Conclusion

In the written sources of the 14th and 15th centuries, it is evident how the Frisians adopted procedural law. The presence and contents of manuals such as the *Processus Iudicii*, as well as the structure of the *Jurisprudentia Frisica*, demonstrate broad adoption of the Romano-canonical procedure of learned law. Sources from legal practice indicate that these procedures were likely to have been used in arbitration, as well as in secular and ecclesiastical courts in Frisia. However, it would be incorrect to refer to this as a comprehensive reception. Frisian jurists changed the Romano-canonical procedure in Frisia to fit their needs; in effect, 'Frisianizing' it. They continued to use the Old Frisian language alongside Latin, and arbitration was shortened and simplified, while the most striking difference was the role played by the traditional Frisian judicial oath.

Glosses from the 14th century show that Frisian jurists were familiar with the various kinds of proof that existed in Romano-canonical procedures. There are indications that they intended to harmonize the two legal traditions by applying the rules of proof for learned law, but not rejecting the traditional judicial oath (of innocence) as a means of proof. In this they were successful, applying witness testimony among oaths and other proofs.

A large amount of deliberation on procedural law was done at the end of the 14th century, with sources such as the *Rechten ende Wilkoeren* reproducing traditional Frisian rules on judicial oaths. Sometimes implied norms and customs were made explicit. At other times, similar concepts were equated and harmonized; the right to prove and the burden of proof are excellent examples of this, with two similar concepts being unified, despite their distinct origins and initially divergent natures.

The most significant challenge to Frisian proofs came from ecclesiastical law. The Church courts preferred witnesses and instruments over other evidence, and this is also stated in Frisian law. However, this preference was not explicitly extended to secular law. Although there are indications that this was the case in practice, it is conceivable that Frisian law continued to hold oaths in high regard. The same cannot be said for ordeals, however. Although they were theoretically prohibited at the Fourth Lateran Council in 1215, late 14th-century sources continued to consider them relevant. While they were explicitly proscribed in the 15th century, legal practice may have lagged behind. In this regard, therefore, more research is needed. Whatever the case, and despite the pressure of ecclesiastical law, Frisians were slow to change how they produced proof.

From the normative sources, it is apparent that judicial oaths remained valid proof and were integrated into the received Romano-canonical procedure. At the same time, these procedures were altered in such a way that made it possible to continue the Frisian procedures. It is clearly observable that oaths were used in much the same way as before, despite procedures being influenced by learned law. The judicial oath thus remained a central proof, albeit now one of many. This fact alone is remarkable, considering the strong reception of the Romano-canonical procedure. Nonetheless, the sources demonstrate that oaths and the procedures applying to oaths did not fundamentally change. In this regard, Immink is right in stating that oaths seemed to be an important aspect of court procedures for Frisians. This is also evident from legal practice, where the oath continued to be used as proof throughout the 15th century.

In conclusion, these developments tell a story of harmonization of the Frisian ways of proof, on the one hand, and the order and structure of Romano-canonical procedures, on the other. Thus, a Frisian-canonical procedure was created.

CHAPTER 4

Theft and the House Search

The previous chapter outlined the Frisian legal procedure and its development in the 15th century. Although the influence of Romano-canonical procedural law was evident, certain elements of Frisian law remained, namely the use of oaths as proof. This chapter focuses on one particular wrongdoing, theft (OF: *thiāfthe*), to provide a case study of how reception changed the Frisians' approach to a specific criminal wrongdoing. After describing in detail how the Frisian indigenous legal system perceived of and dealt with theft, I will examine whether the methods and norms of learned law were applied in respect to this specific wrongdoing.

1 An Overview of Theft in Medieval Frisia

The act of stealing was considered extremely serious in Frisian society. The *Younger Skelta Law* (SkRb 28) details that thief and victim could not come to a private arrangement regarding a theft. Instead, the local judge (*skelta*) had ultimate responsibility and power to punish the thief.[1] Even if the thief and victim attempted to resolve the matter privately, theft remained a public matter and constituted a breach of public peace. In other words, it was not just an issue between two individuals; rather, it was a violation of societal norms, and the victim could not forgive or ignore the crime. No such rules applied to other serious crimes, such as murder or bodily injury.[2]

Medieval Icelandic society shared a similar view of theft. Stealing represented a break with society and was considered a most malicious crime. Thieves were among the lowest members of society, alongside murderers. By stealing, thieves severed their connection to society and stepped outside its conventions.[3] Frisian law treated theft likewise, as the *Younger Skelta Law* (SkRb 28) shows: a thief broke out of the boundaries of society and could no longer partake in its conventions. Compromise between victim and thief was impossible.

1 *D*, XII (SkRb) 28, pp. 308–309.
2 For an exploration of the claim for manslaughter and its status in Frisian procedural law, see Tragter-Schubert, "Zur Totschlagsklage."
3 Miller, *Bloodtaking*, p. 250.

 | DOI:10.1163/9789004712706_005

TABLE 2 Distinctions between theft and robbery in Frisian and Roman law

Frisian law	Roman law
Manifest theft (*epenbēr*) – theft caught in the act	*Furtum manifestum* – theft committed publicly or caught in the act
Non-manifest theft (*hēmelik*) – theft committed secretly	*Furtum non-manifestum* – theft committed secretly
Robbery (*rāf*) – taking away things openly; violence is not a necessary component Forceful robbery (*skākrāf*) – robbery using violence	Rapina – robbery always included violence

Consequently, theft was of great concern to Frisian society, and Frisian law texts include detailed regulations and procedures against thieves.

This chapter categorizes theft into manifest and non-manifest theft. Frisian society distinguished between acts committed openly (*epenbēr; eppe*) and acts committed secretly (*hēmelik*). The secret act was considered particularly reprehensible.[4] This chapter considers theft caught during the act as 'manifest'; theft committed in secret is called 'non-manifest'. These are similar to the terms used in Roman law: theft committed openly or caught in the act (*furtum manifestum*) and theft committed in secret (*furtum non-manifestum*). However, these distinctions are not congruent with those used in Frisian law and as such should not be equated.

According to Frisian law, theft was manifest only when a thief was caught during an act of taking something away without permission. This excluded circumstances when a thief took something away from another person openly and in public. Both cases, however, were included in the Roman legal definition of

4 This general distinction between open and secret wrongdoings is also expressed by the terms *eppe* and *yppe*; see Munske, "Angelsächsich-altfriesiche Beziehungen", p. 42. The Riustringer Codex mentions a manifest robbery (*aubere raf*), Buma, Ebel, *Das Rüstringer Recht*, p. 152. On the term *âubêr* see Munske, "Angelsächsich-altfriesiche Beziehungen", p. 42 f.

furtum manifestum. Frisians, by contrast, considered openly taking something away to be robbery (*rāf*). Robbery was not limited to cases where violence was used, unlike robbery (*rapina*) in Roman law.[5] The table above demonstrates these distinctions.[6]

1.1 *Literature on Theft in Frisia*

Historical research on theft and criminal law in Frisia during the Late Middle Ages is almost non-existent, with the only comprehensive examination having been conducted by Rudolf His and published as *Das Strafrecht der Friesen* in 1901. The work of His, a Swiss legal historian who studied the Medieval criminal law of the Germanic and Frankish periods, is defined by its detailed analysis of primary sources.[7] The result of his life's work was a book on Medieval German criminal law, *Das Straftrecht des deutschen Mittelalters* (1920).[8] Although his book *Das Strafrecht der Friesen* is over a century old, no other historian since then has attempted to investigate the criminal law of Frisia. Consequently, the assertions examined and scrutinized in this chapter are those of His.

To provide context and a contrast with specific facets of theft in Frisian law, comparisons are made with neighboring regions. Berents' 1976 examination of crimes in Medieval Utrecht provides a point of comparison with its neighbor in Frisia,[9] while Van Caenegem similarly explored criminal law in Flanders from the 11th to the 14th centuries.[10]

This chapter examines several aspects: 1) a distinction between petty and grand theft; 2) a further distinction between manifest and non-manifest theft; 3) the boundaries between theft and robbery; 4) the house search; 5) the obstruction of a house search; and 6) recidivism, and 7) presents some statistics from neighboring Utrecht regarding theft. While these statistics do not directly apply to Frisia, they provide some insight into the nature of theft in a neighboring region.[11] An overview of the relevant provisions of classical Frisian law mentioned in this chapter is provided in Table 6.

---

5 His, *Strafrecht*, p. 334 and Munske, *Der germanische Rechtswortschatz*, p. 169. More on this distinction later.

6 Later in the chapter, I explain my conclusions in detail and provide details of the sources supporting these conclusions.

7 According to Küper, "His, Rudolf", p. 248 f.

8 His, *Das Strafrecht des deutschen Mittelalters* I and II.

9 Berents, *Misdaad in de middeleeuwen.*

10 Caenegem, *Het strafrecht in Vlaanderen.*

11 Statistical research was done for the region of Medieval Utrecht by Berents, *Misdaad in de middeleeuwen*, pp. 84–85.

TABLE 6 Frisian provisions regarding theft, their age and where they appear in this chapter

Provision	*Age*	*Topic*
LexF 3.1	*8th/9th century*	*Manifest and non-manifest*
LexF 3.3		*Manifest and non-manifest*
LexF 3.4		*Manifest and non-manifest*
LexF 3.5		*Petty and grand theft*
LexF 3.6		*Petty and grand theft*
LexF 3.8		*Manifest and non-manifest*
LexF 5.1		*Manifest and non-manifest*
LexF 8.1		*Robbery and theft*
SkRa 66	*11th to 13th century*	*House searches*
SkRa 67		*House searches*
SkRa 68		*House searches*
We^{17} 5	*12th century*	*Manifest and non-manifest*
L^{24} 13	*11th century*	*Robbery and theft*
SkRb 29	*12th to 13th century*	*Manifest and non-manifest*
SkRb 30		*Lost and found*
Ska 5	*14th century*	*Robbery and theft*
WuPs 3	*14th century*	*Robbery and theft; House searches; Lost and found*

1.2 *Petty and Grand Theft—Distinctions regarding the Value of Stolen Goods*

A distinction between petty and grand theft (*kleiner und großer Diebstahl*) was a common characteristic of theft in the Medieval German territories. The difference between the two types of theft was based on the value of the stolen goods, and distinct punishments were applied accordingly.[12] The general punishment

12 'Diebstahl' in: Erler, et al, *Handwörterbuch zur deutschen Rechtsgeschichte*, p. 731. See also Eisenhardt, *Deutsche Rechtsgeschichte*, p. 77.

for theft was death by hanging.[13] However, this could be modified. Petty theft often resulted in less severe punishments, such as corporeal markings or monetary fines. In Flanders, petty theft went unpunished for first-time offenders who promised not to steal again in exchange for a lenient sentence. In contrast, grand theft in Flanders was punished with death.[14]

His argues that such a distinction was also present in Frisian law, namely *kleiner und großer Diebstahl*.[15] However, there is no instance in classical Frisian law that mentions the value of stolen goods or makes such a distinction between petty and grand theft. The *Lex Frisionum*, for example, merely states that if a slave is accused of theft, his master will swear an oath on his garment or on a relic if the stolen good was of great value.

> Lex Frisionum 3.5. Si servus furti reus esse dicatur, dominus eius in vestimento suo sacramentum pro illo perficiat.
>
> Lex Frisionum 3.6. Aut si res grandis erat, in reliquiis iuret; aut servum ad iudicium Dei in aqua ferventi examinet.
>
> Lex Frisionum 3.5. If a slave is being accused of being guilty of theft, his master will swear an oath on his garment.
>
> Lex Frisionum 3.6. Or, if it was something of great value, the master swears on the relics; or the slave is tested with an ordeal in boiling water.[16]

The *Lex Frisionum* states nothing about distinct punishments. His also argues that these provisions relate merely to the proof of innocence.[17] Consequently, the textual evidence for a distinction between petty and grand theft regarding punishments is not sufficient, but there may have been a distinction regarding what evidence had to be provided.

---

13 We can also find this in Caenegem, *Het strafrecht in Vlaanderen*, p. 121, and Berents, *Misdaad in de middeleeuwen*, p. 82.

14 Berents, *Misdaad in de middeleeuwen*, p. 82, and Caenegem, *Het strafrecht in Vlaanderen*, p. 122, respectively. In Flanders, banishment could also be a valid punishment instead of hanging. On the death penalty for grand theft in German law, see Eisenhardt, *Deutsche Rechtsgeschichte*, p. 77.

15 His, *Strafrecht*, p. 343.

16 Lex Frisionum 3.5–6.

17 His, *Strafrecht*, p. 343.

Physical punishments for theft were rare because Frisians could compensate their wrongdoings monetarily.[18] In Frisia, being found guilty of theft obligated the thief to 'compensate twice' and pay a fine to the authorities as described in the *Older Skelta Law* (SkRa 67) and the *Younger Skelta Law* (SkRb 35). Frisian law texts make no distinction between petty or grand theft regarding this compensation, as every thief had to compensate the value of the stolen good in the first place.

Thus, petty and grand theft could have referred only to the physical punishments that were applied if the thief failed to compensate the theft. However, there is no concrete evidence for such a distinction in Frisian law texts. It is possible that a distinction existed informally and was unwritten. Neighboring regions, however, did distinguish between petty and grand theft, making Frisia an outlier in this respect. Later sources from Westerlauwers Frisia, such as the city law of Sneek (1456), do mention petty and grand theft:[19]

> 137. Van stelen bouven een Vrancxse scilt.
> Item, soe wie dat stelt bouen een Vrancxsche schilt, die verboert zyn lyf [...][20]
>
> 137. About stealing more than a Frankish shield.
> Item, who steals something above a Frankish shield, has forfeited his life [...]

The death penalty was applied only if the stolen goods exceeded a certain value, but what happened if a thief stole less than a Frankish shield is not stated. These rules and other instances that mention a distinction between petty and grand theft are from the 15th century. It is interesting, therefore, to consider whether foreign law influenced these sources.

In conclusion, a distinction between petty and grand theft was possibly a later development, or such a distinction was simply not visible in classical texts. Until additional evidence is revealed, it is assumed, therefore, that punishments for theft applied regardless of stolen goods' value.

---

18 See the previous chapter on judicial punishments and *D*, VI (K[17]) 16, pp. 200–203. See also His, *Strafrecht*, p. 346.

19 A distinction is especially pronounced in the city books of Frisian cities such as Bolsward 1455 and Sneek 1456. Telting, *De Friesche Stadrechten*, p. 34f. and 105. See also His, *Strafrecht*, p. 343.

20 Telting, *De Friesche Stadrechten*, p. 105. For the same rule in Bolsward, see also Telting, *De Friesche Stadrechten*, p. 34f.

1.3 *Manifest and Non-manifest Theft—Catching a Thief during the Act*

His also argues for the presence of another distinction in Frisian law, namely *handhafter und nicht handhafter Diebstahl*, which was a common feature of Germanic laws.[21] Theft was considered *handhaft* if it was committed openly or thieves were caught in the act or with stolen goods in their hands. If a theft was investigated later and the thief was then tracked down, for example through a house search, the theft was considered *nicht handhaft*.

Roman law also knew a similar distinction (*furtum manifestum* and *nec manifestum*).[22] In fact, the English language has borrowed the terms used for theft in Roman law. Therefore, we will use manifest and non-manifest for both the Frisian and Roman distinctions.

As mentioned above, Frisian law distinguished between theft that a thief committed secretly (non-manifest) and theft in which the thief was caught during the act (manifest). However, this is not entirely congruent with *handhafter und nicht handhafter Diebstahl* in the German territories. In Frisian law, manifest theft included only cases in which a thief was caught in the act. This distinction is not explicitly made in the *Lex Frisionum* or in any of the traditional Frisian law texts, and Frisian legal sources mention no specific term for a thief caught in the act.[23] However, there are indications that specific rules applied to thieves caught in the act of stealing.

> Lex Frisionum 3.8. Si quis in furto deprehensus fuerit, et ab ipso qui eum deprehendit, furti arquatur et negaverit, iuret uterque solus, et ad examinationem ferventis aquae iudicio Dei probandus accedat; si ille qui fur esse dicitur fuerit convictus, componat weregildum suum ad partem regis, et manum LX solidis redimat, et in simplo furti compositionem exsolvat.

> Lex Frisionum 3.8. If someone is caught stealing, and is being accused of theft by the one who caught him, and he denies, then each of them swears alone, and they must be judged in an ordeal with boiling water; if the guilt

---

21 Regarding the presence of such a distinction in Frisian law, see His, *Strafrecht*, p. 345. See also Munske, *Der germanische Rechtswortschatz*, pp. 168–169. In German law, this is referred to as the *Handhafte Tat*, the manifest act. See 'Handhafte Tat' in: Erler, et al, *Handwörterbuch zur deutschen Rechtsgeschichte*, p. 1965; Munske, *Der germanische Rechtswortschatz*, p. 264f.

22 Kaser, *Das römische Privatrecht* II, p. 616. We will discuss this Roman distinction and *furtum* at a later point.

23 Munske, *Der germanische Rechtswortschatz*, p. 169.

> of the accused is proven, he pays his wergild to the king and redeems his hand with 60 solidi and pays the single fine for theft.[24]

Thieves who had been caught still participated in the Frisian legal process and could prove their innocence through an ordeal. However, there is no mention of compurgation or an oath of innocence. The *Lex Frisionum* (3.1) shows that someone accused of theft could generally prove their innocence by swearing an oath: *Si nobilis furtum quodlibet dicitur perpetrasse, et negare voluerit, cum quinque sacramentalibus iuret.* (Translation: "If a nobleman is accused of theft and he wants to deny this, then he swears with five oath-helpers.")[25] Similar provisions, but now for freemen, serfs and slaves, are recorded in LF 3.3–5. The absence of any mention of oath-helpers in the case of a thief caught in the act indicates that compurgation was forbidden. An oath was no longer trusted. Instead, the caught thief had to undergo an ordeal. There is thus demonstrable evidence of a distinction between a thief accused after the fact and a thief caught in the act.

That a thief caught in the act was not allowed to swear an oath of innocence is also evident in the *Exceptions to the Seventeen Statutes* (We^{17} 5). A thief who is caught at night and with stolen goods on their body is not allowed to plead innocence.

> We^{17} 5. Dat fyfta is: hweer so een man oderis gued stelt oen der neyltyuestera nacht binna dorem ende binna drompel endma oen him dat fynt oen syn handen, an sine boesme jefta an sine becke, so ne mey ma dera dede nene wyteed bieda, hwant di bondena tyaef ne mei nene schieldigra baria ende dis jechtiga ne mey ma naet bisecka.

> We^{17} 5. The fifth exception is: if someone steals someone else's goods in the dead of night, passing someone's doors and doorstep whilst doing so and if the stolen goods are found in the thief's hands, tucked in his clothes or strapped on his back, then one is not allowed to swear innocence on the holy relics for this act, because a thief who has been arrested cannot bring forward someone who is more guilty than he, and that which is evident cannot be denied in court.[26]

24 Lex Frisionum 3.8.
25 Lex Frisionum 3.1.
26 *D*, X (We^{17}) 5, pp. 254–255.

It is evident that Frisian law distinguished between manifest theft, where a thief was caught in the act, and non-manifest theft, which a thief committed secretly. Legal consequences for thieves caught in the act were a common feature of many laws in the Medieval German territories, and legal proceedings against such thieves were often a mere formality, leading to their execution. In these proceedings, only the victim was heard, and the verdict was read out publicly.[27]

The *Exceptions to the Seventeen Statutes* (We^{17} 5) provide an example of when oaths of innocence were not allowed, specifically in cases of notoriety.[28] There is no mention of whether the thief had to undergo an ordeal instead. The *Lex Frisionum* (3.8) suggests that an ordeal was the alternative when compurgation was forbidden. However, the last sentence in the *Exceptions to the Seventeen Statutes* (We^{17} 5) indicates that no proof of innocence could be provided at all. In that case, the procedure was a mere formality.

None of the provisions examined so far suggests a death penalty as a punishment. As was typical in Frisian law, the guilty party could compensate for their wrongdoing by paying monetary fines, such as a wergild.[29] The only mention of a death penalty in the *Younger Skelta Law* was presumably in situations where the thief could not or would not pay the fine.

> SkRb 29. Dat is riucht, als di tief finsen is endma him da schelta brinckt, jef him di hals urdeeld wirt, soe ne aegh di schelta dine tief hor hingia ner blinda. So aegh di bannere him to bynden ende to der galga leda. So aegh di man dyne ker hor hine selwa hwe, so hyt mit sine guede winne.

> SkRb 29. This is the law, if a thief has been caught and brought before the *skelta*, and if he is sentenced to death, then the *skelta* is not obligated to either hang the thief or blind him. Then the *bannere* has to bind him and lead him to the gallows. Then the claimant has the choice between hanging him himself and paying someone to do it for him.[30]

One further aspect of manifest theft related to killing a thief is worth noting. In Germanic law, thieves were considered outlawed (*friedlos*); as a result, the

27 'Handhafte Tat' in: Erler, et al, *Handwörterbuch zur deutschen Rechtsgeschichte*, p. 1969.
28 See also the previous chapter 2 on the oath in Frisian procedures.
29 His, *Strafrecht*, pp. 345–346. Called *havedlesene*; see chapter 2 on the judicial punishments.
30 *D*, XII (SkRb) 29, pp. 310–311.

victim of a crime could kill a thief without fear of punishment or fine.[31] His argues that this was also the case in Frisian law, citing the *Lex Frisionum* (5.1), which outlines the circumstances in which someone may be killed, including "[…] a thief, if he (is caught) in a ditch, where he attempts to dig out the house of another […]."[32]

This phrase is rather specific in that it refers to a thief digging a tunnel to break into someone's house and steal their goods. Siems, in his examination of the *Lex Frisionum*, closely analyzed this phrase and discovered that it originates from Exodus 22.2. From there, it made its way into ecclesiastical and Carolingian law and other Germanic laws, including Frisian, Anglo-Saxon and Thuringian.[33]

This provision demonstrates that a thief caught at night in the act of undermining another's house could be killed without incurring a fine. It seems, therefore, that His is correct. This rule was later included in other Frisian law texts, such as the Book of Emperor Rudolf:

> Rud 14. Hwer so dy fria Fresa dis jondis utgeet efter sonnaschyn ende eer sonnaopgongh ende to enis anderis huses geet ende dat inbreckt ende deer incrupt, wirt hi dan in da hole biginsen, so haet hi mitter insmuge syn fria hals urleren ende naet fora to biseken dan itta lioedware aldeer hi syn riucht ontfaen schil. Jef hi in dae hole slain wirt soe is syn hals urleren. Jef hi an dae flechtiga foet ende mit fatiende bernte biginsen wirt, alsodeen riucht. […]
>
> Rud 14. If a free Frisian goes out at night, after sunset and before dawn, and goes to someone else's house and breaks into it and crawls into it, and if he is then apprehended inside the hole he dug, he has lost his free neck because of this burglary, and he will not be permitted to plead not guilty at the court at which he will be tried. If he is killed inside the hole, he will have lost his legal status as a freeman. If he is caught red-handed while fleeing from the site, the same rule applies. […][34]

---

31 'Handhafte Tat' in: Erler, et al, *Handwörterbuch zur deutschen Rechtsgeschichte*, p. 1966. According to the Law of the XII Tables, a thief caught at night could be killed. Moreover, a thief caught during the day, and who defended themselves with weapons, could also be killed. This is mentioned in D. 9.2.4.1, but was no longer valid in late Antiquity.

32 Lex Frisionum 5.1: […] *et furem, si in fossa, qua domum alterius effodere conatur* […] On this, see His, *Strafrecht*, p. 345.

33 Siems, *Studien zur Lex Frisionum*, p. 332. Gerbenzon also comments on this study in Gerbenzon, "H. Siems", p. 173.

34 *D*, XVI (Rud) 14, pp. 392–393.

In summary, the principal distinction between non-manifest and manifest theft was the time at which a thief was apprehended. If a thief was apprehended after the theft had occurred—for example, through a house search—the theft was non-manifest. If, however, a thief was caught in the act, the theft was manifest. A thief caught in the act had limited ability to act in court. It is possible that the accused could still prove their innocence by ordeal, as in the *Lex Frisionum* (3.8). However, the *Exceptions to the Seventeen Statutes* (We^{17} 5) and the *Book of Emperor Rudolf* (Rud 14) forbid such a thief to deny guilt, and a thief caught in the act could also be killed without invoking a fine.

Note that manifest theft did not include theft in the open and in public according to Frisian law. For this we must consider the relationship between theft and robbery.

1.4 *Boundaries between Robbery and Theft*

In Medieval Flemish law, stealing in the open and publicly was considered robbery, while stealing in secret was considered theft. Violence was not required for robbery.[35] His argues that the same applied to Frisia, where robbery was defined as openly taking away someone's property, without any requirement for violence.[36] In Old Frisian, the term *thiāfthe* signifies theft, while *rāf* expresses robbery.[37]

Let us consider the sources in this regard. The *Lex Frisionum* contains a title called "De Notnumfti" (*Lex Frisionum* 8). *Nôtnunft* is defined as taking something away by force, or forceful robbery (*gewaltsamer Raub*). The term is not Old Frisian but Old High German. In the Early Middle Ages, *nôtnunft* expressed forceful robbery, whereas in later centuries it referred primarily to rape and kidnapping of women.[38]

---

35 Caenegem, *Het strafrecht in Vlaanderen*, pp. 120 and 124.

36 His, *Strafrecht*, p. 334.

37 'thiāfte' Hofmann, Popkema, *Altfriesisches Handwörterbuch*, p. 487 and 'rāf' Hofmann, Popkema, *Altfriesisches Handwörterbuch*, p. 393 f. For the different terms and the qualifications of theft and robbery in Old Frisian, see Munske, *Der germanische Rechtswortschatz*, pp. 168–174.

Note that the similar term *rán* in Icelandic law is understood to mean openly and forcefully taking something away. See Miller, *Bloodtaking*, pp. 77 and 326. Icelandic law makes the same distinction between open seizure, on the one hand, and secret and much more serious theft, on the other, even though the punishment for both was the same. On this, see Andersson, "The Thief", p. 497 ff. Miller defines robbery as a forceful act. Consequently, *rán* is not entirely congruent with *rāf*.

38 "nôtnunft". Müller, Benecke. *Mittelhochdeutsches Wörterbuch*, II/1, p. 372a. On the term see *nōtnumft* in connection with robbery in Munske, *Der germanische Rechtswortschatz*, p. 268.

> Lex Frisionum 8.1 Si quis rem quamlibet vi rapuerit, in duplum eam restituere compellatur, et pro freda solidos XII componat, hoc est XXXVI denarios.
>
> Lex Frisionum 8.1 If someone robs something with force, he must restore it twofold, and as peace money he pays 12 solidi, that is 36 denarii.

The existence of a title on forceful robbery (*notnumft*) in the *Lex Frisionum* indicates a distinction between violent and non-violent robbery. The latter is not mentioned anywhere else in the *Lex Frisionum*, and no further mention is made of theft committed in public. Consequently, it is plausible that the author understood robbery as pertaining to taking something openly (either by force or without), while theft was always performed in secret, albeit that the thief could be caught in the act, as we saw above.

The 14th-century text *On Forceful Robberies* (*scaeckraeff*) also details what constituted forceful robbery:

> Hyr biginnet da scaeckraeff
> Ska 1. Dit is een schaeckraef: hwa soe faert onbirades mit onriuchter wald to een standen hus ende deer binimpt da liodem hiara gued deer scholden hiara lyf aff feda ende da seel fan reda, soe brincht hi him self in dera schakera riucht mitta raef. Jef hi deerto bitinged wirt dat hi mitta fia beta schil, so schil hyt al twibeet beta ende dine ferd twifald, alst da liued wilkared habbet.
>
> Here begins 'On forceful robberies'
> Ska 1. This is a forceful robbery: if someone goes to a house without the consent of the court and by illegally using violence takes goods from the people that they need to support themselves and save their souls with, then through this robbery he commits a forceful robbery. If he is tried before court and is sentenced to compensate with money, then the compensation is twofold and he shall pay a twofold penalty for breaking the peace, as the people have determined.[39]

In this provision, using violence to take goods from people in their houses falls under the law of *scaeckraeff* (*skākrāf*).[40] The criminal act is called *raef*.

39 *D*, XIX (Ska) 1, pp. 426–427.

40 '*skākrāf*' Hofmann, Popkema, *Altfriesisches Handwörterbuch*, p. 431.

FIGURE 2 Explanation of the distinctions between robbery and theft in Frisian law

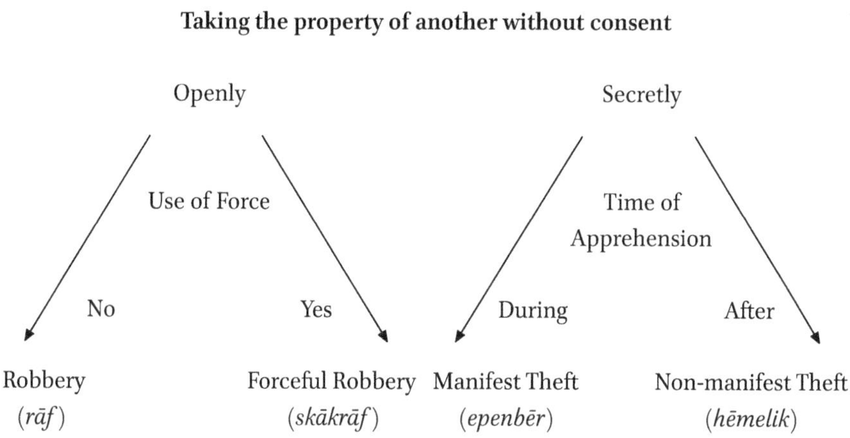

The other provisions of this text detail acts such as ship robbery and robbery of traveling persons. As such, various acts qualifying as violent robbery are mentioned.[41] The specific term of *skākrāf* proves that distinctions regarding robbery were made: *rāf* did not necessarily include violence because a qualification of violent robbery (*skākrāf*) existed.

In conclusion, these textual instances support the assertion of His: robbery (*rāf*) was defined as openly taking something away, regardless of whether violence was used.[42] Therefore, the term 'manifest theft' in relation to Frisian law can only be applied to cases where a thief was caught in the act.

1.5 *House Search*

One of the principal aspects of the Frisian law of theft was the 'house search'. If someone was suspected of having stolen a good, a search party was organized to look for the good in the suspect's house. These search parties followed certain rules and procedures. The concept of 'house search' was not unique to Frisian law; in fact, it was widely used in Europe, with different traditions and rules in different places, such as Denmark, Sweden, Bavaria and Burgundy. The terms used for a house search varied: Nordic laws expressed the house search

41 His asserts that the meaning of *schaeckraf* is lost here because different acts qualifying as robbery are listed. See His, *Strafrecht*, p. 339. However, since all include some form of violence or harm to a victim, we may assume that all these acts indeed pertain to *schaeckraf*.

42 See also Munske, *Der germanische Rechtswortschatz*, p. 268.

as *ransak* or *ransakan*,[43] Middle High German used *hûssuoche*[44] and the term in Medieval Flanders was *huuszoekinge*.[45]

The Frisian house search procedure is detailed in the *Older Skelta Law* (SkRa 66):

> Van tiuftiga gued toe sekan
> SkRa 66. Aldeer ma een man syn gued ofstelt ende hi mitta frana comt to sines bures huis ende deerin seka wil, so schil hi oerlef bidde ende dat gued naemna der hi seka wil. Jef hit soedeen gued se dat met moege oen der hand biluka jefta onder dae schaet bihiella, soe schil di frana ingaen ende saun dis koninges orkenen mit hem, al gripende eermen ende ongert ende onbroket ende berfoet, dat hia neen gued indraga moge deer hya mede schadigie da onschieldiga manne. Jef hia dat tiuftigade gued deerin fyndet, is hit wollen claed ende onfarwed, so moet hyt to sine oenwirke tiaen. Jef hit linnen is, so moet hyt to sine eckere tyaen, deer dat flax oen woex deer ma dat claed of makede. Soe schillet swara tweer synre buren dat hi alsodeen land heed deer dat flax oen woex jefta da scheep hede deer ma dae wolle of scheer. Jef hit wrocht gold is, so moet hyt to sine inwirke tyaen. Jef hit onwrocht is, so schil hyt toe sine warende tyaen jefta to da tolneda merked jefta to da fieldfarende manne.

> How to search for stolen goods
> SkRa 66. If a man's goods are stolen and he comes to his neighbor's house accompanied by the *frana* and wants to search it, he shall ask permission and name the goods he wishes to search for. If it is something that can be held in the hand or hidden under a coat, the *frana* and seven of the king's witnesses with him shall enter with open hands, ungirt, without breeches and barefoot, so that nothing can be carried in with which they might damage the innocent man. If they find the stolen goods inside, and if it is undyed woolen cloth, let him show that it is his own manufacture. If it is linen, let him show his farmland, on which the flax grew out of which the cloth was made. In that case two of his neighbors shall swear that he does own land on which flax grows or that he owns sheep of which the wool was shorn. If it is wrought gold, he must show that it is his own

43 Grimm, *Deutsche Rechts Alterthümer*, pp. 639–643. Schwerin, *Die Formen der Haussuchung*, pp. 5–8.

44 Munske, *Der germanische Rechtswortschatz*, p. 271.

45 As mentioned in Despars, *Cronijcke*, p. 271.

> manufacture. If it is unwrought gold, he must show that it came from his supplier, or the toll-market, or a traveling merchant.[46]

Many European traditions involved some sort of house search. Requirements for clothing to be worn during the search were common in Germanic laws. Norwegian law, for example, required the searcher to enter without trousers.[47] In Sweden, four searchers entered a house bareheaded and ungirded.[48] According to the *Older Skelta Law* (SkRa 66), the reduction of clothing was central because it prevented someone from bringing in any goods and thereby framing the owner of the house.[49] Another provision details what happened if stolen goods were found in the house:

> SkRa 67. Jef ma een gued binna enis mannes huse in synre camer bifaert ende deer een reeckhol in is ende hit soedeen gued se dat ma hit deerin werpa moge, so is hi nyer sexasum op da helligem to witen ende schaedloes dat gued wer to jaen dan hi tief aegh to wessen. Jef hit binna sine huse bidulven se, jefta dat ma hit fynt binna sine tredda slette, soe schil hi schieldich wessa jefta een schieldigra winna. Jef hy aeck neen schieldigra wint so schil hy dat gued eenschet ende dat oder wederjae ende da frana deer dat gued binna sine banne nimmen is dat wederjeld jaen ur al sine hinden deer jerich sint ende hi binna sine dorem haet. So is dat wederjeld iiii einsa ende fyoerteensta trimene penningh.

> SkRa 67. If a good is found in a man's room, and there is a chimney in it, and the good is so small it could have been thrown in, then the owner of the house has more rights to exonerate himself with five compurgators and return the good without having to compensate for it rather than be proclaimed a thief. If it is found buried in his house or locked behind three locks, then he shall be found guilty of theft or produce a guiltier person. If he is unable to do so, he shall return the good and give its value on top of

46 *D*, III (SkRa) 66, pp. 154–157.

47 Schwerin, *Die Formen der Haussuchung*, pp. 5–12.

48 As detailed in the 14th century *Magnus Erikssons landslag*, Þiuua balker, XII pr. See also Grimm, *Deutsche Rechts Alterthümer*, p. 640 and Schwerin, *Die Formen der Haussuchung*, p. 7.

49 Schwerin argues that this reasoning was used retroactively to explain the lack of clothes. He asserts that the requirement to be ungirded stemmed from an older tradition, where nudity was part of a magical ritual or ordeal supposed to counteract the magic of the secret act of theft. See Schwerin, *Die Formen der Haussuchung*, pp. 22 and 26.

> that, and he will pay a wergild for all adult members of his household to the *frana* within whose jurisdiction the good was stolen. And the wergild is 4 ounces and thirteen and a third pence.[50]

If small goods were found, the owner of the house could exonerate themself with the help of five compurgators and by returning the property. If the stolen object was buried or locked away, the owner was guilty of theft and obliged to pay 'compensation' and a 'fine' (these two terms were described in the previous chapter). To summarize: a guilty person had to compensate twofold for the theft and pay a fine to the authorities for disturbing the peace.

1.6 *Hindering Searches for Stolen Goods*

Regarding house searches, the *Older Skelta Law* (SkRa 68) also describes what happened in the event of a search party being hindered or obstructed. If the *frana* was resisted with force, and this was later denied, the *bannere* and seven witnesses had to testify. In this case, the person who resisted had to return the stolen goods and pay a fine.

> Van tiuftiga gueden to sekane
> SkRa 68. Jef di frana mitta lyoden een tiuftigada guede folget ende hi to enis mannes huus comt, soe aech hyt to bariane haet hi deer in seka wil. Jef ma him deer wert mit wighe ende mit wepen ende hy dat binaemde gued deer naet in seka moet, jef hi bisecka wil dat hi da seecknisse na ne werde, so schil dat bitiughe di bannere ende saun synre gaelioed. Als hit di bannere tiughet haet, soe schil hi dat gued jefta alsoe graet gued weerjaen ende da grewa twa pond.

> How to search for stolen goods
> SkRa 68. If the *frana* is tracing stolen goods with the people and he comes to a man's house, he shall declare what he wants to search for in that house. If he is resisted with force and weapons and he is unable to search for the goods, and if the party afterwards denies that they obstructed the search, the *bannere* and seven of his militia will testify to this. If the *bannere* has done so, the party who resisted will return the goods or an equal amount of money and pay two pounds to the count.[51]

---

50 *D*, III (SkRa) 67, pp. 156–157.
51 *D*, III (SkRa) 68, p. 158–159.

The seven who accompany the *frana* and the *bannere* were instrumental in ensuring that searches were done lawfully. Interestingly, the obligations arising after a person resisted a search do not match the obligations resulting from theft in the previous provision of the *Older Skelta Law* (SkRa 67). Those resisting a search have to return the goods once and pay a fine of two pounds to the count. This fine is considerably smaller than the wergild that a thief had to pay. These differences indicate that the two crimes were treated differently. It is plausible that the penalty for hindrance was separate from the penalty for theft. Those who obstructed a search had to compensate once and pay two pounds. If the stolen goods were subsequently found in their home, they had to pay the corresponding penalties for theft on top of the penalties for hindering a search party.

Another law text containing a provision regarding searches and obstruction of searches, and specifically hiding or preventing the recovery of stolen goods, is the *Statutes of Opstalsbam*:

> WuPs 3. Dio oder seeck is, dat ma alle stellen tingh, hoedeen gued hit se, aldeer ma hit fynt dae riuchta hand weder thi jaene sonder leesne ende hwa so dat gued jef di tieff onthalt mit wald, di schil dat gued wederjaen ende dae riuchterem XX merka. Fan rawe ende fan rawede guede schil ma aldusdeen gued riucht halda.

> WuPs 3. The second clause is, that all stolen things, whatever type of goods they may be, if they are found, are to be returned to the rightful owner without asking a price for it and if someone hides the goods or the thief and uses violence when they have been found, he must return the goods and give 20 marks to the judges. The same clause is to be applied in case of robbery and robbed goods.[52]

It is evident that the principle behind the penalty for hindering a search for stolen goods in the *Statutes of Opstalsbam* is consistent with the *Older Skelta Law*: return of the goods and a fine being paid to the magistrate. Despite different amounts of fines, the penalty for hindrance remains the same in various Frisian law texts.

Note the use of *weerjaen* and *wederjaen* (both meaning "to return") in these two texts, respectively. These terms are identical to those used to describe the obligations resulting from theft in the *Older Skelta Law* (SkRa 67). Due to the

52 *D*, XX (WuPs) 3, pp. 430–431.

unspecific use of Old Frisian terms, it is unclear whether the obligation resulting from hindering a search was only reipersecutory or also penal. However, it is most likely to have been a penal obligation rather than reipersecutory because, as explained earlier, the obligations resulting from theft were applied separately.

1.7 *Repeated Acts of Theft—Importance of Recidivism in Frisian Law*

The final assertion of His is that punishments for theft increased with the number of offenses committed. A thief convicted for the first time would receive a less severe punishment than a thief convicted for the second or third time.[53] Frisian sources from the 15th century provide examples of this pattern of punishment. The *Excerpta Legum* (Exc 280) contains a provision setting increasingly harsh penalties for repeat offenders. The first offense is punished by flogging, the second by branding, and the third by hanging.[54]

Additionally, the city regulations of Sneek and Bolsward reveal that juvenile offenders could receive a less severe punishment for theft, unless they already had a criminal record and were repeat offenders ("had a bad reputation before"):

> 137. Van stelen bouten een Vrancxse sculf.
> Item, soe wie dat stelt bouen een Vrancxsche schilt, die verboert zyn lyf, ten zy dat hy is beneden XVIII iaeren ende dat hy nyet eer quaedt geluydt gehadt en heeft. [...][55]
>
> 137. About stealing (something worth) more than a Frankish shield
> Item, who steals something above a Frankish shield, forfeits his life, except when he is under 18 years of age and has not had a bad reputation before. [...]

For comparison purposes, it should be noted that similar regulations existed for petty theft in Utrecht during the 15th century. For a first offense, a thief was punished by flogging, and if they were found guilty a second time, their ear was cut off as a permanent mark. The third offense was always punished by hang-

53 His, *Strafrecht*, p. 347.

54 Exc 280, as well as JF 60:13. The provision has its origins in the *Autentica Riocht* as Aut 6 and, before that, in the *Rechten ende Wilkoeren* as RW 67.

55 From the city regulations of Sneek 1456 as in Telting, *De Friesche Stadrechten*, p. 105. For the same rule in Bolsward (1455), see also Telting, *De Friesche Stadrechten*, p. 34 f. On this, see also His, *Strafrecht*, p. 347 f.

ing.[56] Another example can be found in Medieval Flemish law, where the first offense was not penalized. Instead, the thief had to promise not to steal again in exchange for a lenient sentence. If the thief stole a second time, the penalty was death.[57]

The available sources show that rules for cases of recidivism were a common feature in Frisian law of the 15th century and also in neighboring laws. It is unclear whether the practice of increasing punishments for repeated offenses was a result of the reception of foreign laws in the 14th or 15th centuries or if such penalties existed informally and outside the written sources of Frisian law that we know of.

1.8 *Statistical Information on Theft in the Medieval Low Countries*

Lastly, let us consider some statistical evidence regarding theft in Frisia. Unfortunately, due to a severe lack of records and primary sources, it is difficult to obtain information on how often theft occurred, what kind of people committed theft, and which goods were primarily stolen. Therefore, it is useful and necessary to extrapolate data from comparable areas to gain some insights into these characteristics. Utrecht in the 15th century is a suitable point of comparison since it was a neighboring region to Frisia and shared a rural, agrarian character. While the findings in Berents' comprehensive analysis of crimes in 15th century Utrecht cannot be transferred directly to Frisia, they offer some indications of the nature of theft.

First, Berents' examination revealed that approximately four out of every five thieves were men, while women accounted for a third of victims.[58] Second, regarding stolen goods, Berents argues that these were predominantly trivial household items and animals rather than money. This is unsurprising, considering the agrarian character of Utrecht.[59] By contrast, the *Older Skelta Law* (SkRa 66) mentions rather valuable goods, namely cloth, linen, and wrought and unwrought gold.[60] While Frisia was also an agrarian society, it is possible that valuable goods like gold and linen were stolen more often than in neighboring Utrecht, as the wearing of rich clothes and jewelry was common in Frisian clothing.[61]

---

56 Berents, *Misdaad in de middeleeuwen*, p. 83.
57 Caenegem, *Het strafrecht in Vlaanderen*, p. 123.
58 Berents, *Misdaad in de middeleeuwen*, p. 84.
59 Berents, *Misdaad in de middeleeuwen*, p. 84.
60 *D*, III (SkRa) 66, pp. 154–157.
61 On jewelry and clothing, see Hofmann, "Gold, Silver, Kleinodien" and Spiekhout, "De pracht".

Lastly, an examination of court cases by Berents showed that theft, robbery and fencing together constituted only around 6% of all criminal cases.[62] This low number indicates that theft was a topic of minor importance in the courts of Utrecht. If we assume that this was also the case in Frisia, we can conclude that theft was committed only rarely.

2 Theft in Roman Law—A Brief Overview

In Roman law, the term for theft was *furtum*, which was considered a delict (*delictum*) under private law (*ius privatum*). Roman law distinguished between laws pertaining to the state and public (*ius publicum*) and laws pertaining to individuals. Wrongdoings against the public were prosecuted in public procedure (*iudicium publicum*) and referred to as *crimina*.[63] Delicts, on the other hand, required individuals to bring a private action, which obligated a penalty to be paid to the claimant.[64]

Theft fell primarily under the category of delicts in Roman law, thus obligating the guilty person to pay a penalty to the claimant. However, some theft cases fell under the domain of the *ius publicum*, resulting in corporal punishment, capital punishment, or exile. For example, a theft committed during the night could be prosecuted by a magistrate.[65] Rules regarding *furtum* were quite comprehensive in Roman law, especially in contrast to Frisian law. The most significant information about *furtum* is summarized in the second volume of the handbook by Kaser, and all relevant rules are included in Inst. 4.1 and can be consulted there.[66]

62 Berents, *Misdaad in de middeleeuwen*, p. 85.

63 On *crimina* and public procedure, see D. 48 in its entirety.

64 On the distinction between *ius publicum* and *ius privatum*, see Kaser, *Das römische Privatrecht* II, p. 53 ff. and Ankum, *Elementen*, pp. 69–72. On crimes and delicts, see Kaser, *Das römische Privatrecht* II, p. 425 ff. See also Berger, *Encyclopedic dictionary*, pp. 418 and 430.

65 See in D. 47.2.57(56). For more on this, see Hallebeek, *Lijf ende Goedt*, 238, p. 191. Victims of theft could choose between accusing the thief themselves, or bringing the thief to a magistrate for a criminal charge. In the latter case, the victim could no longer claim a private penalty.

66 Rules regarding theft underwent some developments in Roman history. Some aspects were abandoned, while others remained. On *furtum* in the classical period, see Kaser, *Das römische Privatrecht* I, p. 614 ff. *Furtum* in the post-classical period is more relevant because this is what we can find in Inst. 4.1. On this, see Kaser, *Das römische Privatrecht* II, p. 433 ff. For a recent reference of Roman private law, see Babusiaux, et al., *Handbuch des Römischen Privatrechts*, § 93.

For a theft to be considered *furtum*, several factors had to be met, including taking something away on purpose, taking it for one's own profit, taking movable property that belongs to someone else, taking it in secret, and taking it without permission. *Furtum* also included concealing a thief or stolen goods, aiding a thief, fencing stolen goods, and misusing borrowed property (*furtum usus*). Additionally, taking away property of one's own that was in the possession of another person (as a pledge) was also considered theft and fell under the term *furtum possessionis*.[67]

2.1 Vindicatio *and* Condictio—*Recovery of Stolen Goods*

Roman law distinguished between penal and reipersecutory claims. The latter concerned the recovery of stolen goods or their value, and could be brought separately from the former. There were two options in the case of theft: first, the owner could sue for full restitution of the property. This reipersecutory action was called *rei vindicatio*. Second, if the stolen property was lost and restoration was not possible, the owner could claim the value of the stolen property through a *condictio furtiva*. The *condictio* was always for the simple value of the stolen goods. Both *condictio* and *vindicatio*, but only one of them, could be brought in addition to penal actions.[68]

2.2 Poena—*Penalty for Manifest and Non-manifest Theft*

An action for theft, *actio furti*, could be brought against a thief. This was a penal action, claiming a penalty (*poena*), and was separate from a reipersecutory action. Roman law also made a clear distinction between manifest and non-manifest theft. A *furtum manifestum* occurred when a thief was caught in the act of stealing or at the place of the theft.[69] It was punished with a fourfold penalty: *poena quadrupli*. Non-manifest theft (*furtum nec manifestum*), on the other hand, carried only a *poena dupli*, a twofold penalty. These penalties relate to the *actio furti* and were only penal, not reipersecutory.[70] The relationship between recovery and penalty is explained succinctly in Inst. 4.1.19:

> Inst. 4.1.19 Furti actio sive dupli sive quadrupli tantum ad poenae persecutionem pertinet: nam ipsius rei persecutionem extrinsecus habet dominus, quam aut vindicando aut condicendo potest auferre. sed vindicatio

---

67 Kaser, *Das römische Privatrecht* I, p. 615.

68 Kaser, *Das römische Privatrecht* II, p. 434. On *rei vindicatio*, see p. 292 ff. On *condictio*, see p. 421 ff.

69 Inst. 4.1.3.

70 Kaser, *Das römische Privatrecht* II, p. 434.

> quidem adversus possessorem est, sive fur ipse possidet sive alius quilibet: condictio autem adversus ipsum furem heredemve eius, licet non possideat, competit.
>
> Inst. 4.1.19 The action of theft, whether brought to recover double or quadruple, has no other object than the recovery of the penalty. For the owner has also a means to recover the thing itself, either by a *vindicatio* or a *condictio*. The former may be brought against the possessor, whether the thief or anyone else; the latter may be brought against the thief or the heir of the thief, although not in possession of the thing stolen.[71]

2.3 Rapina—*Robbery in Roman Law*

In Roman law, the crime of taking away by force was called *rapina*, which was equivalent to robbery. Unlike Frisian law, where *raf* did not require the use of violence, this crime always required violence. The *actio vi bonorum raptorum* was the legal action taken against the robber, and it obliged the latter to pay four times the value of the stolen goods if the action was raised within a year, and a single value after a year had elapsed.[72] From the post-classical period onwards, this action was not purely a penal action but became a mixed action. The term "fourfold" included a reipersecutory component, such that the *actio vi bonorum raptorum* obligated the robber to pay a threefold penalty and also to return the stolen goods.[73] Interestingly, a similar arrangement can be found in Frisian law in the form of *twischeet bota*, which required the offender to pay twofold compensation. This similarity between the *actio vi bonorum raptorum* and Frisian compensation should be taken into account when examining whether and how Roman rules regarding penalties were adopted into Frisian law.

2.4 *House Search in Roman Law*

Since the house search appears so prominently in the context of theft in Frisian law, it seems prudent also to examine it briefly in Roman law. This comparison is interesting, but not much more than that. Although there is

---

71 Sandars, *Institutes of Justinian*, p. 408.

72 Inst. 4.2pr: [...] *quae appellatur vi bonorum raptorum et est intra annum quadrupli, post annum simpli.* [...]

73 Inst. 4.2.pr, where is succinctly summarized: [...] *Quadruplum autem non totum poena est et extra poenam rei persecutio, sicut in actione furti manifesti diximus: sed in quadruplo inest et rei persecutio, ut poena tripli sit* [...]

Kaser, *Das römische Privatrecht* II, p. 435.

unlikely to be any connection between the two searches, both legal systems provided for some form of house search, suggesting that it was a common phenomenon.

By the time the *Corpus Iuris Civilis* came into being, house searches were no longer undertaken.[74] The obsolete rules are mentioned at the end of Inst. 4.1.4:

> Inst. 4.1.4. [...] Sed hae actiones, id est concepti et oblati et furti prohibiti nec non furti non exhibiti in desuetudinem abierunt. Cum enim requisitio rei furtivae hodie secundum veterem observationem non fit: merito ex consequentia etiam praefatae actiones ab usu communi recesserunt, cum manifestissimum est quod omnes qui scientes rem furtivam susceperint et celaverint, furti nec manifesti obnoxii sunt.

> Inst. 4.1.4. [...] But these actions *concepti, oblati, furti prohibiti*, and *furti non exhibiti*, have fallen into disuse. Nowadays, a search for stolen things is not performed according to the ancient practice, and therefore these actions have naturally ceased to be in use, as all who knowingly have received and concealed a thing stolen are liable to the *actio furti nec manifesti*.[75]

As this text shows, by the time of Justinian, Roman law no longer contained specific rules for house searches. In Justinian's *Institutes*, however, it is also noted that searches were no longer conducted "according to the ancient practice". Thus, Roman history had indeed once known the concept of a house search.

The term for the ancient house search was *quaestio lance et licio*. This practice is described by Gaius in his *Institutes*.[76] Gaius was a Roman jurist from the 2nd century AD, long after the *quaestio lance et licio* had fallen out of use. But while Frisians certainly had access to the *Institutes* of Justinian and the searches mentioned there, Gaius himself would not have been known at that time. A manuscript of Gaius' *Institutes* was only rediscovered in the 19th century.[77] As such, therefore, we can assume that Frisian jurists were not familiar with Gaius' particular explanations.

---

74 Kaser, *Das römische Privatrecht* II, p. 434 in footnote 17. For the rules in the classical era, see Kaser, *Das römische Privatrecht* I, pp. 616 and 158 ff.

75 Inst. 4.1.4, translation in Sandars, *Institutes of Justinian*, p. 401 f.: [...].

76 Gai. Inst. 4.192–194. Also in Kaser, *Das römische Privatrecht* I, p. 616.

77 Ledlie, "Gaius", p. 12.

According to Gaius, three things were required for a *quaestio*: that a searcher was nude (*nudus*); that he carried a thread or wore a belt (*licium*); and that he carried a bowl (*lanx*). However, some scholars argue that the *licium* and *lanx* were used for measuring, and that no nudity was required.[78] The confusion stems, instead, from the inability of later Roman jurists to comprehend the practice. Gaius's knowledge about house searches was not very accurate because these rules had disappeared in the second century BC and so were long obsolete by the time of Gaius.[79]

Following the *quaestio lance et licio*, a simpler house search developed that included the presence of witnesses. There were several actions for theft that involved house searches. We can find these actions in Inst. 4.1.4, although they had already fallen into disuse by the time the *Institutes* were composed. The *actio furti concepti*, which was applied when stolen things were found in the house, was an action for a threefold penalty. The *actio furti prohibiti* was applied for a fourfold penalty if a search was obstructed by the owner of the house.[80] Two things are noteworthy here. First, both actions are related to the same delict, namely *furtum*. Second, the penalties for these specific kinds of theft are different from the general concept of theft. As in traditional Frisian law, two distinct penalties applied: one for theft and one for obstructing a search.

In conclusion, Roman law before the second century BC had a similar system of house searches to that in traditional Frisian law. However, this is unlikely to have been related to the Frisian or other Germanic forms of house search as, while old Roman law and Frisian law share some characteristics in regard to the house search, they do not share a common tradition. At the same time, the concept of a house search was clearly present in multiple legal systems.

3 Theft in the Late Frisian Sources

Let us now consider what the Frisian sources of the 14th and 15th centuries say about theft. To this end, a brief overview of theft in these sources will be given, before we proceed to the specific obligations resulting from theft and house search, and how these topics were influenced by the learned law.

---

78 Flach, *Gesetze der frühen römischen Republik*, p. 177.
79 Von Schwerin, *Die Formen der Haussuchung*, pp. 11–12.
80 Kaser, *Das römische Privatrecht* I, p. 616.

3.1 *An Introduction to* Furtum *in the* Freeska Landriucht

In the *Freeska Landriucht*, the gloss *Twischet* to the *Older Skelta Law* (SkRa 67) consists of 1) an introduction to manifest and non-manifest theft in Roman private law; 2) a comparison of various punishments in different traditions; and 3) a short section detailing that the intention to commit theft does not make one a thief. For ease of analysis, the gloss is divided here into the same three parts.

> Glossa 47. *Twischet* Res furtiue in duplum sunt restituende, insti. de oblig. que ex maleficio nascuntur § Pena (*Inst.* 4.1.5) et loquitur de furto non manifesto, quia actio furti manifesti est quadrupli, ut in § predicto (*Inst.* 4.1.5). **Quare punitur manifestum magis quam occultum, cum clam facta magis sunt punienda**, ff. de amminist. tuto. l. Non estimo (*Dig.* 26.7.54)? **Sed ymmo magis delinquit qui palam quam qui clam ammouet**, ut Insti. de ui bono. rapto. in princi. (*Inst.* 4.2.pr.); unde magis punitur, ff. de offi. pret. l. Diuus (*Dig.* 1.18.14); concordat xiiii q.v Penale (C. 14 q.5 c.13). Et hec que dicta sunt ad pene persecutionem pertinent, Insti. de oblig. que ex maleficio nascuntur § ult. (*Inst.* 4.1.19[21]). Quia qui furatur, tenetur in quadruplum, cum ipsa re, secundum Accursium ibi.[81]
> [...]

> Gloss 47. *Twischet* (twofold) Things stolen have to be restored in twofold, see *Inst.* 4.1.5. And this text speaks about non-manifest theft, because the *actio furti manifesti* is for fourfold, as in the same text. **Why is manifest theft punished more severely than occult theft, since what is done secretly should be punished more severely?** see D. 26.7.54. **But on the other hand the one who takes something away openly, is misbehaving more seriously than the one who takes something away secretly**, see Inst. 4.2.pr.; hence he is punished more severely, see D. 1.18.14; this is in conformity with C. 14 q.5 c.13. And the things mentioned here refer to claiming the penalty, see *Inst.* 4.1.19(21). Because someone who steals something owes the fourfold value as well as the thing itself, according to Accursius to that text. [...][82]

This gloss relates primarily to obligations resulting from theft, as we can see from the lemma *Twischet* ('twofold compensation'). We limit our focus to the distinction between manifest and non-manifest theft, with the understanding

81 The gloss *condicendo* ad *Inst.* 4.1.19(21).

82 Gloss 47 ad *D*, III (SkRa) 67, pp. 156–159.

that obligations resulting from theft will be analyzed in a later section. The author of the gloss argues that manifest theft should be punished more severely than non-manifest theft, based on the Roman law tradition. However, it is not clear if this was also applicable to Frisian society, as the punishment for theft and robbery varied across different regions.[83] Generally, a thief caught in the act lost the ability to swear oaths, but taking away openly was usually punished less severely than theft. Moreover, Flemish, Islandic and Frisian laws regarded secrecy as more severe than openness.[84] Despite this, the author of gloss 47 intended to argue for the severity of punishment for manifest theft, citing two allegations. The first, *Inst.* 4.2, details penalties for robbery.

> Inst. 4.2 [...] sed in quadruplo inest et rei persecutio, ut poena tripli sit, sive comprehendatur raptor in ipso delicto sive non. ridiculum est enim levioris esse condicionis eum qui vi rapit quam qui clam amovet.
>
> Inst. 4.2 [...] for the recovery of the thing is included in the fourfold, so that the penalty is only of three times the value. And it is the same, whether the robber was or was not taken in the actual commission of the crime. For it would be ridiculous that a person who uses force should be treated more leniently than he who secretly removes a thing.[85]

This argument is not congruent with the one in the gloss (gloss 47 to SkRa 67): "But on the other hand the one who takes something away openly, is misbehaving more seriously than the one who takes something away secretly." Here manifest theft is considered worse than non-manifest theft. On the other hand, Roman law (Inst. 4.2pr) describes the use of force as more reprehensible than taking in secret. In other words, robbery is worse than non-manifest theft. Additionally, there is an allegation to Canon law that is congruent with the argument in the gloss:[86]

83 His, *Strafrecht*, p. 344.

84 Caenegem, *Het strafrecht in Vlaanderen*, p. 124. See also Miller, *Bloodtaking*, p. 250.

85 Translation by Sandars, *Institutes of Justinian*, p. 409.

86 There are two more allegations in this part. First, D. 26.7.54, which concerns tutorship and makes a distinction between a tutor who publicly becomes a debtor of their ward and one who secretly profits from them. This confirms that the secret deed is sometimes worse. It has otherwise no relationship to theft. Second, D. 1.18.14 concerns an insane man who killed his mother. If he did the deed during such a time of insanity, his sentence was to be more lenient than if he did it when of sound mind. It is not clear how this relates to the topic at hand.

> C. 14 q.5 c.13 Poenale est occulte auferre: multo maioris poena est visibiliter eripere. [...]

> C. 14 q.5 c.13 Taking away in secret is punishable; taking away openly is punished much more severely. [...]

The gloss explains that manifest theft is punished more severely than non-manifest theft, which contradicts traditional Frisian law. The author refers to both Roman and Canon law. The argument is justified by reasoning that open misbehavior is more serious than secret misbehavior, attempting to convince the reader through argumentative reasoning. One could easily have imagined only references to provisions of the *ius commune*, but this was not done. This approach is effective because it may convince readers who are unfamiliar or unconvinced by learned law.

That is not to say that the approach of reasoning is not found in the *ius commune*. Indeed, the structure of this argument is very typical for scholastic discussions. A proposition is given ("Why is manifest theft punished more severely than occult theft"), followed by an objection ("What is done secretly should be punished more severely? see D. 26.7.54") and a counterargument ("But on the other hand the one who takes something away openly, is misbehaving more seriously than the one who takes something away secretly; see *Inst.* 4.2.pr.") and a conclusion ("Hence he is punished more severely; see D. 1.18.14; this is in conformity with C. 14 q.5 c.13.").

The second and middle part of the gloss compare various punishments, including comparing corporeal punishments in Roman law and a Medieval Imperial constitution with the Roman fine of the *actio furti manifesti*. The former punishments concern *ius publicum* and were therefore applied to *crimina*. The latter is a private fine of *ius privatum*, theft being a delict and not a crime. Consequently, the gloss compares punishments in public law with fines in private law, with no indication of a preference being given. This part of the gloss consequently has merely a comparative function.

> Gloss 47 continues ...
> [...] Fur de iure autenticorum pro furto non suspenditur, nec occiditur nec membrum ei absciditur, sed aliter castigatur in auct. ut nulli iudic. § Furto (*Auth.* 9.9.13.1) [*Nov.* 134.13.1], sed antiquo iure ff. furca suspenditur ff. de pe. l. Capitalium § Famosos § Grassatores (*Dig.* 48.19.28.15 et 10). Sed secundum constitutionem Fredrici imperatoris, si quis quinque solidos ualens uel amplius furatus fuerit laqueo suspendatur, si minus scopis et forpice excorietur et tondatur, ut in lege Fredrici de pace tenenda uel

> tuenda in c. Si duo homines § Si quinque solidos (*LF* 2.27.18), sed secundum leges furtum manifestum est quadrupliciter restituendum, ut est Inst. ut supra (*Inst.* 4.1.5). […]
>
> […] According to the law of the Authenticum the thief is not hanged, neither killed or deprived of a limb, but chastised in a different way, see *Auth.* 9.9.13.1 (*Nov.* 134.13.1), but according to the ancient law of the Digest he is hanged on the gallows, see D. 48.19.28.15 and 10. But according to a constitution of Emperor Frederick, if someone has stolen something of a value of five *solidi* or more, he gets the rope, if not skinned and shaved with rods and tongs, as in *LF* 2.27.18, but according to Roman law something manifestly stolen has to be restored fourfold, as in *Inst.* 4.1.5. […][87]

The punishments mentioned in this passage range from corporal to monetary. Unlike Frisian law, Roman law did not allow for punishments to be reduced through compensation. Delictual remedies in private law were aimed at monetary fines and public prosecution through physical punishment. In Medieval Danish law, the line between punishment and compensation was blurred: in some cases of theft, a private claimant could choose between inflicting monetary or physical punishments, while in other cases both were part of the final sentence.[88] Consequently, physical and monetary punishment co-existed in various combinations. Nevertheless, gloss 47 provides a comparative view of these punishments without indicating a preference.

The third and final part of this gloss explains that individuals who intended only to commit theft cannot be punished by humans but by God alone:

> Gloss 47 continued …
> […] Item si propterea non facis furtum, quia timens ne uidearis, id est ne iudiceris, intus in corde fecisti reus furti. Teneris, quamuis inde nil tulisti. Teneris quo ad deum, non quo ad hominem, cum rem non tractaueris, ff. de acquiren. possess. (*Dig.* 41.2), quia solo animo furtum non committitur secundum leges ut ibi dicitur.
>
> […] Likewise, if you do not commit theft, but solely out of fear to be detected, i.e. to be sentenced, inside in your heart you have committed

87 Gloss 47 ad *D*, III (SkRa) 67, pp. 156–159.
88 Benham, "Law, language and crime", p. 153.

> theft. You will be held, although you did not take anything. You will be held towards God, not towards men, because you did not touch a thing, see D. 41.2, because according to Roman law one cannot commit theft by the mere intention, as is maintained there.[89]

The referenced text from the *Digest* (D. 41.2.3.18) confirms that theft cannot be committed by mere intent. However, it is not clear from the sources whether Frisian rules addressed mere intention to commit theft.

In conclusion, the function of this gloss is to compare the concepts of theft in Roman law with rules regarding theft in Frisian law. It legitimizes the Roman distinctions by using comprehensible reasoning and provides an overview of physical punishments primarily for the purpose of comparison. As such, we can see that Roman law was not applied in this case.

3.2 *Theft in the* Excerpta Legum

An unfortunate characteristic of the *Excerpta Legum* is that almost no structure is provided for the large collection of material. After collecting all the provisions dealing with theft, I therefore structured them under four topic headings—severity, recidivism, committing theft, and claims—so as to make it easier to examine them. A table is provided for the reader's convenience.

The first topic concerns the severity of theft. Theft is compared to perjury, murder and heresy. Moreover, thieves were limited in their legal capacity. Like a perjurer, a thief was forbidden to be a witness (*Exc 188, Exc 451*). Extrajudicial settlements, too, were forbidden in the case of theft (*Exc 320*), as in the case of murder.[90] Finally, divorce was possible if a spouse committed theft or converted to a heretical belief (*Exc 324, Exc 342*). Given that many of the same restrictions were placed on only the worst of criminals, the severity of theft is apparent. Some of these rules originated in *Thet Autentica Riocht* in the late 14th century.

Thet Autentica Riocht is also an integral source for a second topic, being that of repeated offenses (recidivism). A thief who had been caught before could no longer take an oath of innocence (*Exc 281*).[91] The first offense was punished by flogging, the second by branding, and the third by hanging (Exc 280).[92] This

89 Gloss 47 ad *D*, III (SkRa) 67, pp. 156–159.

90 See for this also the *Younger Skelta Law* (SkRb 28), which forbids thief and victim from coming to a private arrangement.

91 This has some similarities with the fifth exception to the Seventeen Statutes of the Frisian Land Law (We^{17} 5).

92 Very similar punishments existed in Utrecht in the 15th century; see Berents, *Misdaad in de middeleeuwen*, p. 83.

TABLE 7 Overview of relevant provisions in the Excerpta Legum: Selected provisions, the topics that their content is assigned to, their sources, and references to Roman and Canon law

			References to	
Provision	Topic	Source	Roman law	Canon law
Exc 62	3. Committing theft	*Informationes Iuris*	✓	
Exc 93	1. Severity	*Informationes Iuris*		
Exc 188	1. Severity	Arbitration Manual		✓
Exc 236	3. Committing theft	*Informationes Iuris*	✓	✓
Exc 237	4. Claims	*Informationes Iuris*		✓
Exc 238	4. Claims	*Informationes Iuris*	✓	✓
Exc 280	2. Recidivism	RW 67, Aut 6		
Exc 281	2. Recidivism	Aut 55		
Exc 282	4. Claims	Aut 11	✓	
Exc 284	2. Recidivism	Aut 65		
Exc 285	3. Committing theft	Aut 79		
Exc 286	4. Claims	Aut 80–81		
Exc 287	2. Recidivism	Aut 66		
Exc 320	1. Severity	Aut 53		
Exc 324	1. Severity	Aut 63		✓
Exc 342	1. Severity	Aut 63		✓
Exc 451	1. Severity	*Processus iudicii*		
Exc 528	2. Recidivism	*Informationes Iuris*		

topic also specifies how a thief is to be executed, namely that the victim has to hang the thief or pay someone to do so (*Exc 528*). Finally, a thief retained some rights even though the crime was considered exceptionally serious: for example, a thief caught in the act could not be killed without cause (*Exc 284*), while a thief who confessed could still receive the last rites (*Exc 287*).

The third topic consists of ways of committing and assisting theft. These rules were not found in traditional Frisian law. Exc 285 lists nine ways in which theft can be assisted, namely instigation, advice, consent, favor, participation, praise, silence, not preventing theft, and concealment. Exc 62, in turn, provides a general overview of the various ways to commit theft, including obstructing a search for stolen goods, using a borrowed good in a way other than intended, or denying possession of a stolen item and later confessing. A closer examination of this provision and the obstructing of searches follows later. Finally, Exc 236 describes a single possibility of committing theft: borrowing a good for longer than agreed.[93] In contrast to the first (severity) and second (recidivism) topics, these provisions refer primarily to Roman law. They provide a consistent framework and contain no contradictions. Both Exc 62 and Exc 236 originate from case records, thus indicating that Roman law was already present and received in arguments of legal practice.

The fourth topic deals with the claimant in a case of theft. The goods had to be returned to the victim before the thief could claim ownership (Exc 237). The provisions Exc 238 and Exc 282 concern the length of time during which stolen goods can be claimed. Interestingly, they contradict each other as the former (Exc 238) states that stolen goods can be claimed at any time without limitation, while the latter (Exc 282) argues that a claim can only be brought within 10 or 20 years. Finally, this theme also includes the right of claimants to steal back their stolen goods, and the right of servants to steal their wages from their masters (Exc 286).

Both the third and the fourth topics introduce areas of law related to theft that were previously absent. Their contents are more detailed than the arguments of *Thet Autentica Riocht*, and they refer more often to Roman law than to Canon law. Case records were often included in these provisions.

The influence of learned law is evident in all four topics and in most of the provisions on theft in the *Excerpta Legum*. On the one hand, the compilers could refer to *Thet Autentica Riocht* in questions that also had a moral aspect (severity and recidivism). However, *Thet Autentica Riocht* provided little material on the other topics. Instead, the compilers relied on arguments derived from legal practice. Reception took place through pre-existing mixed sources of Frisian and learned law, or through case records, with Roman law obviously being present and authoritative in the arguments presented in Romano-canonical procedures.

3.3 *Theft in the* Jurisprudentia Frisica

An entire title in the *Jurisprudentia Frisica* is devoted to the subject of theft, title 60 'de furtis'. It consists of 24 provisions and 22 glosses, eight of which provisions are copies of provisions of the *Excerpta Legum*. An examination of the glosses in title 60 shows that Roman law is referred to 30 times, while there are only eleven allegations to Canon law. This indicates that the Frisians turned to Roman law more often than to Canon law in matters of theft.

93 This provision includes both borrowing a thing for longer than agreed upon and using it differently than intended.

TABLE 8 Overview of relevant provisions within the Jurisprudentia Frisica, their sources, and whether Roman or Canon law is referenced

Provision *JF*	Description	Source	References to Roman law	References to Canon law
60:1	Penalties		✓	✓
60:2	Assistance		✓	✓
60:3	Assistance	Exc 285	✓	
60:4	Stolen Property		✓	
60:5				
60:6	Stolen Property			
60:7			✓	
60:8	Hiding stolen Goods			
60:9	House Search	SkRa 68, RW 170		
60:10	House Search	SkRa 67, RW 116		
Gloss 10*	House Search	Exc 62	✓	
60:11	Right to a last Rite	Exc 287	✓	✓
60:12	Killing a Thief	Exc 284		
60:13	Repeat Offense	Exc 280		
60:14		SkRb 28, Exc 320		
60:15	Stealing back	Exc 286		
60:16	Stealing back		✓	✓
60:17	Judge and Thief		✓	
60:18	No Oath of Innocence	Exc 281		
60:19	Starvation			✓
60:20	Wage Theft	Exc 286		
60:21	Theft by a Servant	SkRb 35, RW 137		
60:22	Ordeals			✓
60:23	Killing a Thief		✓	
60:24	Arson		✓	

The first provision of the title (JF 60:1) concerns penalties for theft. We will examine this provision in detail later.

The next two provisions concern assisting a thief. Such an act made the accomplice guilty of the same crime (JF 60:2). Nine ways to commit theft by assisting a thief are described (JF 60:3). As the latter is actually a copy from the *Excerpta Legum* (Exc 285), no further elaboration is necessary here.

Four provisions (JF 60:4 to 60:7) detail the relationship between the judge, the thief, and the stolen property, especially the property used to pay the fine.

There are also two traditional Frisian rules, originally from the *Older Skelta Law*, concerning house searches (JF 60:9 and 60:10). In both cases, the original contents of the rules were changed being included in the *Jurisprudentia Frisica* because the altered version already appears in the *Rechten ende Wilkoeren* (RW 170 and 116).[94] Although gloss 10 is thematically related to these provisions, its lemma does not refer to any part of the main text. The gloss is a copy from the *Excerpta Legum*, presumably added later. It has some relevance to house searches and the hiding of stolen goods, and this explains its placement with JF 60:8 through JF 60:10. More on these provisions later.

Several provisions are copied directly from the *Excerpta Legum* (JF 60:11 to 60:15). The changes in this respect are small and insignificant, indicating that they were considered acceptable. These provisions concern the severity of theft and its punishment, and include the right of a confessing thief to the last rites (JF 60:11), penalties for repeated offenses (JF 60:13), the right to steal back one's own property (JF 60:15), and discussion of the killing of a caught thief (JF 60:12). The latter is considered manslaughter if the thief could have been apprehended without violence. The *Lex Frisionum* (5.1) permitted killing without a fine being invoked. In this respect, there seems to have been a change. However, any further investigation of and insight into this question would go beyond the scope of this chapter.

Another provision (JF 60:16) allows the owner to steal back property from a thief without paying a penalty. This is a remarkable provision because it does not specify a condition for allowing the theft to go unpunished. It simply states that one may steal back one's own property.

In addition, a judge who lets a thief go is considered a thief (JF 60:17).

The next provision (JF 60:18) is copied from the *Excerpta Legum* (*Exc* 281) and states that thieves are forbidden to swear an oath of innocence if they have previously been punished for theft.

Two provisions specify the circumstances under which theft is permitted. First (JF 60:19), someone in danger of starvation may steal without committing a sin, but must pay for the stolen goods when able to do so. The act of stealing is not considered a sin, but nothing is said about worldly punishments. In addition, servants may steal wages that are owed to them by their masters (JF 60:20). This provision was copied from the *Excerpta Legum* (Exc 286).

Another provision (JF 60:21) applies to a servant who is involved in theft. It is explained that a servant who steals must compensate twofold and that his master must pay the value of the stolen goods to the court. The origins of this

94 See the table in Gerbenzon, *Excerpta Legum*, pp. 439 and 440.

provision lie in the *Younger Skelta Law* (SkRb 35) and are therefore traditional Frisian law, although the contents have been slightly modified. In the *Younger Skelta Law*, a master had to pay the servant's wergild to the *skelta* instead of the simple value of the stolen goods. This change to the rule appears to have been made sometime in the 14th century, as the *Rechten ende Wilkoeren* (RW 137) already contains the altered version.[95]

The following provision (JF 60:22) is rather curious. It concerns a thief who is found guilty. Interestingly, it mentions an ordeal involving a champion, a custom that was prohibited by that time. The text also mentions both *asega* and *skelta*, two officials who had already disappeared in the 13th century. In contrast to some of the previous provisions containing traditional Frisian law, such as JF 60:09 and 60:10, this provision was not altered at some point, but instead comprises classical Frisian law and so was probably an archaic leftover from an unknown source, which was copied without being changed or updated.[96]

Another provision (JF 60:23) states that killing a thief at night is permitted, with the caveat that the thief should first be prevented from committing the crime before lethal force can be used. This sentiment was already present in the *Excerpta Legum* (Exc 284). This provision corresponds well with another (JF 60:12), although they are not placed next to each other in the manuscript.

The last provision (JF 60:24) seems to be out of place. It specifies that arsonists and robbers are to be beheaded.

In summary, the *Jurisprudentia Frisica* is not merely a continuation of the *Excerpta Legum*, but instead a significant rearrangement and modification. Additionally, this title includes a considerable number of provisions from traditional Frisian law. These findings suggest that there was no linear reception of learned law, but that rules of both Frisian and learned law were altered. A comprehensive and detailed analysis of the obligations resulting from theft and house searches will provide additional insights into these interactions.

4 Obligations Resulting from Theft

4.1 *Twofold Compensation and Roman Law*

Let us return to the subject of 'compensation' in gloss 47 to the *Older Skelta Law* (SkRa 67), which we previously passed over. The gloss is supposed to comment

95 See the table in Gerbenzon, *Excerpta Legum*, p. 440.

96 See also Gerbenzon, "Aantekeningen (Tweede Deel)", p. 348, who dates this text to the early 13th century at the latest. On other archaic paragraphs in the *Jurisprudentia Frisica*, see Gerbenzon, "Aantekeningen (Tweede Deel)", pp. 342–350. On ordeals, see chapter 3.

on the Old Frisian term *twischet*, which we have translated as 'twofold compensation'. This term does not appear in the main text of the *Older Skelta Law*, as reproduced in the *Freeska Landriucht*; instead, the term *eenschet ende dat oder* is used. Since, however, the two terms are congruent, as explained in the previous chapter, this is not a problem. The gloss is likely to refer to an earlier edition of the *Older Skelta Law*.[97]

> Glossa 47. *Twischet* **Res furtiue in duplum sunt restituende**, Insti. de oblig. que ex maleficio nascuntur § Pena (*Inst.* 4.1.5) et loquitur de furto non manifesto, quia actio furti manifesti est quadrupli, ut in § predicto (*Inst.* 4.1.5). Quare punitur manifestum magis quam occultum, cum clam facta magis sunt punienda, ff. de amminist. tuto. l. Non estimo (*Dig.* 26.7.54)? Sed ymmo magis delinquit qui palam quam qui clam ammouet, ut Insti. de ui bono. rapto. in princi. (*Inst.* 4.2.pr.); unde magis punitur, ff. de offi. pret. l. Diuus (*Dig.* 1.18.14); concordat xiiii q.v Penale (C. 14 q.5 c.13). **Et hec que dicta sunt ad pene persecutionem pertinent**, Insti. de oblig. que ex maleficio nascuntur § ult. (*Inst.* 4.l.19[21]). Quia qui furatur, tenetur in quadruplum, cum ipsa re, secundum Accursium ibi.[98] […]

> Gloss 47. *Twischet* (twofold) **Things stolen have to be restored in twofold**, see *Inst.* 4.1.5. And this text speaks about non-manifest theft, because the *actio furti manifesti* is for fourfold, as in the same text. Why is manifest theft punished more severely than occult theft, since what is done secretly should be punished more severely? see D. 26.7.54. But on the other hand the one who takes something away openly, is misbehaving more seriously than the one who takes something away secretly, see Inst. 4.2.pr.; hence he is punished more severely, see D. 1.18.14; this is in conformity with C. 14 q.5 c.13. **And the things mentioned here refer to claiming the penalty**, see *Inst.* 4.1.19(21). Because someone who steals something owes the fourfold value as well as the thing itself, according to Accursius to that text. […][99]

The gloss being analyzed here relates to the connection between Frisian law and Roman law, and how they are linked. The gloss equates the Frisian term *twischet wederjaen* with the Latin term *in duplum restituende*, which refers

97 In contrast to the text of the *Older Skelta Law*, the Latin gloss was not likely to have been updated and therefore reflects an earlier or different version of the *Freeska Landriucht*. See Nijdam, et al., *Frisian Land Law*, p. 33f.

98 The gloss *condicendo* ad *Inst.* 4.1.19(21).

99 Gloss 47 ad *D*, III (SkRa) 67, pp. 156–159.

to Inst. 4.1.5, where it is stated that in the event of non-manifest theft, the twofold penalty can be claimed.[100] However, there are considerable differences between the two. The Frisian obligation is aimed at twofold compensation, which includes both reipersecutory and penal parts, while Inst. 4.1.5 deals with the fine that can be claimed through the *actio furti nec manifesti*, which has a purely penal nature.[101]

The gloss then goes on to link twofold restitution with non-manifest theft, while manifest theft and the corresponding *actio furti manifesti* are linked to the fourfold. This part of the gloss implies initially that the Roman text concerns some form of *restitutio*, but only in the second highlighted sentence, with references to Inst. 4.1.19(21) and to Accursius, is the link to *poena* made explicit.

An analysis of the reasoning in the gloss leads to the following. In a first step, the gloss equates a Frisian term with a similar Latin term: *twischet wederjaen* with *in duplum restituende*. Frisian law is thus written in the language of Roman law. This necessarily ignores the proper use of the term *restitutio*. In a second step, the gloss equates the same rule of Frisian law (rendered in Roman terms) with the correct term (*poena*). The latter part of the gloss could also be a later addition intended to correct the preceding suggestion that *twischet wederjaen* of Frisian law was congruent with the Roman fines of the twofold or fourfold, which is not the case.

The overall reception of Roman law in the Frisian law texts occurred through an artificially constructed connection between rather unspecific terms of Frisian law (*twischet*) and more specific terms of Roman law (first *restitutio*, then *poena*), which are only comparable to a limited extent. The 'twofold compensation' of Frisian law is still functionally different from the Roman penalties for theft.

4.2 *Obligations in the* Jurisprudentia Frisica

The distinction between manifest and non-manifest theft is also present in the *Jurisprudentia Frisica* (JF 60:1), where the thief is obliged to pay the fourfold in the former case and the twofold in the latter case.

---

100 Inst. 4.1.5. *Poena manifesti furti quadrupli est tam ex servi persona quam ex liberi, nec manifesti dupli.*

There is no mention of *compensatio* or *restitutio* here. Recovery of stolen goods was always separate and consisted of the simple value; see *condictio* or *vindicatio*. On theft in Roman law, see earlier in this chapter. See Kaser, *Das römische Privatrecht* II, p. 432 ff. and 592 ff., respectively.

101 We can find a similar arrangement in *Lex Frisionum* 3.2. There, *restituere* is also used in Latin. As, however, there is no explicit connection to Roman law, a literal translation of the Frisian terms may have been plausible.

> JF 60:1: Dyo tijeffta is twyrahanda Als hemelick ende openbeer. Openbeer is als een man bygripen wirth mitter deda inda loegh deer dijo tijeffte schijd ende dat schelma **fijower fald weer jaen.** Hemelick tijeffta is deer naet openbeer is dat schelma **dubeld weer jaen.**

> JF 60:1 There are two kinds of theft, namely covert and public. Public theft means that someone is caught in the act at the spot where the theft takes place, and it should be restored fourfold. Covert theft means that it is not public, and it should be restored twofold.[102]

The gloss to this text makes a connection to the Roman distinction between *furtum manifestum* and *furtum non manifestum*. This distinction is similar to the one in the Frisian main text (JF 60:1) as both involve the same obligation to pay the victim, namely the fourfold in the case of manifest theft and the twofold in the case of non-manifest theft.

> Glossa 1. Dijo tijefte is Item nota duo esse genera furtorum, Instit. de obligacionibus que ex maleficio (*Inst.* 4.1.3), concordat l.ii ff. eo. (*Dig.* 47.2.2), scilicet manifestum et non manifestum. Manifestum dicitur, ubi deprehenditur cum furto uel in loco, quo furtum fit. Et contra, ffurtum non manifestum dicitur omne illud, quod non est manifestum. Et **pena** furti manifesti quadruplum, que descendit de iure pretorio, Instit de perpetuis et temporalibus accionibus § i (*Inst.* 4.12.1), non manifesti ad duplum et descendit ex legibus xii tabularum, Instit de noxaliis § Sunt autem (*Inst.* 4.8.4). [...]

> Gloss 1. *Dijo tijefte is* Also note that there are two kinds of theft, see Inst. 4.1.3, confirmed by D. 47.2.2, namely manifest and non-manifest. Theft is called manifest, when one is caught with the stolen thing, or at the location where the theft took place. And on the other hand, theft is called non-manifest, when it is not manifest. And the **penalty** for manifest theft is the fourfold and has its origin in praetorian law, see Inst. 4.12.1, for non-manifest theft the twofold, which originates from the Law of the Twelve Tables, see Inst. 4.8.4. [...][103]

---

102 *Ro*, III (JF), tit. 60, no. 1.

103 *Ro*, III (JF), tit. 60, no. 1.

It is questionable, though, whether the Frisian rule here was equated in every respect with the Roman rule. As we saw above, the Frisian *openbeer/epenbēr* did not originally coincide with the Roman *furtum manifestum*. *Openbeer* meant caught in the act, whereas *furtum manifestum* was theft committed openly or caught with the stolen goods. This difference still seems to be present. The Frisian text speaks about *bygripen wirth mitter deda*, and the gloss about *ubi deprehenditur cum furto uel in loco*. Additionally, while the penalties for theft in Frisian law originally included restitution or monetary compensation for the loss (the *wederjaen* in SkRa 67), Roman law only imposed a fine for the stealing and had a separate remedy for recovery of the stolen good or its value (*rei vindicatio* or *condictio furtiva*). If the gloss were a further explanation of JF 60:1, this would imply that Frisian law was altered over time, that the remedies for *wederjaen* had become penal and that another reipersecutory remedy was available. Another possibility would be that the gloss did not interpret or explain the Frisian provision, but merely provided some comparison.

To determine whether a reipersecutory remedy was available in 15th-century Frisian law, we need to examine the *Jurisprudentia Frisica's* preceding title, "de restitutione spoliatorum" (JF 59). This deals with both petitory and possessory claims for the recovery of things taken away, with possessory remedies being more prevalent. In the case of a petitory claim, one should maintain legal entitlement to the thing. In the case of a possessory claim, one should maintain that factual possession of the thing was infringed. The most important of these remedies was the *actio spolii* or *condictio ex canone redintegranda*, based on the words *redintegranda sunt omnia expoliatis* in Gratian's decree.[104]

Moreover, a thief or robber claiming to be entitled to the possession was still required to restore it and then bring a petitory claim in court:

> JF 59:9 Hwamsoma syn gued ontraweth dat riucht is schyldich dat raeffgued weer in da riuchta hand to dryuuen sonder aller handa jen spreeck.

> JF 59:13 Hweerso een man een orem syn gued off winth onredelick off mit macht onthalt jnt arst so is hy deer by raweth is ner nymmen fan syner wegena schyldich to andryen eer hy da bysittinge fanda gued altomael weer haet.

104 C.3 q.1 c.1–4. The heading of the title 'de restitutione spoliatorum' (JF 59) is the same as in title X 2.13 of the *Liber Extra* and VI. 2.5 of the *Liber Sextus*, and seems to be strongly influenced by Canon law.

JF 59:9 If someone robs someone else's good, the court is obligated to return the robbed good to its rightful owner, without any objection/contradiction.

JF 59:13 When someone unreasonably (by court sentence) comes into possession of another person's good or takes possession (of it) by force, then first of all neither he who has been robbed, or anyone acting on his behalf, is obligated to defend himself before court before he has retained full possession of the good.[105]

What remains unclear is the relationship between the twofold and fourfold payments regarding stolen things in title JF 60 and the recovery of stolen things in title JF 59. Were these remedies competing or complementary? Although, unfortunately, the sources do not provide sufficient insight to answer this question, there seems to be some connection between the two titles in their arrangement in the manuscript. First, the recovery of stolen goods is dealt with (JF 59), and subsequently the possibility to claim the twofold or fourfold of their value (JF 60).

If the two remedies did not exclude each other, the remedies for the two- and fourfold (JF 60:1), which were originally aimed at restoring the goods and claiming a penalty, were now exclusively used for the penalty. That could explain why the gloss *dijo tijefte is* to JF 60:1 equated the Frisian remedies for the twofold and fourfold with the Roman *actio furti nec manifesti* and *actio furti manifesti*, since the Frisian remedies had also acquired an exclusively penal nature.

The use of the Old Frisian language is revealing in this case. The Roman penalties are written in the same manner and terms as compensation was in the Frisian law: *wederjaen*. The continued use of these terms implies a continuance of legal tradition. Consequently, a link between Frisian and Roman law is created, whether deliberately or unintentionally.

When comparing this relationship between Frisian and Roman law to the one present in *Freeska Landriucht* (gloss 47 to SkRa 67), we find almost a reversal. Gloss 47 attempted to connect and equate the Frisian twofold compensation with the Roman twofold penalty. To this end, the legal language of Roman law was altered to fit the Frisian terms, with a connection to the correct Roman term being created afterwards.

The *Jurisprudentia Frisica* (gloss 1 to JF 60:1) devised a new, hybrid rule: the distinction between manifest and non-manifest theft is still Frisian, although

105 *Ro*, III (JF), tit. 59, nos. 9 and 13.

it appears Roman. However, the obligations are evidently Roman and written in the vernacular language. Both the *Freeska Landriucht* and the *Jurisprudentia Frisica* aimed to connect Frisian and Roman law, implying congruency and continuation between the different legal traditions. However, the dynamics and relationships of power between them changed in the intervening period. By the end of the 15th century, the Old Frisian language was being utilized to express a concept of Roman law.

The similarities between Roman *furtum* and the classical Frisian rules regarding theft may have been a reason for this reception. Frisian law was familiar with private penalties for theft—even though they had reipersecutory elements—and was therefore not fundamentally different from Roman law. Ultimately, small differences between the two remained, namely the slightly different definitions of manifest theft.

Looking ahead to the 17th century, we can see an entirely different development. Delicts such as *actio ex lege Aquilia* lost their punitive nature and were transformed into reipersecutory offenses. Consequently, claimants were only able to demand compensation for damages.[106] This development contrast with the changes that occurred in the 15th century, when obligations resulting from theft became solely punitive. Further research may shed light on the reasons for these changes in the 17th century.

5 House Searches in the 14th and 15th Centuries

5.1 *The Gloss to the* Older Skelta Law *in the* Freeska Landriucht

One of the key features of legal proceedings related to theft was the search of a suspected thief's home. This search was crucial in determining whether or not the suspect had actually stolen something and, as such, it was an important aspect for learned jurists to consider when incorporating elements of Roman law into their own legal systems. Medieval jurists could not ignore the significance of the house search as it played a central role in these proceedings. To gain further insight into the topic, we can examine the glosses to the *Freeska Landriucht*, particularly gloss 48 to the *Older Skelta Law* (SkRa 68), which deals with obstruction of a house search.

> Glossa 48. Pena recusantis, qui negat inquisitionem rei furtiue. Ex presumptione iuris reus dicitur furti, Extra de presump. c. Nullus (X 2.23.4).

---

106 Lokin et al. *Roman-Frisian Law*, p. 206 ff. and 225 f.

> Gloss 48. As punishment for the obstinate one who opposes the search for the stolen thing. By presumption he is regarded culpable of stealing it, see X 2.23.4.[107]

According to the *Older Skelta Law* (SkRa 68), anyone who obstructs a search is required either to return the stolen goods or to provide an equivalent amount of money, and pay a fine of two pounds to the count. However, because the above gloss lacks a specific lemma, it remains unclear whether the "punishment" (*pena*) applies to the return of goods, to the fine, or to both. It is possible that the two pounds are intended as a type of fine, while the requirement to return the goods or pay an equivalent amount has a more punitive character.

It is important to note that obstructing a house search is viewed as a confession of guilt, with the individual who obstructed the search being presumed to be the thief. This presumption is based on a decretal from the *Liber Extra*, which considers obstruction of a house search to be an admission of hiding stolen items.

> X 2.23.4. Nullus dubitat, quod ita iudicium nocens subterfugit, quemadmodum ut absoluatur, qui est innocens quaerit. Confitetur enim de omnibus quisquis se subterfugere iudicium dilationibus putat.

> X 2.23.4. No-one doubts that just like a guilty person evades judgment, someone innocent seeks it in order to be absolved. Because the one who thinks he can evade judgment by delays, confesses to all charges.

The presumption of guilt for obstructing a house search functioned as justification for the penalty outlined in the main text (SkRa 68). Regardless of whether the individual was actually a thief, they were required to "return the goods or an equal amount of money and pay two pounds to the count." However, it appears that this presumption did not make one liable in the same way as when stolen goods were found in a house without a search having been obstructed. In such cases, the *Older Skelta Law* (SkRa 67) ruled that the inhabitant had to "return the property and give its value on top of that, and he will pay a wergild for all adult members of his household to the *frana*." There were, therefore, two distinct obligations.

It remains unclear how these two provisions relate to each other. It seems unlikely that resisting a house search would be more advantageous than allow-

107 *D*, III (SkRa) 68, pp. 158–159.

ing it, particularly if stolen goods were actually hidden in the house. There is no rational justification for such a difference between the obligations. It is more likely that both obligations could apply, one for the obstruction and one for the theft itself.

Alternatively, the above gloss and the presumption of guilt could imply a different approach. If an individual obstructing a house search is presumed to be a thief, then they are equally punishable and liable as a thief. This reasoning is not explicitly stated in the gloss to the *Older Skelta Law*, but it opens up the possibility of this idea, which would make the specific punishments outlined in the main text (SkRa 68) redundant.

5.2 *In the* Excerpta Legum

Surprisingly, the *Excerpta Legum* does not contain any explicit provision on house searches, despite their prominence in relation to theft. It is possible that traditional written laws and customs were deemed sufficient, and that further input from learned legal scholars was considered unnecessary. However, there is one provision in which obstruction of searches is mentioned:

> Exc 62. Jtem. Dit js riucht, dat ma thiefta bigaen mey mitta bisecken, want di heller ende di steller allike schildich sint, quia confessus in iure pro conuicto habetur: C. De confessis, I. una.
> Sed iste absque tormentis et uinculis negat se non habere tunicam, postea coram amicabili compositore confessus est, et quod talis confessio facit eum furem, hoc sic probatur, quia furtum committitur quando quis contrectat rem inuito domino, sed iste sic fecit, ergo etcetera; hoc probatur lnst. De obligacionibus que ex delicto nascuntur, quasi per totum. **Quia actio furti competit aduersus eum qui furtum querere testibus presentibus uolentem prohibuerit** et eciam furtiua apud se inuenta non exhibuit, sed iste primo negauit et postea coram iudice exhibuit, et sic commisit iste furtum, quia iste fuit creditor et quando creditor pignore in alium usum utatur furtum committit: lnst., eodem tytulo, § Itaque.[108]

> Exc 62. Item. This is the law, that one can commit theft through denial, because the fence and thief are equally guilty, because someone, who confessed in court, is considered sentenced, see C. 7.59.1.
> However, this person denies without torment and shackles to have the tunic. Subsequently, towards a friendly arbiter he has acknowledged to

108 *A*, I (Exc) 62, pp. 50–52.

> have it. That such an acknowledgment makes him a thief, is proven, because theft is committed, when someone takes hold of another's thing without the consent of the owner. However, this person did so, and thus etc. These things are proven in the entire title Inst. 4.1. **Because the claim for theft is granted against the one who impeded someone who wanted to search for a stolen good in the presence of witnesses**, and also was not willing to exhibit the stolen goods found with himself. But this person has first denied and later he has yet exhibited them to the judge, and thus he has committed theft, because he was a creditor and when a creditor uses the pledged thing for another purpose, he commits theft, see Inst. 4.1.6. i.m.

This provision, which originates from a case record, begins by stating the thesis that theft can also be committed by denial. The latter part of the gloss is written in Latin and provides supporting arguments and allegations. Something relevant for house searches is mentioned in the middle of the gloss: "Because the claim for theft (*actio furti*) is granted against the one who impeded someone who wanted to search for a stolen good in the presence of witnesses." This implies that anyone who obstructed a house search was considered just as liable as the thief themselves, and thus subject to the *actio furti*, which carried a twofold penalty. This penalty was more severe than the *Older Skelta Law* (SkRa 68), which only required the return of the goods or an equal amount of money, and a payment of two pounds to the count.

It is worth noting that, according to Roman law, the *actio furti* could be brought not only against the thief but also against anyone who assisted them, or similar persons. In the above provision (Exc 62), we see that this broad application of the *actio furti* was apparently received in Frisian law as well. Although Roman law was unfamiliar with house searches and individuals obstructing them, the *Excerpta Legum* (Exc 62) makes it clear that these persons belong to the same category as fences, those who confessed in court or to an arbiter, and pledgees who used the pledge for another purpose. As a result, someone who obstructs a search could be presumed equally guilty of theft. However, it should be noted that this provision is only a fragment of an argument in a court case, specifically a case concerning theft by denial. The main thesis of the provision mentions a fence, and thus it may not be applicable to cases of obstructing house searches.

5.3 *In the* Jurisprudentia Frisica

Of the 24 provisions in title 60 of the *Jurisprudentia Frisica*, only two pertain to house searches (JF 60:9 and JF 60:10). This suggests that house searches were less relevant for theft at the end of the 15th century. Moreover, these two provisions derive originally from the *Older Skelta Law*, but already appear in their altered form in the *Rechten ende Wilkoeren* (RW 170 and 116), which means that they were customary Frisian legal provisions that were modified in the 14th century. When these two sources are compared, it is evident that the practice of house searches underwent changes over time.

Van tiuftiga gueden to sekane SkRa 68. Jef di frana mitta lyoden een tiuftigada guede folget ende hi to enis mannes huus comt, soe aech hyt to bariane haet hi deer in seka wil. Jef ma him deer wert mit wighe ende mit wepen ende hy dat binaemde gued deer naet in seka moet, jef hi bisecka wil dat hi da seecknisse na ne werde, so schil dat bitiughe di bannere ende saun synre gaelioed. Als hit di bannere tiughet haet, soe schil hi dat gued jefta alsoe graet gued weerjaen ende da grewa twa pond.	JF 60:9 JEffter een man folget tiuftiget gued to enis mannis huus ende hy deer seecknis jn jared endma hym deer sekenisse werde myt wige ende myt wepen jeff myt wirden so is hy al schyldich to blijwen **Autentica**
How to search for stolen goods SkRa 68. If the *frana* is tracing stolen goods with the people and he comes to a man's house, he shall declare what he wants to search for in that house. If he is resisted with force and weapons and he is unable to search for the goods, and if the party afterwards denies that they obstructed the search, the *bannere* and seven of his militia will testify to this. If the *bannere* has done so, the party who resisted will return the goods or an equal amount of money and pay two pounds to the count.[109]	JF 60:9 If someone suspects that stolen property is in someone's house, and he wants to search there and this search is refused by fight and weapons or by words, then he (the owner of the house) is to be held guilty. **Autentica**[110]

---

109 *D*, III (SkRa) 68, pp. 158–159.
110 *Ro*, III (JF) tit. 60, no. 9.

Gerbenzon noted that this provision (JF 60:9) is present in *Rechte ende Wilkoeren* (RW 170) and is likely to have been copied from there, as indicated by the word *Autentica* at the end of the provision.[111] It also closely follows the *Older Skelta Law* (SkRa 68), suggesting its origin in traditional Frisian law. However, several details are missing in the 14th century version (RW 70) and the late 15th-century version (JF 60:9) of the provision. For instance, no person is specified to lead the search, neither *frana* nor *bannere*, and there is no mention of witnesses or punishment for obstruction. The owner of the house is merely labeled "guilty," but the crime they are guilty of is unspecified. This development from *Older Skelta Law* to the *Rechten ende Wilkoeren* and *Jurisprudentia Frisica* indicates an abandonment of the separate obligation for obstruction, likely influenced by Roman law.

Additionally, there is one gloss (gloss 10) relating to the *actio furti* and applying it to those who hinder searches: "[...] Because the claim for theft is granted against the one who impeded someone who wanted to search for the stolen good in the presence of witnesses [...]."[112] It is a direct copy from the *Excerpta Legum* (Exc 62), and an obstructionist was to be punished in the same way as a thief. The penalties for obstruction in the *Older Skelta Law* (SkRa 68) were no longer necessary in the *Jurisprudentia Frisica* (JF 60:9) as they had been replaced by the penalties of the *actio furti*.

Despite the growing influence of learned law, it is clear that the house search continued to be an important part of Frisian legal practice, probably due to its prominent role in legal procedure. As a result, seeking to entirely eliminate such a significant indigenous tradition would have been challenging, and legal scholars may not have been inclined to do so. Assuming that the *Jurisprudentia Frisica* reflects legal practice to some extent suggests that house searches were still being carried out at the end of the 15th century.

---

111 Gerbenzon, "Aantekeningen (Tweede Deel)", p. 341f.

112 Gloss 10 ad *Ro*, III (JF) tit. 60, no. 7: [...] *Quia actio furti competit aduersus eum, qui furtum querere testibus presentibus uolentem prohibuerit* [...]. The lemma in gloss 10 does not correspond to any text in title 60 of the JF. Instead, it contains some parts of the beginning of provision 62 of the Exc. The gloss was presumably copied from that source into the JF, without relating it to any other part. There are some minor differences that do not diverge in any significant way from how the gloss appears in the *Codex Aysma*. The transfer of this provision underlines that obstruction fell under the claim of theft. The lack of a relationship of the lemma, and the position on page 239 in the manuscript, where there is no provision dealing with any similar topic, indicates that it was added later, or that the previous point of reference was removed or moved. This arrangement shows that the *Jurisprudentia Frisica* in *Codex Roorda* was not finished in its conception, and that gloss 10 was presumably added later in the process.

However, the modifications made to the *Older Skelta Law* (SkRa 68) in the *Rechten ende Wilkoeren* (RW 170) and *Jurisprudentia Frisica* (JF 60:9) indicate that the practice of house searches was updated to align with the changing legal landscape at the end of the 14th century. Archaic officials, such as the *frana* and *bannere*, were removed and the provision was made more consistent with Roman law. Additionally, elements incompatible with other parts of learned law, such as the specific obligation resulting from obstruction, were eliminated. It is plausible that the intention behind these changes was to adapt the practice of house searches so that it could continue to exist within the framework of Roman law pertaining to theft.

A second provision (JF 60:10) detailing the rights of a person in whose house stolen goods were found also reveals how the practice of Frisian house searches was altered. If the goods were small and could have been brought in secretly, the owner of the house had a greater right to exonerate themselves than to be proclaimed guilty. However, this was not the case if the goods were hidden or locked behind doors. Although this provision (JF 60:10) is very similar to a text in the *Older Skelta Law* (SkRa 67), it omits the distinct penalties. Presumably the *Jurisprudentia Frisica* considered the remedies for theft to be applicable and thus that these did not need to be restated here.

SkRa 67. Jef ma een gued binna enis mannes huse in synre camer bifaert ende deer een reeckhol in is ende hit soedeen gued se dat ma hit deerin werpa moge, so is hi nyer sexasum op da helligem to witen ende schaedloes dat gued wer to jaen dan hi tief aegh to wessen. Jef hit binna sine huse bidulven se, jefta dat ma hit fynt binna sine tredda slette, soe schil hi schieldich wessa jefta een schieldigra winna. Jef hy aeck neen schieldigra wint so schil hy dat gued eenschet ende dat oder wederjae ende da frana deer dat gued binna sine banne nimmen is dat wederjeld jaen ur al sine hinden deer jerich sint ende hi binna sine dorem haet. So is dat wederjeld IIII einsa ende fyoerteensta trimene penningh.

JF 60:10 HWeersoma een gued fijnt bynna enis mannis huus ende hit alzo deen gued se datmet deer **onwytlick inbringa** mey So is hy **nyer synre sikeringa** dan hyna se ymmen to wrwinnen. hit ne se datmet fijnde in sloten bysletten jeffta onder da eerda bydolen inda kaueeren. so fijr so hya in seck wird se Sintse iechtich so schellet se schyldich blywe jeffta een schyldigra wynna **Autentica.**

(*cont.*)

SkRa 67. If a property is found in a man's room, and there is a chimney in it, and the property is **so small it could have been thrown in**, then the owner of the house has more rights to exonerate himself with five compurgators and return the property without having to compensate for it rather than be proclaimed a thief. If it is found buried in his house or locked behind three locks, then he shall be found guilty of theft or produce a guiltier person. If he is unable to do so, **he shall return the property and give its value on top of that**, and he will pay a wergild for all adult members of his household to the *frana* within whose jurisdiction the property was stolen. And the wergild is 4 ounces and thirteen and a third pence.[113]	JF 60:10 If property is found in someone's house, and if the property is of such nature, that it could have been **covertly brought into** the house, then he (the owner of the house) has a right to **exonerate himself rather than being pronounced guilty**, unless the property is found behind closed locks or buried in the soil of the room. This is valid if the defendants have denied. If they have confessed, they will be found guilty, unless they are able to point out someone who is more guilty. **Autentica.**[114]

Note the reference to the oath of innocence (*sikeringa*) in JF 60:10, which suggests that oaths continued to play a crucial role in Frisian procedural law. Although the specific punishments were removed, the house search was still part of a Frisian legal system in the late 15th century that received many foreign elements while also retaining Frisians elements.

Additionally, JF 60:10 has the signifier *Autentica* written at the end, hinting at its origin in the *Rechten ende Wilkoeren*:[115]

> RW 116. Van guet tho vynden
> Dyt ys recht soe we eenych guet vyndet bynnen ens mans husse ende dat also dane guet ys dat men aldar hemelycken jn brengen mach off moge soe ys he nare tho ontgan dan hem yemant tho verwynnen thensy datmen

113 *D*, III (SkRa) 67, pp. 156–157.

114 *Ro*, III (JF) tit. 60, no. 10.

115 As noted by Gerbenzon, "Aantekeningen (Tweede Deel)", p. 341f. However, it is not found in *Thet Autentica Riocht*.

> dat vyndet in sloten besloten off onder de erden begrauen jn kameren also ver als dee zaeke werdych ys so sullen see schuldych blyuen off eynen schuldygen tho maken.
>
> RW 116. About the finding of goods
> This is law: Who finds a good inside the house of a man, and it is a good that could be brought inside secretly, then the man [owner of the house] is more entitled to swear an oath of innocence than someone is entitled to declare him guilty. However, if the good is found hidden behind locks or underground in the rooms (in so far it is worth a lawsuit), then they [the inhabitants of the house] must be guilty, or accuse someone else of being guilty.

This provision is remarkably similar to the one from the *Jurisprudentia Frisica* (JF 60:10), which suggests that alterations to the house search had already been made by the end of the 14th century. The *Rechten ende Wilkoeren* was composed in Westerlauwers Frisia at the end of the 14th century.[116]

Evidently, the authors of the *Rechten ende Wilkoeren* (RW 170 and 116) and, by extension, the authors of the *Jurisprudentia Frisica* (JF 60:9 and 60:10) consulted and transferred the Frisian rules for house searches into a new text, and the alterations reveal what they discarded and retained. First, they removed distinct obligations resulting from theft or obstruction from the framework as these were no longer necessary. There was only one (penal) action that could be brought against both the thief and the person who obstructed a house search. The authors of the *Rechten ende Wilkoeren* and *Jurisprudentia Frisica* arguably altered the provisions regarding searches and obstruction of searches to align them with the rules of Roman law.

Second, neither the *Excerpta Legum* nor the *Jurisprudentia Frisica* mention how a house search had to be conducted. Presumably, the old rules, as in the *Older Skelta Law* (SkRa 66), continued to apply, although this is not certain. Regardless, house searches were still significant at the end of the 15th century.

We can compare this change to the house search in the 14th century to the remnant of ordeals mentioned in the *Jurisprudentia Frisica* (JF 60:21). This provision clearly contains archaic elements of Frisian law, such as the *skelta* and *asega*, and the judicial duel. The provisions pertaining to the house search (JF 60:09, RW 170 and 60:10, RW 116), on the other hand, contain no such elements and were apparently altered and updated to fit into the new legal system.

116 Meijering, Nijdam, '*Wat is Recht?*', p. 30.

This suggests that jurists harmonized the house search, while not attempting the same with the ordeal, which simply remained as an archaic remnant in the text. Therefore, their approaches to ordeals and house searches were fundamentally different.[117]

In conclusion, jurists around the end of the 14th century began modifying the traditional house search to fit it into a Frisian legal framework increasingly influenced by learned law. In doing so, they removed the specific obligation resulting from obstruction and replaced it with an action for theft (*actio furti*), which can be ascribed to the influence of Roman law. Despite this influence, however, the house search remained part of the Frisian legal system, and the way in which it was altered demonstrates an attempt to harmonize the traditional Frisian house search with a concept of theft primarily influenced by Roman law.

6 Conclusion

It is evident that, in the Late Middle Ages, Frisians adopted aspects of Roman and Canon law regarding theft. This was made possible by the similarities between Frisian and Roman law as both allowed for private penalties and differentiated between various forms of theft. The reception of Roman law occurred in the 14th and 15th centuries and resulted in various changes to Frisian law. Firstly, obligations resulting from theft became exclusively penal, whereas in classical Frisian law they were both penal and reipersecutory. Secondly, Frisian law adopted the Roman penalties of fourfold punishment for manifest theft and twofold punishment for non-manifest theft, despite the severity of secret acts in Frisian society. Thirdly, new ways of committing theft, such as assisting or hiding a thief, were included in written texts. Finally, all forms of theft were included under the claim of theft (*actio furti*), whereas classical Frisian law considered acts such as obstructing a house search as separate claims.

Despite the adoption of elements of learned law, certain aspects of Frisian law remained unchanged, such as the distinction between manifest and non-manifest theft, which remained distinctly Frisian. Manifest theft included only theft caught in the act and not theft committed openly, unlike in Roman law. But although Frisian law resisted aligning this distinction with the Roman one, the two were expressed in terms of each other, allowing for continuity. Additionally, the house search remained an integral aspect of legal procedure

117 On the ordeals in Frisian law, see Chapter 3.

regarding theft, but was modified to align with the new framework; for example, by removing the specific obligations resulting from obstructing a search party.

In the examination of primary sources, it was possible to observe one way in which reception was undertaken: 1) Frisian legal terms were compared with Roman legal terms; 2) These terms were equated, despite obvious differences; and 3) This equation of terms (such as *wederjaen* and *restitutio*) made it possible to receive Roman norms on *furtum* and create continuity between the old Frisian and new Roman rules. This 'clothing' of the latter in the terms and understanding of the former made reception and its acceptance possible.

In conclusion, the reception of elements of learned law in this field occurred in Frisian society primarily because of the similarities between Frisian and Roman law regarding theft. Frisians made their own choices about which elements to adopt and retain, thus creating a hybrid legal tradition that combined Frisian and Roman law and that retained traditional Frisian elements such as the house search because they were integral to the Frisian legal system. We can see some similarities in this respect with the retaining of oaths in the new Frisian legal procedure described in the previous chapter

CHAPTER 5

The Development of a Frisian Testament

In 1401, Clothus Bentha, a Frisian from Rawerderhem, left his property to three heirs:

> **Testament of Clothus Bentha** **1401 July 27/28**
> [...] In primis Sicconem Ydszarda, Tzalenghum Fethza et eius fratrum Poptatum, parochianos Popengwere, Rawerderhem et Solis, haeredes s instituo meorum omnium bonorum mobilium et immobilium, legatis et donationibus exceptis, in modum qui sequitur. [...][1]
>
> [...] In the first place, I institute Sicco Ydszarda, Tzalenghus Fethza and his brother Poptatus, parishioners of Popengwere [Poppingawier], Rawerderhem [Rauwerd] and Solis [Terzool], as heirs of all of my movable and immovable goods, legacies and donations excluded, in the following way. [...]

In this manner, Clothus ensured in his last will and testament that his goods would go to the people and institutions he intended to receive them. Verhoeven and Mol identified this document, in their comprehensive collection *Friese Testamenten tot 1550*, as the earliest surviving written testament from Westerlauwers Frisia. While Frisians may have made wills earlier, no evidence of such documents has survived. Traditional Frisian law made no provision for testaments, and succession was intestate. Consequently, Clothus' will is the earliest documented evidence of Frisians making written wills in Frisia. However, an earlier testament made by Syborch in Hamburg in 1376 demonstrates that Frisians outside of Frisia were already writing wills at an earlier date.[2]

1 *FT* 3, pp. 3–4, r. 36 and 1–3.

2 Verhoeven, Mol, *Friese Testamenten*, p. XVI. Some testaments written even earlier concern property being left to Frisian institutions and persons. See Verhoeven, Mol, *Friese Testamenten*, p. XVII and in footnote 25.

 | DOI:10.1163/9789004712706_006

1 Last Wills and Testaments

A testament, in the context of inheritance, refers to a stated desire for the distribution of one's property after death, and is also known as a will or last will. Historically, last wills and testaments were made both orally and in written form, and a testator had to follow specific formalities, depending on the legal framework, to make a valid testament. Other documents of distribution after death, such as codicils, required different formalities.[3] A detailed description of the Roman codicil follows later in this chapter.

Testaments are particularly useful as historical sources for a variety of legal and societal aspects and provide insights into cultural, religious, social and economic relations.[4] In the context of the reception of learned law in Frisia, testaments promise an additional avenue of examination: an interaction between different traditions of intestate and testamentary succession. Two traditions of making wills are relevant in this chapter, each with its own formal requirements for validity.

The first tradition was the will in conformity with Roman law, which was of a secular nature and intended to determine the ultimate destination of one's assets. The second tradition was the will made in conformity with the rules of Canon law, which was of an ecclesiastical nature and commonly concerned the salvation of the testator's soul.

Disputes concerning the execution of a testament could be brought before secular as well as ecclesiastical courts. In principle, secular courts could take note of the dispute, but some exceptions applied. The litigating parties could agree to bring the dispute before an ecclesiastical court, which could be competent to rule on those dispositions in the will that favored the Church. In some regions, such as in England, ecclesiastical courts were competent in inheritance cases on the basis of customary law. Ecclesiastical courts could also acquire competence if secular courts failed to do justice, i.e., a competence *ex defectu justitiae*.[5]

It is possible that the oldest testaments in Frisia were drafted in accordance with the requirements of Canon law and were primarily aimed at leaving certain assets to ecclesiastical and charitable institutions. However, the Medieval Frisian law texts handed down discuss rules concerning testaments considered

3 For an overview of the history of testaments in the Netherlands, see Meijers, Eggens, *Het Testament*.

4 Verhoeven, Mol, *Friese Testamenten*, pp. IX–X.

5 See X 2.2.11 and its glosses. See also Hannan, "Canon law of Wills", p. 528.

valid in a secular domain and enforceable in secular litigation. That does not exclude the possibility, though, that these rules had emerged from various legal traditions.

In addition to the old tradition of testaments according to the rules of Canon law, a Roman testamentary law was received. Consequently, competition and interaction existed between these two testamentary traditions (Roman and Canon). Investigation of the sources may reveal why testaments of a secular nature appear to have come to prevail, which Roman elements were received and which factors contributed to the reception of such elements.

Additionally, it should be noted that the making of wills could also be influenced by traditions of customary law. An example of such interaction is found in the Frankish kingdom of the 9th century, when Germanic legal concepts managed to change the way the Roman testament was constituted, and therefore also its contents, to create a hybrid testament.[6] Naturally, conclusions from a 9th-century Frankish context cannot simply be transferred into 15th-century Frisia. However, a hybrid form of last wills—containing elements of both legal traditions—is one possible result of an interaction between divergent legal traditions of testamentary succession. In this chapter, therefore, we explore whether such a hybridism also existed in Frisia.

1.1 *Primary Sources and Literature*

Verhoeven and Mol have collected all surviving Frisian testaments between 1400 and 1550.[7] In total, they found 212 documents: two from the end of the 14th century, 58 from the 15th century, and the remaining 152 from the first half of the 16th century. All 210 documents from the 15th and 16th century were made in Westerlauwers Frisia. They also include documents that can be classified as codicils in the sense of Roman law. Codicils instructed the heir to perform a specific act, and required five instead of seven witnesses.[8] Verhoeven and Mol state that all the documents are similar only insofar as they concern distribution of property after death, weather as a testament or a codicil.[9] Both men and women are testators, and presumably were of wealthy families who had

6 Spreckelmeyer, "Zur rechtlichen Funktion", pp. 112–113.

7 They assert that their collection is as complete as possible and that it is unlikely that earlier written wills existed, see Verhoeven, Mol, *Friese Testamenten*, p. XVIII. Although Verhoeven muses that the existence of earlier testaments is plausible. Verhoeven, "De beoorkonding", p. 13.

8 More on codicils later. On the codicil, see Kaser, *Das römische Privatrecht* II, p. 495 ff.

9 For information on the collected documents and some considerations, see Verhoeven, Mol, *Friese Testamenten*, pp. XIV–XVII.

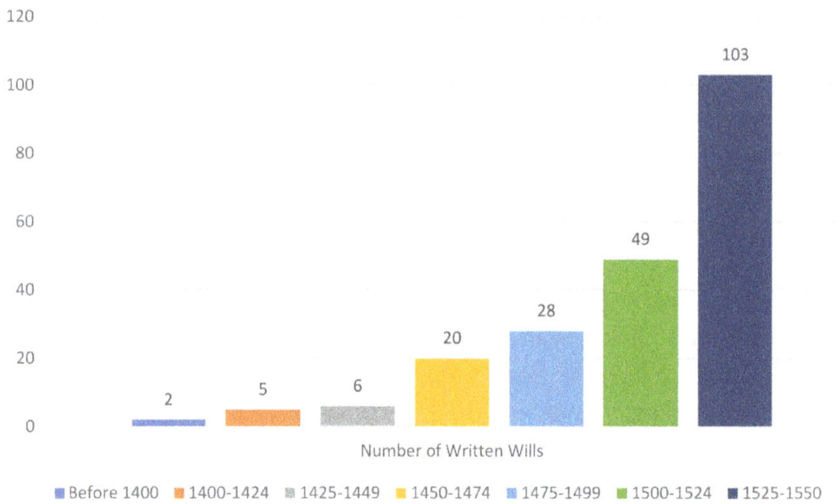

FIGURE 3 The number of preserved written wills over time, in periods of 25 years. All wills are from Westerlauwers Frisia except for the two from before 1400.

property to distribute. This is evident in the high number of testators from influential Frisian families, such as the Camminga and Camstra families.[10]

The chart above shows a sharp increase in Frisians making testaments during the late 15th and 16th centuries, assuming the surviving documents are representative of the actual number of testaments from that period.

These sources have aroused considerable interest among historians of Medieval Frisia. Not long after the publication of *Friese Testamenten tot 1550*, several scholars examined them and conducted further research on wills and succession in Frisia. Their contributions are collected in the volume *Zorgen voor Zekerheid*.[11] This provides valuable insights and information on the subject, ranging from the institution of heirs and the authentication of wills to how Frisians distributed money to pious causes and the Church. The insights of these scholars form an important basis for this study of reception. This chapter expands on their findings and contextualizes the changes and developments of Frisian law in the 15th century. By including late Medieval normative sources, we create an even larger and more complete picture of Frisian testamentary succession in the 15th century.

Additionally, research in neighboring regions offers the promise of gaining further insight into Westerlauwers Frisia. In East Frisia, testaments drawn up

10 To an extent that Verhoeven and Mol have included details of relationships between members of these families. Verhoeven, Mol, *Friese Testamenten*, pp. 485–543.

11 Mol, *Zorgen voor zekerheid*.

according to the rules of Canon law were the only valid forms of wills.[12] The question of whether this corresponds to or differs from Westerlauwers Frisia is therefore also considered in this chapter, with appropriate comparisons providing insights into the emergence of the testament in Frisia.[13]

This chapter explores testaments in Frisia and their development in the 15th century, particularly the formalities for making a will. Consider those to whom Clothus Bentha turned when making his last will. Requirements such as the ability to testate, the institution of an heir, the number of witnesses required to be present and the role of authenticating persons (priests or notaries) are examined to reveal why and how Frisians made testaments in the manner they did. This examination contributes to the overarching question about the reception of learned law in Frisia, specifically to when and the extent to which Roman law was received and applied, and to gaining an understanding of the possible reasons for reception in Frisia.

One source that sheds light on the ability to make a testament and the requirements applying is the gloss to the *Older Skelta Law* in the *Freeska Landriucht*:

> Glossa 41. *Ende di ora deel to goedes tyenst* Item libere apud eos qui uolunt sponte suscipere liberam habeant testandi facultatem, dummodo legittime testentur, C. de ino. testa. l. Si quando (*Cod.* 3.28.35) et nota de sacrosanctis et l. i. (*Cod.* 1.2.1).
>
> Gloss 41. *Ende di ora deel to goedes tyenst* Likewise, it is at the discretion of those who wish to do this by their own free will, that they have the free competence to make a last will and testament, as long as they do so in a legitimate way, see C. 3.28.35 and notice C. 1.2.1.[14]

This gloss raises a fundamental question: how was a testament legitimately made (*legittime testentur*)? The references to Roman law at the end of this gloss suggest that Roman law played a role in determining how a testament should be made. This chapter investigates this question in detail and explores its implications for the tradition of making wills according to Canon law. Additionally, it examines the interaction between the two testamentary traditions of learned law in Frisia. These questions are of particular interest for the reception

12 Buss, *Letztwillige Verfügungen*, p. 50.

13 See, for example, the comprehensive study of the emergence of the testament in Utrecht in: Cappon, *De Opkomst van het Testament in het Sticht Utrecht*.

14 Gloss 41 ad *D*, III (SkRa) 52, pp. 146–149.

of learned law as they shed light on the ways in which testaments were made and how the requirements and formalities of a testament developed during the 15th century.

2 Succession in Frisian Law and Customs

Classical Frisian law, like other Germanic laws, was not familiar with testaments providing for succession and the distribution of the testator's assets. All goods and lands were inherited intestate. Like many Germanic laws, the Frisian law of intestate succession was customary and not anchored in legislation.[15] In general, the closest relatives of the deceased inherited. These included the mother, father, sister, brother, daughter and son of the deceased (known as the 'six-hands').

> L^{24} 16. Dat xviste landriucht is: so hwer so lawa lawiget wirdet utoer sex handen ende deer is nen fader ner moder, broder ner suster, bern ner bernsbern, dat hetet onween lawa. Soe hwa so deer dan sibst to is, di nime da lawa. Jef dat aeck ne se, so dele da oder frionden al like deer hia lyc sib se ende di aesga nime deer of deer hi fander deelscip aeg: een penningh fan allerlikes hand.

> L^{24} 16. The 16th land law is: if an inheritance falls outside the six-hands and there is no father nor mother, brother nor sister, children nor grandchildren, then this is called an unhoped-for inheritance. Whoever is closest related to the deceased then, shall take the inheritance. If there is none, then all relatives shall have an equal share according to their degree of relatedness and the *asega* shall take the fee he is entitled to for the partitioning: one penny from each party.[16]

Although the six-hands included both daughters and sons, the text (L^{24} 16) refers to "children" in general and also extends the category to grandchildren. Unfortunately, the text does not specify how the six-hands would inherit, as it concerned a case of succession by heirs not belonging to the six-hands. It is likely that the rules concerning succession by the six-hands were never recorded, and were simply customary law. The only principle mentioned in the

15 Meyers, "Het Friese erfecht", p. 54.
16 *D*, VIII (L^{24}) 16, pp. 234–235.

text (L^{24}) regarding this succession is that "Whoever is closest related (*sibst*) to the deceased then, shall take the inheritance (*lawa*)."

According to secondary literature, sons inherited equally from the family goods, while daughters received only half of what a son obtained.[17] Traditionally, the oldest son received the familial home so that he could continue living in it, while daughters did not inherit once they had moved out of the parental home and received a dowry.[18] This is clearly stated in the Fivelgoer Law, which concerns the four promises that are made to a bride.

> fon frowm.
> Fro 3. Sa hwersa ma ene frowa vtjeft, sa racht ma hire fior wed. [...] Thet thredde, thet se vrweddade th ene becfeng anda lawm, and sa weddade hire hir feder wither tha bedlinze alle hredde.[19]

> Concerning women
> Fro 3. When one gives a woman into marriage, one has to provide four promises. [...] The third is that she renounces her claim of the parental inheritance and her father definitively guarantees her again the dowry.

In this manner, inheritance in Frisia took place by intestate succession. It should be noted, however, that even after the introduction of testaments, most cases of inheritance were probably still intestate. The low number of surviving last wills from the 15th century supports this assumption.

3 The Medieval Testament

3.1 *Roman* testamentum

The Roman testament (*testamentum*) served as the basis for Medieval wills, taking various shapes over time. One such form was the testament of Canon law, which evolved from the *testamentum* over the centuries. The Roman testament was codified in the laws of Justinian (*Corpus Iuris Civilis*) and is encountered

17 Algra, *Oudfries Recht*, pp. 355–356; Meyers, "Het Friese Erfrecht", p. 58ff.; Noomen, "Consolidatie", p. 77. The literature refers to the Inheritance Law of Fivelgo and Hunsingo in Richthofen, *Friesische Rechtsquellen*, p. 324f. I am not certain whether this source alone suffices to make accurate claims about the inheritance of sons and daughters in Westerlauwers Frisia. More research is needed.

18 Algra, Oudfries Recht, p. 352.

19 *F*, XIV (Fro) 3, p. 152.

in the Frisian sources. One of the principles was that testamentary succession excluded intestate succession (*ab intestato*), meaning that a will always took priority over succession by heirs-at-law.[20]

Roman law required several formalities for a testament to be valid.[21] First, testacy was obtained when reaching puberty (*pubertas*), which was at the age of twelve for girls and fourteen for boys. Second, the right to testate had to be intact, meaning it could not have been revoked because of an individual having committed a crime, for example. Third, a testator had to be of sound mind, and neither deaf nor mute, when making their last will.[22] All these requirements pertained to the testator.

Another crucial formal condition was that an heir had to be instituted (*heredis institutio*). A testament drawn up without instituting an heir was not valid.[23] The primary function of a will was to secure succession, and so if someone wanted to disinherit or substitute an heir-at-law, they had to name that heir specifically. This applied only to descendants; an heir-at-law who was not a child or grandchild did not have to be mentioned in the testament.[24] However, children could not be completely disinherited without a sound reason. They were entitled to a share of a third or half of the inheritance, which was known as the legitimate portion (*portio legitima*). This also limited the possibility of bequeathing to the Church and charitable ends.[25] Instituting an heir required clear and intentional words, but no specific arrangement of words or sentences.[26]

For a will to be valid, seven witnesses had to be present.[27] Alternatively, a *testamentum* could be made orally (*per nuncupationem*), in which case seven witnesses had to be present. Other forms of distributing property after death also existed, such as the codicil (*codicillus*). The primary difference between a testament and a codicil was the number of witnesses: a codicil required only five witnesses. A second difference was that a codicil did not institute an heir,

---

20 D. 50.17.7.

21 For details of these formalities, see Kaser, *Das römische Privatrecht* II, p. 477 ff. See also Rüfner, "Testamentary Formalities" and Rüfner, "Substance", p. 320.

22 *Inst.* 2.12. On these requirements, see also Mousourakis, *Fundamentals*, p. 287.

23 *Inst.* 2.13. pr. See also Kaser, *Das römische Privatrecht* II, p. 490 ff., and Johnston, *Roman Law*, p. 202. The institution of an heir is seen as the core and foundation of the testament (*Inst.* 2.20.34). As a principal rule, every testament should start with such institution (D. 28.5.1).

24 *Inst.* 2.13.1 and in Johnston, *Roman Law*, p. 202.

25 *Nov.* 18 and *Nov.* 115.

26 Mousourakis, *Fundamentals*, p. 289; Kaser, *Das römische Privatrecht* II, p. 491 f.

27 C. 6.23.21. On the Roman testament, see Kaser, *Das römische Privatrecht* II, pp. 477–482.

but contained only *fideicommissa* (i.e., requests to the heir or legatee to perform certain acts).[28]

In the Western half of the Roman Empire, testaments and codicils gradually blended over time: instituting an heir was no longer prohibited in a codicil and, conversely, no longer required in a testament. As a result, the instituting of heirs was entirely absent in early Medieval testaments in the Frankish kingdom. In the East, however, Roman law retained these strict distinctions.[29] A written clause also enabled a testament to be treated as a codicil if it was deemed invalid as a testament. Such a *Kodizillarklausel* was necessary because an invalid testament could not be considered a codicil by implication alone.[30]

3.2 *Canonical Last Will*

Wills under Canon law were made from at least the 9th century onwards in Western Europe. They were drawn up according to the precepts of Canon law and fell under the jurisdiction of ecclesiastical courts, especially when they contained bequests for the Church or charitable institutions. With the Christianization of Frisia in the 8th and 9th centuries, these institutions and the making of wills also appeared in Frisia, with members of the clergy usually present for the drawing up of last wills.[31] As previously mentioned, the Canon law testamentary tradition preceded the emergence of secular testaments and secular jurisdiction in hereditary disputes in the 15th century.

The ecclesiastical precepts for drawing up a testament differed from the Roman rules. It was first and foremost a spiritual and religious act, not a means to direct succession. A central part of religious life was to give alms, often at the end of one's life or even on the deathbed. The dying were expected to leave part of their property to charitable institutions and the Church in a *donatio pro anima*. In this manner, they hoped to gain salvation, with the amount of this donation varying from a modest gift to the entirety of one's property, as long as the *portio legitima* of the children was observed.[32] These donations were the primary purpose of such a will, which is also apparent from their position in the documents: placed right at the beginning, with any distribution of property to family members and so on coming afterwards.[33]

---

28 *Inst.* 2.25. On the codicil, see Kaser, *Das römische Privatrecht* II, p. 495 ff.

29 Kaser, *Das römische Privatrecht* II, p. 490.

30 Kaser, *Das römische Privatrecht* II, p. 497.

31 Hannan, "Canon law of Wills", p. 528.

32 On the *portio legitima*, see Hallebeek, "Dispositions".

33 Epstein, *Wills and Wealth*, pp. 6 and 136–137.

Since most donations were given to the Church or its charitable institutions, clergy and ecclesiastical institutions had a strong interest in enabling people to make wills. At the same time, they endeavored to control how testaments were made. To increase the number of people donating *pro anima*, the Church wanted to make drawing up a testament easy. The formalities of Canon law for a last will were much simpler than those in Roman law.[34] Instituting an heir was no longer required and two witnesses sufficed for attestation. Aside from these two witnesses, a priest was present to authenticate the will.[35] This simplicity greatly contributed to the spread of testaments.

After the revival of Roman law, requirements for a valid testament were discussed by learned jurists. In the 12th century, Pope Alexander III (1100/1105–1181) argued that the stricter formalities of Roman law were not necessary and issued a decree stating that two witnesses and a priest sufficed (X 3.26.10).[36] Canonists subsequently debated which form was valid. Some argued that two witnesses and a priest were adequate only for charitable disposals, while others argued that they sufficed for all forms of the testament. Pope Alexander III asserted that charitable disposals did not require the presence of a priest (X 3.26.11).[37] Different regions came to different conclusions on this debate: in England, for example, the simple Canon law form prevailed without much discussion.[38] The influence of the last will according to Canon law in Frisia and the conclusions reached by Frisian jurists are discussed below.

4 Last Wills in Frisian Law before 1400

Frisians had two main reasons for making wills or will-like acts. Firstly, they were interested in providing for their own salvation by making donations to charitable institutions. Secondly, they wanted to organize succession and distribute property according to their own wishes.[39]

Wills or will-like acts are documented in Frisian sources from the 13th century onwards, including in the *Book of Emperor Rudolf*:

34 Hannan, "Canon law of Wills", p. 535.
35 X 3.26.10. On the formalities of wills and others, see Hannan, "Canon law of Wills", pp. 534–541.
36 X 3.26. Hannan, "Canon law of Wills", p. 528.
37 Bassani, "A Coffer for the Will", p. 241. The two opinions are also present in X 3.26.11.
38 Sheehan, *The will in medieval England*, p. 176.
39 Epstein, *Wills and Wealth*, pp. 136–137.

> Rud 5. Dit is dat aerst fan da fiowerem: hweer so een man leyt oen da lesta eynde, haet so hi dan deth bi sines papa rede, so aech ma da oenspreeck foerd toe fyndane.

> Rud 5. This is the first exception of these four:[40] when a man is lying **on his deathbed**, whatever he then does with the approval of his priest, the court shall find in favor of the claimant.[41]

This has some similarities to a Canonical last will, namely the presence of a priest at a person's final moments. However, there is no mention of two witnesses. Nonetheless, this text probably still refers to last wills under Canon law. First, the *Book of Emperor Rudolf* itself was written in the 13th century and was influenced by Canon law.[42] Second, Cappon argues for the existence of oral testaments before the 15th century.[43] Such wills were made according to ecclesiastical requirements and left no traces. Moreover, neighboring regions support this assumption, with Canon law wills being made in Utrecht from the late 13th century onwards.[44]

A similar formulation to *oen da lesta eynde* appears in the 14th-century *Statutes of Opstalsbam*, where a priest is also mentioned:

> WUps 17. Dio sexteensta seeck is, dat alle lawa deer lawiget wirdet fan gode, dat se aldeer lawie deer se di daed brenghe, hit ne se dat hi **op syn lesta tiid mit siin biegtris** rede oderis ordinerie. Hwa so dat inbrect mit onriuchter wald di uerbert xx merka.

> WUps 17. The sixteenth clause is that all inheritances which consist of goods are brought there wherever death brings them, unless a man decides otherwise **in his last hours with the approval of his confessor**. If someone infringes on this with illegal force, he has to pay a fine of 20 marks.[45]

---

40 There are four exceptions to the provision in the *Book of Emperor Rudolf* (Rud 4), which states that a defendant is favored in all reasonable cases. Rud 5 contains the first of these exceptions.

41 *D*, XVI (Rud) 5, pp. 384–385.

42 Gerbenzon, "Kanonisches Recht", p. 41.

43 Cappon, "De erfstelling", pp. 51–52.

44 Including two witnesses. Cappon, *De opkomst van het testament*, p. 97 ff.

45 *D*, XX (WUps) 17, pp. 432–435.

Cappon argues that this provision is evidence of a presence of testaments before the 15th century.[46] Although there is no direct mention of a testament (OF: *testament*) or a last will (OF: *lesta/ ūtersta willa*), the distribution of property after death is said to be according to the will of the deceased person. This could also refer to other actions enabling distribution of property after death, such as the *donatio post obitum*. Nevertheless, another characteristic of testamentary succession is present: a person's will overrules "wherever death brings them" (*deer se di daed brenghe*). This provision indicates that a decision made in an individual's final hours overrules intestate succession, which leads me to believe that it indeed refers to a last will. The mention of a priest in the role of a confessor (OF: *biechter*) indicates that Canon law norms were present and applied, although no mention is made of the number of witnesses required. Testaments were made orally in the presence of a priest from at least the 13th century onwards. Although no written documents of last wills or records of Canon law wills survive, the two texts examined suggest that it is probable that wills were made in Frisia before 1400.

4.1 *In the* Freeska Landriucht

The *Freeska Landriucht* contains several glosses that specifically mention testaments. These glosses are from no later than the end of the 14th century, but may be older. Therefore, it is plausible that they are commenting on an already existing tradition of making wills in Frisia. The first relevant gloss, mentioned at the beginning of this chapter, was a gloss to the *Older Skelta Law* (SkRa 52).

> SkRa 52. Dit is riucht: jefter een ovirlandich man sterft, so aech di frana dat gued to ontfaen jeer ende dey to haldene. Jof deer enich eftercomt fan syn eerven binna jeer ende binna dei, dae eerfnamen toe jaen. Jef deer nimmen comt: di frana nym een deel ende di ora deel to Godes tyenst.
>
> Glossa 41. *Ende di ora deel to goedes tyenst* Item libere apud eos qui uolunt sponte suscipere liberam habeant testandi facultatem, dummodo legittime testentur, C. de ino. testa. l. Si quando (*Cod.* 3.28.35) et nota de sacrosanctis et l. i. (*Cod.* 1.2.1).
>
> SkRa 52. This is the law: if a foreigner dies, the *frana* shall take custody of his goods and keep them for a year and a day. If any of his heirs come

46 Cappon, "De erfstelling", p. 51, footnote 54.

for them within a year and a day, he shall give them to the heir. If no-one comes then the *frana* takes half and the other half goes to the church.

Gloss 41. *Ende di ora deel to goedes tyenst* Likewise, it is at the discretion of those who wish to do this by their own free will, that they have the free competence to make a last will and testament, as long as they do so in a legitimate way, see C. 3.28.35 and notice C. 1.2.1.[47]

The main text (SkRa 52) concerns succession by a foreigner. Consequently, it may be argued that the assertion that a testament can be made to arrange succession applies only to foreigners. However, it is implausible that a testament was available only to foreigners, given the presumed existence of wills from 13th-century sources onwards. Instead, a testament is presented as a valid alternative to intestate succession for all, not just foreigners.

It is noteworthy that both allegations in the gloss reference Roman law. This is unusual, given that previous sources implied that the earliest wills were made according to Canon law. This could indicate a shift towards testaments being governed by secular norms. Additionally, the Frisian text identifies the *frana* as the competent authority for succession.

Both references agree on a right to make a testament. In the first allegation (C. 3.28.35) we find a very similar phrase as in the gloss: [...] *nisi ut habeat consuetam et legitimam testamenti factionem* [...]. (Translation: "[...] that one may have the customary and lawful right to make a testament.") The second allegation (C. 1.2.1) concerns this testamentary right in the context of leaving property to the Church. People are free to leave property to this institution because they are free to make a will.[48] That this particular provision is referenced may indicate that the making of wills and the bequeathing of one's assets in those wills still primarily took place in favor of charitable and ecclesiastical institutions.

Neither in the text nor in the references can we find any information or details on how a testament was to be made "in a legitimate way". It is possible that Roman norms were to be applied, based on the predominance of Roman law in the glosses. However, no formalities of Roman law are mentioned here. Conversely, if Canon law still supplied the only valid norms for last wills, the absence of any references to Canon law is equally puzzling. Let us examine the other instances where testaments are mentioned. The *Older Skelta Law* details what happens to an estate subject to litigation by the heirs-at-law:

---

47 *D*, III (SkRa) 52, pp. 146–149.

48 C. 1.2.1: *Nihil est quod magis hominibus debetur, quam ut supremae voluntatis.*

SkRa 71. **Van bodel riucht dine sibsta in dat huis to wisane**
Hweer so een bodel laweged is ende di sibsta mit tinge to da huis comt, soe aegh di aesga dine alre sibsta in to delen to da forma tinge. Als hi incommen is, so aegh hi een ferd oen da gued an fara flette alont hit bitinget is, huckera hiara di aeftera eerwa se. Ende huckera fan hiarem deer dat biradeth dat hi aeftera eerwa se, so aegh hi dine ferd oen da gued.

Glossa 53. *Den alre sibsta* Verum est ab intestato uenienti, secus in herede scripto qui primo mittendus est in possessionem omnium rerum testatoris que fuerunt ipsius tempore mortis testatoris, ut in dicta l. iii C. de edic. diui adri. toll. libro sexto *Codicis* (*Cod.* 6.33.3).

SkRa 71. **Concerning temporarily allotting an estate to the next of kin**
Whenever an estate has been bequeathed and the relatives come to the house to litigate their claims, the *asega* must allot the right of entry to the next of kin on the first court session. When the next of kin has entered, he shall have a right to peaceful possession of the property in the front part of the house until the question has been litigated as to which of them is the more lawful heir. And which of them shows that he is the more lawful heir, let him have a right to peaceful possession of the property.

Gloss 53. *Den alre sibsta* (*the next of kin*). This is true for the heir-at-law. It is different for the testamentary heir who first must be authorized to take possession of all the testator's things, which were his from the time of the testator's death, as in C. 6.33.3 mentioned above.[49]

The Frisian text deals exclusively with intestate succession, where the next of kin dispute who should inherit. However, the gloss not only acknowledges testamentary succession, but also emphasizes that it supersedes intestate succession. A testamentary heir who is named replaces the heirs-at-law. The gloss explicitly states that the presence of a testamentary heir changes the course of succession, making an addition to the provision and Frisian law in general.

This is not merely a comparison or interpretation of the Frisian text; rather, the choice of words in the gloss shows that it considers the provision to be valid (*Verum est ab intestato uenienti*), and the addition of a testamentary heir

49 *D*, III (SkRa) 71, pp. 160–161.

to be authoritative and valid (*secus in herede scripto*) as well. As such, it can be concluded that the glossator considered this additional rule to be valid and applicable for the Frisian context.

Yet, again, only Roman law is referenced. The allegation (C. 6.33.3) states that an heir appointed by will is placed in possession of an estate.[50] As previously seen in the *Freeska Landriucht* (gloss 41 to SkRa 52), the secular Roman rules of wills are considered, instead of the ecclesiastical ones. However, the rule that a testament excludes intestate succession is not in contradiction with Canon law. The testament in this gloss relates solely to succession. Roman testaments were primarily intended for the settlement of succession, while Canon wills were a means to distribute property to the Church in the hope of spiritual salvation.[51] The connection of testaments with Frisian succession indicates that testaments belong to the realm of secular law and are primarily positioned in the context of succession. This could explain why Roman law is referred to in this gloss.

The final gloss concerning testaments is attached to the *Book of Emperor Rudolf* (Rud 5) analyzed above and discusses a situation in which a person made a last act on their deathbed.

> Rud 5. Dit is dat aerst fan da fiowerem: hweer so een man leyt oen da lesta eynde, haet so hi dan deth bi sines papa rede, so aech ma da oenspreeck foerd toe fyndane.
>
> Glossa 173. Testamentum, pro quo habes ff. de testa l. Si pars iudicancium (*Dig*. 5.2.10). Quando agitur de inofficioso testamento, pocius pro testamento est iudicandum, ff. de inoff. test. l. Si pars (*Dig*. 5.2.10).
>
> Rud 5. This is the first exception of these four:[52] when a man is lying on his deathbed, whatever he then does with the approval of his priest, the court shall find in favor of the claimant.
>
> Gloss 173. A last will and testament, for which there is the provision of D. 5.2.10. In legal proceedings concerning an 'undutiful last will' (*testa-*

---

50 *Cod.* 6.33.3: [...] *mittatur quidem in possessionem earum rerum, quae testatoris mortis tempore fuerunt* [...]

51 Epstein, *Wills and wealth*, p. 137 ff.

52 There are four exception to Rud 4, which states that a defendant is favored in all reasonable cases. Rud 5 contains the first of these exceptions.

> *mentum inofficiosum*) one should sooner judge in favor of this last will, see D. 5.2.10.[53]

The first important point to note is the context of the gloss. The gloss is attached to the *Book of Emperor Rudolf* (Rud 5) and its contents should therefore be considered in connection with this. We can observe the word *testamentum*, indicating that the glossator identified the last act of a person in the main text (Rud 5) with the making of a testament.

The second noteworthy aspect of this gloss is that it refers to a specific term in Roman law, a *testamentum inofficiosum*. This term refers to a situation where someone claimed that a testament was not valid because it had unlawfully excluded or passed them over by, for example, disinheriting them without a sound reason. In such cases, they were granted a *querela inofficiosi testamenti*.[54] If a testament was declared 'undutiful', intestate succession occurred instead. The presence of such a specific aspect of Roman testaments demonstrates how intimately familiar Frisian jurists were with Roman law.

Upon examining the allegations, we can see that they concern only the *testamentum inofficiosum*. D. 5.2 is entitled *De inofficioso testamento* and states that a decision by one judge in favor of an allegedly undutiful will is preferred over a decision against it by the other judge.[55] However, no further details are provided on the making of wills. The gloss itself functions primarily as another comparison, providing an example of when a will is favored even when disputed. Based on the available information, no other conclusion is plausible. It is consequently unlikely that the rules of the *testamentum inofficiosum* were applied.

4.2 *Some Conclusions about Frisian Testaments*

Wills, or acts resembling wills, have been documented since the 13th century, and appear to have been drawn up using ecclesiastical formalities, often in the presence of a priest. This suggests that disputes concerning succession may have initially fallen under the jurisdiction of the Church. However, the classical sources do not provide any rules or formalities for making a will, indicating that the Church had complete control over this practice. As a result, secular Frisian

53 Gloss 173 ad *D*, XVI (Rud) 5, pp. 384–385.

54 D. 5.2. as a whole. See also Kaser, *Das römische Privatrecht* II, p. 512.

55 D. 5.2.10: "*Si pars iudicantium de inofficioso testamento contra testamentum, pars secundum id sententiam dederit, quod interdum fieri solet, humanius erit sequi eius partis sententiam quae secundum testamentum spectavit: nisi si aperte iudices inique secundum scriptum heredem pronuntiasse apparebit.*"

law texts do not include any detailed formalities for making a will because these rules were established in Canon law.

The first instances of Roman law being referenced in connection with testaments are found in the glosses to the *Freeska Landriucht* (gloss 41, 53 and 173). Interestingly, these glosses refer only to Roman law and not to Canon law, despite the earliest wills most likely having been drawn up using Canon law. Individuals evidently had the freedom to make a will, but these glosses and allegations mention no specific requirements. This lack of information on how to make a will also extends to which court—secular or ecclesiastical—had jurisdiction over matters of wills.

There are two possibilities for the role of the glosses found in the *Freeska Landriucht*. First, the allegations to Roman law could be seen as confirming Canon law. None of the glosses and allegations details norms that conflict with Canon law, and they all fit into the existing ecclesiastical and testamentary tradition. As this tradition was also the dominant form of making a will in Frisia, it is plausible that a learned jurist would not want to contradict it. The lack of specific formalities in the glosses may be due to the fact that secular law only confirmed the right to make a will, while the formalities and arbitration of wills fell within the domain of ecclesiastical institutions.

However, certain factors make this solution less likely. Most notably, the references were exclusively to Roman law, whereas if the glosses were intended to confirm a right to make a testament according to Canon law, one would expect a reference to Canon law. Alternatively, these allegations to Roman law may have been copied from works of canonists, meaning they are connected to Canon law and are not indicative of an application of Roman law.

The second possibility is that the glosses were intended to create a secular testament. The absence of any ecclesiastical references indicates that the last will and testament in the glosses of the *Freeska Landriucht* (glosses 41, 53 and 173) was secular and modeled on secular Roman formalities rather than on Canon law ones. The texts in which the instances of wills appeared were also secular texts, and the magistrates who had competence over wills were secular (*frana* and *skelta*), as, for example, in the *Older Skelta Law* (SkRa 52 and 71).

However, there is no mention of specific formalities for testaments. A potential explanation for this lack of specific formalities for a secular testament is that someone making one could refer directly to Roman law, as implied by the gloss to the *Older Skelta Law* (gloss 41). Nonetheless, there is no clear expression of a secular will following the Roman testamentary tradition, and no evidence that Frisians made written wills according to the Roman form before 1400.

In conclusion, it is unclear why the allegations in the glosses to the *Older Skelta Law* and the *Book of Emperor Rudolf* in the *Freeska Landriucht* refer only to Roman law. Of the two possible explanations provided, the most plausible would seem to be that there was indeed an intention to create a secular testament in the gloss. In that case, the nearest source of secular norms for a testament could be found in Roman law. However, the lack of details suggests that this was far from a complete application of Roman law. Rather, the glossators sought to include testaments in secular law, without indicating which specific formalities were to be followed.

Regarding the question of how wills were made in Frisia, it should be noted that comprehensive information is lacking. In the various provisions and glosses to classical texts of the *Freeska Landriucht*, the only requirement that is mentioned multiple times is the presence of a priest or confessor. This, along with the lack of more detailed norms in secular texts, indicates that, from the earliest times, testaments were made according to the formalities of Canon law. In the remainder of this chapter, we will analyze the changes and developments in this regard in the 15th century.

5 Frisians' Wills in the 15th Century—What Frisians Distributed

From the 15th century onwards, Frisians made more and more wills, with the number of surviving wills increasing from 58 between 1400 and 1500 to 152 between 1500 and 1550.[56] These provide examples of what Frisians left to their heirs and other beneficiaries. Land, for example, was often distributed among friends and family, as in the case of the testament of Doitia Albada from 1466.

> **Testament of Doitia Albada** **1466, May 6**
> [...] Item soe maeckt hy erffgenamen syn kynderen in al syn ander guedt die hy afterlaten hevet, in sulcken manier als hiernae geschreven staet. Int eerste soe sal Rienck, syn zoon, hebben hondert pondematen landts in Latingha gued toe Wywert. Item Lyuwa, syn zoon, hondert pondemate landts toe Flansem. Item Syt, syn dochter, dat groete guedt toe Abbinghawier. Item Hilke, syn dochter, dat gued daer Ids op woent toe Abbinghaweer. [...][57]
>
> [...] Item, he makes all his children his heirs of all his other goods that he has left behind, in the manner which is described here: first, his son

56 Verhoeven, Mol, *Friese Testamenten*, pp. XIV–XVII.

57 *FT* 24, p. 41, r. 12–17.

> Rienck shall have 100 *pondematen*[58] of land in the estate Latingha near Wywert [Wieuwerd]. Item, his son Lyuwa shall have 100 *pondematen* land in Flansem [Flansum]. Item, his daughter Syt shall have the large estate in Abbinggawier [Abbengawier]. Item, his daughter Hilke shall have the estate in Abbinghaweer [Abbengawier], where Ids lives. […]

Another significant way in which property was distributed was through charitable donations to monasteries, churches and clergy. This, too, we can see in Doitia's will:

> **Testament of Doitia Albada** **1466, May 6**
> […] Item toe Betanien in Sneeck tuie postulatsguldens. Item die vier biddende orden elcs een pondt. Item toe Rordahusum drie klinckerts. Item toe Rawert drie klinckerts. Item toe Irnsem toe die personaetschip tuie pondemate landts, leggende in de personnes landt. Item die jongerschip toe Irnsem een acker die by die jonger priesters huys leyt, ende den mollenwier. Item elcke kercke in De Hem tuie flamsche, halff die kerck ende halff die priesters. […][59]
>
> […] Item, to Betanien in Sneek two *postulatsgulden*.[60] Item, to the four mendicant orders each one pound. Item, to Rordahusum [Roordahuizum] three klinkerds. Item, to Rawert [Rauwerd] three klinkerds. Item, to Irnsem [Irnsum] for the priesthood two *pondemate* land, located in the priest's land. Item, for the youth of Irnsem [Irnsum] a field that lies close to the young priest's house, and the mill. Item, each church in De Hem two *flamsche*[61] (coins), half for the church and half for the priests. […]

Giving money or land to ecclesiastical institutions was still an important part of making a testament, with the salvation of one's soul being a primary concern of many Frisians who wrote a will.

Money, of course, was left not only to charity, but also to relatives and others for whom one wished to provide:

58 An Old Frisian unit of area. 'pundesmete' Hofmann, Popkema, *Altfriesisches Handwörterbuch*, p. 391. Roughly equivalent to an English acre or 0,375 hectares. Nijdam, et al., *Frisian Land Law*, p. 19.

59 *FT* 24, p. 41, r. 6–11.

60 A type of gold coin. See Heenstra, *Evolution of Money Standard*, p. 244.

61 A Flemish silver coin. Also *vleemse groten*. See Heenstra, *Evolution of Money Standard*, pp. 153 and 244.

Titardus carpentator **1442 November 17**
Item legavit Jeselick, sorori suae, et filio suo Hermanno, decem klinckardos.[62]

Item, he leaves to his sister Jeselick and her son Hermannus ten klinkerds.[63]

Land and money were not the only things passed down in wills. Teeta Jellama, for example, left his best coat to his wife Alle: *Item Alle, myn huusfrouwe, myn besta hoythia.*[64] Leaving the best clothes to the surviving spouse was actually a tradition in intestate succession.[65] Such practical objects were of great importance in everyday life and could be expensive.

6 The Formalities of Making a Testament

Having established the presence of last wills in Frisia during the 13th and 14th centuries, it is worth examining their form and shape in Frisian law during the 15th century. By exploring the formalities that accompanied the making of a testament, we can gain insight into which elements of Roman law were applied and which elements of the Canonical testamentary tradition were retained or abandoned.

Four aspects of making a testament are examined here: the testator's requirements to testate, the institution of an heir, the number of witnesses present, and the role of authenticating persons such as priests or notaries. These are all relevant to an analysis of Frisian testaments and are present in the sources of the 15th century.

While the *Rechten ende Wilkoeren* and *Thet Autentica Riocht* offer little insight into testaments, the *Excerpta Legum* provides a rich variety of information.[66] Of the nearly 600 provisions, 40 mention a testament. Some of these

62 *FT* 12, p. 17, r. 12.
63 A type of coin struck in Holland after 1400. See Heenstra, *Evolution of Money Standard*, p. 153.
64 *FT* 26, p. 44, r. 31.
65 As detailed in the *Older Skelta Law*. Although they were not to have any precious materials such as gold, silk or expensive colors. See *D*, III (SkRa) 74, pp. 164–165.
66 There is only one instance in *RW*: *RW* 69, which will be discussed later in detail. This text is also in *Aut* 8.
Aut 2 is a text concerning disinheriting; it is copied from Canon law (Glosa *exhaeredet* ad X 2.24.23) and before that found in *Nov.* 115.3. On this, see also Brouwer, *Autentica Riocht*, pp. 112–114.

provisions only mention a testament briefly or are tangent to it, and are therefore of little significance for examining formalities. However, one rubric in the manuscript (*Codex Aysma*) of the *Excerpta Legum* is titled "de donationibus et testamentis", indicating that testaments were significant enough to warrant a title of their own. This is particularly interesting, given that the *Freeska Landriucht, Thet Autentica Riocht*, and the *Rechten ende Wilkoeren* contain only a few mentions of wills.

Based on this observation, we can surmise that there was an increase in the significance and occurrence of testaments from the late 14th to the mid-15th century, or at the very least that more was written and collected during this period. This corresponds with the increasing number of written wills in the 15th century.

The connection between *donatio* and *testamentum* in the rubric can be traced back to the historical development of the testament in Western Europe. In the Middle Ages, donations were used in place of testaments to devolve property after death, as in the case of a *donatio post obitum* (donation after death).[67] Consequently, the link between donation and testament in the rubric can be viewed as a vestige of this historical background. It is notable that such a title was absent from Canon law, where donations (X 3.24) and testaments were clearly distinguished (X 3.26).

In the *Jurisprudentia Frisica*, testaments had their own title (JF 46 'De testamentis et ultimis voluntatibus'), possibly deriving from a title of the Liber Extra with the same name (X 3.26). A preceding title, 'De donationibus mortis causa' (JF 45), serves to separate donations and testament. Title 46 is considerably longer than the rubric in the *Excerpta Legum*, consisting of 79 provisions and 105 glosses. Of these provisions, 27 are also present in the *Excerpta Legum*, indicating that a significant number of provisions were retained.[68]

Written wills of the 15th century provide evidence of the secular formalities involved in making a testament.[69] This chapter will examine these formalities in detail. There was a growing interest in making wills that adhered to secular norms. What prompted people to prefer making a secular will over a will governed by Canon law? The primary advantage of testamentary succession was that testators could organize succession according to their wishes. However, the surviving Frisian testamentary documents demonstrate that the heir-at-

67 Cappon, "de erfstelling", p. 41. For an overview of the relationship between testaments and donations, see Rüfner, "Substance", p. 321. The same for the *donatio mortis causa* from Roman law.

68 According to a table of concordance by Gerbenzon, *Excerpta Legum*, pp. 436–441.

69 For example, the frequent instituting of an heir; see Cappon, "De erfstelling", p. 52.

TABLE 9 Overview of the provisions to be examined, including their origins, the section in which they are relevant and whether they refer to sources of Roman or Canon law

Provision	Origin	Section	References to Roman law	References to Canon law
RW 69		Witnesses		
Exc 48	Case Records	Testators	✓	
Exc 58	Case Records	Witnesses	✓	
Exc 59	Case Records	Witnesses	✓	✓
Exc 60	Case Records	Witnesses		✓
Exc 61	Case Records	Witnesses		✓
Exc 74	Case Records	Institution	✓	
Exc 76	Case Records	Institution	✓	
Exc 88	Case Records	Witnesses		✓
Exc 295	RW 69; Aut 8	Witnesses		
Exc 488	Case Records	Authentication		✓
Exc 496	Case Records	Authentication	✓	
Exc 530	Case Records	Testators	✓	✓
JF 46:1	Exc 488	Witnesses		
JF 46:21	Exc 488	Institution, Authentication	✓	✓
JF 46:24	Exc 488	Authentication		
JF 46:25	Exc 488	Witnesses		
JF 46:43	Exc 488	Authentication		✓
JF 46:44	Exc 488	Witnesses		✓
JF 46:45	Exc 488	Witnesses, Authentication	✓	✓
JF 46:52	Exc 488	Testators		
JF 46:53	Exc 488	Testators		✓
JF 46:55	Exc 48	Testators	✓	
JF 46:59	Exc 496	Authentication	✓	
JF 46:62	Exc 295	Witnesses		
JF 46:72	Exc 74	Institution	✓	
JF 46:74	Exc 76	Institution	✓	
JF 46:79	Exc 530	Testators	✓	✓

law was predominantly still appointed as the testamentary heir.[70] Thus, the intention was not to supplant or disinherit an heir, but rather to ensure the secure devolution of property. This was primarily to prevent potential conflicts between heirs, which could arise in intestate succession. Additionally, it ensured that property could be distributed exactly as intended, provided the legitimate portion was observed.

While spiritual matters were still significant aspects of wills, they were no longer the sole and central characteristic. The growing prevalence of wills following secular law indicates that Frisians were increasingly concerned with the distribution of property.[71] Spiritual needs were not necessarily neglected, but secular testaments and the Roman rules regarding testaments were deemed more appropriate for settling one's inheritance. It is not surprising, therefore, that Frisians increasingly adopted testaments following Roman law rather than Canon law, given that the former was primarily focused on succession, whereas the latter prioritized salvation.

The table above summarizes the provisions to be explored in this chapter, together with their origins and concordance with other sources, and other pertinent information. The section with the most provisions in the *Excerpta Legum* is 'witnesses', which occurs 12 times and specifies their number and quality.

6.1 *Requirements for Being a Testator*

The first group of formalities for making a testament concerns what was required of a testator. In the gloss to the *Older Skelta Law* (gloss 41 to SkRa 52), we have seen that anyone "who wishes to do this by their own free will, that they have the free competence to make a last will and testament, as long as they do so in a legitimate way". Accordingly, free competence was a prerequisite for a valid testament.

6.1.1 Minimum Age

The *Excerpta Legum* contains more detailed requirements, including a minimum age of a testator, which was fixed at 14 years old:

70 Cappon, "De erfstelling", p. 69.

71 Cappon, "De erfstelling", pp. 72–73. A comparison can be made with the adoption of Roman wills by Germanic people in the Early Middle Ages. Making a will allowed individuals to distribute specific goods to specific people, according to the wishes of the deceased. Janes asserts that this made them advantageous over traditional succession; on wills in the Early Middle Ages, see Janes, "Treasure Bequest", p. 368.

> Exc 48. Dit is riucht, dat een kynt, **diir binna xiiii ierum is**, mey nen testament makya ende mey aek nat hlya an syn vaders testament, want also dene yelde weet nat hoth hy deth. **Dit steet screwen in des keysers riucht**: C. De falsa moneta I. i (*Cod.* 9.24.1), ff. De iuris et facti ignorancia, lege vltima (*Dig.* 22.6.19); et Inst. Quibus non permissum est testamenta, § Preterea (*Inst.* 2.12.1).[72]
>
> Exc 48. This is law that a child that is **younger than 14 years old**, may not make a testament; and it may not attest to the testament of its father,[73] because at such an age, it does not know what it is doing. **This is written in Roman law**: C. 9.24.1; D. 22.6.10; *Inst.* 2.12.1.

The references to Roman law in this provision are meant to support the claims being made. However, the first reference (C. 9.24.1) concerns counterfeit money and not testaments, although wards (*pupilli*) are excluded from liability at the end of the title (C. 9.24.7) due to their age. The term *pupilli* referred to children under the ages of puberty (*impuberes*), which officially began at the age of 12 for girls and 14 for boys.[74] Full legal capacity was not attained until the age of 25. This confirms the principle that children were incapable of acting. In Canon law, the age of majority was similarly set at 12 and 14 years, respectively.[75]

The second reference (D. 22.6.10) also confirms this principle: *Impuberes sine tutore agentes nihil posse vel scire intelleguntur.* [Translation: "Children under the age of puberty acting without a tutor are considered to be able to do or know nothing."] This particular provision concerns ignorance of fact and law. The third reference (*Inst.* 2.12.1) directly connects to last wills, stating that *impuberes* cannot make wills.[76]

---

72 *A*, I (Exc) 48, p. 38.

73 The meaning of this part of the sentence is not entirely clear. The translation of Buma et al. is: *und es darf sich auch nicht mit seines Vaters Testament einverstanden erklären*. See Buma, et al., *Codex Aysma*, p. 39. I have chosen to translate this as 'attest to the testament of its father'. This is based on the term *hlya* which itself has many translations; see 'hlīa' Hofmann, Popkema, *Altfriesisches Handwörterbuch*, p. 224, including (*öffentlich*) *aussagen, erklären, bezeugen*. Moreover, this provision originated in a case record. As, therefore, the context may have been lost, we cannot know the meaning for certain.

74 Inst. 1.22 pr. See also 'Pupillus (pupilla)' Berger, *Encyclopedic dictionary*, p. 662. For more information on capacity to act and puberty, see Kaser, *Das römische Privatrecht* II, p. 116.

75 For the age of discretion according to Canon law, see X 5.38.12 (*Omnis utriuque sexus*) of the Fourth Lataran Council. It should be noted that 12 and 14 were common ages of majority in the Low Countries in the Middle Ages, Ankum, "Cessation de la Minorite", p. 294.

76 Inst. 2.12.1. *Praeterea testamentum facere non possunt impuberes, quia nullum eorum animi iudicium est.*

It is evident that age restrictions were present in Roman law. The first two allegations in this context relate to limitations on liability and ignorance regarding fact and law. These restrictions were part of the more extensive age restrictions on *impuberes*, which applied in various contexts. Therefore, we cannot merely speak of a reception of an age limit for making a testament, but of the entire Roman system of children's capacity to act.

Classical Frisian law was already familiar with certain limitations regarding children. For example, and as the *Twenty-four Land Laws* and the *Calculated Tariffs* show, children were not liable for damages they inflicted.[77] However, there is no mention of a distinction between girls and boys, as there was in Roman law. The Frisian text above (Exc 48) refers only to a "child" and 14 years of age. As such, Roman law was not received in detail. Alternatively, it is possible that the author intended to annul this distinction and simplify the minimum age to 14 years for both genders. This is plausible within the context of traditional Frisian law, where the age of majority (*jerich*) was 12 years for both girls and boys, without any gender distinction.[78] Therefore, the provision sets an age limit for testaments that was higher than the general age of majority in Frisian law. It is possible that the author intended to receive Roman law, but to retain an identical age of majority for both genders.

Within the *Jurisprudentia Frisica* (JF 46:55), we find similar requirements, namely that a girl had to be 12 years of age and a boy 14 to make a testament. In contrast to the *Excerpta Legum* (Exc 48), however, a clear distinction between genders is apparent here.

> JF 46:55 Eer dat testament een kneppens machtich is so schel hy wessa fyoertyen jeer aud al fol, datter naeet een dey oenbreckt ende dyo famne toliff jeer, want alzo deen jeeld weet naet haetze deth.
>
> 46:55 The last will of a boy is only valid when **he is fourteen years old**, in full, that there is not a day missing, and for a girl if **she is twelve**, because if they are younger, **they do not know what they are doing.**[79]

77 *D*, VIII (L^{24}) 12, pp. 230–231 and *D*, XIV (BBr) 244, pp. 370–373. Interestingly, the first text requires only half compensation, while the second text requires full compensation. Both texts are linked to damage caused by animals and mention unintentional injury and injury by wives in the same manner as children.

78 This can be seen, for example, with regard to the age at which a girl could choose to marry; see Dom 1. See also the age at which a son would reach majority and become his mother's guardian, SkRa 11. On ages of minority, see Algra, *Oudfries Recht*, p. 306 f.

79 *Ro*, III (JF), tit. 46, no. 55.

As such, this element of Roman law was now comprehensively received. In two glosses (75 and 76), this argument is supported by a large number of allegations to Roman law. Gloss 75 contains two allegations to C. 9.24.1 and D. 22.6.10, both of which have already been discussed.

6.1.2 Soundness of Mind

Additional requirements stemming from Roman law can also be found, including the fact that a testament of a 'mentally unfit' person is invalid.

> Exc 530. Jtem. Dit is riucht: En menscha, der is in dwalinghe zyns zennes of mit quader siocte byfinzen, dat testament, dar di menscha danne makath, dath hath nen macht ney da riuchte, want der steet aldus fan screwen: Quia si testator fuerit furiosus uel extra mentem positus, non valet eius testamentum, ut probatur C. Qui testament a facere possunt, I. Furiosum (*Cod.* 6.22.9); Extra, De successionibus ab intestato, Cum dilectus (X 3.27.3); Inst., De testamentis, § Sed quod (*Inst.* 2.10), et De inofficioso testamento, § I (*Inst.* 2.18.pr.)[80]

> Exc 530. Item. This is law: If a person is mentally disturbed or suffers from the falling sickness, then the testament that this person has made under these conditions has no legal validity, since about that the following is written: If the testator is insane or not in possession of his mental faculties, then his testament is not legally valid, as is shown from C. 6.22.9; X 3.27.3; *Inst.* 2.10 … and *Inst.* 2.18. pr.

The text provides three allegations to Roman law. Firstly, according to C. 6.22.9, a person who is insane is not capable of making a will. Secondly, *Inst.* 2.10 deals with the execution of wills and with witnesses, and specifies that an insane person cannot be a witness (*Inst.* 2.10.6). However, no such requirement is given for testators in this title. Thirdly, *Inst.* 2.18 concerns undutiful wills, where children allege insanity after their parents left them out of the will. At the very end of the principium, it is stated: *nam si vere furiosus est, nullum est testamentum.* [Translation: "For if one is truly insane, the testament is void."] Therefore, the mentally ill (*furiosi*) were also among those restricted in their capacity to act.[81]

The provision also contains an allegation to Canon law (X 3.27.3), which states that a testator cannot be "out of their mind" (*non mentis compos*).[82] This

80 *A*, I (Exc) 530, p. 370.

81 C. 5.70. See also Kaser, *Das römische Privatrecht* II, p. 120.

82 X 3.27.3 in the paragraph *Nos causam.*

is consistent with Roman law (C. 6.22.9).[83] The *Jurisprudentia Frisica* (JF 46:52 and 46:79) also requires a mentally sound testator, and essentially contains a slightly modified version of the aforementioned provision (Exc 530). Both provisions emphasize the need for a testator to be of sound mind.

6.1.3 Malicious Intentions

An additional requirement appears in the *Jurisprudentia Frisica* and concerns deceit in making a testament:

> JF 46:53 Wjrt deer een testament maketh myt laesheed ende myt falscheed dat aegh neen stal ende haet neen macht.
>
> Glossa 73. *Wirt dijr een tes* Quia fraus et dolus nemini patrocinari debet, de rescriptis c. Sede apostolica (X 1.3.15). Qui enim falsa narrat, nichil impetrat, quia fraus nemini debet esse uiciosa, ut extra de iudiciis, c. Intelleximus (X 2.1.7) et de dolo c. Ex litteris (X 2.14.2) et de appella. c. Insinuacione (X 2.28.50) et c. Suggestum (X 2.28.15) cum suis concordantibus, iii q.i Episcopi, in glosa.[84]
>
> JF 46:53 If a last will is made with deceit and falsehood, it has no force of law and is not valid.
>
> Gloss 73. *Wirt dijr een tes* Because fraud and deceit should for no-one be an excuse, see X 1.3.15. Because who tells lies, obtains nothing, because fraud should for no-one be harmful as in X 2.1.7, X 2.14.2, X 2.28.50, X 2.28.15 with their concordant provisions and in the gloss obiicere to C. 3 q.1 c.2.[85]

Of note here is the reference to Canon law. The references reflect what is written in the text, namely that one should not benefit from an act of deceit or fraud.[86] This suggests that Canon law was also seen as a source of testamentary requirements in secular law. While Roman law also contains rules regarding deceit, they are not referenced here.[87]

---

83 There is even a gloss in the *Liber Extra* that refers to that provision in Roman law. See Glossa *compotem* ad X 3.27.3.

84 Glossa *obiicere* ad C.3 q.1 c.2.

85 *Ro*, III (JF), tit. 46, no. 53.

86 X 1.3.15: [...] *quia fraus et dolus ei patrocinari non debent.* And in X 2.1.7: [...] *de sua militia commodum reportare.*

87 On *dolus malus*, see D. 4.3.1.2. Fraud invalidated a contract or testaments; see Kaser, *Das römische Privatrecht* II, p. 90. Mousourakis, *Fundamentals*, p. 290.

In conclusion, it is clear that Roman law played a significant role in determining the requirements for age and mental capacity in relation to testaments. The *Excerpta Legum* and the *Jurisprudentia Frisica* contain numerous provisions reflecting the influence of Roman law on secular testaments. Although these rules did not conflict with Canon law, Roman law was the primary source for establishing some formalities of making a testament, namely those related to the capacity of the testator. Furthermore, jurists relied on Roman law, while also incorporating norms of ecclesiastical law, as seen in gloss 73, which deals with deceit in making a will. It is worth noting that Canon law existed in Frisia before the reception of Roman testamentary law, and that Frisians thus received Roman law on top of a layer of Canon law.

Moreover, we can observe an increasing adoption of Roman law in Frisia. In the *Excerpta Legum*, the minimum age requirement for both genders was the same (14 years); this was also the case in traditional Frisian law, albeit a different age (12 years). In the *Jurisprudentia Frisica*, however, the Roman distinction between boys (14 years) and girls (12 years) was more extensively embraced.

6.2 *Instituting an Heir*

A crucial requirement for a Roman testament was the appointment of an heir (*heredis institutio*). Without an appointed heir, a testament was considered invalid.[88] By examining the presence or absence of this characteristic in the Frisian testaments of the 15th century, we can thus determine how comprehensively Roman law was received and which of its norms were applied to the making of wills.

Cappon conducted research on this subject in his article "De erfstelling in de Friese testamenten".[89] He focuses primarily on the appearance of the *heredis institutio* in the Frisian testamentary documents collected by Mol and Verhoeven, which depicts how Frisians constructed their wills in practice, rather than what theory and law dictated. Cappon concludes that the instituting of an heir was not a fixed formality, pointing to a lack of clear provisions in the *Jurisprudentia Frisica*.[90] This chapter examines this claim, based on the available legal sources, so as to enable us to compare the theoretical legal framework with the reality of making testaments.

88 *Inst.* 2.13. pr. See also Kaser, *Das römische Privatrecht* II, p. 490ff., and Johnston, *Roman Law*, p. 202.
89 Cappon, "De erfstelling".
90 Cappon, "De erfstelling", pp. 55–57.

Regarding legal practice, Cappon asserts that the instituting of an heir was widely common in Frisia and at times perceived as a condition for validity.[91] For example, the testament of Ducko Onnama from 1423 demonstrates that a testator could believe it to be a necessary part of a will.

> **Testament of Ducko Onnama** **1423 May 27**
> [...] Insuper sepenominatus testator proinde, considerans testamentum fore cassum et irritum absque institutione heredis, ideoque Bettekam et Wapekam, duas sorores Ewyngha, instituit heredes veras et legitimas domus et domistadii Onnama [...][92]
>
> [...] In addition, the often-named testator, contemplating that a testament will be void and invalid without an institution of an heir, therefore institutes Bettekam and Wapekam, the two sisters Ewyngha, as true and lawful heirs of the house and estate Onnama [...]

As is apparent, the appointing of an heir was sometimes considered necessary for a testament. Ducko Onnama's will was written shortly before the *Excerpta Legum* was compiled in the first half of the 15th century. Let us therefore examine whether the *heredis institutio* is included in this compilation.

6.2.1 In the Excerpta Legum

An answer to the question of whether it was necessary to mention an heir is found in the *Excerpta Legum*, where the appointment of an heir is described as an obligation for a valid testament.

> Exc 74. Item. Dit is riucht, dat elk man schildich is, syn **riuchta weerhaftigha eerwa** to scriwen in syn testament, oers hath hit nene macht, als deer screwen steet in des keysers riucht: C. De inpuberum et alliis substitucionibus, l. Humanitatis (*Cod.* 6.26.9), et Inst. De pupillari substitucione, post principium (*Inst.* 2.16). Ende dit aldeer omme, hoe dia falskheit des testamentis openberat wirde ende hoe dyo falskheit vrbec gunge ende hoe dattet playt dar mey legarath wirde, als der steet screwen in des keysers riucht: C. De episcopis et clericis, Si quis ad declinandam (*Cod.* 1.3.48); Inst. De fideicommissarijs hereditatibus, § Inprimis (*Inst.* 2.23.2).[93]

---

91 Cappon, "De erfstelling", pp. 55–57.

92 *FT*, no. 6, p. 9, r. 22–26.

93 *A*, I (Exc) 74, p. 58. The Frisian part of this provision is also found in *A*, I (Exc) 18, p. 14.

> Exc 74. Item. This is law that everyone is obligated to write his **lawful and true heir** in his testament, otherwise it is invalid, as is written in Imperial law, see C. 6.26.9 and *Inst.* 2.16. And this (the rule about institution of an heir) happens so that the invalidity of a testament is revealed, and the false claim is rejected, and litigation comes to an end, as is written in Roman law, see C. 1.3.48; *Inst.* 2.23.2.

This provision seems to refute Cappon's assessment. A requirement to institute an heir is clearly detailed here. However, we must consider who this "lawful and true heir" (*riuchta weerhaftigha eerwa*) refers to.

We can imagine two possibilities. First, that the *riuchta weerhaftigha eerwa* refers to the heir-at-law. This seems to be the opinion of Buma, Gerbenzon and Tragter-Schubert, who translate the words as "einen gesetzlichen und wahren Erben".[94] In this case, the provision (Exc 74) states that the heir-at-law must be mentioned in the testament for it to be valid. This clashes with Roman law because testamentary succession excludes intestate succession. The testamentary heir is not the heir-at-law because, in the case of a testament, there is no heir-at-law. According to Roman law, the heir-at-law had to be mentioned in the testament only if this heir was a descendant, entitled to a legitimate portion, and the testator wanted to disinherit them.[95] However, there is no indication whatsoever in the text (Exc 74) that we are dealing with such a specific situation. If, consequently, the *riuchta weerhaftigha eerwa* is indeed the heir-at-law, this would mean that this provision (Exc 74) interprets a general requirement to name the heir-at-law in the testament, presumably either to institute them or to disinherit them. This would be an interpretation going beyond the intentions of Roman law.

The second possibility is that the *riuchta weerhaftigha erwa* refers to the testamentary heir. Someone would have to name the testamentary heir in order for that heir to be instituted. If we interpret the provision in this way, we can understand it as a requirement to name whoever one wants to institute as testamentary heir.

Maybe the allegations can throw some light on these two possibilities. Curiously, the first allegation (C. 6.26.9) concerns substitution of a child, instituted as heir, and is not one of the instances in Roman law stating the instituting of an

94 Buma et al., *Codex Aysma*, p. 59. "Gesetzlicher Erbe" refers to intestate succession. Moreover, they use the same translation for *riuchta eerwa* ("gesetzlicher Erbe") in Exc 76, Buma et al., *Codex Aysma*, p. 61.

95 See, for example, *Inst.* 2.13, D. 28.2.2 and Johnston, *Roman Law*, p. 202.

heir to be a requirement for validity.[96] The second allegation (*Inst.* 2.16) is also about testamentary substitution of the heir. Neither of these texts confirms the statement of Exc 74, namely that a *heredis institutio* is needed for a last will to be valid.

The third allegation (C. 1.3.48) also concerns a specific case of appointing an heir: namely instituting captives as heirs in order to provide their ransom.[97] Again, this does not confirm that an heir had to be instituted and that a testament without an heir was invalid. We find such a requirement only in the last allegation (*Inst.* 2.23.2).[98] We find another reference to this passage of the *Institutes* in the *Excerpta Legum*, namely in Exc 76. As such, we have two provisions that explicitly require a lawful heir to be instituted and refer to Roman law for the origins of this requirement.

> Exc 76. Item. Dit is riucht: Hwa syn riuchta eerwa nat scrijft in syn testament ende namt hine nat in sine testament, so is al dat hele testament on machtich, als der steet screwen ⟨lnSI. 1⟩, De fideicommissarijs hereditatibus, § Inprimis (*Inst.* 2.23.2).[99]

> Exc 76. Item. This is law: If someone does not enter his lawful heir into his testament and he does not name him by name in his testament, then the testament is entirely invalid, as is written in *Inst.* 2.23.2.

The connection with *Inst.* 2.23.2 can also shed light on a possible meaning of the term *riuchta* (lawful) *eerwa* (heir). Buma, Gerbenzon and Tragter-Schubert also translate this as "seinen gesetzlichen Erben".[100] The above text states that the rule that the *riuchta eerwa* should be mentioned in the testament was written in *Inst.* 2.23.2. The latter provision speaks about someone who is lawfully instituted as heir in the testament (*recto iure testamento heres instituatur*). The problem can be resolved by accepting *riuchta eerwa* as a translation of or equivalent to *heres recto iure*; in view of the connection between the concept and the provision of *Inst.* 2.23.2, this is certainly arguable. *Riuchta eerwa* is not the heir-

96 Neither do any of the glosses.

97 C. 1.3.48: *Si quis ad declinandam legem Falcidiam, cum desiderat totam suam substantiam pro redemptione captivorum relinquere, eos ipsos captivos scripserit heredes* [...].

98 *Inst.* 2.23.2: *In primis igitur sciendum est, opus esse ut aliquis recto iure testamento heres instituatur, eiusque fidei committatur ut eam hereditatem alii restituat: alioquin inutile est testamentum in quo nemo heres instituitur.* [...]

99 *A*, 1 (Exc) 77, p. 60.

100 Buma et al., *Codex Aysma*, p. 61.

at-law, nor the testamentary heir, but instead any heir who can be considered the legitimate heir, either based on testamentary or on intestate succession.

This solution implies that the translation of Exc 74 and 76 by Buma, Gerbenzon and Tragter-Schubert may put the reader on the wrong track by implying that *riuchta eerwa* ("lawful heir") specifically denotes the heir-at-law ("gesetzlicher Erbe"). This, however, is far from certain, given that the term also referred to testamentary heirs and is therefore not clearly congruent with heir-at-law. This demonstrates how important it is to study the primary sources in their original language and not only in translations.

It is also noteworthy that the contents of *Inst.* 2.23.2 concern trust estates specifically and not wills in general. One must wonder why the writers of these allegations did not include the explicit requirement to institute an heir, as, for example, in *Inst.* 2.20.34 and D. 28.5.1.

A possible explanation may be found in the origins of this provision, which was copied from a case record. As such, therefore, the original thesis may have been different and the context lost.[101] All allegations in this provision concern testamentary heirs, which supports the second possibility that *riuchta weerhaftigha eerwa* refers to the testamentary heir. However, we should not overemphasize the connection between the allegations and the main argument of the text. This provision (Exc 74) originated in a case record, reconstructs an argument made during litigation, and delivers allegations as support.

The main argument, written in Frisian, states that "Everyone is obligated to write his lawful and true heir in his testament, otherwise it is invalid." If we take this argument at face value, the allegation may simply have been placed to support it. However, we do not know the context of the case, and it is therefore possible that this case concerned the substitution of a testamentary heir. Consequently, the allegations alone are not sufficient to prove what the term *riuchta weerhaftigha eerwa* refers to.

This term also appears in other places, such as another provision of the *Excerpta Legum* (Exc 18), where it clearly refers to heirs-at-law, who had to be mentioned in the testament if they were to be disinherited. As previously stated, this was indeed Roman law.

> Exc 18. Dit is riucht: Hwaso syn riuchta weeraftigha erwa on erwya wol om een misdeda, dyn scel hy by nama naemnya in syn testament, oers soe

101 The context may have been a case of disinheritance or substitution of an heir. Exc 75 concerns both these topics. If both originated from the same case record, the allegations may have made more sense in that context. This also indicates that this provision referred only to descendants as "lawful and true heirs".

> mey hem naet on eerwya; dit steet screven in da keyser riucht, De liberis et posthumis, l. Nominatim (*Dig.* 28.2.2).[102]
>
> Exc 18. This is law: if someone wants to disinherit his lawful and true heir because of a wrongdoing, he shall name (the heir) by name in his testament, otherwise he cannot disinherit him; this is written in Imperial law, see D. 28.2.2.

In this text, the term *riuchta weerhaftigha eerwa* clearly refers to the heir-at-law because the latter (if they were a descendant) had to be mentioned in a testament if they were to be disinherited (see D. 28.2.2). This indicates that the previous provision (Exc 74) also referred to the heir-at-law, and argued that such person in general had to be named in the testament, although such statement is incompatible with Roman law.

The term *riuchta weerhaftigha eerwa* also appears outside the *Excerpta Legum*. When, for example, Ducko Onnama considered that "A testament will be void and invalid without an institution of an heir", he was not thinking of his own descendants. Instead, he institutes the two sisters Betteka and Wapeka Ewyngha as "true and lawful heirs" of the family's house and estate.[103] This suggests, again, that the *riuchta weerhaftigha eerwa* was the testamentary heir. Onnama made the two sisters his testamentary heirs, indicating that they were the "true and lawful heirs". If these sisters were unrelated to Onnama, this implies that the *riuchta weerhaftigha eerwa* was not the heir-at-law, as unrelated individuals were not heirs-at-law.

Nevertheless, a definite answer as to who *riuchta weerhaftigha eerwa* refers to cannot be given at this point. Further research is required to determine precisely what the term refers to. Alternatively, the term might not be precise and could refer both to heirs-at-law and to testamentary heirs.

A final point to consider is that all three provisions examined (Exc 18, 74 and 76) begin with the words *Dit is riucht/This is law*. This phrase is traditionally the opening of Frisian provisions.[104] Yet, we know that both the above provisions are from case records and not derived from recordings of customary law. No such rules existed in Frisian legal sources. Then why do we find such a traditional opening to a rule received from Roman law? It is plausible that this

---

102 *A*, I (Exc) 18, p. 14.

103 See above and in *FT*, no. 6, p. 9, r. 22–26. The sisters Ewyngha were possibly also related to Ducko in some form. See Verhoeven, Mol, *Friese Testamenten*, p. 486.

104 Vries, "Thet is ac londriucht", p. 583.

phrase was added to make the text appear more familiar. The intention may have been to assert that this rule was indeed an indigenous Frisian rule and not an entirely new addition. Alternatively, it was already considered part of Frisian law and could therefore be written in this manner. Both possibilities are supported by the fact that the rule is written in Frisian and not in Latin. Whether this occurred when the case was being recorded or when it was being copied into the *Excerpta Legum* is unknown. However, it is clear that a Roman rule regarding the instituting of an heir was 'Frisianized.' Consequently, Frisians appear to be much more familiar with the Roman testamentary tradition than previously assumed.

6.2.2 In Frisian Documents

The hereditary documents containing testaments from the 15th century also demonstrate an heir being instituted, with 74 % of the testaments between 1400 and 1550 containing such a clause.[105] Even if we consider only the period to 1500, a similar pattern emerges, with all but 13 of the 58 testators in this period appointing an heir in their last will.[106] This amounts to a share of around 78 %, which does not deviate significantly from the collection as a whole. It is clear, therefore, that the instituting of an heir was a common part of Frisian testaments.[107]

However, the absence of an instituted heir in the remaining documents may not necessarily indicate that these wills were not made in accordance with Roman law. Codicils also did not require a *heredis institutio*, but were equally valid. Moreover, even if we assume institution of an heir to have been a requirement for a valid testament, there is no certainty as to whether Frisians always adhered to this rule in practice. Wills in which no heir was instituted may have been seen as valid according to Canon law, and the requirements for a valid testament may not have been uniform across the different regions. Consequently, the presence or absence of an institution cannot definitively inform us as to whether these documents were valid under Frisian law at the time.

Nonetheless, it is evident that Frisians were familiar with the Roman law of succession and its various types of bequests. To illustrate this, we return to the testament of Clothus Bentha, who names his heirs in the second paragraph of the document:

105 Cappon, "De erfstelling", p. 52. For example, the testament of Feddricus Hummama from 1455 (FT 17, p. 28, r. 36 ff.).

106 These are the documents *FT* 15, 16, 21, 23, 26, 27, 31, 32, 33, 34, 45, 49, and 56.

107 As Cappon also notes; see Cappon, "De erfstelling", p. 53.

Testament of Clothus Bentha **1401 July 27/28**

[...] In primis Sicconem Ydszarda, Tzalenghum Fethza et eius fratrum Poptatum, parochianos Popengwere, Rawerderhem et Solis, haeredes instituo meorum omnium bonorum mobilium et immobilium, legatis et donationibus exceptis, in modum qui sequitur. [...][108]

[...] In the first place, I institute Sicco Ydszarda, Tzalenghus Fethza and his brother Poptatus, parishioners of Popengwere [Poppingawier], Rawerderhem [Rauwerd] and Solis [Terzool], as heirs of all of my movable and immovable goods, legacies and donations excluded, in the following way. [...]

The words chosen here leave no doubt as to the connection with Roman law: *haeredes instituo*. From this paragraph and the document as a whole, it is evident that Clothus Bentha was quite familiar with Roman law and the requirement to institute an heir. He uses *bona mobilia et immobilia*[109] to refer to his property and makes a clear distinction between property left to his heirs, as successors under universal title, and legacies (*legata*) and donations (*donationes*) left to others.

6.2.3 In the Jurisprudentia Frisica

The *Jurisprudentia Frisica* also mentions the institution of an heir on several occasions. In fact, the provisions of the *Excerpta Legum* (Exc 74 and Exc 76) reappear as JF 46:72 and JF 46:74. There is a slight difference in the Latin allegations; these were separated from the text and placed in glosses instead of being part of the main text. There were also other provisions dealing with the appointment of an heir; these were not part of the *Excerpta Legum*.[110] As an example, consider the following provision:

JF 46:21 Hweerso een testament maketh wirth jn een presters andert ende in gueda lyoeden andert, ende dy eerffnama deer oen byscryown se, so is dat testament noeglick ende aegh een stal to habben.

108 *FT* 3, pp. 3–4, r. 36 and 1–3.

109 A Roman categorization of things into 'movable' and 'immovable'. See Kaser, *Das römische Privatrecht* II, p. 245 f.

110 These provisions and their glosses include JF 46:21 and gloss 33, JF 46:24 and gloss 36, JF 46:25 and gloss 38, and JF 46:28 and gloss 41.

> Glossa 33. *Hweerso een testament maket* ut C. de testamentis l. Nec codicilis (*Cod.* 6.23.14), § Illud (*Cod.* 6.23.16.1), extra de testamentis c. Cum omnes in glosa ii.[111] Et quod heres debet nominari, cauetur l. Iubemus titulo preallegato Codicis (*Cod.* 6.23.29), quia ultima uoluntas testatoris pro lege seruanda est, xiii q.ii c. Vltima uoluntas (C. 13 q.2 c.4). Et ultimum testamentum hominis immobile perseuerat, ut de celebracione missarum c. Cum Marthe (X 3.41.6). Et nichil est quod magis debeatur hominibus quam ut supreme uoluntatis liber sit stilus C. de sacrosanctis ecclesis l. ii (*Cod.* 1.2.1)

> JF 46:21 When a last will is made in the presence of a priest and in the presence of good people, and the heir is mentioned in it, the last will is valid and has legal validity.

> Gloss 33. *Hweerso een testament maket* as in C. 6.23.14, C. 6.23.16.1 and the gloss improbamus ad X 3.26.10. And that the heir should be mentioned is decreed in C. 6.23.29, because the testator's last will should be observed as the law, see C. 13 q.2 c.4. And man's final testament invariably may persist, as in X 3.41.6. And nothing is more owed to people than that the composition of their last will is unrestricted, see C. 1.2.1.[112]

The provision states that an heir must be named for the will to be legally valid. Moreover, a priest and good people must also be present. We will return to this topic at a later point.

Reference is made to both Roman and Canon law. C. 6.23.14 states that the institution of an heir is what distinguishes a testament from a codicil.[113] The same is stated by the second reference (C. 6.23.29).[114] We find the same argument in gloss 38:

> Glossa 38. Nota testamentum dicitur ubi heres instituitur, codicillus non instituitur sed alias quis de rebus suis disponit, C. eodem Non Codicillus (*Cod.* 6.23.14). [...]

---

111 Glosa *improbamus* ad X 3.26.10.

112 *Ro*, III (JF), tit. 46, no. 21.

113 C. 6.23.14: "*Non codicillum, sed testamentum aviam vestram facere voluisse institutio et exheredatio facta probant evidenter.*"

114 C. 6.23.29: "*Iubemus omnimodo testatorem, si vires ad scribendum habeat, nomen heredis vel heredum in sua subscriptione vel in quacumque parte testamenti ponere, ut sit manifestum secundum illius voluntatem hereditatem esse transmissam.* [...]"

> Gloss 38. Note that something is called a last will when an heir is instituted and something is called a codicil when this is not the case, but someone disposes of his assets otherwise, see C. 6.23.14. [...][115]

The gloss (gloss 33 to JF 46:21) then includes an allegation to Canon law. The gloss *improbamus* makes no mention of an heir to be instituted: this requirement did not exist in Canon law. However, it does mention the presence of a priest and two or three witnesses.[116] The other two allegations to Canon law concern the duty to respect a will and its perpetuity. C. 13 q.2 c.4 states: *Ultima voluntas defuncti modis omnibus conservari debet.* (Translation: "The last will of a deceased person must be observed in all ways.")

6.2.4 Codicils

The instituting of an heir was a significant aspect of Frisian wills, as evidenced by the Frisian testaments and the collected provisions in the *Excerpta Legum* and the *Jurisprudentia Frisica*. However, Cappon argues that these instances alone are insufficient evidence of an heir being required for validity. He asserts that property distribution in a testament was possible even without appointing an heir, indicating that the *heredis institutio* was not universally accepted in Frisian law or practice.[117] Cappon cites a few examples to support his argument. Of particular importance is the testament of Jarich Epa Hotnya from 1475, which does not institute any heirs, yet still directs the inheritance. However, the following is written at the end:

> **Jarich Epa Hotnya** 1475 May 25
> Item disses lesta willa wol Jarich datma steed ende fest halda schel, ende duga schel in all syn articulen als een testament jeff als een codicil jeff als een oer lesta willa, als hi alderbest gued wessa mey ney dae riochten, hya sye gastelick jefta wraulsc.[118]
>
> Jarich wants that this last will be held solid and that it shall be valid in all its articles as a testament or as a codicil or as another type of last will, as it may be as good as possible according to the laws, whether it be ecclesiastical or secular.

115 Gloss 38 ad *Ro*, III (JF), tit. 46, no. 25.

116 X 3.26.10: "[...] *quae parochiani coram presbytero suo, et tribus vel duabus aliis personis idoneis* [...]."

117 Cappon, "De erfstelling", pp. 55–56 in footnote 67.

118 *FT* 34, p. 60, r. 28–31.

Jarich Epa Hotnya intended for his will to be valid as a codicil if it was not considered a valid testament. Although Cappon argues that property could be disposed of without an heir being instituted, this did not contradict Roman law. In such cases, the document was considered a codicil, and its contents could be executed as such while still observing the testator's will. The intention of testators was to provide an alternative should the testament be considered invalid because of failing to follow certain formalities. We also find such clauses in Medieval German testaments, as well as in the collected Frisian documents. They were included for the same reason.[119] As such, documents that did not institute an heir but that contained such a clause still followed Roman law. This includes the document of Jarich Epa Hotnya.

However, the presence of a clause attempting to validate the document as either a testament or a codicil suggests that Frisian testators in the 15th century faced confusion and uncertainty. Jarich Epa Hotnya, for example, was not sure whether his will would be regarded as a valid testament. Different types of wills existed, some instituting an heir and others following Canon law formalities more closely, but containing a codicillary clause. According to Cappon, some wills contained neither.[120]

This diversity of forms shows that there were no definitive, universal formalities for making a testament. The uncertainty and confusion regarding formal requirements explain why Jarich Epa Hotnya and others included a codicillary clause.

In conclusion, the practice of making a testament was much more uncertain than normative sources would have us believe. Although the *Excerpta Legum* and the *Jurisprudentia Frisica* clearly required an heir to be instituted, the existence of ecclesiastical rules and competence regarding testaments created an environment where a testator was uncertain about the requirements needed for a will to be deemed valid. This resulted in the appearance of codicillary clauses when no heir was instituted. While, therefore, Cappon was correct that the reality did not reflect the formalities firmly established in law, he was incorrect in stating that the instituting of an heir was not a formality firmly established in law.

6.3 *Number of Witnesses*

A crucial difference between Roman and Canon law was the number of witnesses required to attest the drawing up of a testament. According to Roman

119 Brandt, "Mittelalterliche Bürgertestamente", p. 5 f. and Verhoeven, Mol, *Friese Testamenten*, p. xv f.

120 Cappon, "De erfstelling", pp. 55–56 in footnote 67.

law, seven witnesses were required for a testament and five for a codicil, while Canon law required only two or three witnesses.[121] Consequently, the Roman form excluded a testament with fewer witnesses and considered it invalid, meaning that the two requirements could not exist simultaneously. By examining the formalities of testaments in Frisia, we can determine which of these two requirements was established in written law. This can help us understand whether Roman law was comprehensively received, and which elements were rejected or applied. It will also shed light on the extent to which testamentary law was secularized.[122]

Neither of the classical Frisian sources nor the *Freeska Landriucht* mention a specific number of witnesses. As explained earlier, it is likely that the exact formalities existed within the Church in Canon law and that testaments were made accordingly. The first mention of the number of witnesses is found in *Rechten ende Wilkoeren*, followed by *Thet Autentica Riocht*. Both texts date back to the end of the 14th century. However, the *Rechten ende Wilkoeren* survived only in its later Ommelander form, while *Thet Autentica Riocht* is found in parts in 15th-century manuscripts, such as the *Codex Unia* (*U*), *Codex Aysma* (*A*) and *Codex Roorda* (*Ro*).

> **RW 69. Van testament tho maken.**
> Wat so een man doe op syn leste tyt by syn bichtvaders rade tho wthynge ende net tho ynnigen, also vere als de prester dar **twe trouwe tuygen** by heft, soe ys dee daet schuldych een stall tho holden.
>
> **RW 69. Of the making of a testament.**
> Whatever a man does on his deathbed on the advice of his confessor—as long as it concerns donations and not claims[123]—is valid if the priest has two reliable witnesses with him.

Below follow the three versions of *Thet Autentica Riocht* as they appear in the three manuscripts (*U*, *A* and *Ro*).[124] The translation is identical to the one above.

121 See earlier on testaments in learned law.

122 An earlier version of this section was presented at the conference 'Ius commune and local testamentary succession laws and customs (c. 1400–1620)' in January 2023 in Krakow and published as Wiegand, "'As good as possible'".

123 The exact meaning of *tho wthynge ende net tho ynnigen* is unclear. It is possible that *ynnigen* refers to outstanding debts.

124 On all three versions, see: Brouwer, *Thet Autentica Riocht*, p. 42. The *Codex Aysma* version is found in Exc 295, the *Codex Roorda* version in *Ro*, III (JF), tit. 46, no. 62.

> Aut 8 (U): Hot so en man bi siner bichters rede op sine lesta tijd deth thi wttigum and naut thi ingum also fir so thi prester habbe **een jefta tween trowe orkenen**, so aech thet tho staen.
>
> Aut 8 (A): Item. Dit is riucht: Hot en man deth op syn leste tyt bi syn presters reda ty vtingum ende nat to ynnegum, so fijr so di prester **twer trouwe orkenen** habbe, so acht to stane.
>
> Aut 8 (Ro): Haetso een menscha deth op sijn off lesta testament by syn presters reed to wtingen ende naet to ynigem so fyr so dy prester **tweer trowe orkenen** habbe so aegt to staen. [...]

All four instances mention the need for two reliable witnesses (*tuygen/orkenen*) to be present beside a priest. This corresponds to the requirements of Canon law, which mandates a priest and at least two witnesses. We can conclude from this that both the *Rechten ende Wilkoeren* and *Thet Autentica Riocht* exclusively reproduce Canon law regarding witnesses. Whether this meant that the Canon law testament was anchored in secular Frisian law, or that it was merely reproduced, is unclear. Gerbenzon argues that Frisian law, in general, became Canonized.[125] If we concur with this assertion, this text demonstrates that Frisian law followed the testamentary tradition in Canon law. This affirms the above supposition that the earliest testaments were drawn up according to Canon law and that the Canonical testamentary tradition preceded the secular one.

Lastly, the instance in the *Codex Unia* (*U*) mentions that one or two witnesses are needed (*een jefta tween trowe orkenen*). This does not correspond to Canon law. It is unclear why only one witness is mentioned as being sufficient.

6.3.1 In the *Excerpta Legum*—Three or Seven Witnesses?

In contrast to *Thet Autentica Riocht*, norms in the *Excerpta Legum* appear to have been received from Roman law.

> Exc 58. Jtem. Dit is riucht, datter iii orkenen nat nochliic sint to barian een testament, mer der herat to wel vii: C. De testament is, l. Si unus (*Cod.* 6.23.12), et eciam l. ultima (*Cod.* 6.23.31).[126]

125 Gerbenzon, "Enkele nieuwe gegevens", p. 137.

126 A, I (Exc) 58, p. 48.

> Exc 58. Item. This is the law that for an attestation of a testament three witnesses are not enough, but that seven are necessary, see C. 6.23.12 and C. 6.23.31.

The rejection of the Canon law requirement for three witnesses in favor of the seven witnesses needed in Roman law is evident in this provision. It shows that testaments had to be drawn up according to Roman law, at least regarding the number of witnesses.

The two allegations are to a title in the *Codex Iustinianus* concerning how a testament had to be made ('De testamentis: quemadmodum testamenta ordinantur'). The first allegation states that a will with even one of the seven witnesses missing was void: *Si unus de septem testibus defuerit* [...], *iure deficiat testamentum*.[127] (Translation: "If one of the seven witnesses is missing [...], the testament is void by law.") This highlights that seven witnesses were obligatory and that any lower number, including three, was insufficient. The second allegation (C. 6.23.31) details exceptions: in a rural area where seven witnesses could not be found, five were sufficient. However, under no circumstance were fewer than five allowed: *minus autem nullo modo concedimus*.[128] (Translation: "However, under no circumstance do we allow fewer (than five).") Thus, these allegations confirm the required number of witnesses and explicitly forbid any number of witnesses below seven (or five in a rural area). This rule excludes the possibility of making a valid secular testament by following Canonical legal norms.

Could Frisians, however, still make testaments with fewer than seven witnesses? To answer this question, we can examine another provision in the *Excerpta Legum*, where the various forms of testaments are discussed:

> Exc 59. Jtem. Dit js gastlijc riucht, dat dia biwysinghe ief dyo biprouinghe van ⟨en⟩ testament machtich ief nochlic is, der en man makat vor syn persona ende vor ij orkennen. Dit is to verstane van guede, der heilgum iefta herum iefta to Godis erum bispritzen is. Dat steet screwen De testibus, Cum a nobis (X 2.20.28),[129] et c. Relatum (X 3.26.11), in glosa per

127 C. 6.23.12.

128 C. 6.23.31.3.

129 The manuscript that Buma et al. worked with led them to conclude that X 2.20.28 is referenced here. See Buma, et al. *Codex Aysma*, pp. 48–51. There is certainly mention of two or three witnesses in that provision. However, in the context of the next allegation (X 3.26.11), it appears more likely that it was not X 2.20.28 (*de testibus et attestatiobinus*, c. *Cum a nobis*) but X 3.26.10 (*de testamentis et ultimis voluntatibus*, c. *Cum esse*) that was referenced. The

doctores,[130] et De noui operis nunciacione, c. i (X 5.32.1) per Joannem Andree.[131] Want oers so scold di paeus des keysers riucht al to lijchtlike weer ropt habba, der nat reedlijc were dat hy dat dwaen scolde, sonderlingha in da logum ief in da stedum, der hem beyda gaestlijc riucht ende wraldisk riucht nat to biherat, als deer steet screwen. Argumentum de hoc De iudicijs, Nouit ille (X 2.1.13); et c. De appellacionibus, ⟨Si⟩ duobus (X 2.28.7); et C. De inofficioso testamento, l. Quoniam (*Cod.* 3.28.32). Ende dat dy keyser wold, datter vij orkenen vr dat testament scolde wasa, dat is al deer omme, datter inda testament nene falskheit bysighat worda, als dijr steit screwen Jnst., De fideicommissarijs hereditatibus, § vltima (*Inst.* 2.23.12).[132]

Exc 59. Item. This is ecclesiastical law that the proof or confirmation that someone has drawn up a last will in the presence of his priest and two witnesses is valid and sufficient. That must be understood in such a way that it concerns property that is left to saints and lords (church and clergymen) or in the honor of God. This is written by the scholars in X 2.20.28 and X 3.26.11 in the glosses *relictis* and *decretorum*, and by Johannes Andreae in his commentary to X 5.32.1. Because otherwise the pope would revoke Imperial law all too lightly, which would not be correct that he would do so and in particular in those places and locations where he has no control over both ecclesiastical and secular law. The Argument for this is in X 2.1.13, X 2.28.7 and C. 3.28.32. And that the emperor wanted seven witnesses to be present when drawing up a last will, so that there would be no forgery in a last will, is written in *Inst.* 2.23.12.

It appears that wills made according to Canon law could still exist, albeit for limited purposes and restricted to ecclesiastical matters, *heilgum iefta herum iefta to Godis erum bispritzen*. This provision thus created two forms of testament: secular wills requiring seven witnesses and ecclesiastical wills requiring only two witnesses, but limited to charitable donations to the Church. The Church retained jurisdiction over the latter, as in previous centuries.[133] The first

same provision and its allegations reappear in JF 46:70 and gloss 90, where reference is made to X 3.26.10. Consequently I believe that there may have been an error of transcription or interpretation and so will not examine X 2.20.28 in any further detail.

130 Glosa *relictis* and *decretorum* ad X 3.26.11.

131 Giovanni d'Andrea. *In quintum decretalium librum novella commentaria*, ad X 5.32.1.

132 *A*, I (Exc) 59, pp. 48–50.

133 Seif, "Römisch-kanonisches Erbrecht", p. 101.

line of the text, *Dit js gastlijc riucht*, clarifies that what follows, a priest and two witnesses, constitutes ecclesiastical, not secular law. Wills concerning anything other than charitable purposes should fall under secular jurisdiction and follow secular Roman law, except for dispositions that favored the Church.

The debate about how and when to use Roman and Canon norms for testaments was familiar among Medieval learned jurists. In the twelfth century, for example, Pope Alexander III (1100/1105–1181) issued a decree stating that two witnesses and a priest sufficed.[134] This decree is found in X 3.26.10 and a similar one can be found in X 3.26.11, and is even referred to in the text above (Exc 59). The former states that ecclesiastical law should be followed instead of secular law when making a testament. The latter states the same, but specifically refers to cases in which the Church is favored by a testament. These wills were valid and could not be challenged, according to Pope Alexander III. However, the provision above (Exc 59) directly challenges the pope by stating that only testaments for charitable purposes were allowed to have only two or three witnesses. All others had to follow Roman law.

The two glosses mentioned in the context of X 3.26.11 confirm unequivocally that two or three witnesses were sufficient for charitable wills only: *Ad hunc casum restringe cap. proxi. s. eo. in quo favore ecclesiae sufficiunt duo vel tres testes.*[135] ("Restrict this to this case and to the preceding case in which two or three witnesses suffice in favor of the Church."); *Sic nota causas ultimae voluntatis defunctorum ad ecclesiasticum iudicem pertinere, quod verum est in relictis ecclesiae, et pauperibus.*[136] ("Thus, note that cases of last wills of the deceased pertain to the competence of the Church, which is true in the case of things left to the Church or the poor."). The same was supposedly said by Giovanni d'Andrea in his commentary to X 5.32.1 However, no such argument is found there. It is probable, therefore, that this allegation had become corrupted. Alternatively, Giovanni d'Andrea makes a similar argument in a commentary to X 3.26.11: *Valet legatum ad pias causas coram duobus testibus factum.*[137] ("A legacy to charitable ends is valid when it is made in presence of two witnesses.")

The provision above (Exc 59) presents the opinion of those canonists who believed that the canonical formalities for a testament applied only to charita-

134 Bassani, "A Coffer for the Will", p. 241.

135 Glosa *relictis* ad X 3.26.11.

136 Glosa *decretorum* ad X 3.26.11.

137 Ioannes Andreae (c. 1270–1348). *In tertium decretalium libros novella commentaria*, ad X 3.26.11, n. 1.

ble purposes. Therefore, any testament that was not entirely dedicated to the Church required seven witnesses, as stated in the provision. The reason given for this is that the pope would not want to revoke Imperial law, especially in regions under secular jurisdiction. Three references are presented to support this argument.

The first reference (X 2.1.13) explains that the Church is concerned only with spiritual law, not secular law. This comes from a letter of Innocent III (1161–1216) to French prelates regarding a dispute between the Kings of England and France. Innocent III writes that while he has no jurisdiction over secular matters, his ecclesiastical competence extends to cases where someone committed a sin. Although this reference is not directly relevant to testaments in Frisia, it demonstrates the porous borders between secular and ecclesiastical jurisdiction.[138]

The second reference (X 2.28.7) concerns an appellation from a secular judge. One cannot appeal a decision by a secular judge to the pope unless the pope has secular jurisdiction in that region. This reference also serves primarily to demonstrate the limits of ecclesiastical competence.

The third reference (C. 3.28.32) is unclear and does not seem to provide a suitable explanation. In another version of the provision (Exc 59) in the *Jurisprudentia Frisica* (gloss 91 to JF 46), the reference is to C. 3.28.35. This reference concerns the legal and ordinary testamentary right granted by the emperor. The two decretals show the limits of ecclesiastical competence, while the reference to Roman law explains the interest of the emperor in last wills and testaments. This was an argument for why the Church could not simply disregard secular law.

In conclusion, this provision limits Canon law wills to charitable purposes only, which fell under ecclesiastical jurisdiction. In the case of all other testamentary dispositions, Roman law (secular law) had to be followed. The same argument was previously made in X 3.26.11 in opposition to Pope Alexander III's decretal. However, it is unclear how this would work in a will that included both property disposals and charitable donations. Presumably, such a will had to be made according to Roman law.

Interestingly, two consequent provisions in the *Excerpta Legum* state that two witnesses were sufficient:

138 Alternatively, not respecting the will of the testator can be considered a sin, and could therefore fall under the competence of the Church. The Church claimed competence in cases of sin, as by the 'reason of sin' *ratione peccati*. X 2.1.13.

> Exc 60. Jtem. Dit js riucht, dat ij orkenen iefta iij mogen ful wird hoda. Quia in ore duorurn uel trium stat omne verbum uel testimonium in c. Relatum, De testamentis (X 3.26.11), et Jhoannis viij.[139,140]
>
> Exc 61. Jtem. Dit js riucht, dat ij orkenen steet to lewan. Dat steit screwen aldus in sacra scriptura ut Matthei xviij[141] et Deuteronornio xix[142] et in lege Moysayca.[143] Jn iure canonico expresse cauetur et in c. Cum esses, De testamentis (X 3.26.10); et c. Licet vniuersis (X 2.20.23); et in c. In omni negocio, De testibus (X 2.20.4), jn quibus iuribus scripturn est expresse: Jn ore duorum etcetera.[144]
>
> Exc 60. Item. This is the law, that two or three witnesses are able to fully attest to the truth. "Because in the mouth of two or three people all words and testimonies persist." X 3.26.11 and John 8.17.
>
> Exc 61. Item. This is the law that two witnesses are to be believed. That is written in the Holy Scripture in Math. 18 and Deut. 19 and in the law of Moses. In Canon law this is expressly said in X 3.26.10, X 2.20.23 and X 2.20.4, where is expressly written: In the mouth of two etc.

The contrast to the previous provisions may be explained in two ways. First, there was no certainty among or decision by the compilers of the *Excerpta Legum* regarding the number of witnesses. They collected case records arguing for opposite points, with the intention being to decide on the number of witnesses when the collection was transformed into a law text. The second possibility is that these two contrasting examples do not refer specifically to testaments but to testimonies in general. It is possible that seven witnesses were required to attest a testament, while in other cases two or three sufficed. While neither of the two provisions mentions a last will and testament, they follow immediately after the previous provision (Exc 59), which concerns witnesses for making wills. Moreover, reference is made to both X 3.26.10 and 11, which

139 John 8.17: *et in lege vestra scriptum est quia duorum hominum testimonium verum est.*

140 *A*, I (Exc) 60, p. 50.

141 Matthew 18.16.

142 Deuteronomy 19.15.

143 A reference to Mosaic Law, i.e., the Torah. For example in Yad, Edut 5:1, which in turn refers to Deut. 19.15.

144 *A*, I (Exc) 61, p. 50.

we have previously discussed. These references declared that two or three witnesses were sufficient for Canon law wills.

Additionally, a new argument is brought up in another provision:

> Exc 88. Jtem. Dil js riucht, datma vij orkenen bet lewa scel danma breef ende sygel van twam of van iij. Dat steil screwen: Quia viua vox pocior est quam mortua: De probacionibus, Tercio loco (X 2.19.5).[145]
>
> Exc 88. Item. This is the law that seven witnesses are more to be believed than a document sealed by two or three. This is written: because the living voice is mightier than the deceased, see X 2.19.5.

It is possible that testaments could be made with only two or three witnesses present, but it is more likely that this provision (Exc 88) is dealing with witnesses in the context of providing evidence in litigation. Theoretically, it is possible for testaments made according to both Roman and Canon formalities to exist and to be valid at the same time. However, the contradictions and possibilities within the collected texts explain why Frisian testators were not entirely certain about what a valid testament required.

6.3.2 In the Jurisprudentia Frisica

In the title *de testamentis* (JF 46) in the *Jurisprudentia Frisica* we find seven witnesses being prescribed in the very first provision:

> JF 46:1 Dit is riucht dat to een noeglyck testament schellet wesse sawn orkenen dyr aldeer to baeden sint. Ende ist een leya testament deerma alzo manich l nae krya moge, so ist a noegh oen fyff orkenen. Ende om dissen willa dat disse seeck in dat wralsche riucht is so meyma naet myn habba dan sawn off fyff orkenen.
>
> JF 46:1 This is law, that seven witnesses who have been called there must be present when a last will is drawn up. And if it is a layperson's last will, for which one is not able to procure so many witnesses, then five witnesses suffice. And because these cases are dealt with in a worldly court, one is not allowed to have less than seven or five witnesses.[146]

145 *A*, I (Exc) 88, p. 68.
146 *Ro*, III (JF), tit. 46, no. 1.

It is noteworthy that this provision places the making of a testament under the jurisdiction of a secular court. This indicates that Frisian secular law not only had competence regarding testaments but also followed the requirements of Roman law in terms of the number of witnesses. This includes an exception: five witnesses are sufficient if there are not enough people present, such as in sparsely populated areas.[147] Additionally, other provisions in the *Jurisprudentia Frisica* (JF 46:1, 46:25, 46:43, 46:45, 46:69, and 46:70) mention the requirement for seven witnesses in Roman formalities.

However, if this provision concerns the secular court, was it still possible to make ecclesiastical testaments requiring two or three witnesses? There are indeed parallel or contradictory rules.

> JF 46:44 Jtem Een prester mit twam orkenen moghen een testament machtich hoda.
>
> Glossa 65. *Item Een prester* ut in c. Cum esses titulo de testamentis (X 3.26.10). Et duo testes sine presbitero sufficiunt ad pias causas, de testamentis c. Relatum (X 3.26.11).
>
> JF 46:44 Item. A priest and two witnesses can confirm the validity of a last will.
>
> Gloss 65. *Item een prester* as in X 3.26.10. And two witnesses without a priest suffice for charitable ends, see X 3.26.11.[148]

This provision contains rules of Canon law and contradicts the previous provision. It also references the two decretals by Pope Alexander III recorded in the *Liber Extra* (X 3.26.10 and 11), which imply that two or three witnesses were sufficient for a testament. The gloss in this text states that two witnesses were enough for charitable ends, and thus two witnesses and a priest should have been sufficient for all other testaments, including those not for charitable ends. It is unclear, however, whether this refers to secular wills or only to the existing Canon law for ecclesiastical wills.

A second provision (JF 46:70 and gloss 90) also mentions the Canon law requirements, but this provision was already present in the *Excerpa Legum* (Exc 59). It states that two or three witnesses were enough for testaments for

---

147 On this, see also C. 6.23.31.

148 *Ro*, III (JF), tit. 46, no. 44.

charitable ends, but that seven witnesses were needed for other testaments. It is clear, therefore, that this line of thought continued into the *Jurisprudentia Frisica*. Once again, this is also detailed in another gloss (gloss 66 to JF 46:45). The main text mentions a priest and a notary, which is another interesting aspect of Frisian wills that will be examined later in this chapter.

> JF 46:45 En testament fan wralsche secken ende aeck fen lawen ende eerffscip deer sint netrefftich sawn orkenen toda prester jeffta keysers orkenen deer al deer al jowns to ropen wirdeth, ende middelste dat sint vijff dat is in een huusmans testament, ende in een litika gae deer naet fule folkes wrgaria mey.
>
> Glossa 66. [...] Item et quod dicitur de testamentis et ultimis uoluntatibus in c. Cum esses (X 3.26.10) et c. Relatum (X 3.26.11), intelligitur tantum de relictis ad pias causas uel ad pias usus, ut dicunt doctores, quia non est uerisimile quod dominus papa unico uerbo tot legibus derogare, arg. ad hoc C. de inofficioso testamento l. Si quinque (*Cod.* 6.28.35), ne falsitas in testamento committerentur, uoluerant ut talis certus numerus adhiberetur, C. de fidei commissis l. ultima (*Cod.* 6.42.32)
>
> JF 46:45 For a last will concerning worldly affairs and also of legacies and inheritance, seven witnesses are needed alongside the priest or notary who are called up at the same time, and on average five, that is in a farmer's last will and in a small parish where not many people can gather.
>
> Gloss 66. [...] Similarly, what is stated about testaments and last wills in X 3.26.10–11, is understood as concerning only things left to charitable ends or for charitable use, as the scholars say, because it is not very likely that the pope with one single word derogates so many provisions, see C. 6.28.35. They wanted that such a distinct number is called upon, so that in the last will no fraud is committed, see C. 6.42.32.[149]

It is stated here that the decrees of Alexander III (1100/1105–1181) pertain only to charitable dispositions and not to secular ones, as in the provision (JF 46:45) itself. It appears, therefore, that Roman rules were applied when a testament not exclusively benefiting the Church was made. References to a testament made with two or three witnesses according to Canon law related, therefore,

149 *Ro*, III (JF), tit. 46, no. 45.

to a testament for charitable ends falling under the competence of an ecclesiastical court. Jurists may have had personal reasons for including in the compilations of law texts a simple way for people to leave property to the Church and its institutions. Some of them were themselves clerics who had studied learned law at universities in Europe and worked at monasteries in Frisia. Therefore, they were some of the principal beneficiaries of charity to ecclesiastical institutions.

How, however, is it possible for JF 46:44 to state that a priest and two witnesses can validate a will when it appears that this number of witnesses was valid only for charitable ends, as claimed in JF 46:70 and gloss 66 to JF 46:45? No mention is made in JF 46:44 of a restriction for charitable ends. Indeed, charitable ends require only two witnesses and no priest to be present.[150] A potential answer can be found in another provision, JF 46:25, concerning the will made latest.

> JF 46:25 Jof een man een testament maketh haet ende dyr sawn fol orkenen wr wessen habbet, ende hy dan deer ney dat foerlibbe fyff of sex of tyen jeer langera of kortera, ende sterue, dan so schel dat testament staen ende een folle macht habbe. Ende ist seeck datter een oer testament maketh eer hy dan sterfft so schel dat machtich blywe dyr lest mecket is ende dat arst naet. Ende al heder al sawn orkenen wr dat arste testament wessen dat scholde allycual onmachtich blywe, ende dat lest schel staen, al weer deer naet meer dan twyr orkenen wr wessen. Ende sinter sawn wr dat leste so ist alzo fule festera ney riucht.

> JF 46:25 If a person has made a last will and seven true witnesses were present, and after that he lived for five or six or ten years, longer or shorter, and then died, then the last will will be valid and fully legal. And if he makes another last will before he dies, then that last will that was made last and not the first will have legal validity. And even if there had been seven witnesses to (making) the first testament, that would nevertheless no longer have any legal validity and the latter will be valid, even though there would have been no more than two witnesses. And if seven were present at the latter, then that is all the more powerful by law.[151]

150 As we have seen in gloss 65 to JF 46:44.

151 *Ro*, III (JF), tit. 46, no. 25.

As with previous provisions, seven witnesses are stated to be required. A will that was made chronologically last always invalidated all previous wills. This provision also includes a notable exception: even if the last will was only attested by two witnesses, it was still considered valid and superseded all previous wills. This contrasts with other parts of the title, which state that fewer than seven witnesses meant a will was invalidated (JF 46:1).

One possible explanation for this exception is that a will represents the final wishes of a dying or deceased person, and those intentions were to be protected.[152] In this case, ensuring that the last will persists, even if it does not meet the usual formal requirements, may be seen as a way of honoring the testator's wishes. However, the provision also notes that a testament with seven witnesses is still considered stronger.[153]

Another possibility is that the first will was a secular one and had the required seven witnesses present. The second will, however, was ecclesiastical and left all the testator's assets to the Church or other charitable ends, and therefore only two witnesses were needed. In this scenario, the second will would overrule the first will, even if it was made according to different formalities.

In conclusion, both the *Excerpta Legum* and the *Jurisprudentia Frisica* establish that seven witnesses are required for the creation of a secular testament, indicating that Roman law was received and applied. Even, however, in the late 15th century, the *Jurisprudentia Frisica* mentions two or three witnesses, which may have been limited to dispositions and wills for the Church and charitable ends, or to replace a previous will attested by seven witnesses.[154] Secular testaments were thus made according to secular Roman law.

While the number of witnesses and references to Roman law indicate a secularization of testaments, it is important to note that testaments with the Church as only beneficiary could still be validly drawn up according to Canon law, and disputes concerning these testaments fell under the jurisdiction of the ecclesiastical court.

Although JF 46:44 may have applied exclusively to this category of testaments, this is unclear because the gloss (gloss 65) mentions wills for charitable ends requiring only two witnesses and no priest. As a result, it is possible that

152 Bassani, "A Coffer for the Will", p. 231 f.
153 See also Exc 88 for the same line of thought.
154 On limitation to charitable wills see, for example, Exc 59 and gloss 66 to JF 46:45. There are other instances where this number of witnesses is not limited to charitable wills; see, for example, JF 46:44.

JF 46:44 allowed any last will to be drawn up according to Canon law, including secular wills, which would contradict earlier rules requiring seven witnesses (JF 46:1). However, the exact requirements for witnesses remain unclear, and the *Jurisprudentia Frisica* remains ambiguous on this issue.

It may be asked why such texts on Canon law testaments as JF 46:44 were adopted in a compilation of an explicitly secular nature. This could have to do with the affinity of these two categories of testaments and the social importance of testaments in favor of the Church.

Some of the documents of wills from the 15th century demonstrate that, in practice, the situation was uncertain. This is exemplified by codicillary clauses by testators such as Jarich Epa Hotnya,[155] who was not certain whether the number of witnesses present for his will were sufficient. Since he had fewer than seven witnesses present, he included a clause in case his will proved not to be valid under Roman formalities. This demonstrates the uncertainty facing Frisian testators when considering which testamentary requirements to apply.

6.4 *Priest,* Scriwer *and Notary—Authenticating Persons*

6.4.1 The Priest

The role and presence of priests in the making of testaments has until now been ignored. According to Canon law, a priest's presence was necessary to attest and authenticate the content of a testament.[156] The *Freeska Landriucht* contains multiple instances of a priest being present during the making of a will, such as in the *Book of Emperor Rudolf* (Rud 5): "When a man is lying on his deathbed, whatever he then does with the approval of his priest, the court shall find in favor of the claimant." The priest played the role of a pastor and confessor to individuals just before their death, but also witnessed and recorded their last will. Being able to write and being trusted by the populace, a priest (OF: *prester*) was one of the few people suited for this role as an authenticating person (*persona autentica*).[157]

Verhoeven examined the authentication of Frisian wills and noted that 81% of testaments between 1400 and 1550 mention the presence of a member of the clergy.[158] This suggests that priests remained crucial in this role even into the

155 *FT* 34, p. 60, r. 28–31.

156 X 3.26.10.

157 Vellinga, "Keysers Orkena", p. 8 f.; Verhoeven, "De Beoorkonding", pp. 22–26.

158 Verhoeven, "De Beoorkonding", p. 22. There are several possible reasons why the remaining 19% did not have priests. First, they could have been made according to Roman law, i.e., they did not require a priest. Second, they could have included only charitable donations and therefore would not have required a priest under Canon law. Third, exceptions

16th century. Verhoeven believes that this was due to their traditional connection to testaments and last rites. Priests encouraged people to make wills as a means of providing charity for their own salvation and, as members of ecclesiastical institutions, also benefited from such disposals.[159] The question arises as to whether normative sources reflect the continued importance of the priest as *persona autentica*, and whether this changed with the increasing reception of Roman law and its application.

In this regard, a provision in the *Excerpta Legum* raises an interesting question.

> Exc 488. Jtem. Dit js riucht: Hwerzo der en testament makath werth zonder ene prester, dat en hath ney da gastlike riuchte nenne macht. Quia testamentum confectum siue conscriptum sine sacerdote non valet, ut ponit Spéculator, De instrumentorum edicione, quia sacerdos, qui est persona autentica, maxime requiritur: § 2 Compendiose.[160] Sed numquid eciam et secundum consuetudinem patrie, que est optima legum interpres?[161]
>
> Exc 488. Item. This is the law. If a testament is made without the participation of a priest, it has no validity according to ecclesiastical law, because a testament made and written without a priest is not legally binding, says the Spéculator, De instrumentorum edicione. Because a priest, who is a *persona autentica*, is very much required (§ 12). However, does this also apply according to customary law of the fatherland, which is the best interpretation of the laws?

The text discusses the role of priests in the authentication of testaments ("Because a priest, who is a *persona autentica*") according to ecclesiastical law. Guillaume Durand is referenced to support the requirement for a priest as a *persona autentica* when making a will. Durand also states that customary law may allow for deviations from formalities, such as the absence of a priest, if the testator was competent.[162]

in Canon law or local laws may have enabled attestation without priests. On this, see also Guillaume Durand below.

159 Verhoeven, "De Beoorkonding", p. 23.

160 Guillaume Durand, *Speculum Iudiciale*, lib. 2, part. 2, de instrumentorum editione, § Compendiose, n. 12, p. 134.

161 *A*, I (Exc) 488, p. 340.

162 Guillaume Durand, *Speculum Iudiciale*, lib. 2, part. 2, de instrumentorum editione, § Compendiose, n. 14, p. 134: *Sed numquid de consuetudine possunt praemissae solemnitatis*

However, the text also raises the question of whether a priest is necessary for making a Frisian will ("of the fatherland"). No answer to this question is provided. This text derives from a case record, and an answer may have been given in the full case record, or the answer may have been self-evident. Yet, we do not know it. If we follow what Durand writes, it is possible for the customary law of the fatherland to override the formalities of learned law and not to require a priest to be present. However, no rule in Frisian law explicitly states that a priest was not needed for making a testament. The text suggests possible alternatives to priests for authenticating wills could be investigated. For example, were there other individuals trusted by the populace who could perform this role? Further investigation is needed to answer this question.

6.4.2 The Scriwer

Reference to two other individuals can be found in another case record in the *Excerpta Legum*. This states that an error by a priest or writer/scribe does not invalidate a will:

> Exc 496. Item. Dit is riucht: al wert secke, dat **di prester jefta dy scriwer enis testaments** onriuchte scriwe iefta netreftige punten vrsumathe in da testamente als om wan wysheit ief om ore vorsuminghe, zo scolde dat testament allike machtich bliwa ende der versumat were fanda prestere jefta van ⟨da⟩ scriwere, darma bywysa mochte, dat scolde allike machtich blywa ende dat testament aech allike machtich to bliwen. Patet quod error **notarii seu alterius testamentum alicuius scribentis** non uiciat testamentum, quin firmum permaneat et inconcussum, dummodo constat de intentione testatoris in l. Errore, C. De testamentis et quemadmodum testamenta ordinantur (*Cod.* 6.23.7), ubi dicit dare, quod error notarii uel omissi testatoris non uiciat dispositionem, dummodo constat de eius uoluntate. Idem patet in l. Ambiguitates, C. eiusdem tituli (*Cod.* 6.23.24), ubi omissio erronea tabellionis eciam notariorum non uiciat dispositionem. Et sic dare patet iste articulus.[163]

> Exc 496. Item. This is the law. Even if a priest or a writer/scribe of a testament writes something untrue or leaves necessary points out of a tes-

remitti? Dico quod sic, cum non prohibeatur consuetudo haec admitti. (Translation: "However, is it possible to relax the previously mentioned formalities by customs? I say that it is so, because it is not prohibited to allow this custom.")

163 *A*, I (Exc) 496, pp. 346–348.

> tament, because of ignorance or another fault, then the testament shall still remain valid. And what the priest or writer has verifiably left out, that shall be valid as well, and the remainder of the testament shall also be legally effective. It is shown that a mistake by the notary or another writer of someone else's testament does not inhibit the testament insofar that it is invalid or decrepit, if the intention of the testator is certain, see C. 6.23.7. There is said, that a mistake of the notary or an omission by the testator does not influence the disposition if it is certain what he (the testator) wished. The same is shown in C. 6.23.24, where is said: If the *tabellio* or *notarius* leave something out by mistake, then this does not impair a disposition. And thus, this article is explained.

The argument presented here originates from Roman law, specifically from two provisions in the *Codex* (C. 6.23.7 and C. 6.23.24), which assert that mistakes do not invalidate a testament. However, the focus of interest lies on the officials mentioned in the Old Frisian part of the provision.

The provision mentions a *prester* (priest) writing down the will, but that is not the only person mentioned. There is also a *scriwer* (writer/scribe), while in the Latin part two other professions are mentioned: *tabellio* and *notarius*. Roman law made a distinction between a *tabellio*, who was a public notary whom parties could consult independently, and a *notarius*, who was employed by the state.[164] The two terms became largely synonymous in the Middle Ages, when the Medieval notary (*notarius publicus*) came into existence in the 6th century under the rule of the Lombards by combining the roles of a *tabellio* and a *notarius*. The Roman-Catholic Church and the Holy Roman Emperor facilitated the spread of the notary, who was commonly used for verifying documents. In Northern Europe, notaries were used in episcopal adjudication and were thus widespread.[165] A notary was responsible for writing down a person's will and verifying its contents. We can be certain that learned Frisian jurists were familiar with the office of notary since it was an element of the *ius commune*.

Both the priest and *scriwer*, as well as the *tabellio* and *notarius*, are mentioned in pairs, which could suggest a relationship between them. However, this is unlikely to have been the case. While the *tabellio* and *notarius* were both authentication officials in Roman law, and their roles were largely the same, the priest and *scriwer*, by contrast, were very different professions. It is more

164 Cappon, "Het notariaat", p. 5.

165 Cappon, "Het notariaat", pp. 6–10.

likely, therefore, that the author of this provision simply named the two most prevalent professions involved in writing down wills: priests and scribes.

A priest not only wrote down the will but also served as a *persona autentica*, meaning that their role was to authenticate the will. It is unlikely that the *scriwer* fulfilled the same role as a priest. The two professions had distinct functions. A *scriwer's* task was likely to have been limited to writing down what they were told, with no official role in authenticating the will.[166] This was in contrast to the priest according to Canon law, who attested the testament and provided the necessary legal weight.[167] Therefore, a *scriwer* was not a notary and should not be equated with one. The text (Exc 496) also does not associate the *scriwer* with the notary, except in the former's role as a scribe.

Additionally, 15th-century Frisian cities had secretaries that fulfilled the same roles as the clergy in writing and attesting documents. These secretaries were also called *scriweren*, and it is possible that they are referenced in the *Excerpta Legum* (Exc 496).[168] However, since secretaries existed only in larger cities, priests and non-authenticating *scriweren* were much more common.

6.4.3 The Notary

Notaries spread through various regions at different times. The first notary in Utrecht was documented at the end of the 13th century, whereas they did not appear in Holland until the 14th and 15th centuries.[169] Similarly, notaries were first mentioned in Frisia, including East Frisia, in the 15th century.[170] However, the presence of notaries and the situations in which they were used were initially modest, and their numbers remained low for some time. Of all testaments collected before 1550, only 35 were signed by a notary, with only six before

166 'schriver' Verwijs, Verdam. *Middelnederlandsch woordenboek*. (20.08.2020); 'skrīvere' Hofmann, Popkema, *Altfriesisches Handwörterbuch*, p. 445.

167 Verhoeven, "De Beoorkonding", p. 26.

168 An example of this is the city regulation of Sneek, art. 51: "*Wie die brieuen schryuen zal, die den borghers anghaet. Item, alle die brieuen, die die Burgermeesters, Schepenen ende die Raedtsluyden zullen besegelen van saicken, die die burghers aengaen, to gheuen ende to nemen, die brieuen sal onser stadt Clerck schryuen; of zy en zullen die brieuen nyet besegelen, ten zy by zynen wille.*" In: Telting, *Friesche Stadrechten*, p. 80.

Mention is made here of a *stadt Clerck*, i.e., a city clerk. Since the clerk's role is to write and seal documents (*besegelen*), his function is similar to that of a notary. On this, see also the second meaning of 'schriver' Verwijs, Verdam, *Middelnederlandsch woordenboek*, (20.08.2020).

169 Cappon, "Het notariaat", pp. 12–13.

170 Buss, *Letztwillige Verfügungen*, p. 56.

1500.[171] The first mention of a notary is in the testament of Arnt and Hille of Suerhusum [Surhuizum], who wrote a joint testament in which they each gave the other, as surviving spouse, a third of their property, including gold, silver and land.

> **Testament of Arnt van Suerhusum and Hille, his wife 1459 January 12**
> [...] Hyrum heb wy, Arnt ende Hille voirs., her Rippert toe Steens,[172] cureit ende en keysers oerkene, ghelovet mit hande ende mit monde dat wy dese ordinancie ende vrye ghyfte als voirs. is, sonder alle weerropinghe steed ende vaste holden willen onwerropelyc tot unse lyfs eynde, sonder arghelyst. [...][173]
>
> [...] Therefore we, the aforementioned Arnt and Hille, have vowed with 'hands and mouth' to pastor Rippert of Steens [Stiens], curator and notary, that we will keep to all the aforementioned ordinances and gifts without revoking them until the end of our life, without trickery. [...]

This clause, namely that the ordinances could not be revoked, was contrary to Roman law, as any will could always be revoked.[174] However, we can interpret this clause as a joint promise by both spouses not to change their will after the other dies. Nonetheless, Roman law was evidently not followed in this respect.

Of more interest are the descriptors used for pastor Rippert of Steens (*cureit ende en keysers oerkene*). In Old Frisian, a notary was generally denoted by *keysers orkena*, meaning 'emperor's witness', indicating that notaries were connected to the emperor. When looking for references to notaries in texts written in Frisia, we can expect, therefore, to find this term. In the *Excerpta Legum* (Exc 496), however, *keysers orkena* is not mentioned. In the testament of Arnt and Hille, pastor Rippert of Steens is referred to as both a notary (*keysers oerkene*) and a clergyman (*cureit*), suggesting that notaries were not necessarily secular. In fact, it is plausible that notaries were either members of the clergy or secretaries (*scriweren*) in cities, as only these people would have the necessary

171 Verhoeven, "De Beoorkonding", p. 29. The documents in question are FT 20 (1459), FT 23 (1465), FT 28 (1472), FT 37 (1476), FT 42 (1481) and FT 55 (1496).

172 Rippert is identified by Mol and Verhoeven as a pastor in Stiens. See Mol, Verhoeven, *Friese Testamenten*, p. 471. In the margin, he is called *presbiteri*, clearly identifying him as a cleric.

173 FT 20, p. 37, r. 3–7.

174 As, for example, in C. 6.22.6. On the revocation of wills, see Kaser, *Das römische Privatrecht* II, p. 494f.

education and experience to write and attest wills.[175] As previously mentioned, the Church played a significant role in the spread and use of notaries.

The lack of clear and frequent mentions of notaries in testaments and in the *Excerpta Legum* indicates that their presence was still limited. Instead, it was often priests who fulfilled the authenticating function, as they had also done previously. One reason for the late appearance of notaries in Frisia may be connected to the low level of urbanization in the region.[176] With smaller populations in cities, this particular administrative profession was not sustainable. Others point towards the clergy itself for the scarcity of notaries. With a strong clergy, priests remained viable competitors of notaries, thus reducing the need to seek out secular, public officials.[177] On the other hand, the scarcity of notaries also incentivized people to turn to priests to verify their wills, thus making the latter indispensable.[178] This may explain why we find priests in written secular law.

6.4.4 Clarity in the Jurisprudentia Frisica?

Given the increasing secularization of wills, a change can be expected in the normative sources of the late 15th century. We can specifically expect to see more mentions of notaries. On the other hand, several provisions of the *Jurisprudentia Frisica* require the presence of a priest, including the following:

> JF 46:43. Hweerso dy **persona** naet is wr een testament dat is naet machtich.

> JF 46:43. If there is no priest present when a last will is drawn up, then it is not valid.[179]

Notably, the word used here for a priest is *persona*, a loan word from Latin. Previously, we have seen primarily *prester*. In fact, *persona* refers only to a priest and not to a *persona autentica* in general.[180] Moreover, there is no further mention of a number of witnesses in this provision. A provision immediately following it (JF 46:44) mentions two witnesses, along with a *prester*. Accordingly,

175 Vellinga, "Keysers Orkena", p. 12.
176 Zijlstra, *Het geleerde Friesland*, p. 230.
177 Cappon, "Het notariaat", p. 15.
178 Verhoeven, "De Beoorkonding", pp. 26–29. Verhoeven also gives reasons here when and why this changed, with the clergy becoming less important in the 16th century.
179 *Ro*, III (JF), tit. 46, no. 43.
180 'persōna' Hofmann, Popkema, *Altfriesisches Handwörterbuch*, p. 382.

it is possible that this requirement for a priest was necessary only for ecclesiastical testaments. That this was not the case, however, can be seen in two other provisions:

> JF 46:21. Hweerso een testament maketh wirth jn een presters andert ende in gueda lyoeden andert, ende dy eerffnama deer oen byscryown se, so is dat testament noeglick ende aegh een stal to habben.
>
> JF 46:24. Hweerso een menscha een testament jeffta lesta willa haet mecket by syn persona reed ende in orkenscips andert, ende haet een eerwa inda testament bynaemd, so mogen da jeen deer wtoer sex handen sint dat testament naet wrsprecka. Als dat landriucht seyt dat sint fader ende moder sister ende broder kynd ende kyns kynd. Ende al weer dat seeck datter al weer broer jeffta suster soe mogen hyae ietta dat testament naet leckya, als neen onnaetlicke handen in dat testament sint to eerua maketh.
>
> JF 46:21. When a last will is made in the presence of a priest and in the presence of good people, and the heir is mentioned in it, then the last will is valid and has legal validity.[181]
>
> JF 46:24. If someone has made a testament or last will with the consent of his priest and in the presence of witnesses and has mentioned an heir in the will, then those outside the six-hands may not contradict the will. As the land law says, these are father and mother, sister and brother, child and grandchild. And if there were a brother or sister, then they still shall not disapprobate the last will, as long as no unrelated persons are made heirs in the last will.[182]

Although these provisions do not specify the number of witnesses required, both contain a requirement to appoint an heir, which was a formality of the Roman *testamentum*. It is possible that the absence of notaries at the time meant that priests were indispensable as authenticating individuals, resulting in this hybrid form of a will that combined the *heredis institutio* with clergy as *persona autentica*. Other texts, such as JF 46:44, 46:45, 45:59, 46:62 and 46:70, also mention the need for a priest to be present for a valid testament.

181 *Ro*, III (JF), tit. 46, no. 21.
182 *Ro*, III (JF), tit. 46, no. 24.

The *Jurisprudentia Frisica* mentions the *scriwer* only once, in JF 46:59, which is a copy of a provision in the *Excerpta Legum* (Exc 496). This provision also mentions a *notarius*. Although the Medieval *notarius* was present in Frisia by the end of the 15th century, only one other text, which we have previously seen in relation to the required number of witnesses, mentions a notary:

> JF 46:45. En testament fan wralsche secken ende aeck fen lawen ende eerffscip deer sint netrefftich sawn orkenen toda prester jeffta keysers orkenen deer al deer al jowns to ropen wirdeth, ende middelste dat sint vijff dat is in een huusmans testament, ende in een litika gae deer naet fule folkes wrgaria mey.

> JF 46:45. For a last will concerning worldly affairs and also of legacies and inheritance, seven witnesses are needed alongside the priest or notary who are called up at the same time, and on average five, that is in a farmer's last will and in a small parish where not many people can gather.[183]

In this provision, we see that either a priest (*prester*) or a notary (*keysers orkena*) is required to be present, along with seven witnesses. This demonstrates the entanglement of various testamentary traditions. Firstly, the priest and notary are considered to have the same authentication role. The phrase *wralsche sicken* ("worldly affairs") indicates that priests were also used for secular testaments and, as previously explained, were uniquely qualified to fulfill this role in the absence of notaries.

Secondly, these formalities contain elements of both Roman and Canon law. The presence of a priest is an element of Canon law, while Roman law required a *notarius*. However, the provision specifies the need for seven witnesses and not two or three, following Roman law. Therefore, we see that while a secular testament followed Roman testamentary law, some elements of ecclesiastical wills were retained. Priests had a twofold role: they could draw up a testament according to Canon law if two witnesses were present, and they could also authenticate a secular will drawn up in the presence of seven witnesses. Consequently, a hybrid testament existed that included elements both of Roman law (seven witnesses) and Canon law (priest). This is summarized in a gloss to the above provision (JF 46:45):

183 *Ro*, III (JF), tit. 46, no. 45.

> Glossa 66. *Een testament fan wrald* Sic patet quod in testamentis requiruntur septem testes cum notario cum presbitero, C. de testa. l. Hac consultis. (*Cod.* 6.23.21), C. qui testamentum possunt l. Hac consultissima (*Cod.* 6.22.8) et extra de testibus c. Licet uniuersis (X 2.20.23), C. l. Si unus uel plures (*Cod.* 6.23.31.4). [...]

> Gloss 66. *Een testament fan wrald* And so it appears that for last wills seven witnesses are required together with a notary or a priest, see C. 6.23.21, C. 6.22.8, X 2.20.23 and C. 6.23.31.4. [...][184]

As the second half of this gloss has been examined in the context of the number of witnesses, I will focus entirely on the first sentence, which simply restates what was said in JF 46:45. Curiously, the Latin reads *cum notario* ***cum*** *presbitero*, suggesting that both a priest and notary were required. However, it seems more likely that only one of them was needed, and this was probably an error in transcription.

Several allegations are presented to confirm the need for seven witnesses and a notary/priest. In C. 6.23.21 an eighth person is required to write the will down if the testator is not able to do so.[185] Since many people in the Middle Ages were illiterate, a literate priest would often document their dying wishes. In C. 6.22.8, seven witnesses and a notary are specifically mentioned as being necessary.[186] The decretal X 2.20.23 mentions the two or three witnesses required by Canon law for attestation in general, but not specifically for wills.[187] A gloss to this decretal also mentions seven or five witnesses, but does not mention a need for a priest or other authenticator.[188] It is surprising that there is no allegation to Canon law that mentions a priest, given that the intention of these allegations is to support the argument that a notary or priest was needed. Finally, C. 6.23.41.4 concerns rustic ignorance and allows witnesses to sign for other witnesses who cannot write their own signature. This is related to the mentioning of a farmer's last will in the main text (JF 46:45), which required

184 Gloss 66 ad *Ro*, III (JF), tit. 46, no. 45.

185 According to the Codex, this applied only when a testator was unable to write. In other cases, seven witnesses alone sufficed. [...] *Quod si litteras testator ignoret vel subscribere nequeat, octavo subscriptore pro eo adhibito eadem servari decernimus.* [...]

186 This concerns cases where a testator was blind and the will was consequently conducted verbally. *Hac consultissima lege sancimus, ut carentes oculis seu morbo vel ita nati per nuncupationem suae condant moderamina voluntatis, praesentibus septem testibus, quos aliis quoque testamentis interesse iuris est, tabulario etiam* [...].

187 X 2.20.23: [...] *non minus quam duorum vel trium virorum* [...].

188 Glosa *quaedam* ad X 2.20.23.

only five witnesses. Both the main text and the allegation take into account the fact that the population in rural villages was often sparse and uneducated.

In conclusion, the Frisian sources reveal the crucial role and function of priests as authenticating persons until the late 15th century. They were central to the documentation and authentication of testaments, a role that persisted even after the secularization of testaments and the arrival of notaries in the mid-15th century. In fact, the majority of Frisian wills were written by priests (81%).[189] The dominance of priests in this role is also evident in normative sources, where they are mentioned even when other formalities had been received from Roman law, such as the number of witnesses. Consequently, the priest as a *persona autentica* continued to be essential even after a secular Frisian testament had been established.

The strong clerical involvement in drawing up testaments hindered the spread of notaries throughout Europe, as also seen in Frisia.[190] The continued use of priests made notaries less useful and less needed. This situation changed in the 16th century, however, with the increasing secularization of testaments leading to priests ultimately being replaced by notaries.[191] The beginnings of this development were evident in the 15th century, along with the obstacles impeding it. But while notaries penetrated the law of testaments and were available, albeit to a limited degree, to testators, the historically strong relevance of priests for authentication purposes prevented them from being fully replaced until the 16th century.

7 Conclusion

Before 1400, Frisian wills were made according to Canon law, requiring two witnesses and a priest as *persona autentica*. These ecclesiastical testaments primarily concerned pious bequests and fell under the jurisdiction of the Church. If we consider there to have been a Frisian testamentary tradition in this period, it was a Canon-(Frisian) tradition. However, primary sources of the 14th century, particularly the texts compiled in the *Freeska Landriucht*, indicate that Frisian jurists were interested in creating a testament governed by secular law, exclusively referencing Roman law.

189 Verhoeven, "De Beoorkonding", p. 22.
190 Cappon, "Het notariaat", p. 15.
191 Verhoeven, "De Beoorkonding", p. 18. Verhoeven argues that the Reformation in the latter half of the 16th century was crucial for this development; see page 28.

This intention to create a secular testament was realized in the 15th century, as written primary sources demonstrate. The reason for this endeavor is still largely unclear, but it is possible that Frisians increasingly turned to testaments, rather than religious instruments, as instruments for settling succession. Frisian jurists may have developed formalities based on secular Roman law to govern how wills were written. Roman law was subsequently the primary source of such formalities, and we can see a clear reception of Roman testamentary law in this respect.

Secular written sources state that a *heredis institutio* was required for validity, and Frisians perceived this to be so. Consequently, most wills made between 1400 and 1500 instituted an heir. Frisians were also familiar with codicils and included codicillary clauses in their writings. Law texts describe seven witnesses being required for a valid will. Frisian law received all these formalities from Roman law, thus showing that this was the foundation for a new, secular Frisian testamentary law.

Despite this reception of Roman testamentary law, however, neither law texts nor testamentary documents were uniform. Not all Frisians included a *heredis institutio* in their will, and those who wrote codicillary clauses were often unsure what form a valid testament should take. Law texts such as the *Excerpta Legum* and *Jurisprudentia Frisica* often still stated that two or three witnesses were sufficient. Moreover, in practice, Frisians continued to write wills that were attested by only two or three witnesses. Similarly, the majority of testamentary documents were authenticated not by secular notaries, but by priests who adopted a secular function as authenticators of last wills.

These elements of the new Frisian testamentary tradition demonstrate that, for a long period of time, no unified system for writing a will in Frisia existed. Written law drew no clear boundaries between testaments made according to Canon or Roman law. Consequently, Frisian testators were often uncertain as to how to write a valid testament, leading to a flexible practice of making wills that contained elements of both Canon and Roman law. The practicality of making a will, even when it included only two witnesses and required a priest to be present, could in some instances override any formalities written in the law texts. For Frisians and Frisian jurists, it was essential that someone could write a will and settle the inheritance of their assets. The exact requirements for a valid testament were of secondary importance.

Nonetheless, it is evident that Frisian jurists endeavored to create a secular testament according to Roman testamentary law. When practicality impeded complete reception, a hybrid testamentary tradition emerged. In conclusion, the Canon-(Frisian) testamentary tradition was, for the most part, Romanized.

CHAPTER 6

Widowhood and Guardianship

It was not only men like Ducko Onnama and Jarich Epa Hotnya who wrote wills. In 1451, the widow Site Kammingha left all her property and goods to her four children:

> **Testament of Site Kammingha** **1451 April 18**
> Item jo hat macket toe erven al her gueden, replick, onreplick, byhala bockinge ende lieffgifte, Rienick, Sicken, Tiemck ende Sacken, ende hattet macket om een scheidenge herrer kinderen als ney folget. Int eerst had jo achthondert pondameten, dat laugit hyo ende deelt aldus dat her zynnen, als Rienck ende Sicke, schillet ieder habbe treddeheelhondert pondameten, ende Tiemck ende Sacke schiller yder habbe oerheelhondert. Ende in disse 300 pondameten der da dochteren schillit habbe, soe schilit hya habbe dat land te Teghum ende to Meedum, ende het dat land minder is dan da thryahondert pondameten, dat schil men hemmen foert uutwyse to Leckum.[1]
>
> Item, she appoints as heirs of all her goods—movable, unmovable, except *bockinge* (legacies to the Church) and 'love gifts'—Rienick, Sicke, Tiemck and Sacke, and has made the following distribution among her children. First, she possesses eight hundred *pondameten* which she leaves and divides thus, that her sons, Rienick and Sicke, shall each have two hundred and fifty *pondameten*, and that [her daughters] Tiemck and Sacke shall each have one hundred and fifty. And in these three hundred *pondameten* that her daughters shall have, they shall have the land which lies in Teghum and in Meedum, and however much less than three hundred *pondameten* that land measures, they shall receive the remaining part (from the land which lies) in Leckum.

This fragment of a testament shows that wealthy widows managed and passed on considerable amounts of property. Site had been married to Peter Kammingha of the wealthy Kammingha family near Leeuwarden, who had died years earlier. This was Site's second marriage. Her first husband was Peter

1 *FT* 14, p. 21, r. 23–30.

 | DOI:10.1163/9789004712706_007

Camstra, from another influential Frisian family.[2] Both marriages left the widowed Site with a large estate, which she subsequently passed on to her children.

1 Some Aspects of Medieval Widows and Widowhood

Information about the life, social standing and legal position of women and widows in Medieval Frisia is scarce. Both secondary and primary sources require closer examination as there is a lack of comprehensive scholarship on this topic. To gain a deeper understanding of the experiences of women and widows in Frisia, we must therefore draw upon broader literature examining women and widows in surrounding regions of Northern and Western Europe.[3]

It was not uncommon for widows to have significant control over large amounts of land and property in Medieval Frisia and Northern Europe in general. Women in this region could own property and had the right to dispose of it freely, including the ability to acquire new property or sell their existing property. Inheritance and marriage customs also allowed women to receive land and other property, which meant that they were directly involved in its control and ownership.[4]

In Medieval Frisia, women like Site Kammingha could bring their own goods and lands into their new households upon marriage, and retained ownership of them throughout the marriage. There was no joint ownership (common estate) of all goods between the two spouses.[5] During the marriage, the wife's property was under the administration of her husband but remained her property. As a result, a husband could not legally sell or transfer the property without his wife's consent.[6] This arrangement gave both spouses property rights during the marriage, and this provided women with a degree of autonomy through ownership of land and goods.[7]

2 For some additional information regarding Site and her husbands, see Mol, Verhoeven, *Friese Testamenten*, pp. 478 and 538.

3 With special consideration being given to the Low Countries, Germany and England.

4 Goody, "Inheritance, property and women", p. 10.

5 According to Algra, *Oudfries Recht*, p. 341.

6 The Fivelgoer law mentions that she gives her goods to the husband "for safekeeping", *F*, XIV (Fro) 3, p. 152. On this, see also in late Medieval cities, Howell, *Women, production, and patriarchy*, p. 15.

7 This also meant that both spouses contributed to the household's income during the mar-

But while women in Medieval Northern Europe, including Frisia, enjoyed significant rights to property ownership, their legal status as persons was restricted. As noted by Edith Ennen, women were not completely devoid of rights, but their legal capacity, at least in theory, was severely limited. For instance, they were generally unable to appear in court or pursue legal action independently.[8] The Medieval perception of women as vulnerable and in need of protection, regardless of whether this was accurate in practice, meant that they were often placed under the authority of a guardian. The role of the guardian was to provide protection and representation in legal matters.[9]

In Old Frisian, the guardianship that women were placed under was known as *mundskip*, with a *mund* being a protector or guardian.[10] *Mundskip* signified the authority that someone held over their family. For women, this meant that they were under the control of male figures: unmarried women who were still part of their parental household were under the *mundskip* of their father or other male relatives. Married women came under the authority of their husbands and were subject to their husband's *mundskip*.[11] In theory, this legal arrangement meant that women obtained their legal status as persons only through their guardians and not on their own.[12]

In practice, the position of Medieval women was more nuanced, and guardianship was less strict. Consequently, guardianship and lack of legal capacity were not always enforced or interpreted very narrowly. Women often had legal capacity even without guardians, and regional differences existed across Northern Europe, as well as differences pertaining to marital status. In 16th-century Holland, for example, unmarried women had full legal capacity in court, in contrast to their married counterparts.[13] Furthermore, widows attained legal status

---

riage, meaning it was beneficial for both of them to do so. See De Moor, Zanden, "Girl power", pp. 7–8.

8 Ennen, *Frauen im Mittelalter*, p. 34. This was certainly the case in the Early Middle Ages. Ennen also claims that women could not administer property. I have shown above that this was no longer the case in the Late Middle Ages.

9 For example, in Antwerp; see Aert, "The legal possibilities", p. 285.

10 Also referred to as *mund, munt* or *mond*. Not to be confused with the person of the *mund*, also written as *foermond*. I have chosen to use *mundskip* for the guardianship itself, while *mund* will refer to the person of the guardian from now on. *Mundskip* was Latinized as *mundium*. The authority of the family was also called *were* in early Frisian sources. On this last point, see Algra, *Oudfries recht 800–1256*, p. 293.

11 On the guardian in the Medieval German territories, see Ennen, *Frauen im Mittelalter*, p. 34 and Floßmann, *Gleichberechtigung der Geschlechter*, p. 120.

12 As noted for Medieval Ghent in Nicholas, *The domestic life*, p. 18.

13 Aert, "The legal possibilities", p. 285.

and greater legal independence in the Late Middle Ages, which is significant for the study of Frisian widowhood.[14]

The legal status of widows is particularly relevant for historical research because primary sources often obscure the lives of Medieval women, such that they become 'invisible'. In many cases, women's public actions were performed on their behalf by their husbands, and they were usually represented by their guardians in legal matters such as signing documents. As a result, women's lives have often proved to be more elusive to scholars than the more publicly visible lives of men.[15]

The issue of the 'invisibility' of Medieval women in primary sources should not be overstated. Sources from the city of Nuremberg in the Medieval and Early Modern period show, for example, that women, including married ones, represented themselves in court and signed contracts.[16] Moreover, even women under guardianship were not entirely invisible as they could act against bad guardians (OF: *balemund*) in the event of perceived shortcomings. Moreover, a guardian's consent was implied in all acts by women in 14th-century Ghent, even without explicit approval.[17] Even women under guardianship, therefore, were not entirely invisible.

Upon becoming widowed, a woman's visibility and agency increased.[18] This makes widows an especially interesting subject for examination. No longer hidden behind their husbands, widows were thrust into the public sphere with increased legal capacity and the potential to manage their lives independently. They could act on their own in business and legal matters, and in England and the Medieval German territories were even allowed to continue their late husband's craft.[19] While still subject to other social and legal constraints, widows were theoretically more autonomous than any other women.

The legal framework of widowhood and the concerns of widows can provide a first impression of the constraints and opportunities they faced.[20] While prac-

14 As Howell notes for late Medieval cities and Ennen for late Medieval Germany. See Howell, *Women, Production, and Patriarchy*, p. 15; Ennen, *Frauen im Mittelalter*, p. 138.

15 On the visibility of widows and women, see Aert, "The legal possibilities", p. 282.

16 Wiesner, *Working women*, p. 25. Some women acquired civil status in legal matters despite being under guardianship; see Howell, *Women, Production, and Patriarchy*, p. 15 f.

17 Nicholas, *The domestic life*, p. 18.

18 Cavallo, Warner, *Widowhood*, p. 3. On visibility of widows and women, see Van Aert, "The legal possibilities", p. 282.

19 Ennen, *Frauen im Mittelalter*, p. 136. On the economic rights of widows and their relationship to their husband's business and guild access, see Froide, "Marital Status as a Category", pp. 243–245.

20 Aert, "The legal possibilities", p. 282.

tice and theory certainly differed, insights into a society's norms and understandings can be gained from such examination. Additionally, sources other than normative ones, such as documents and testaments, help to contrast norms with lived reality.

The most important aspect to note about widowhood is that it was a common occurrence in Medieval times. A demographic study of Medieval England, France and Germany shows that the number of unmarried women (including widows, divorced and never-married women) was relatively high at approximately 30–40% of the adult female population.[21] While there are certainly issues with identifying and analyzing demographic data from this period, indications suggest that widows were a frequent occurrence in late Medieval life. This is further corroborated by an estimation that 14.9% of the adult female population in Early Modern England was widowed.[22]

One possible reason for this phenomenon was that husbands commonly died before their wives. In Southern Europe, this was primarily due to their age difference at marriage. Women tended to marry older men at a very young age, usually outliving them. In Northern Europe, however, the age at which couples married was higher, and women married later than in the south. Therefore, the main reason for widowhood in Northern Europe was more likely to be the comparatively shorter lifespan of men. Women, on average, lived longer, and men were more likely to die early due to external factors such as violence.[23]

Violence is also a potential factor that may have contributed to the prevalence of widows, as feuds could have been a common cause of men's death in Frisia. When feuds between families or clans occurred without reconciliation, participating men were more likely to be killed than women were.[24] This may have contributed to the frequency of widowhood.

However, this notion has been challenged by a counterargument that it was not until the twentieth century that women lived longer than men. Instead, in this view, the high frequency of remarriage among widowers is a more plausible reason for the commonness of widowhood. Accordingly, widowhood was "often a permanent position" for widows but less so for widowers.[25]

---

21 Kowaleski, "Singlewomen: The Demographic Perspective.", p. 237. This was much higher than in Southern Europe, for example.

22 Froide, "Marital Status as a Category", p. 237. In late Medieval Sussex, too, widowhood was common; see Mate, *Daughters, Wives and Widows*, p. 94.

23 Goody, Goody, *The development of the family*, p. 64.

24 On the importance of feuds, see Noomen, "De Friese vetemaatschappij".

25 Buitelaar, "Widow's Worlds", p. 5.

This second option seems more probable as feuds were not excesses of violence creating chaos and death among the population but rather controlled means of conflict resolution.[26] Therefore, feuds are unlikely to have been a reason for shorter lifespans of men in Medieval Frisia. Consequently, shorter lifespans of men in general may not have been the primary reason for frequent widowhood. It is more likely that widows simply remarried less frequently than widowers. More research is needed in this regard.

This leads us to one final aspect that must be emphasized: widowers. While they may share some characteristics with widows, an examination of widowers would be less fruitful and less significant. Cavallo and Warner provide a short overview of widowers in their book *Widowhood in medieval and early modern Europe*.[27] First and foremost, a man's status did not change upon becoming a widower. He retained authority over his estate and children, which he also had during marriage. Moreover, a man had full legal capacity, and this did not change when he became a widower. Widowers also remarried more often than widows, possibly because widowers were looking for the sort of help in the household that was missing in the absence of a wife.[28] Additionally, widowers were not often identified as such, unlike widows, in Medieval sources. For all these reasons, widowers play no role in this study of Frisian widows: there were no specific arrangements for 'widowerhood' in Frisian custom, and widowers could expect to continue their lives largely unchanged.

1.1 *Historiography of the Influences of the Reception of Roman Law on Family Law*

Examinations of the German territories in the Late Middle Ages and Early Modern Period reveal significant changes in the status and situation of women. However, family law remained one of the least changed fields of law, being "lived law" and therefore resistant to change.[29] Nevertheless, historians have noted several developments. Firstly, the authority of the father of a family was strengthened through the reception of Roman law. This was connected to the reappearance of the Roman concept of *patria potestas*, the paternal power over a family. Consequently, the head of a household received powers granted to a

---

26 See also Noomen, "De Friese vetemaatschappij", p. 44 ff.

27 Cavallo, Warner, *Widowhood*, p. 3 ff.

28 On this, see also Buitelaar, "Widow's Worlds", p. 5, who emphasizes a husband's inability to run the household.

29 Floßmann, *Gleichberechtigung der Geschlechter*, p. 129; see Wiesner, *Gender, Church and State*, p. 85.

pater familias in Roman law. Such a development was observed in Medieval Italy, while in Germany, this authority was equated with the *mund*.[30]

Consequently, the power of guardians in the 16th century also increased.[31] In Germany, court cases saw guardians being appointed for widows and women more often than in the Late Middle Ages, leading to stricter male control over women.[32] Additionally, gender-based guardianship reappeared after having faded in the Middle Ages. Roman law contributed to its return, not directly, but through linking guardianship over women to tutelage over children.[33] Women were seen as in need of oversight, like children. This strengthened the role of legal guardians over them. Lastly, historians note that joint parental authority disappeared with the reception of Roman law. This authority had gradually increased in the Late Middle Ages, but vanished again in the 16th century.[34]

In conclusion, reception of Roman law is thought to have put additional limitations and constraints on the legal capacity of Medieval widows. Most of this historical research concerns the 16th century, when a significant reception of Roman law occurred. However, such conclusions are merely general trends that varied between territories.[35] To investigate whether the same trends were found in Frisia in the 15th century, we need to examine the subject of Frisian widows. Areas of particular interest in this examination are the financial assets given upon widowhood, widows' authority over their children, and guardianship over a widow herself. We can observe how changes in these fields—and in family law—occurred through the reception of Roman law, such that it will be possible to ascertain how the limitations and freedoms of a Medieval Frisian widow like Site Kammingha changed in the 15th century.

2 The Financial Security of a Frisian Widow

A Frisian woman who became widowed was not left destitute. All the property she owned but that had been in her husband's safekeeping was returned to her. This was likely to have constituted a significant portion of her financial secu-

30 Garlati, "Women's Succession", p. 209 and Floßmann, *Gleichberechtigung der Geschlechter*, p. 130.

31 Franklin, "Peasant Widows", p. 204; as also noted for Nuremberg in Wiesner, *Working women*, pp. 24–25.

32 Aert, "The legal possibilities", p. 285.

33 Wiesner, *Gender, Church and State*, p. 86.

34 Floßmann, *Gleichberechtigung der Geschlechter*, p. 129; see Wiesner, *Gender, Church and State*, p. 86.

35 As stated by Wiesner, *Gender, Church and State*, p. 86.

rity, including the goods she brought into the marriage that were solely hers and not her husband's. Additionally, endowments made for the wedding and marriage became the wife's property. The two principal endowments were the 'dowry' and the 'morning gift', about which little has been written. Therefore, only a brief overview is provided here.

Several Old Frisian terms, such as *birns, bedlinze* or *fletieve*, are used to refer to a 'dowry'.[36] However, the term 'dowry' is used cautiously as the English understanding of the word cannot be directly transferred to the Frisian context. Other potential terms for this 'dowry' are 'marriage gift' or 'wedding gift'. In Medieval Frisia, both the bride and groom received such gifts from their respective families. The bride received a 'dowry' from her family, which she subsequently owned, and the groom received a 'dowry' from his family. Such gifts were determined in marriage contracts concluded between the two spouses' families.[37]

When a bride received such a 'dowry', she relinquished all claims on her part of her parents' inheritance. The Fivelgoer law states: [...] *Thet thredde, thet se vrweddade th ene becfeng anda lawm, and sa weddade hire hir feder wither tha bedlinze alle hredde.*[38] (Translation: "[...] Third, that she relinquishes her claim on the parental inheritance and (fourth) that her father assures her of the dowry.") Therefore, a bride was no longer considered an heir-at-law to her own blood relatives. We can understand the 'dowry' as an advance of the parental inheritance because she received it before her parents died.[39] No such arrangement was mentioned for the groom, who continued to inherit from his ancestors. The bride owned the 'dowry' herself and, after it had been in her husband's safekeeping during their marriage, she could rely on it if she became a widow.

The second endowment during the wedding was the 'morning gift' (German: '*Morgengabe*'). A bride received this gift from her husband on the morning after the wedding to signify that the marriage had been consummated. The 'morning gift' was a Germanic custom.[40] In Old Frisian sources we find the term

---

36 Vries, "Altfriesische Eheverträge", p. 255.

37 Vries, "Altfriesische Eheverträge", p. 243.

38 *F*, XIV (Fro) 3, p. 152. More on this provision later.

39 Algra, *Oudfries Recht*, p. 352. We find a similar situation in Medieval Ghent, where siblings of a bride were entitled to recover assets in the amount of the dowry from the parents' estate. See Nicholas, *The domestic life*, pp. 26–27.

40 'Morgengabe' in: Erler, at al., *Handwörterbuch zur deutschen Rechtsgeschichte*, p. 678ff. Also 'Morgengabe' in: Frühneuhochdeutsches Wörterbuch online. http://fwb-online.de/go/morgengabe.s.1f_1604988245 Accessed: 10 October 2022.

halsepund, although this is not used frequently.[41] If a marriage was contracted against the will of the spouses' parents, a morning gift was the only property that a bride received during the wedding because no other gifts from the families would have been forthcoming.[42]

Aside from these endowments, other means of supporting the financial security of Frisian widows included the *wetma*, 'love gifts' and more.

2.1 *A 'Widow's Portion' or* wetma

Wetma refers to property such as money, goods and land specifically intended to support a widow during her widowhood.[43] After a husband died, his estate was divided, and the heirs transferred the *wetma* to his widow. The specifics of how and from whom the widow received this *wetma* will be explained later. In Frisian society, widows were a particular focus of concern, especially among husbands who wanted to ensure their wife's well-being after their death. However, no such concern was extended to widowers, probably because a widowed man did not need to recover his own goods from his deceased wife's administration.[44]

According to Algra, the *wetma* was a continuation of another gift that a bride received when she was wedded: the *mundsket*. This gift could take the form of money, as well as other valuable goods and land. According to Algra, it was kept separate and returned to the woman as a *wetma* when she became widowed.[45] A *mundsket* was a Germanic marriage custom that involved paying a price for transferring guardianship over a woman. A man wanting to marry a woman had to pay this *mundsket* to her legal guardian in order to acquire the *mundskip*. Originally, this payment was made to the woman's father, but later developments meant that the woman herself received the gift, although it is unclear when this started occurring in Frisia. Importantly, this payment was not for the purchase of the bride, but only for transferring of guardianship.[46]

---

41 The only mention is in *F*, XIV (Fro) 4, p. 154: "*Hire halsepund thet sen xiij enza ende viij panningan.*"

42 Algra also speculates that this was the case in marriages between spouses from different (i.e., unequal) classes, although there is no definitive evidence for this. See Algra, *Oudfries Recht*, p. 352.

43 German: 'Wittum'; Dutch: 'weduwengoed'; English: 'dower'. See also 'Wittum' in: Erler, at al., *Handwörterbuch zur deutschen Rechtsgeschichte*, p. 1469 ff.

44 Cavallo, Warner, *Widowhood*, p. 12.

45 Algra, *Oudfries Recht*, p. 350. Mehringer also makes a connection between the Scandinavian *mundr* when comparing the Old Frisian *mundsket*, and the *wetma*; see Mehringer, "Wörter und Sachen", p. 290.

46 German: 'Mundschatz'; Latin: 'mundium'. See 'Munt' in: Erler, at al., *Handwörterbuch zur*

Frisian sources mention the *mundsket* multiple times, such as in the *Older Skelta Law*, where the future husband was required to pay two shillings.

> **Fant mondschet der famna**
> SkRa 9. Deer famna riucht is: dy jen deerse aeftighet tweer schillinghen des mondes.
>
> **On the guardianship of a maiden**
> SkRa 9. This is the law concerning a maiden: he who marries her has to pay two shillings for the guardianship.[47]

This provision requires a future husband to pay two shillings as a *mundsket* but does not specify to whom the payment should be made. Moreover, the amount of two shillings seems improbably low for a *mundsket*, which typically consisted of a substantial amount of value. It is possible that the sum mentioned here refers only to the part of the *mundsket* that the bride herself received, but this is unlikely, given that in Frankish customs from the 6th century onwards, the full *mundsket* was paid to the bride.[48] Alternatively, the two shillings may have been part of the *mundsket* still paid to the father or even the minimum amount that had to be paid as a *mundsket*, irrespective of the giver's wealth. While there is no evidence to support any of these suppositions, and it remains unclear as to how this provision relates to the *mundsket*, this practice was clearly anchored in Frisian law.

Algra argues that the *mundsket* became a *wetma* upon the husband's death, and he sees two ways in which this was supposed to happen. First, the *mundsket* may have been a fixed amount of money or valuable goods that were kept separate during the marriage. For example, the wife may have given valuable goods and money to the husband for safekeeping; the latter then stored them separately from his own property. When the husband's estate was being divided, the *mundsket* would then be transferred to the widow as support for her life in widowhood (*wetma*).[49] This would mean that the transformation from *mundsket* to *wetma* was purely semantic, with the actual property remaining the same, but being referred to as *wetma* when the woman became a widow. However,

deutschen Rechtsgeschichte, p. 752. Regarding the difference to 'purchasing' a bride, see Ennen, *Frauen im Mittelalter*, p. 35. In 6th-century Frankish law, this price was already paid to the bride. See Floßmann, *Gleichberechtigung der Geschlechter*, p. 122.

47 *D*, III (SkRa) 9, pp. 122–123.

48 Floßmann, *Gleichberechtigung der Geschlechter*, p. 122.

49 Algra, *Oudfries Recht*, p. 350.

Algra provides no primary sources to substantiate such a connection between *mundsket* and *wetma*, and so it is difficult to know whether the *mundsket* was actually used in this manner by the Frisians.

Second, Algra suggests that a *wetma* could be structured as *half be ende bodel*. This arrangement requires further explanation. Algra defines it as half of the profits during the marriage (*be*) and half of the inventory of the front of the house (*bodel*).[50] This allowed a wife to exchange her *mundsket* for a portion of her husband's profits and estate. In this case, she would no longer receive the money and goods she had given to her husband for safekeeping, but would instead receive *half be ende bodel*. Algra concludes that a *wetma* was a continuation of a *mundsket*, either in the form of a fixed amount or *half be ende bodel*.

However, the term *half be ende bodel* is not clearly defined. Although Algra claims that *bodel* refers to the inventory of the front of the house ("*de inventaris in het voorhuis*"), this definition is not entirely convincing. The Old Frisian term *bodel* can mean 'movables' or 'assets', and the Middle Dutch term *boedel* can refer to an estate (*huis en hof*) but also 'movables' (*roerende goederen*) or 'matrimonial property' (*huwelijksvermogen*).[51] Therefore, Algra's interpretation may not be accurate. It is more likely that *half bodel* referred to half of the movables of the entire property of the husband, or even half of the estate itself. The latter arrangement may also have allowed the widow to remain on the husband's estate.

To gain a better understanding of the acquisition of *half be ende bodel*, it is essential to consult the primary sources. The Fivelgoer law states, for instance, that a wife could give her *mundsket* to her husband in exchange for *half be ende bodel*. Four promises are made to a woman regarding her marriage, including her free choice of partner and the 'dowry'. The only promise of interest to us on this occasion is the second promise, which concerns *half be ende bodel*.

> fon frowm.
> Fro 3. Sa hwersa ma ene frowa vtjeft, sa racht ma hire fior wed. Thet forme, thettere thi feder freikap weddade, with wane sa hio hire lif wolde ledza. **Thet other, thet (se) kapade met scat ende mith skillinge, ther hio hire frudelf ief in tha hude, half be ende bodel, iefta xiij mere and viij panningan.** Thet thredde, thet se vrweddade th ene becfeng anda lawm, and sa weddade hire hir feder wither tha bedlinze alle hredde.[52]

---

50 Algra, *Oudfries Recht*, p. 351.

51 'bodel' Hofmann, Popkema, *Altfriesisches Handwörterbuch*, p. 72.
'boedel' Verwijs, Verdam. *Middelnederlandsch woordenboek*. (09 March 2023).

52 *F*, XIV (Fro) 3, p. 152.

> About women
> Fro 3. When one gives a woman into marriage, one gives her four promises. First, that her father assures her the free choice to whom she wants to give her body. **Second, that she buys with goods and money, which she gave to her husband for safekeeping, half of the profits and half of the *bodel*, or with 13 marks and eight pennies.** Third, that she relinquishes her claim on the parental inheritance and (fourth) that her father assures her of the dowry.

Two ways of acquiring *half be ende bodel* are mentioned here. First, there is the *met scat ende mith skillinge*, which may refer to the *mundsket*, given by the wife to the husband for safekeeping. As Algra suggests, a *mundsket* was used to 'buy' (*kapade*) *half be ende bodel.* Second, a fixed amount of money (13 marks and eight pennies) is mentioned, which could be an equivalent to a *mundsket.*

If the *met scat ende mith skillinge* is indeed the *mundsket*, the link to *half be ende bodel* is evident. However, there is no mention here of a *wetma*, and therefore no connection between *half be ende bodel* and *wetma* (and, by extension, the *mundsket*). The primary sources provide no concrete evidence of Algra's argument that these concepts are linked.

A similar concept of taking care of a widow's financial needs existed in Medieval England through an English dower, which was an endowment given by a groom to his bride. The purpose of the dower was to support the bride in the event of her potential widowhood and only became effective upon the husband's death. The husband managed the dower, which constituted between a third and half of his property.[53]

The dower shared similarities with the second form of *wetma*, where a widow received *half of be ende bodel.* This could suggest that *half of be ende bodel* included half of all property, rather than just the inventory of the front house.

Moreover, a dower often required a widow to behave in a certain manner. For instance, a husband could presuppose that his wife should remain unmarried for the rest of her life if she wanted to retain the dower.[54] These requirements for obtaining a dower indicate that there may have been significant differences between dower and *wetma*. If *wetma* was indeed the *mundsket* by another name, it would already have been under the ownership of the widow, and there would not have been any need to obtain or keep it.

53 Goody, "Inheritance, property and women", pp. 16–17.
54 Goody, "Inheritance, property and women", p. 17.

Insights into how a widow obtained her *wetma* can be found in the Fivelgoer law, which describes a situation in which a groom was killed during the wedding ceremony, with the result, therefore, that the marriage was not fully concluded. The question then arising was whether the bride was already considered a wife and entitled to the *wetma* for her widowhood. Details of this situation were written down precisely because it was both rare and exceptional. Nonetheless, this example allows us to observe how a newly widowed woman received her *wetma*.

> breidgoma.
> Fro 4. Sa thi breydgoma slain is in drecht, sa fulgat thio breyde tha lyke to howe ende to grewe and to huse and wint thermithe here drechtpund and thene wetma, thet sent xviij enza, and thet inreste iefta thet vterste rider, vndschawidis kern. Sa ach thet mundlase meydene to kiasan hire fremeda formunde. Thet kapade se mi th schette ende mith scillinge, tha capstedene. Hire halsepund thet sen xiij enza ende viij panningan.[55]

> (Concerning) a groom
> Fro 4. If a groom was killed during the wedding procession, the bride follows the body to the churchyard and to the grave and to the house (of the parents-in-law); and this way she earns her *drechtpund* and the *wetma*, which are eighteen ounces and the inner-most or outermost cow, chosen blindly. Further, the girl without a guardian has the right to choose her new husband. That she buys with her good and money, (that is) the validity of the marriage contract. Her morning gift is thirteen ounces and eight pennies.

It appears that the widow received *wetma* from her husband's family, which suggests that they held significant power over its acquisition. Without their consent, a widow may have faced difficulties in obtaining what was rightfully hers. Conflicts over such matters were not uncommon in Medieval Europe.[56]

However, the fact that a widow "earns her *wetma*" according to the above provision (Fro 4) raises questions about whether *wetma* was truly the same as the *mundsket*. It should be recalled that the *mundsket* was fully owned by the bride, and that she would not have needed to "earn" it. This issue can be resolved if we interpret "earning" in the following way: when the wedding

55 *F*, XIV (Fro) 4, pp. 152–154.

56 On conflicts between a widow and her husband's family and heirs, see Mate, *Daughters, Wives, and Widows*, p. 94 ff.

procession was interrupted by the husband's death, the question arose as to whether the marriage was sufficiently advanced for the bride to be considered the deceased's widow. By following the body and demonstrating her loyalty to the deceased, she proved that the marriage had been concluded, and she had become his wife (however briefly) and his widow. Therefore, all arrangements made for the wedding, including payment of the *mundsket*, were valid. If she had not followed the body, the bride would not have been considered married, and all arrangements made for the wedding, including payment of the *mundsket*, would have been canceled. In this interpretation, *wetma* could indeed be the same as the *mundsket*, as Algra claims.[57]

2.1.1 Comparing the Monetary Values of a *wetma* and a *mundsket*

Another way to examine whether the *wetma*, the *mundsket* and *half be ende bodel* were related is to analyze their equivalent monetary values. The amount of a *mundsket* is mentioned in Fro 1, which states that: "*Sa isti mundsket xiij scillingan and xiij panningan jef en som skildwepem.*" (Translation: "The *mundsket* is 13 shillings and 13 pennies or an equivalent sum in *skilden.*")[58] This amounts to approximately 169 pennies.[59]

Fro 3 states, meanwhile, that a woman can purchase *half be ende bodel* with *scat ende mith skillinge*, or *xiij mere and viij panningan* ("13 marks and eight pennies"). If this amount refers to the *mundsket*, it corresponds to approximately 164 to 178 pennies, which is similar to the sum mentioned in Fro 1. Therefore, it is plausible that a *mundsket* was used to acquire an entitlement to *half be ende bodel*.

Based on Algra's assertion, this sum must also be roughly equivalent to a *wetma* since it was supposed to be a *mundsket* or *half be ende bodel*. However, the mention of *wetma* in the Fivelgoer law (Fro 4) is less informative. The provision states that a widow receives both a *drechtpund* and the *wetma*. A *drechtpund* is a 'pound for the wedding procession' (German: *Brautzugsgeld*[60]) and possibly another gift given to a bride during the wedding. The combined (converted) value of *drechtpund* and *wetma* is 360 pennies plus a cow. This is much more than the other two sums (Fro 1 and 3). However, as there is no information on the value of a *drechtpund*, it cannot be separated from the total. See figure 4 for an overview of the monetary values.

57 Algra, *Oudfries Recht*, p. 350.
58 *F*, XIV (Fro) 1, p. 152.
59 A conversion table can be found in: Henstra, *Evolution of Money*, p. 5.
60 'drechtpund' Hofmann, Popkema, *Altfriesisches Handwörterbuch*, p. 104.

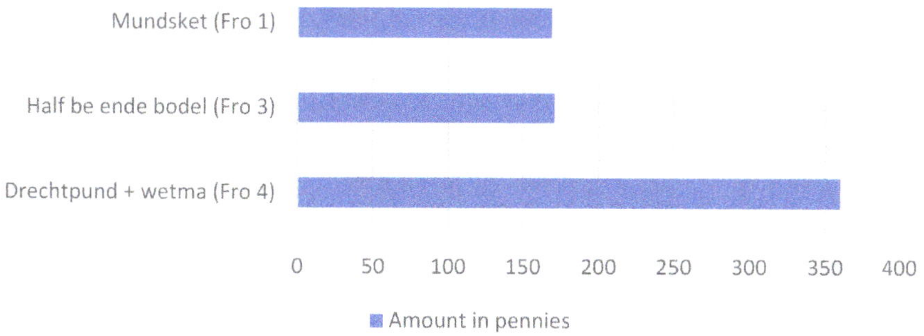

FIGURE 4 Comparison of monetary amounts in the Fivelgoer law

It is possible, therefore, that Algra's assertion is correct and that these three terms describe the same thing. Although a relationship between *mundsket* and *half be ende bodel* can be observed in the Fivelgoer law (Fro 1 and Fro 3), the relationship between these two terms and the *wetma* is less obvious. There is no direct evidence that a *wetma* is a *mundsket* or takes the form of a *half be ende bodel*. However, when considering the widow as her husband's beneficiary, we encounter *half be ende bodel* again. More on this later. Thus, it is plausible that a *wetma* indeed represented continuation of the payment for the *mundsket*.

We can also briefly consider the mentions of *wetma* in the *Freeska Landriucht*. As we have already seen, the *mundsket* in the *Older Skelta Law* (SkRa 9) was only two shillings (about 24 pennies), which is a considerably lower sum than the amounts in the Fivelgoer law. It is unlikely that the *Older Skelta Law* actually refers to the entire *mundsket*. The *Twenty-four Land Laws* (L^{24} 21) also mention a fixed sum of a *wetma* for a noblewoman, showing that a *wetma* depended on a widow's social status.

> L^{24} 21a. Elkes wives weetma dat is acht pond acht einsa ende acht peninge.
>
> L^{24} 21b. Enis edeles wives weetme is c. pond.
>
> L^{24} 21a. Any woman's *wetma* is eight pounds and eight ounces and eight pennies.
>
> L^{24} 21b. The *wetma* of a noblewoman is 100 pounds.[61]

61 *D*, VIII (L^{24}) 21a/b, pp. 238–241.

There is debate surrounding the meaning of the term *wetma* in this particular provision. Some argue that it refers to the wergild, despite the use of the term *wetma*, because the sum is identical to the sum for a wergild.[62] However, a gloss (gloss 147) attached to the provision in the *Freeska Landriucht* concerns the provision of widows, which suggests that the text pertains to a 'widow's portion' rather than to a wergild. However, the exact meaning of the text is uncertain. According to the provision, the *wetma* for a woman would be approximately 2,088 pennies, and around 24,000 pennies for a noblewoman. Both sums are much higher than any previous amount stated.

Consequently, these provisions provide no clarity on a *wetma* or its exact value. While Algra's argument about a connection between *mundsket* and *wetma* is plausible, the primary sources are unclear. Further research is therefore necessary to fully comprehend the nature of *wetma*.

2.2 *'Love Gifts'*

Sources from the 15th century include another term, *liafjefte*, meaning 'love gift'. This was a gift that one spouse gave to the other, and which the recipient obtained after the giver's death. It is similar to a *donatio post obitum* (donation after death), which was also received after the donator's death. As the name suggests, it was given out of affection for a spouse.[63] Testators often gave 'love gifts' to their loved ones in testamentary documents, where we can find numerous mentions of them.[64] However, the exact nature of a 'love gift' needs further elaboration.

Liafjefte is found in the Medieval register (RgJ) of the *Jus Municipale Frisonum* manuscript (*J*), where it is used to describe the twenty-second of the *Twenty-four Land Laws* (L^{24} 22): *xxij landriucht: En edelis wiuis liafiefta ney hier mannis daed.*[65] As we have previously seen, this text addresses the *wetma*. However, it is unlikely that a 'love gift' was just another term for a *wetma* since it is not used elsewhere in the manuscript in this manner. In other instances, the context for *liafjefte* is also different.

In the *Jurisprudentia Frisica*, a love gift is identified in the title 'De secundis nupciis' (On second marriages) as something given by a husband to his wife. A widow who remarried within the 'weeping year' lost her 'love gift':

---

62 See Nijdam et al. *Frisian Land Law*, pp. 239 and 241, who translated it as wergild.

63 It could also be given to other people whom the giver considered worthy of his or her love, such as children.

64 For example, in the testaments of Andlef Abbengha (*FT* 9, p. 13, r. 15 and 30) and Grathie Kammingha (*FT* 37, p. 65, r. 39–40). More on these later.

65 *J*, I (RgJ) 49, p. 40.

JF 87:1 Hweerso een frow her so naet seth ner regered haet ney her mannes daed dat hyo lyaeff jeffta wirdich se, dyo meyse mit riuchta naet ontfaen ner byhalda. Dit is dyo reden om dat hio boestged haet ende een oren man nymen al fiir bynna da aersta jeer ende dey deer neen edeler frouwa to byheert ner wel bytimeth. Ende deer aeck jn scryouna riucht to maniger steed is wrbeden, alsma inda keysers riucht claerlick ende wel bywysa mey deer in een loegh aldus seyt. Een frow deer bynna der tyt dis weermodis off der seerfaldicheed dat is bynna da scryel jeer is haesten ende nympt een oren man, dyo is infamis dat is hio is eerloes, ende hio mey buppa den trymdeel fan al her gueden oenden lettera man naet toe birnse bringa ende aeck jn her lesta testament naet mey jaen buppa den trymdeel ende da lyaef iefta deer her byspritsen ende toe leyd sint fan her ara man ende da lawa deer fan syner wegena oen stoeren sint haet hio foerbeerd [...]

Glossa 1. *Hweerso een frou her so naet seth* in l.i C. de secundis nupciis (*Cod.* 5.9.1), ubi cauetur "Si qua mulier nequaquam luctus religionem priori uiro nupciarum festinacione prestiterit, iure quidem notissimo sit infames. Preterea secundo uiro ultra terciam partem bonorum in dotem nec det, neque ei testamento plus quam terciam partem relinquat. Omnium preterea hereditatum legatorum fideicommissorum suprema uoluntate relictorum, mortis causa donacionum sit expers." [...]

JF 87:1 If after her husband's death a wife does not behave or has arranged her life in such a way that she is not worthy of the love gift, she may not lawfully take or keep it [the love gift]. This is the reason: because she married and took another man well within the first year and a day, which does not behoove or befit an honorable woman and which is also prohibited in many places in written law, as can be proven clearly under imperial law which reads thus in one place: a woman is *infamis*, that means 'dishonorable', if she hastens to take another man within the period of mourning or grieve, that is within the 'weeping year', and she may not give her second husband more than a third of all her goods as a dowry, nor may she give more than a third in her last will, and she has lost by guilt and forfeited the love gifts which her first husband gave her, as well as the inheritance he left her. [...]

Gloss 1. *Hweerso een frou her so naet seth* as in C. 5.9.1, which rules "If a wife through a rash marriage did not show any respectful mourning towards her previous husband, she should be infamous according to the

> widely-known provision. Moreover, she may not give her second husband more than one third of her estate as dowry and neither may she leave him by testament more than one third. Moreover, she will not share in any inheritances, legacies, fideicommissa by last will, or death-bed gifts." [...][66]

Two points are noteworthy in this text. Firstly, a widow would lose her 'love gift' if, not acting "appropriately", she remarried within a year of her husband's death. Besides the love gift, she would then also lose her husband's inheritance, and was not allowed to give her second husband more than one third of her own property. This restriction limited widows in their ability to remarry freely as they risked losing property if they remarried within a year.

This rule was derived from Roman law, as evidenced by an Old Frisian translation of C. 5.9.1, which is also quoted in the gloss. The reason why this was of particular concern for the authors of the *Jurisprudentia Frisica* is unclear. The *Codex* states the reason to be for preventing "violation of morality", which is also given in the Frisian provision.[67] It is possible that prompt remarriages were seen as a problem by the latter half of the 15th century. Moreover, the year of mourning may have had a practical basis. By waiting a year before remarrying, the family of the deceased could be sure that the widow was not pregnant from her deceased husband. Any children born to the widow during the first year of widowhood could be identified as her deceased husband's.

Secondly, in the Old Frisian translation of C. 5.9.1, *lyaef iefte* stands in for various Roman terms, such as legacies, fideicommissa, and death-bed gifts. As none of these concepts existed in traditional Frisian law, 'love gift' appears to have been used as a collective term to describe bequests made from affection for a widowed spouse. Another provision of the *Jurisprudentia Frisica* also mentions this term:

> JF 87:5 Djt is keysers riucht hweerso een man sterft ende lyout kynden haet dio moder onfucht fanda man, fan testament, fan lyaeff ieftem, fan jouwen fan bysprekim, jefta fan enigerhanda gued deer dy man dat wyff jout, dat gued schel dyo moder da mannes kynden weer lauwigia. Ende mey dat gued her setta ner sella ner nenirhanda wijs wrbringa, mer hio aegh dyo netticheed also langh als hyo lyuweth.

66 *Ro*, III (JF), tit. 87, no. 1.

67 C. 5.9.1.2: *"quibus correctionem morum induximus"*.

> JF 87:5 This is imperial law. When a man dies and leaves behind children, then the mother must in turn leave whatever (goods) she received from her husband—whether by will, by love gifts, by donations, by bequests or whatever goods the husband gave to the wife—to the children of that man and she is not allowed to pledge the property, nor sell or alienate it in any way, but she has its usufruct as long as she lives.[68]

Although 'love gifts' are mentioned alongside donations and bequests, no definition of such a gift is given, and nor is an explanation provided of how it differs from these other forms of giving. The above text is an altered version of C. 5.9.3, which lists several things a woman received from her husband: *aut quidquid mortis causa donationibus factis aut testamenti iure directo aut fideicommissi vel legati titulo vel cuiuslibet munificae liberalitatis praemio ex bonis.* ("or what they received as a death-bed gift, or in view of a last will, either directly, or as a fideicommissum, legacy or any kind of reward for generosity"). However, it is unclear which of these terms 'love gift' is supposed to replace.

There is consequently insufficient evidence to define 'love gift' in any narrower terms than a broader, unspecific term for gifts given upon the death of the giver. Since all instances of *liafjefte* mentioned so far date back to the 15th century, it is possible that this term only emerged in the Late Middle Ages to describe a variety of newly emerging *ius commune* legal terms, such as *legatum* and *donatio*. However, further research will need to be conducted in this regard.

The documents from the 15th century also include instances of 'love gifts' being given. In 1438, for example, Andlef Abbengha provided his son Sywert with *lyafyeften ende legaten*, but the nature of these gifts is not further specified.[69] Later in the same testament, he also gives his wife Hylka a 'love gift'.[70] Here, 'love gifts' are clearly distinguished from legacies, indicating that *liafjefte* as a collective term may not have encompassed legacies after all.

Similarly, in 1478, Grathie Kammingha left her mother Doede a 'love gift' on top of instituting her as heir of all movable and immovable property, excluding *bokinge* (donations to the Church) and 'love gifts'.[71] Grathie was a granddaughter of Site Kammingha, who was mentioned at the beginning of this chapter.[72] It is in her testament that we also find evidence of what such a gift could entail. Besides her mother, Grathie also provided her husband with a 'love gift' in the

---

68 *Ro*, III (JF), tit. 87, no. 5.

69 *FT* 9, p. 12, r. 30.

70 *FT* 9, p. 13, r. 15.

71 *FT* 37, p. 65, r. 39–40.

72 Mol, Verhoeven, *Friese Testamenten*, p. 538.

form of all the land that they had bought together during the marriage.[73] Land bought during marriage was part of the profits (*be*) and was therefore divided between the spouses upon death or divorce. Through this 'love gift', Grathie was able to transfer her half of this land to her husband. Her testament does not mention any children, and she died childless. She left her goods not only to her mother and husband, but also to other female relatives, including her aunts Tyemck and Sacke, and her niece Hidda.[74] Grathie clearly took special care of her female relatives.

These examples demonstrate that a 'love gift' took many forms. It was a broad term that eluded precise definition. Broadly speaking, it encompassed all forms of gifts given by a dying person to family members and partners whom they considered worthy. For a widow, such a gift could be substantial and very fortunate for her life in widowhood. At the same time, she herself determined where her own goods would go after her death. As we have seen with Grathie Kammingha, this freedom enabled women to support other women.

Finally, 'love gifts' appeared primarily in the context of inheritance and wills. As such, it is possible that this term was used principally when succession and inheritance were recorded in writing. This would distinguish it from a *wetma*, which was given to a widow independently of any arrangements made by her husband. Even if succession was intestate, a *wetma* had to be given. Obviously, this was not the case for a 'love gift'. As such, this gift may have been a product of increased testamentary practice. Alternatively, a 'love gift' may have been related to a *donatio post obitum*, a donation that came into effect with the death of the donator.[75] In that case, it would fall outside the scope of testamentary succession. Closer examination of this term and possible appearances before the 15th century will be needed to discover its possibly more extensive history.

2.3 *The Widow as a Beneficiary of Her Husband's Inheritance*

The last aspect to consider is the role of a widow as a beneficiary of her husband's inheritance. In the Frisian system of inheritance, wives did not inherit from their husbands. In fact, only children received their father's inheritance, and if there were no children, the husband's family inherited.[76] However, it

73 *FT* 37, p. 65, r. 41–42 f.

74 *FT* 37, p. 66, r. 9–10.

75 For the relation between donations and testaments in Roman law, see Rüfner, "Substance", p. 321. Donations, such as the donatio post obitum predate the Medieval testament in Frisia, see Cappon, *De opkomst van het testament*, p. 75 ff.

76 On Frisian succession, see chapter 5, which explains that the 'six-hands' were called to succession. See also Algra, *Oudfries Recht*, p. 338 f.

was possible for a wife to become a beneficiary and to claim one third of her deceased husband's inheritance. Such a procedure is outlined in the *Younger Skelta Law*:

> SkRb 33. Jeff een frowe her des foermeth dat hio oen her manne voercoft habbe half be ende half bodel ende trymene syn ain, lawiged ende onlawiged, jeff di eerfnama des bisecka wil, soe is hio nier hyne to jechten mit saun orkenen—dat schillet wessa fiower an syner sida ende tre an her syda—dan di eerfnama mitta seckwird ty ongane. Nu ist riucht dat dio frowe schil dat her half in bringa jeff hio dat trymene habba wil. Jef ma deerom monnia schil, so spreckt ma aldus: "Ic monie jo bi da ede deer y da koningh to hulde sworen ende bi juwer selwis sele dat i dae wird sidze hor disse frowe an disse manne foercaped habbe half be ende half bodel ende trymene syn ain ende hi se mit cape an da wara latte ende hio nu an da wara sitta schil mit mara riucht dan hioet enigh man rema thoer." Nu schellet da sex folgia ende da schillet elkerlyc sidza mit sonderlinga ede deer hi da koninge to hulde swoer ende by syner selwes sele, dat hi dae wird sidze, dat dis man riucht seide, nu dat deer hi hyr seide om dat eerwe.
>
> SkRb 33. If a woman declares that she transferred to her deceased husband half of the profit the estate yielded during their matrimony and half of the movables and (she can therefore claim a right to) one third of the entire property, both acquired through inheritance and otherwise, and if the heir wants to deny this, then she has a stronger right to prove her case with the help of seven witnesses—four from his side and three from her side—than that the heir may invalidate her argument by denying. Now it is the law that a woman must bring in her half if she wants to have a third (of the inheritance). If one wants to enjoin over this, one shall speak thus: "I enjoin you on the oath you swore to the king and on your own soul to tell the truth, whether this woman gave this man half of the profit the estate made during their matrimony and half of the movables and that in return for this he has given her a third of the entire inheritance, and that he legally installed her into the inheritance and that she now legally owns the property and does not have to concede it to anybody." Now the other six will follow and they must each declare under oath—which they swore to the king—and on their own soul tell the truth, that the first man spoke correctly when he spoke about the inheritance.[77]

77 *D*, XII (SkRb) 33, pp. 312–315.

As we can see here, a wife could sell (*forkāpia*) her share of the *be ende bodel* to her husband and instead receive a third of his inheritance after he died. This arrangement bears some resemblance to the English concept of a dower, which could be specified in a marriage contract or be based on local customs. In the latter case, it often took the form of a third of a husband's property, but could also amount to up to half.[78]

There is a connection between the Frisian *wetma* and the English dower, with the similarities between the two having been previously outlined. In Frisian law, a widow received a *wetma* as security for widowhood, which in one form could potentially constitute *half be ende bodel*. In that case, the wife may have been able to give up her own *wetma* to obtain the status of a beneficiary. This would mean that the arrangement of the *Younger Skelta Law* (SkRb 33) was also a form of a widow's provision or *wetma*.

Algra asserts that by becoming a beneficiary of her husband's inheritance, the wife was instituted as an heir of her husband, and therefore received the same share as a daughter, i.e., one third. This was supposedly more beneficial to the widow than keeping her half of the *be ende bodel*.[79] However, it is doubtful whether a widow was truly considered an heir of her husband, or whether she simply received a third of his inheritance. In the latter case, this third would be independent of any other heirs, among whom the rest would be divided. The above provision (SkRb 33) mentions only her claim to a third of his property, but does not call her an heir. Definitive evidence for Algra's claim is consequently lacking. It is also possible that a widow received a third of the inheritance without being considered a daughter in terms of inheritance (i.e., receiving a third share).

The existence of such arrangements suggests that the *wetma* and other assets given to widows at the time of marriage were often insufficient to provide a comfortable life in widowhood.[80] Receiving a third of her husband's inheritance was a potential solution to this problem. It is important to note that the value of the properties involved depended on the social status of the spouses, and the intention may have been to maintain the same standard of living in widowhood as during marriage, rather than merely providing for basic needs.

Testamentary bequests became increasingly common, enabling husbands and wives to provide for each other after death. This reduced the need for the aforementioned arrangements.

78 Goody, "Inheritance", pp. 16–17.

79 Algra, *Oudfries Recht*, p. 355. A daughter's share of the paternal inheritance was half of a son's. See Noomen, "Consolidatie van familiebezit", p. 76.

80 Algra, *Oudfries Recht*, p. 353.

There is no evidence of spousal succession in the late 15th-century sources. The *Jurisprudentia Frisica*, title 50 'De legitimis heredibus' (On the legitimate heirs), concerns intestate succession and does not mention whether a wife or husband could inherit from their spouse. In Roman law, a spouse inherited when there were no other possible heirs, such as ascendents, descendants or collaterals.[81] However, it is unclear whether this rule was adopted in Frisian law or applied in practice.

Grathie Kammingha's testament, which appointed her mother as heir and not her still-living husband, suggests that inheritance was still primarily settled within the husband's or wife's family.[82] It therefore remains unclear as to whether a surviving spouse could inherit in intestate succession in the 15th century, or whether inheritance was limited to blood relatives, as in classical Frisian law. It is also uncertain as to whether the arrangements described in the *Younger Skelta Law* (SkRb 33) remained valid. However, spouses were able to make a testament to ensure that their partners received a share of their property upon becoming a widow or widower.

2.4 *'Swaddling-Payment' and Usufruct*

A widowed mother with children could expect additional financial support to care for any minors. The main form of this was the 'swaddling-payment' (*luterslaen*), details of which can be found in the *Older Skelta Law*. A son was obliged to pay his mother for every year until the age of twelve that she kept him safe from harm. This obligation had to be fulfilled when the son married as he was then no longer under his mother's guardianship.

> **Fant laen des mondschypes des moers vant kynd**
> SkRa 11. Dit is riucht luterslaen, dat dy soen aegh syne moeder toleff jera aller jeerkis toe laen toe jaen fyff schillinghen, als hy synre breid halled, so fyr dat hi onwemed see fan warlasheed fan fyf seckum: fan swynes tusch, fan honna eetsle, fan hundes bythe, fan hynxstes hoeff ende fan reederis hoerne.
>
> **On the payment for the mother's guardianship of the child**
> SkRa 11. This is the lawful 'swaddling-payment', that the son has to pay his mother five shillings for each of the twelve years (he was underage) when he brings his bride home, when he has remained uninjured as a conse-

81 Kaser, *Das römische Privatrecht* II, p. 507 and, for the *Novels*, p. 510.

82 *FT* 37, p. 65, r. 39–40.

> quence of neglect by these five things: the tusk of a swine, the spur of a cock, the bite of a dog, the hoof of a horse and the horn of cattle.[83]

It is likely that this provision concerned widowed mothers as the mother is named as the child's guardian, whereas the guardian would have been the father if he had been present. The provision lists five cases in which a son was exempt from paying the swaddling-payment, all of which relate to injuries caused by farm animals, indicating that these laws primarily applied to rural landowners.

The same rule is found in the *Eight Provisions* (Dom 2), with an addition that specifies that a widow has full control over her swaddling-payment: [...] *Soe mei hio mitta lutterislaen capia ende sella ende oen jefta jowa sonder des mondes oerlef ende jelkirs haet hyo nates wald oers dan her ayn ledena.* (Translation: "[...] With this 'swaddling-payment', the mother may buy and sell, or give away from it, without having to ask the consent of her guardian and apart from that she does not have any competence, save over her own body.")[84] This suggests that the swaddling-payment was one of the few things a widow-mother had complete control over. The payment itself, totaling 60 shillings (approximately 720 pennies), appears to be a substantial amount compared to the *mundsket*, and likely comprised both movable and immovable property.

Furthermore, a widow-mother had usufruct rights over her husband's and children's property as long as she lived in the familial household to care for minor children.[85]

2.5 *Summary*

The mechanisms and arrangements mentioned above were designed to provide widows with financial security. However, the amount of property a widow had access to depended on what she received from her family and husband. Some widows were left with barely enough to feed themselves, while others retained a significant amount of property. Nonetheless, Frisian law demonstrates that supporting widows was important, and many rules obligated husbands and their families to ensure a widow's continued well-being.

Beyond financial security, attaining money, land and other goods allowed widows to exercise a greater degree of independence than during marriage. In 14th-century Ghent, for instance, a significant number of moneylenders and

83 *D*, III (SkRa) 11, pp. 122–123.
84 *D*, IX (Dom) 2, pp. 244–245.
85 Algra, *Oudfries Recht*, p. 353.

moneychangers were widows.[86] Similarly, in many European cities, a widow inherited her husband's trade and gained access to rights, privileges and networks of local guilds.[87] Although no precise data is available for Frisia, it is reasonable to assume that wealthy Frisian widows also gained considerable economic capacity to act. Therefore, widowhood could provide women with power, influence and independence that were not attainable before or during a marriage.

However, the situation of a widow became more complicated in the event of minor children. While financial goods from the marriage provided the basis for a widow's financial security, they do not present the entire picture of widows in Medieval Frisia.

3 Who Governed the Children?—A Widow-Mother as Guardian

The presence or absence of children had a significant impact on the life of a widow.[88] If the marriage produced children, the mother would typically remain in the familial household with any minor children, with her role being to raise them until they could take over the household themselves. During this time, she would enjoy usufruct of the estate. When the children reached adulthood, they would pay their mother for the time she had been their guardian (see SkRa 11).

The relationship between a mother and her children regarding inheritance and property was complicated. In societies where spouses had continuing rights to an estate, the death of one spouse did not transfer complete rights to the heirs. Only when both spouses had died did the heirs inherit the entirety of the property.[89] In Frisia, there was no common estate between husband and wife; instead, their property was kept separate, except for the *bodel*, which was the common good. The *bodel* was not immediately divided upon the death of one of the spouses and remained unified until all claims of heirs were brought forth.[90] The surviving widow then had a right to half of the *bodel*, while the rest was distributed among the husband's heirs. As long as the children were minors, responsibility for administrating the *bodel* and all inheritances fell to the mother. Upon her death, her half of the *bodel* was then transferred to her heirs.

86 Nicholas, *The domestic life*, p. 84 ff.
87 Froide, "Marital Status as a Category", p. 244 ff.
88 Cavallo, Warner, *Widowhood*, p. 18.
89 Goody, "Inheritance", p. 11.
90 Algra, *Oudfries Recht*, p. 331.

There is some uncertainty about whether a widow-mother was a *mund* to the same extent as the father had been. The rubric of the *Older Skelta Law* (SkRa 11) in the *Freeska Landriucht* explicitly refers to the mother as a *mund*. However, other redactions of the *Older Skelta Law* do not.[91] Being a *mund* entailed having specific competences over the children and their property. The following text suggests that a mother's authority was more limited than that of a male *mund*:

> **Als dyo moeder her kindes eerfschip forkaped**
> L^{24} 2. Dat oder landriucht is, hweer so dyo moder her kyndes eerwe foerkapet jefta foerwixled mit her fryonda reed eer dat kind jerich is, als hit jerich se, likie him di kaep, so halde hitten ende likiet him naet so fare hit oen syn ayn eerwe son der stryd ende sonder schulde. So hwa so dat kynd bifiucht jefta birawe | op syn ayn eerwe so breckt hy tyen lyoedmerck tojens dine frana dat sint xxi schillingen. Ende alle dae lyoed agen him to helpen ende di frana dat hy comme op syn ayn eerwe deer hy eer bi riuchta aechte, hit ne se dat hioet seld habbe jef seth jef wixled truch dera tria haudneda een, deer hio dis kyndes des lives mede hulp.
>
> **If a mother sells her child's inheritance**
> L^{24} 2. The second land law is that when a mother sells her child's inheritance or exchanges it with the consent of her relatives before the child comes of age, and if the child then comes of age and the transaction pleases him, let it stay firm, but if he does not like it, let him take possession of his own inheritance without having to undergo an ordeal over it or without having to pay any penalty to the people. Whoever then attacks the child or robs him on his own land is fined with ten marks, to be paid to the *frana*, which nowadays makes 21 shillings. And all people are obligated to help the child and the *frana* has to install him on his own land, which is lawfully his, unless the mother sold or mortgaged or exchanged it because of any of the three major emergencies, which forced her to sell his inheritance in order to save her child's life.[92]

In this provision, the authority of the widow-mother seems to be limited. The sale of a child's property required the consent of her relatives, specifically her

91 In the Jus Municipale Frisonum, the rubric refers only to "*lutherislaen*". *J*, III (SkRa) 11, p. 78. No rubric exists in either the *Dousa* manuscript (*Do*, 10, pp. 22–23, r. 12–15.) or the fragment present in *Codex Roorda*.

92 *D*, VIII (L^{24}) 2, pp. 214–215.

fryonda, or blood relatives. This implies that a widowed mother did not have complete freedom and independence in managing her children's assets. Algra and Sterringa assert that a widow required the approval of a guardian because all widows had guardians assigned to them.[93] However, the provision does not explicitly mention a *mund*, but rather unspecified relatives.

The deceased husband's family had an interest in preserving the children's inheritance, which explains why their consent was necessary.[94] In this provision, however, it is not the husband's relatives but the widow's blood relatives (*fryonda*) who give consent.[95] It is also unlikely that the approval pertained only to the transfer of property. The husband's family would still have wanted to ensure that the inheritance remained intact. Thus, we might expect to see their consent, rather than that of the widow's family, being required.

Despite this ambiguity, widowed mothers clearly faced restrictions in how they could manage their children's inheritance as they needed their relatives' permission to dispose of these assets. Later Frisian sources reveal that widow-mothers received a guardian from the husband's family. The *Book of Emperor Rudolf* (13th century) states that the husband's brother assumed responsibility for the widow and her children's guardianship.

> Rud 21. Dit is dat sexte: hwer so een man nimpt een frowa ende hi deer kinden bitiucht, jef di man dan sterft eer da kinden jerich sint, **soe aegh syn broder jefta syn broders soen da bischirmense an da guede ende an da kynden ende an der frouwa, dat him ymmen dwe wald jefta onriucht ont dae kynden jerich sint, hit ne se dat dio frouwe ene oderne man nime. Soe aegh hy dis mondschettes fan dera frouwa een Colensche pond also fyr soe hy riucht mond habbe wessen der frouwa ende der kyndena.** Haet hi dan der frouwa ende der kindena een urrader hiara guedis wessen ende dat openbere se, so is hi een baelmond, also fyr so hit biprowat se mit riuchta landriuchte.
>
> Jef di mond da kinden to bosta jout eer hia to hiara jerem commen sint, buta rede der moder, soe ne mei dio dede naet staen, want hit di

93 Sterringa, "The most miserable women", p. 290. Algra comments on the blood relatives: "haar bloedverwanten [die vogd over haar zijn]". See Algra, *Oudfries Recht*, p. 359.

94 A similar situation is found in Medieval Ghent. A relative of the husband was appointed to oversee the mother's activities with regard to the children; see Nicholas, *The domestic life*, p. 121.

95 'friūnd' Hofmann, Popkema, *Altfriesisches Handwörterbuch*, p. 175. The same terminology is also used in other versions of this rule: for example, in *J*, VIII (L[24]) 2a, p. 152.

keyser urbeden haet alle needmonda. Jef hit dioe moder deth buta reed dis mondis, so aegh dio dede eft naet to staen, want him di keyser dae mondschip toedeeld haet.

Aldeerom aegh neen frow neen deda toe dwaen buta her manne; hioe ne mei her winna ner forliesa. **Da frowen aghen da bihode der kinden ende dis guedis, hit ne se dat hiaet urliese mit trim tingem. Dat aerste is als hia ene oderne man nimet, so ist urlerren, hit ne se dat hioet biburgie da kynden also gued weer toe jouwen als hioet ontfucht. So mei hio foerd in der hoda bliuwa alont dae kynden jerich sint.** Dat oder is jef hio dera kyndena eerwe urbrinckt buta rede dis mondis, soe haet hio se eefta urloren. Dat tredde is jef hio se in een claester bringha wil, so ne aeg hia neen abbet to ontfaen eer hia jerich sint. Jef dat eerwe urbrocht is mit clasterferd jefta mit kape, als hia jerich sint, so fee hia oen hiara ain eerwe mit lioda landriuchta deer him di koningh Kaerl joe. Want alle needmonden fan onjeriga kinden buta reed dis mondis ende dera bihield dat haet di paeus ende di keyser urbeden.

Rud 21. This is the sixth key provision: if a man marries a woman and he begets children with her, and if the man then dies before the children are of age, **then his brother or his nephew have to take the guardianship of the goods and the children and the woman upon themselves, so that no-one will do them any harm or injustice until the children are of age, unless the woman marries another man. Then the guardian is entitled to a fee of one pound of pennies of Cologne from the woman if he has been a just guardian to the woman and the children.** If, however, he showed no care for the woman's or the children's goods and if this is publicly known, he is a bad guardian, provided that he has been found guilty of this in court according to the land law.

If the guardian lets the children enter into matrimony before they are of age, without the consent of the mother, this act shall not be considered to be legally binding because the emperor has forbidden all forms of imposed guardianship. If the mother does this without the consent of the guardian, this shall also not be considered to be legally binding because the emperor has given the guardianship to the guardian.

For this reason, a woman is not allowed to perform a legal act without her husband; she can win nor lose a case. **Women have the right to take care of the children and their property, unless they lose this right because of three things. The first is when she marries another man, then she has lost it unless she can provide security that she will give the children back their goods in the same condition and value as she had**

> **received it. Then she may continue to look after the goods of the children until they are of age.** The second is, if she alienates the inheritance of her children without the consent of the guardian. Then she has also lost it. The third is, if she wants to bring them into a monastery, then no abbot must accept them until they are of age. If the inheritance has been alienated because of entry into a monastery or because of selling it, and if the children then come of age, they can take possession of their own inheritance according to the land law which was given to them by King Charles. Because all imposed guardianships against underage children without the consent and monitoring of the guardian have been forbidden by the pope and the emperor.[96]

A comparison of the functions of the brother and the widow-mother shows some differences. The brother's primary responsibility was *beschirmense*, which means 'protection' or 'legal protection'.[97] Later he is referred to as a *mond*, indicating that his duty was to serve as a guardian for both the mother and the children. The widow-mother, by contrast, had the right to *bihode*, which can be translated as 'care', 'supervision' or 'custody'.[98] This suggests that she was not a formal guardian (*mund*) of her children, thus limiting her legal capacity to act in matters related to property. However, her right to 'custody' was acknowledged, and she retained this right even if she remarried. In such cases, she was required to promise to return the children's property in the same condition. Therefore, a widowed mother had some authority over her children through this 'custody'.

This provision (Rud 21) highlights two scenarios in which the authority of a widow-mother was limited. Firstly, she needed a guardian's consent to alienate her children's inheritance, with the brother-guardian, as a representative of the husband's clan, having a significant interest in ensuring that the inheritance remained intact within the family of the deceased husband. Secondly, the widow-mother required the guardian's consent to arrange marriages for her children; however, the guardian also needed the mother's approval to do the same. Therefore, the guardian and the mother were mutually dependent on each other.

During the Middle Ages, joint parental authority became increasingly common in Germany.[99] Mothers previously had little say in the upbringing of their

---

96 *D*, XVI (Rud) 21, pp. 397–399.

97 'biskirmenisse' Hofmann, Popkema, *Altfriesisches Handwörterbuch*, p. 60.

98 'bihōde' Hofmann, Popkema, *Altfriesisches Handwörterbuch*, p. 46.

99 Cavallo, Warner, *Widowhood*, p. 16; Wiesner, *Gender, Church and State*, p. 86.

children, but over time their authority increased and their role aligned closely with that of a husband's *Vormundschaft*.[100] However, information on the situation of widow-mothers in classical Frisian law is sparse, and neither the *Older Skelta Law* nor the *Twenty-four Land Laws* mention any guardian or caretaker besides a widow-mother. As such, we cannot quite reconstruct the same development. Indeed, a guardian of a widow and children appears only to be present in the later sources. It is uncertain whether this is due to a lack of information or to a change in guardianship. In the 13th century, a widowed mother in Frisia exercised most functions of *mundskip* over her children, but formally she and her children were under the guardianship of a male relative of her deceased husband.

A useful comparison can be made with Medieval Ghent, where a surviving parent did not automatically become the legal guardian. Instead, a relative from the husband's clan was appointed, and the surviving spouse acted as a 'supervisor' of the appointed guardian to make sure that he acted on the children's behalf.[101] Similarly, in Frisia, a relative of the husband was appointed guardian (*mund*), but the widowed mother retained custody of the children (*bihode*). Thus, a widowed mother maintained authority and administration over her children and their property.

In Medieval Ghent, it was also possible for a widowed mother to become a legal guardian with the consent of the deceased's family. In this case, a 'supervisor' was provided by the family, and the roles were reversed.[102] The surviving spouse and the deceased's family jointly administered the children and their property, with one serving as the legal guardian and the other as a 'supervisor'. However, it is not known whether this reverse situation was also possible in Frisia.

3.1 *First Influences of Roman Law—A Mother's Tutelage*

Frisian jurists commented quite extensively on the provision in the *Book of Emperor Rudolf* (Rud 21) dealt with above. Some of the glosses raise interesting questions regarding a comparison with and an application of Roman law regarding widows as guardians of their children. The previous analysis of this text (Rud 21) neglected to include and discuss a short paragraph at the end of the provision:

---

100 Floßmann, *Gleichberechtigung der Geschlechter*, p. 127.

101 Nicholas, *The domestic life*, p. 109. It is important to note here that, since Frisian law did not have fixed legal terms, words such as 'overseer' should be understand in a general way, i.e., as someone who oversees others.

102 Nicholas, *The domestic life*, p. 121.

> [...] Emen ende eeftersusterlinghen fan der modersida sint alsoe nei toe dae mondscip onjerigha kindena soe dae fedrien ende dae susterlingen fan des faders sida.

> [...] Uncles and cousins from the mother's side have the same right to become guardian of underage children as uncles and cousins from the father's side.[103]

This is a rather curious paragraph. At the beginning of the provision, it was stated that the husband's brother or nephew would become the guardian of the widow and children. However, the inclusion of the mother's side seems illogical if the purpose of the guardian was to represent the father's side and oversee the mother. It is possible that this paragraph was added later as it does not fit well with the rest of the provision in the *Book of Emperor Rudolf* (Rud 21). Furthermore, this paragraph is not included in the *Jus Municipale Frisonum* (*J*) version of the text.[104] It is likely that this addition was influenced by Roman law, where guardianship over minors was known as *tutela*, hence the use of "tutelage" in referring to it. The term "guardianship" still denotes the Frisian *mund*. Additional insights can be gleaned from the first gloss to this provision in the *Book of Emperor Rudolf* (gloss 183 to Rud 21):

> Glossa 183. *So aegh syn broder iefta syn broders soen* Instit. de legi. ag. tutela § i (*Inst.* 1.15.1), C. eodem titulo (*Cod.* 5.30). Hodie uero nouo iure auctenticorum agnati simul et cognati. Et proximior gradu prefertur in tutela, sicut in successione, in auct. de success. que ab intestat. deferuntur § Ex his (*Auth.* 9.1.5 [*Nov.* 118.5]), ff. legi. tute. l. Si plures et l. Si relinquero (*Dig.* 26.4.9 et 8) et Insti. de capi. diminui. § Vltimo (*Inst.* 1.16.7) in glosa.[105]

> Gloss 183. *So aegh syn broder iefta syn broders soen* See *Inst.* 1.15.1 and C. 5.30. Nowadays, however, according to the new law of the *authenticae*, those related through males together with next of kin in general. And the one most closely related has preference in the tutelage just as in the succession, see *Auth.* 9.1.5 (*Nov.* 118.5), D. 26.4.9 and 8, and in the Gloss to Inst. 1.16.7.[106]

---

103 *D*, XVI (Rud) 21, pp. 398–399.
104 *J*, XVIII (Rud) 16, p. 362.
105 The gloss *gradu* ad *Inst.* 1.16.7.
106 Gloss 183 ad *D*, XVI (Rud) 21, pp. 398–399.

The lemma states that the brother of the deceased husband becomes the guardian, but the gloss and the aforementioned paragraph extend guardianship from the father's side to both sides. However, this was not the case in traditional Frisian law.[107] It is likely that this extension was influenced by Roman law, which was received into Frisian law. The fact that it is written in Old Frisian as part of the *Book of Emperor Rudolf* (Rud 21) demonstrates the profoundness of this reception.

The rules of Roman law referenced in the gloss relate to tutelage in general. According to Roman law, both sides are equally preferred for tutelage, as stated, for example, in Auth. 9.1.5 (*Nov.* 118.5), which is mentioned in the gloss: [...] *Sancimus enim unumquemque secundum gradum et ordinem, quo ad hereditatem vocatur aut solus aut cum aliis, et functionem tutelae suscipere, nulla neque in hac parte differentia introducenda de agnatorum seu cognatorum iure* [...].[108] (Translation: "[...] We order that all of them, according to their degree of relationship, and in the order in which they are called to the succession, either alone or along with others, shall take up the guardianship, and that no distinction shall be made in this respect between agnates and cognates; [...].") Additionally, it is interesting to note that *mundskip* is interpreted as *tutela*. Therefore, guardianship over children and widows was equated with tutelage in Roman law.

Gloss 185 refers to the first case in which a widow-mother can lose her guardianship, which is when she remarries.[109] It contains only allegations that confirm this loss in several instances of Roman law.

Another gloss (gloss 186) refers to the requirements placed on a mother who wants to be the tutor of her children according to Roman law. In this case, the mother must provide security to continue looking after the goods of her children.

> Glossa 186. *Hit ne se dat hiaet biburgie* Nota antequam mater admittitur ad tutelam puerorum, debet primo coram iudice obligare res suas et renunciare senatusconsulto uelliano et abdicare secundas nupcias, ut in auct. unde sine prohibitione matris § finali collatione vii (*Auth.* 7.4.2 [*Nov.* 94.2]). Et si secundas nupcias contraxerit, antequam pecierit tutorem fi-

107 Although it is interesting to consider that this may be why the Twenty-four Land Laws (L^{24} 2) refer to the blood relatives of the widow instead of those of the deceased husband. Nonetheless, the Book of Emperor Rudolf (Rud 21) is clear that a brother or nephew on the male side was to take over guardianship.

108 *Auth.* 9.1.5 (*Nov.* 118.5).

109 Gloss 185 ad *D*, XVI (Rud) 21, pp. 398–399.

liis dari et antequam racionem tutele et totum quidquit inde debet reddiderit, non solum bona matris sed uitrici sunt filiis obligata. Aliis penis abiectis, in auctentico de nupc. § Si autem tutelam (*Auth.* 4.1.40 [*Nov.* 22.40]). Et debet mater compelli, ut rationem tutele reddat et quidquit inuentum fuerit eam debere integre persoluat, ut ibi.

Gloss 186. *Hit ne se dat hiaet biburgie* Note. Before the mother is admitted to the tutelage, she must first provide security with her assets before the judge, renounce her appeal to the *Senatusconsultum Velleianum*, and abdicate a second marriage, see *Auth.* 7.4.2 (*Nov.* 94.2). And if she enters into a second marriage before she has requested that a tutor be given for the children and before she has given account of the tutelage and has restored all she accordingly owes, not only the mother's assets but also those of the stepfather will serve as security for the children. For other humiliating punishments see *Auth.* 4.1.40 (*Nov.* 22.40). And the mother should be compelled to give account of the tutelage and whatever appears that she owes, she will fully pay, as is stated there.[110]

The role of the mother as caretaker is defined as one of tutelage (*tutela puerorum*). A tutor's primary duty was to care for and protect their wards. Since the time of Justinian, women were allowed to be tutors in the same manner as men.[111] In Frisia, widow-mothers fulfilled essentially the same function as a guardian.[112] However, while they had the ability to administer property, they also needed a 'proper' guardian's permission for alienation and other legal action. It is possible that the mother and a male relative of the father oversaw children together, as in Medieval Ghent. As such, mothers were likely to have remained dependent on a male figure. This is different from Roman law, where a mother could be a tutor in the same manner as a father and was therefore not formally restricted by other male guardians.[113]

There were also other differences in tutelage requirements. According to Roman law, a mother who wanted to acquire tutelage over her children had to renounce the protection provided by the *Senatusconsultum Velleianum*. She was also forbidden from marrying again. The SC *Velleianum* forbade women

110 Gloss 186 ad *D*, XVI (Rud) 21, pp. 398–401.

111 See Kaser, *Das römische Privatrecht* II, p. 229 ff. for the duties of a tutor and p. 227 f. for the admittance of women to tutelage.

112 For example, in *D*, III (SkRa) 8, pp. 120–121.

113 Roman law makes no explicit distinction between the tutelage of a woman or man. See Kaser, *Das römische Privatrecht* II, p. 461 f. I will return to this later in this chapter in detail.

from giving guarantees or standing surety so as to protect them from possible claims.[114] By renouncing this decree a mother could stand surety with her own property for any debts incurred on behalf of her children. A similar situation can be found in the Frisian provision, where a mother had to provide security for the goods of her children. These rules were intended to ensure that the paternal inheritance remained intact.

However, the *Book of Emperor Rudolf* (Rud 21) states that a mother was required to provide such security only if she wanted to retain care of her children after marrying a second time. Roman law, by contrast, required renouncement of the SC *Velleianum* in order to acquire tutelage in the first place. A second marriage immediately made a woman unsuitable to be a tutor, as stated in Auth. 7.4.2 at the end: [...] *mox tamen ut secundas contraxerit nuptias, repente expelli tutela* [...].[115] (Translation: "[...] nevertheless, as soon as she has contracted a second marriage, she is deprived of tutelage [...].") Gloss 186 does not mention this difference and does not specify that a second marriage terminates tutelage. However, this is stated in the next gloss:

> Glossa 187. *Soe mei hio foerd inder hode* Sed non in tutela, quia alius dabitur tutor pupillis a iudice, ut in auctentico de nup. § Si autem in fine (*Auth.* 4.1.40 [*Nov.* 22.40]).

> Gloss 187. *Soe mei hio foerd inder hode* But not remain tutor, since the judge will provide the pupils with a tutor in a different way, as in *Auth.* 4.1.40 (*Nov.* 22.40).[116]

The lemma *Soe mei hio foerd inder hode* refers to a line in the *Book of Emperor Rudolf* (Rud 21) that allowed a woman to continue taking care of her children's property if she guaranteed that it would remain intact. However, the gloss states that she cannot remain a tutor. Despite this, in context, the gloss does not refute her right to take care of the children or their property. Instead, she can still act as a caretaker according to the Frisian provision, but not as a tutor according to Roman law. As a result, an intermixture of Frisian and Roman rules emerged.

In conclusion, the analyzed glosses demonstrate how Frisian jurists interpreted the role of a widowed mother with tutelage in Roman law. However,

114 Kaser, *Das römische Privatrecht* II, pp. 461–462.
115 *Auth.* 7.4.2 (*Nov.* 94.2).
116 Gloss 187 ad *D*, XVI (Rud) 21, pp. 400–401.

this did not reflect the Frisian reality, where mothers who took care of their children needed a *mund* to take legal action concerning the children, such as alienation of their assets.

The interconnecting of Frisian and Roman concepts is significant in terms of reception. It shows how Frisians incorporated elements of Roman law into their legal system. By linking Frisian and Roman concepts, irrespective of their differences, Roman law gained authority and familiarity, which enabled later jurists to apply its elements. Additionally, the interpretation of a Frisian concept through a Roman law concept directly influenced the formation of legal norms and reality. Identifying guardianship over children with Roman tutelage served to strengthen the legal position of mothers as they became the sole authority over their children, without needing to refer to a more authoritative male relative.

Furthermore, certain characteristics of Roman law regarding a mother's tutelage emerged, primarily the formalities for becoming a tutor: providing security, giving an oath not to remarry, and renouncing the protection of the SC *Velleianum*. It is argued that the renunciation of the SC *Velleianum* became a principle of becoming a guardian according to the *ius commune*.[117] This limited what a widow could freely do if she wanted to retain guardianship over her children. These formalities contrasted with what was written in the *Book of Emperor Rudolf* (Rud 21), where a mother was able both to administer her children's property and to remarry as long as she provided security for their assets. The glosses did not disallow the caretaking of children and their property by a widow: while she lost tutelage over her children and their assets, she could retain care (*bihode*) of them. Accordingly, as a tutor in the sense of Roman law, a widow had much the same authority and power as a Frisian *mund*. However, if she could not be tutor, Frisian law still allowed her *bihode* of her children, which meant that a widow would not have to relinquish all the influence over her children as far as the text and gloss detail.

3.2 *The Case of N. against R. concerning Guardianship by a Mother—A Case Record from the 15th Century*

Sometime before the mid-15th century, an unknown widow with a child appeared before a Frisian court to contest guardianship over her child being assigned to a relative. A partial record of this case was included in the *Excerpta Legum* in *Codex Aysma* under the rubric 'de tutelis'. The woman was unlikely

117 Floßmann, *Gleichberechtigung der Geschlechter*, p. 130.

to have been able to represent herself and was thus represented by someone else in court.[118] This woman (N.) remains largely unknown, except that she may have been wealthy enough to bring the case to court.[119] The other party (R.) claimed to be the child's guardian and was related to N. in some way, as N. argued that he was a cognate, not an agnate, of the child. Unfortunately, the records do not provide evidence of how the case was resolved.

N. made five distinct claims against R., and her arguments reveal the interweaving of Frisian *mundskip* and Roman *tutela* that has already been observed. The inclusion of this case record in the *Excerpta Legum* suggests that the compilers agreed with some of N.'s arguments, providing insight into how Frisian jurists may have interpreted the rules regarding widows as guardians. The case also illustrates how a widow could assert her own rights and viewpoints in court. The case record is laid out in separate parts, allowing for a detailed analysis of each claim.

3.2.1 First Claim

> Exc 260. Item. Dit is N. riucht to yens R. als om dat mundscip.
> Int arsta dat R. nen mond nys ende dat mondscip des kyndes ende guedis N. to heert ney riucht, als hio en moder is; dit in scrioun riucht to biwisen.[120]

> Exc 260. Item. This is the claim of N. against R. concerning guardianship. First of all, that R. is not the guardian and that according to law the guardianship over the child and goods falls to N., because she is the mother; this I will prove with written law.

We have already seen in the Frisian sources discussed above that a mother had a right to care for children and property. However, N. explicitly claimed a right to guardianship (*mundskip*) and not to 'custody' (*bihode*). According to Roman law, a mother could be a tutor in the same way as a man. We find confirmation of this in the *Excerpta Legum*:

---

118 See also *A*, I (Exc) 454, p. 312, where it is stated that a woman could not be a legal representative.

119 This is most probably an abbreviation for *nomen*, i.e., the claimant. Other names were also abbreviated, such as R. (potentially *reus*) and B. These are unlikely to have been abbreviations of proper names.

120 *A*, I (Exc) 260, p. 210.

> Exc 274. Item. Der mey nen wyf mond wasa buta der moder ende alde moder, ut in Auctentico, De heredibus ab intestato venientibus, § Mulieribus (*Auth.* 9.1 [*Nov.* 118.5]).[121]
>
> Exc 274. Item. No woman may be a guardian, except the mother and grandmother, as in *Auth.* 9.1 [*Nov.* 118.5].

This rule comes directly from Roman law, specifically the allegation at the end. No such rule was found in Frisian law. The addition of this rule meant that guardianship was limited to mothers and grandmothers. At the same time, it is now clear that a mother could be a guardian (*mund*) and not just have 'custody'. Another text is explicit regarding the joint administration by a guardian and a mother:

> Exc 273. Item. Dit is riucht, dat da kynden agen an mond to habben, vnt hia ierich sint, der hemman reda ende hiara gued walde mitter moder. [...][122]
>
> Exc 273. Item. This is law, that children ought to have a guardian until they come of age, who cares for them and administers their goods together with the mother. [...]

This rule is similar to what is written in the *Book of Emperor Rudolf* (Rud 21) and was also the case in Medieval Ghent. When examining other primary sources of the 15th century, we find similar arrangements in practice. In 1440, Peter Kammingha, husband of Site Kammingha, stated the following on the administration of the children's property in his testament:

> **Testament of Peter Kammengha** **1440 May 8**
> [...] Ende Sicke, zyn lya, scil habba da bihielde der statthene to Kammenghabuer, ende scil bruka ende regeria alla da guide ond tha kynden to bueckwesta kommeth, by rede der mondena der hy da kynden ende da guide byfellen had, als Menno Jayama, Gerrard Kammengha, Renyck Kampstera ende Syko Mirtena. [...][123]

121 *A*, I (Exc) 274, p. 222.
122 *A*, I (Exc) 273, p. 222.
123 *FT* II, p. 16, r. 2–6.

> [...] And Sicke [Site], his love, shall have the custody of the *statthene*[124] at Kammenghabuer, and shall use and administer all the goods until the children come of age, by consent of the guardians to whom he has entrusted the children and the goods, that is Menno Jayama, Gerrard Kammengha, Renyck Kampstera and Syko Mirtena. [...]

It is noteworthy that the will appointed multiple guardians (*mondena*), instead of just one. Moreover, Site was assigned the role of *bihielde* (compare *bihode*), meaning she had 'custody' but not guardianship. It is unclear whether the requirement for guardians' consent is the same as 'joint' guardianship in the *Excerpta Legum* (Exc 273). The appointment of testamentary guardians became more common in 15th-century Frisia with the rise in the use of testaments.[125] According to Roman law, a tutor appointed by testament was preferred to all others.[126] Peter Kammingha's last will shows that guardians could be instituted alongside a mother as someone who had 'custody' (*bihode*) of property and children. In contrast, a testamentary tutor according to Roman law excluded the mother as guardian. It is not clear whether a similar form of joint administration by the mother and guardian existed in Roman law. Roman law allowed a mother to administrate the estate or even act as an aid to a tutor, but whether this was possible in Frisian law is not clearly indicated.

In this context, the first claim by N. is that she had the right to be her children's guardian, and her relative R. did not. As there is no mention of any other guardians, we may assume that she claimed to be the sole guardian. That would have meant increased authority and competence, as well as being independent of any relatives who sought control of her or her child.

The Early Modern Period in Europe saw an increase in women's capacity to act as sole guardians of their children. There was an important reason for this: mothers did not inherit from their children. If a child died before its mother, she did not succeed to the child's property, whereas a father did.[127] Therefore, there was no conflict of interest between a mother's authority and her children's inheritance from their father. Consequently, mothers were seen as removed from potential disputes and self-interest. The logical reasoning behind this was that they were thought to be removed from the inheritance but still interested

---

124 The plot of land where the residence stood. Compare 'stathe' Hofmann, Popkema, *Altfriesisches Handwörterbuch*, p. 460.

125 On the development of last wills and testaments in Frisia, see Chapter 5.

126 On this, see *Inst.* 1.15.2. For more on tutors, see Kaser, *Das römische Privatrecht* II, p. 224f. This is also stated in Frisian law in *A*, I (Exc) 275, pp. 222–224.

127 On widows in general, see Cavallo, Warner, *Widowhood*, p. 16.

in acting for the well-being of their children. Thus, their priority would be the children rather than themselves. It was for this reason that women were preferred as guardians of the children rather than uncles and other relatives.

We can already observe these changes in Frisia in the 15th century owing to a strong reception of Roman law. The link between *mundskip* and *tutela*, as seen in the gloss of the *Freeska Landriucht* (glosses 183–187 to Rud 21), enabled mothers to have sole guardianship over their children. This particular circumstance may well have been connected to a comparatively early reception of Roman elements. From the 14th century onwards, guardianship was interpreted as *tutela*. This had consequences for how women were able to administer their children's assets, with the claim of N. showing that elements of Roman law were present, authoritative and applied in the 15th century.

3.2.2 Second Claim

The second claim reveals another aspect. It appears that N. remarried or intended to remarry, and this may have been the reason for bringing the court case in the first place. N. claimed that, as a mother, she could remain guardian of the children and the property even if she remarried.

> [...] Item. Dat dyo moder mey bliwa in bi hielde ende inder monscip des kyndis ende guedis, ist dat dio moder bi borgie da kynde dat gued al so gued weder als hioth ontfoecht, ende dat wanneer dat hio al orsta tyt mannye, so mey si vord mond bliwa, als hio al eer wesen hath; dat to biwisen mit scrioun riucht, mit keysers Rolef riucht.
> Item. Dat dio moder mey mond bliwa, wan hio wel itta dat orste tyt mannye, ut jnfra patebit. [...][128]

> [...] Item. That the mother can continue to be custodian and guardian of the child and the good, if the mother can guarantee that the good is returned in the same value as it is attained. And that when she marries a second time, she may remain guardian as she has been before; this I will prove with written law, with the law of Emperor Rudolf.
> Item. That the mother may remain guardian when she marries a second time, is shown below. [...]

Her claim refers directly to the *Book of Emperor Rudolf*, which we have examined extensively. According to this source, a mother could continue to take care

128 *A*, I (Exc) 260, p. 210.

of her children and their property if she provided security for them. The same is stated here under the term *borgie*, i.e., to provide surety.[129] This is followed by several arguments in Latin, with references to Roman law in support of this claim.

> [...] Nota: mater hodie nouo iure tutrix in filiis sine iuramento: C. eodem, autentica Sacramenturn (auth. post *Cod.* 5.35); Extra, De appellationibus, Ex parte ij (X 2.28.67); et hoc dum tamen renunciat Velleyano, et prefertur omnibus tutoribus legitimis et datiuis, non autem testamentarijs: in Auctentico, De heredibus ad intestato, § Ex hiis, collatione ix (*Auth.* 9.1 [*Nov.* 118.5];) et in Auctentico, ut matres sine prohibitione, § Quia vero ii collatione vii (*Auth.* 7.4 [*Nov.* 94.2];) et C. eodem, auctentica Matri (auth. post *Cod.* 5.35.2). [...][130]

> [...] Note: According to the new law, the mother is nowadays tutor over her children without an oath, see the auth. *Sacramentum* (post C. 5.35); X 2.28.67. This only applies when she renounces the protections of the [Senatusconsultum] Velleianum; and she is preferred to all statutory and appointed tutors, but not the testamentary ones. See *Auth.* 9.1 [*Nov.* 118.5] and *Auth.* 7.4 [*Nov.* 94.2] and the auth. *Matri* (post C. 5.35.2). [...]

This argument follows the developments in Roman law described in *Auth.* 7.4 [*Nov.* 94.2]. In the *Codex*, a widowed mother still had to take an oath not to remarry if she wished to obtain tutelage of her children. This was later changed in the *Novels*. It is noted that this oath was often broken and so the requirement was changed. Instead, if she wanted to become a tutor, she had to renounce the protection of the SC *Velleianum*. However, this was in order to become a tutor in the first place. If she remarried, her position as tutor was lost regardless of the renouncement. The argument continues:

> [...] Et quam cito ad secundas uolauerit, finita est tutela, quasi sit mortua, ut in § Quia uero (*Auth.* 7.4 [*Nov.* 94.2]). Tamen si voluerit esse tutrix, ut dictum est, debet cauere rem pupilli saluam fore et facere inuentarium: in Auctentico, Vt sine prohibitione, § finali, collatione vii (*Auth.* 7.4 [*Nov.* 94.2]); et oportet, quod sit maior, ut Insti., Qui tutores in testamento dari possunt, § Furiosus (*Inst.* 1.14.2). Item. Debet dare fideiussorem, qui

129 'borgia' Hofmann, Popkema, *Altfriesisches Handwörterbuch*, p. 76.

130 *A*, 1 (Exc) 260, p. 210.

> promittit rem pupilli saluam fore: in Auctentico, Vt sine prohibitione matres, § finali (*Auth.* 7.4 [*Nov.* 94.2]). Item. Quod mater bene potest esse tutrix cum solemnitate illa, que est quando mulier tutele officium fungi potest, ut C. Quando mulier tutele officium fungi potest, l. finali, § Si enim (*Cod.* 5.35.3.2), ubi sic tenetur: "Si enim in filiis iustis", id est legitimis, "in quibus testamentarie et legitime sunt tutele, tamen matribus hiis", scilicet testamentariis et legitimis tutelis, "deficientibus ad prouidentiam filiorum suorum venire conceditur, multomagis in huiusmodi casibus, vbi legitima tutela euanescit, saltem alias dari eis", id est filiis, "humanissimum", benignissimum, misericordissimum. [...][131]
>
> [...] And as soon as she marries a second time, the tutelage is ended, see *Auth.* 7.4 [*Nov.* 94.2]. However, if she wants to be tutor, she has to guarantee the estate of her ward and draw up an inventory, see *Auth.* 7.4 [*Nov.* 94.2]. And she has to be of full age, see *Inst.* 1.14.2. Item. She has to provide a surety, who guarantees that the estate of her ward remains intact, see *Auth.* 7.4 [*Nov.* 94.2]. (I claim), that the mother can very well be tutor, if she undergoes the formalities that are required of a woman in order to exercise guardianship, as in C. 5.35.3.2, where the following is stated: "When namely in case of conjugal" that is legitimate "children, for whom exists a testamentary and statutory tutelage, the mothers are entitled to custody over their children, if those" that is the testamentary and statutory tutors "are missing, so it is more humane", more benign and compassionate "for them" that is the children "in those cases in which statutory tutors are missing, to at least appoint other tutors."

According to this text (and Roman law), a mother could remain tutor of her children if she followed certain formalities, such as guaranteeing the preservation of her children's property, drawing up an inventory, and providing surety for any contracts. However, these formalities were necessary for tutelage in general, not specifically for a mother who wanted to remain tutor after remarriage. In fact, *Auth.* 7.4 [*Nov.* 94] explicitly states that a mother loses her tutelage when she remarries: [...] *mox tamen ut secundas contraxerit nuptias, repente expelli tutela* [...]. (Translation: "[...] nevertheless, as soon as she has entered a second marriage, she is quickly removed from guardianship [...].") Therefore, the claim that a widow-mother who remarried could be the tutor of her chil-

131 *A*, I (Exc) 260, pp. 210–212.

dren was incompatible with Roman law. This is also confirmed by the quote at the end, C. 5.35.3.2, which states that a mother is a preferred tutor but cannot remarry while having tutelage.

In conclusion, N.'s argument does not hold up to scrutiny when we examine the sources closely. In fact, Roman law states the opposite of her claim. The compilers of the *Excerpta Legum* seem not to have minded this and copied this case record into their collection. It is evident, therefore, that Frisian law (Rud 21) was disguised as Roman law. While Roman law was known and used, it was applied only when it was deemed beneficial for the claimant. Frisians adapted and transformed elements of Roman law, rather than adopting them in their entirety. Hence, the legal system in 15th-century Frisia was shaped by how Frisians used learned and Frisian law.

Other instances in the *Excerpta Legum* provide additional reasons for a mother's loss of guardianship. One provision (Exc 271) implicitly refers to the same three reasons for loss as given in the *Book of Emperor Rudolf* (Rud 21), demonstrating once again the authority of this source on the topic. A mother would also lose her inheritance if she failed to appoint a new guardian within a year of remarriage.

> Exc 271. Jtem. Dit is riucht, datter sint iii punten, dar dyo moder da mondscip mey vrliest. Dat scelma finda in da landriucht, ende en punt ister, der dyo moder dis kyndis erfscip mey vrliest, wanner hio da bihode des kyndis guedis hath ende nymt en man ende ieft da kynden nen orin mond binda jeer in lege vltima C. Ad senatusconsultum Tertulianum (*Cod.* 6.56.3).[132]

> Exc 271. Item. This is law: there are three reasons for a mother to lose guardianship. This is found in the land law. And there is one case in which the mother loses the (management of the) inheritance of her child, (namely) if she manages the goods of the child and marries again and does not appoint another guardian for the children within a year, see C. 6.56.3.

The phrase *in da landriucht* must refer specifically to the *Book of Emperor Rudolf* (Rud 21), where three reasons are given for loss of guardianship. The latter part of the above provision (Exc 271) refers to loss of inheritance rather than

132 *A*, I (Exc) 271, pp. 220–222.

loss of guardianship. Although the reference to Roman law certainly relates to the loss of a child's inheritance, there are some important differences between the two:

> *Cod.* 6.56.3. Matres, quae puberes amiserunt filios, licet impuberibus eis tutores non petierunt, praescriptione non petiti tutoris ad excludendam eorum successionem minime debere praescribi certum est.[133]

> C. 6.56.3. It is certain that mothers who have lost their children after the latter arrived at puberty should not be excluded from the succession to their estates by an exception on the ground that they did not demand tutors for them before they reached that age.

There is no mention of remarriage in this Roman rule: it required the appointment of a tutor even if the mother did not remarry. It is possible that the Frisian provision was altered to fit the Frisian context, where a mother could retain guardianship, but it is unclear why *Nov.* 22.40, which states that inheritance is lost upon remarriage unless a guardian is provided, was not referenced.

It is also possible that the above provision (Exc 271) and the phrase *dis kyndis erfscip mey vrliest* refer to loss of the right to manage the children's inheritance rather than to loss of the inheritance directly. This loss of the right to administer the children's property is also found in another provision, namely the directly following Exc 272:

> Exc 272. Item. Dit is riucht: Hwerso en frouwe dis arre mannis iefta thera kyndera fynd nymt, so hath hio da **bihodinghe** van da gueden vrlerin.[134]

> Exc 272. Item. This is law: when a woman marries the enemy of her husband or (the enemy of) her children, she has lost the administration of the property (of her children).

This rule seems to be specifically of Frisian origin. The expression "enemy of the husband or her children" must certainly be seen in the context of Medieval Frisian society and its many feuds. Marrying one's husband's enemy may have been considered a betrayal of his family. In such a case, the estate and the children were in danger of coming under the authority of their father's enemy.

133 C. 6.56.3.

134 *A*, I (Exc) 272, p. 222.

While we do not find such a rule in the *Freeska Landriucht*, it is found in *Thet Autentica Riucht* (Aut 13) and the *Rechten ende Wilkoeren* (RW 75).[135] In the latter, the mother loses guardianship over the children, not just the administration of property:

> RW 75. Van voermunderschop.
> Soe waer ene vrouwe oers eersten mans, offte syne kynder, viant nempt, soe heft se de **voermunderscop** orer kynderen verloren.

> RW 75. Concerning guardianship.
> When a woman marries her first husband's, or his children's, enemy, then she has lost the guardianship over her children.

Other instances of this rule, including the one in *Codex Aysma*, as well as those in *Codex Unia* and *Codex Roorda*, all refer to the administration of goods rather than guardianship.[136] The relationship between *bihodinghe* and *mundskip* was already explained in the context of the *Book of Emperor Rudolf* (Rud 21). There are three possibilities: first, both the *Excerpta Legum* (Exc 272) and the *Rechten ende Wilkoeren* (RW 75) are in agreement and differ only in their choice of words. Second, there may have been a difference in regions: in Westerlauwers Frisia, a mother lost custody and administration of goods, while in the Ommelanden she lost guardianship. Third, a change occurred between the 15th century (Exc 272) and the 16th century (RW 75). In this case, it is possible that a mother having custody was equated with guardianship. Neither of these possibilities can be proven at this point. What remains clear is that a mother could lose some degree of authority over her children and their property if she married an enemy. On the other hand, it also indicates that if she married someone who was not an enemy, she could remain the administrator or guardian.

3.2.3 Third Claim

> EL 261. Item. Dat dio moder mey tzieza her weselkinden an mond hwam dat hio wol, wanneer dat ze needreft hede, al ist datze wttera ferre mannye; dat to biwisen mit scrioun riucht.[137]

135 See the table of concordances in Gerbenzon, *Excerpta legum*, p. 438.

136 For a comparison of all three instances in *U*, *A* and *Ro*, see Brouwer, *Thet autentica riocht*, p. 43f.

137 *A*, I (Exc) 261, p. 212.

> EL 261. Item. (I claim) that the mother can chose as a guardian over her half-orphaned children who she wants, even when she marries a second time. This I will prove with written law.

N. claims that it was her right to choose the guardian. This is in contrast to the *Book of Emperor Rudolf*, where it is stated that a relative from the husband's side became guardian. In Medieval Ghent, too, the husband's family appointed a guardian. N.'s claim is therefore quite extraordinary. By appointing a guardian herself, N. would have been able to increase her own influence in the matter. The remaining paragraphs do not contain any evidence in written law to support this assertion. Roman law has no such rule.[138]

3.2.4 Fourth Claim

In the fourth claim, N. argued that she excluded all other guardians because she was the child's mother:

> Item. Dat dyo moder mey da monscip bihalda, als vorscrioun is, ende dat keysers riucht wr bieth ielkeren dat mond scip als vaderen ende moderen, ende dyo moder is to fera set ende bislut van alle sibdelen, der vander sida wt sprutan sint, als B. is, ende dat neyder ordyneringe des erfscipes des keysers riuchtes, ut patet in Auctentico, De heredibus qui ab intestato veniunt, § Ex hiis (Auth. 9.1 [Nov. 118.5]) […].[139]

> Item. (I claim), that the mother as previously mentioned may retain guardianship, because imperial law forbids to transfer guardianship to others than male and female relatives in ascending line; and the mother has preference and excludes all relatives who are from the side (collaterals), as for example B.; and this corresponds to the succession of imperial law, as appears from Auth. 9.1 [Nov. 118.5]. […]

A third unknown person, B., is mentioned here. B. was a collateral relative who could potentially also have claimed guardianship over N.'s child. N. clearly sought to exclude all potential guardians not appointed by her. In this way, she

---

138 According to Roman law, there were three ways to obtain guardianship: by testament (*tutor testamentarius*), on the basis of law as an agnate (*tutor legitimus*) and by court order (*tutor dativus*). See Kaser, *Das römische Privatrecht* II, p. 224ff. These three ways are also found in the *Excerpta Legum* in Exc 275.

139 *A*, I (Exc) 261, p. 212.

attempted to exercise control and authority over her children and their property against her own and her husband's relatives. Roman law is referenced as an argument.

3.2.5 Fifth Claim

Lastly, N. claimed that R. was not entitled to guardianship:

> Exc 262. Item. Neydam dat R. vander swerdsyda nat en is, so hert dat mondscip hem nat to, als dit latyn seit infra: Insti., De legitima agnatorum tutela (Inst. 1.15 pr.), ubi dicitur: "Quibus ex testamento tutor datus non sit, hiis ex lege xii tabularum agnati sunt tutores, qui vocantur legitimi. Agnati sunt autem cognati per virilis sexus cognationem coniuncti" et dicuntur quasi agnati[140] etcetera. De isto vide textum Insti., De legitima agnatorum tutela (Inst. 1.15), per totum.[141]

> Exc 262. Item. Because R. does not belong to the 'sword-side', he is not entitled to guardianship, as the Latin text below says: see Inst. 1.15 pr., where is said: "To those, to whom no tutor is appointed through a testament, the agnates are according to the Law of the Twelve Tables (their) tutors, who are called statutory tutors. Agnates are cognates connected through consanguinity of the male gender" and they are called quasi-cognates. etc. For this see the entire title of Inst. 1.15.

N.'s argument is based on the fact that R. was her relative and not her late husband's ('sword-side'). In this way, she tried to exclude him from claiming guardianship. The argument was categorized in its own provision (Exc 262) by the compilers of the *Codex Aysma*, indicating that it may have been considered as a separate rule for a future law text. We must remember that the *Excerpta Legum* was merely a collection and compilation of rules, norms and arguments that were to be organized into an actual law text. N.'s claim contrasts with what is written in the *Book of Emperor Rudolf* (Rud 21), where it is stated that both sides of the family had the right to be guardians.

3.2.6 Outcome of N.'s Case

N. made five claims in her case against R, in which she aimed to gain control over her child and its goods, while excluding all other potential challengers for

140 Read: *cognati*.

141 *A*, I (Exc) 262, p. 214.

guardianship. N.'s references to Roman law were not always accurate, however, including her arguments for retaining guardianship after remarriage. Although this was allowed according to Frisian law, it was not in line with Roman law.

In conclusion, N. trod a fine line between Frisian law and Roman law, using the latter whenever it suited her to support her five claims. This widow-mother thus took advantage of the different legal systems in order to further her own case.

Unfortunately, we do not know the outcome of this case for certain. However, the fact that such arguments were made in court and adjudicated suggests that they were well-regarded rather than considered unconventional. Furthermore, the inclusion of this case record in the *Excerpta Legum* implies that the claimant's action was successful. As the compilers of the *Excerpta Legum* would have wanted to retain valid arguments from legal practice, it is likely that N. won her case or at least argued convincingly. Other sources may shed more light on this matter.

3.3 *Female Guardians at the End of the 15th Century*

Many of the rules found in the *Excerpta Legum* are reflected in the late-15th-century *Jurisprudentia Frisica*. Indeed, many of these rules were copied without change, as shown below in the table of concordances between the two sources.

TABLE 10 Concordance between title 26 'de tutoribus et curatoribus' in the Jurisprudentia Frisica and the Excerpta Legum

JF	26:1	26:2	26:3	26:6	26:10	26:15	26:18	26:19	26:20	26:21	26:28	26:29
Exc	273	263	263	263	262	275	274	260	261	261	271	272

Joint administration is mentioned in JF 26:1, which is a copy of Exc 273. It is also stated elsewhere that the consent of the court and the minor's relatives was required:

> JF 26:7 Jtem fyarde tyt so seyt dat keysers riucht dat dy mond aegh inda bewaringe des kyndes gued to gaen by des riuchtis reed, ende dera fryondena. Ende deth hy dat naet so aegh hy bettringe to dwaen.
>
> Glossa 8. *Jtem fyarde tyt so seyt dat* ut in ff. de confirmacione tutorum l. Qui a patre (*Dig*. 26.3.3) et l. Si filius (*Dig*. 26.3.6) et ff. de administracione tutorum l. Tutores (*Dig*. 26.7.39).

> JF 26:7 Item, fourthly, imperial law says that in maintaining the child's good the guardian must seek the consent of the court and of its relatives, and if he does not do so, he must pay compensation.
>
> Gloss 8. *Jtem fyarde tyt so seyt dat*, see D. 26.3.3 and D. 26.3.6 and D. 26. 7.39.[142]

This text emphasizes the dependence of a guardian on other individuals close to the child. While referencing Roman law, neither of the three allegations specify that the consent of any relatives is needed. D. 26.3.3 and D. 26.3.6 confirm the need for court consent, but do not mention relatives. Although court consent was an element received from Roman law, the requirement of consent from relatives was already anchored in older Frisian laws.

Notably, the fifth claim of N. (Exc 262) is found in this source, with the exact same wording being used as in the *Excerpta Legum*, suggesting that it was directly copied from this source. Her argument that a guardian had to come from the 'sword-side' (JF 26:10) was apparently accepted and became part of this law text.

Another provision of particular interest is the following:

> JF 26:16 Dat keysers riucht seyt: Monscip to feren dat is een hlest deer een man berth, ende alsuke denigha hlest geet buppa da wyfflicke cranckheyt, want een wyff steet onder mondschip ende selff neen monschip feert.
>
> Glossa 20. *Dat keysers riucht* "Tutelam administrare uirile munus est et ultra sexum feminee infirmitatis tale officium est", l.i C. quando mulier tute. offi. fungi (*Cod.* 5.35.1).
>
> 26:16 Imperial law says: taking on guardianship is a burden which belongs to a man, and such a burden is beyond the strength of a woman, for a woman is under guardianship and cannot be a guardian herself.
>
> Gloss 20. *Dat keysers riucht* "Exercising a tutelage is a task for men, because such an office exceeds the weak feminine gender", see C. 5.35.1.[143]

142 *Ro*, III (JF), tit. 26, no. 7.

143 *Ro*, III (JF), tit. 26, no. 16.

Guardianship in this context is restricted to male persons, with an exception made for mothers and grandmothers, as stated in another provision (JF 26:17). Both follow Roman law, which is detailed in the text. Two reasons are given: first, the perceived "weakness" of women, and second, women being under guardianship themselves. We will examine the second argument in the context of guardianship over women and widows at a later point. The first argument is supported by a gloss (gloss 20) that quotes C. 5.35.1. We can see that this argument either derives from or is congruent with Roman law.

In practice, it is unlikely that the above provision (JF 26:16) was widely enforced. A contract of sale from 1431 shows that Anna Knoestens acted as "*myn zuster mond*", her sister's guardian.[144] It is unclear what capacity she held as a guardian outside this sale. However, since Anna was a guardian of her own sister, women were clearly able to be guardians of people other than their own children. Furthermore, she was able to put her own seal on the letter. This demonstrates that practice regarding women's guardianship over others was more lenient than the norms may indicate.

Within these norms, only mothers and grandmothers were permitted to be guardians. Furthermore, provision of surety, renouncement of a second marriage, and renouncement of the invoking of the SC *Velleianum* were required (JF 26:19) in the same manner as in the *Excerpta Legum*. Mothers were preferred over all others as guardians (JF 26:21, 26:23; 26:25). This confirms the fourth claim made by N. (Exc 261), of which JF 26:21 is in fact a copy. A mother's ability to appoint a guardian of her choice when she wanted to, as in the third claim of N. (Exc 261), is also confirmed (JF 26:20).

Some of N.'s claims were clearly deemed appropriate and suitable for the new law. The inclusion of these arguments indicates that such rules had not existed in written form in Frisian law. Otherwise, jurists could have copied them from written law instead of from case records. It appears, instead, that they were valid in practice, i.e., in Romano-canonical court procedures.

However, there is one crucial exception to the concordance between N.'s claims and what is found in the *Jurisprudentia Frisica*. None of the provisions in title 26 mention a mother's right to remarry and keep guardianship. In fact, only the requirement to renounce remarriage is stated (JF 26:17; 26:19). Evidently, the authors did not agree with N.'s second claim. It is unclear whether this constitutes a development between the middle and the end of the 15th century. Whether N.'s second claim was confirmed by the court in the procedure she initiated is also unknown. Assuming it was accepted, this would imply that remar-

144 Iterson, "Vrouwenvoogdij", p. 96.

riage and guardianship were compatible from at least the time of the *Book of Emperor Rudolf*, where we found this arrangement for the first time, until the mid-15th century. By the end of the century, this right no longer appeared in written law. While this change may have been due to the reception of Roman law, it is also possible that N.'s claim was unsuccessful but nevertheless copied into the *Excerpta Legum*. This would indicate that a right to continue guardianship after remarriage diminished sometime before the end of the 15th century, with this likely also to have been due to an increasing influence of Roman law.

The *Excerpta Legum*, which was a compilation of rules and cases intended to be worked into a proper law text, does not provide a satisfactory answer to this question. The inclusion of N.'s second argument indicates, however, that the compilers at least thought it was a valid argument. Consequently, remarriage and guardianship were most probably still reconcilable in practice around the mid-15th century. By the end of the 15th century, however, due to the reception of Roman law, the *Jurisprudentia Frisica* no longer included the possibility of remarriage and remaining a guardian.

The *Jurisprudentia Frisica* also retains other reasons for losing guardianship. Marrying an enemy of the husband or of the children also ended a mother's guardianship over the latter (JF 26:29), as did remarriage within a 'weeping year' or 'thereafter' (JF 87:3): [...] *Ende aeck foerliest hio da mondscip der kyndena hwaneer hio boestiget bynna da jeer jof aldeer ney*. (Translation: "[...] and she also loses guardianship of the children if she marries within a year or thereafter.")[145] The phrasing of this rule is curious as, technically, it encompasses both the 'weeping year' and all the time coming after that, thereby making the reference to the former redundant. It is possible that this example refers only to a short period after a husband's death. However, the text is not sufficiently clear on this. Given the provisions of title 26, it is more plausible that loss of guardianship on remarriage was the rule. Nevertheless, it is possible that the norms applying in practice may not have been so clear.

4 Guardianship over Widows

Scholars have studied the topic of guardianship over widows in Medieval Frisia. In 1888, Fockema Andreae argued that all Medieval Frisian women were subject to gender-based guardianship. However, widows still had a significant degree of agency, as guardians were only necessary for certain legal matters, such as when

145 *Ro*, III (JF), tit. 87, no. 3.

alienating a child's goods or arranging the child's marriage. Therefore, Fockema Andreae maintained that while a gender-based guardianship applied in theory, in practice, a guardian was required only for certain specific legal matters.[146]

In 1937, W. van Iterson responded to Fockema Andreae's argument in "Vrouwenvoogdij," asserting that widows were not universally under guardianship. A guardian was appointed only when children were involved, with the primary objective being to preserve what the offspring had inherited from their father. Once all children came of age, the estate was divided, requiring the appointment of a guardian.[147]

The *Older Skelta Law* explicitly specified who held guardianship over a woman.

> Fan mondscypes lawa ander wedua
> SkRa 8. Dit is riucht, datter nimmen aech dyne mondscet oen der wedue dan her soen, so fyr als hi jerich se, jefta dy selva deer dan da aeftingha aech. Lywet ny dy soen, soe aegh hy dan des mondes fyower penninghen min dan twa merck.

> On Passing on the Guardianship of a Widow
> SkRa 8. This is the law, that no man shall have guardianship of a widow but her son, provided he is of age, or **the man she remarries.** If there is no son alive anymore, the new husband shall receive four pennies less than two marks for the guardianship.[148]

Scholars have debated the exact meaning of the phrase *dy selva deer dan da aeftingha aech.* Some argue that it refers to "the one who has the right to give her in marriage", while others assert that it refers to a new husband, as translated above.[149] The question of whether widows were under guardianship when no son was alive depends heavily on the interpretation of this phrase. In the former case, it would appear that all widows were under guardianship, either by a son or someone unspecified, presumably a relative. In the latter case, by con-

146 Fockema Andreae, "De onzelfstandigheid der vrouwen", p. 41.

147 Iterson, "Vrouwenvoogdij", p. 89.

148 *D*, III (SkRa) 8, pp. 120–121.

149 On the former translation, see Sterringa, "The most miserable women", p. 293. Others also argue for such a translation: Algra, *Oudfries Recht*, p. 303f.; and Buma, Ebel in their translation of *J*, III (SkRa) 8, pp. 76–77.
On the latter translation, see Iterson, "Vrouwenvoogdij", p. 83; Breuker, *Landrecht der Vriesne*, pp. 22–23; Meijering, Nijdam, '*Wat is recht?*', pp. 90–93; Fairbanks, *Skeltana Riucht*, pp. 74–77 and note one on page 126.

trast, only a son or subsequent husband held guardianship over a widow, and she otherwise enjoyed great legal autonomy. I am inclined to follow the second interpretation. The absence of guardianship under usual circumstances is emphasized by the phrase "no man shall have guardianship". Thus, it appears more logical that guardianship over widows existed only in the stated circumstances. Consequently, a widow who did not remarry remained free of the authority of a male figure.

On the other hand, a widow under guardianship of her son was severely limited in her capacity to act. This is exemplified in a provision of the *Eight Provisions* (Dom 2) concerning primarily the swaddling-payment. While the first half is congruent with the *Older Skelta Law* (SkRa 11), the second part has some additional details regarding guardianship over a widow-mother.

> Dom 2. […] Hit ne se dat hi swara wil als hi saun jeer ald is, dat hy syn gued moge bigaen ende bistaen ende bireda. Ende di aesga aegh him dine eed to stowiane. Ende hi jouwe dan synre moder xxxv schillingen ende hi wesse dan mond synre moder. Soe mei hio mitta lutterislaen capia ende sella ende oen jefta jowa sonder des mondes oerlef ende jelkirs haet hyo nates wald oers dan her ayn ledena.

> Dom 2. […] It is also possible for a son to declare himself capable of handling his own affairs and taking care of his property when he is seven years old.[150] In that case, the *asega* has to administer the required oath to him. After that, he shall give his mother thirty-five shillings and from then on be the guardian of his mother. With this 'swaddling-payment', the mother may buy and sell, or give away from it, without having to ask the consent of her guardian and apart from that she does not have any competence but over her own body.[151]

According to this provision, a mother had full control only over her swaddling-payment. It is explicitly stated that she otherwise had no competence, except over her own body. This implies that guardianship held by a son was as rigid as that held by a father or husband. Consequently, a widow whose son was of age did not experience independence or autonomy, at least in theory. However,

150 Seven years is a very young age to attain legal capacity. Frisian law made this exception and allowed sons to declare themselves capable at seven years old. However, this rule is not found outside the *Eight Provisions* in the *Freeska Landriucht* and in the manuscripts *J*, X (Dom) 2, pp. 196–198 and *F*, VII (Dom) 2, p. 60.

151 *D*, IX (Dom) 2, pp. 244–245.

practice may have varied widely, especially considering the financial assets a widow had control over.[152] In this light, it is implausible that she had competence only over her swaddling-payment.

According to the *Book of Emperor Rudolf* (Rud 21), a mother and her minor children were under the guardianship of the late husband's brother. However, this does not indicate a universal, gender-based guardianship. Instead, it is plausible that a guardian was appointed only when there were minor children.[153] A guardian was primarily appointed to ensure that the children's inheritance stayed intact.

In summary, guardianship over widows existed under two circumstances: first, a widow with an adult son became subject to guardianship by that son; second, if a widow had minor children from her deceased husband, a relative of that husband acted as the guardian of her and her children. In the latter case, he was needed for certain legal actions, such as alienation of property, but otherwise, in theory, a widow administered her children and their property independently. A widow without children did not have to have a guardian, but was able to appoint one if needed. This corresponds to what has been written about widows in the Late Middle Ages. In the Medieval German territories, widows chose guardians when they were needed for actions at court, but otherwise had greater legal independence than other women.[154]

Having a guardian who provided support and protection could also be beneficial for widows. In Late Medieval Sussex, for example, women sometimes came into conflict with their heirs or stepsons over inheritance and property rights.[155] Without a guardian, it was more difficult for them to withstand such harassment. Second marriages also offered security, despite a loss of autonomy.[156] In Frisia, too, guardianship was perceived as beneficial. Women without the protection of a *mund* (*mundlas meiden*) lacked legal capacity and could not act in court or administer property.[157] It was the duty of a *mund* to provide his charges with protection, support and legal representation.[158] As *mundlas meiden* theoretically had no legal capacity and could not act in court or administer property, many widows may have voluntarily chosen a guardian for the benefits that such protection brought.

---

152 On these assets, see the sections on *wetma*, etc.

153 See also Iterson, "Vrouwenvoogdij", p. 86, who makes the same argument.

154 Ennen, *Frauen im Mittelalter*, p. 138; Wiesner, *Working Women*, p. 23.

155 Mate, *Daughters, Wives and Widows*, p. 94 ff.

156 Mate, *Daughters, Wives and Widows*, p. 134.

157 Algra, *Oudfries Recht*, p. 305.

158 Algra, *Oudfries Recht*, p. 293.

In conclusion, women gained considerable autonomy during widowhood. As mothers, they administered their children's property independently or with the help of their husband's relatives. As childless women, they retained control over their own properties and could appoint a guardian if needed. Depending on the properties received after their husband's death, widows enjoyed financial and social independence.[159] However, the reality may have been different from the theory, as relatives could have asserted authority over childless widows and widow-mothers, preventing them from effectively exercising their independence. Legal and social practice may indeed have been more strict than the norms indicate.[160]

While the conclusion is that a widow's life was relatively autonomous compared to that of other women, the reality may have been different. Establishing greater clarity in this respect would require the legal status and capacity of widows, especially in Frisia, to be examined in more detail. Medieval documents, including testamentary documents, may provide insight into the reality of guardianship, especially in contrast to normative sources. Unfortunately, this is outside the scope of this study.

4.1 *Legal Restrictions and Guardianship over Widows in the 15th Century*

Looking at guardianship chronologically, we can see that, by the mid-fifteenth century, the *Excerpta Legum* contained some additional restrictions on women's capacity to act. Women needed a guardian, for example, to enter into a contract (Exc 79):

> Exc 79. Item. Dit is riucht, dat een wyff buta her mundis rede ende consent mey nene forwert meckya. Redene weer omme: want hyo ne mey nen burga werda ner nen consent iefta wolla der to dwaen, der scataftich2 an wirda mey. Van disse twam ponten so biwyse ic den arsta in da keysers riuchte: ff. Ad Vellianum, l. i et ii. (*Dig.* 16.1.1–2) Thine lettera bewys ick Inst., De auctoritate tutorum, § Sed neque hereditatem (Inst. 1.21.1); Jnstit., Quibus alienare licet uel non, § Nunc admonendi sumus (Inst. 2.8.2).[161]

> Exc 79. Item. This is law, that a woman may not conclude a contract without permission and consent of her guardian, because she can neither vouch for nor give consent or agreement to something, through which

159 Sterringa, "The most miserable women", p. 301.
160 Aert, "The legal possibilities", p. 283.
161 *A*, I (Exc) 79, p. 62.

> damage can be done to her. The first of these two points I prove with imperial law: D. 16.1.1 and 2. The second I prove with Inst. 1.21.1; Inst. 2.8.2.

This text may seem specific to contracts that could disadvantage women, but I believe it has a more general claim. The text originated from a case record, where the claimant argued in court that women could not enter into contracts without a guardian. The reason given for this was that women may not be able to fully consent to something that could be harmful to them. The claim is about a general lack of capacity to enter into contracts, with the potential disadvantage for women being used to legitimize such a claim. It seems unlikely, therefore, that the claim refers only to potentially disadvantageous contracts.

This provision (Exc 79) is not significantly different from classical Frisian law because both limit the legal matters women could engage in. What is more interesting is how learned law is used to support this argument. The provision cites Roman law as a reference for limiting the legal capacity of women. D. 16.1 details the *SC Velleianum*, which we have discussed before: women were not able to stand surety to protect them from financial dangers. The *Institutes* (*Inst.* 1.21.1 and *Inst.* 2.8.2) explicitly forbid wards with guardians from taking certain actions, such as accepting an inheritance or alienating property. Women were classified similarly to children and thus required a guardian. Such restrictions were also present in the law of the Medieval German territories, but the reasoning in this provision was received from Roman law.[162]

Because of this provision, widows who were not under permanent guardianship (i.e., those without children; see SkRa 8) also lacked legal capacity to enter into contracts. This was one case in which a widow needed a guardian, and why it may have been beneficial to appoint one, even if she may not have wanted one otherwise.

Lastly, this shows how elements of Roman law were adopted in Frisian law. As we have seen in Chapter 2, written Frisian law did not contain many norms regarding contracts. When contract law was expanded, rules of learned law were adopted. The same is true in this case.

4.2 *The Return of Gender-Based Guardianship?*

The *Jurisprudentia Frisica* provides some additional insights into the legal status of women in the late 15th century. It forbids women from being guardians (JF 26:16), with one reason given for this norm being that women themselves

162 Ennen, *Frauen im Mittelalter*, p. 34.

were under guardianship.[163] However, it is unclear what form this guardianship over women took, and whether it was universal or limited to women under the guardianship of a father or husband. The *Jurisprudentia Frisica* is the only instance that seems to mention a universal guardianship over women, and it is unlikely that this was an element received from Roman law because gender-based tutelage had been abolished in the empire.[164]

It is argued that the reception of Roman law led to a re-emergence of gender-based guardianship, not because Roman law supported such a guardianship, but because tutelage over children was extended to women. Jurists at the time intended to reinstitute gender-based guardianship by utilizing Roman law, with the reason given in the *Jurisprudentia Frisica* (JF 26:16), inspired by Roman law (C. 5.35.1),[165] being the weakness of the female gender. However, women could still be guardians over their children and even others, thus contradicting the idea of universal guardianship over them.[166]

A study of women in Late Medieval Leiden and Cologne showed that widows could obtain the same legal capacity as an adult man, and that even married women could occasionally acquire this status in legal matters, despite being under their husbands' guardianship.[167] Frisian women may have had similar opportunities to transcend the strict limitations imposed on them in written law. Therefore, while the *Jurisprudentia Frisica* suggests a universal guardianship over women, it is not necessarily irreconcilable with the evidence of women being able to have legal capacity in certain circumstances.

---

163 Only mothers and grandmothers were allowed to be guardians. See also the previous section on widows' guardianship over their own children.

164 The *tutela mulierum* was probably abolished in the 4th century, before the compilation of laws by Justinian. See Domingo, "The Family in Ancient Roman Law", p. 6. And Kaser, *Das römische Privatrecht* II, p. 222.

165 Wiesner, *Gender, Church and State*, p. 86.

166 This is also supported by Iterson, "Vrouwenvoogdij", p. 96.

167 Howell, *Women, production, and patriarchy*, p. 15 f.

CHAPTER 7

Conclusion: A Frisian Reception of Learned Law

This study has shown that Frisian law underwent significant development between the 11th and 15th centuries, and particularly in the 14th and 15th centuries. It is the first comprehensive and extensive examination of Frisian law in the Late Middle Ages, and while much remains to be discovered, a first, pioneering step has been taken towards understanding Frisian law. By examining five legal concepts in five chapters, the study explores the extent to which learned law was received into the Frisian legal system. This broad approach has enabled insights to be gained into the reception of learned law in Frisia as a whole, revealing that Frisians did indeed receive elements of learned law into their legal system.

Previously, scholars believed that the change from a classical Frisian legal system to a Roman-Frisian legal system occurred in the 16th and 17th centuries. They asserted that the new rulers of Frisia introduced Roman law because the Frisian legal system of the 15th century was dysfunctional and unusable. However, this book rejects this idea of a "lawless 15th century," given that the primary sources analyzed here demonstrate that a vast amount of new legal sources were recorded, collected and compiled in the 15th century. These sources included the classical Frisian texts in the *Freeska Landriucht*, and new rules and provisions in the *Excerpta Legum* and *Jurisprudentia Frisica*. The existence and contents of these texts leave no doubt about the growth and vibrancy of the Frisian legal system in the 15th century. The collection of material in the *Excerpta Legum* and its subsequent restructuring into a practical law text in the *Jurisprudentia Frisica* prove that Frisian law was not stagnant, but instead changed with the times. Moreover, the many case records included in these sources suggest that the Frisians themselves participated in a changed legal system, one they shaped by their own practices and arguments in court. Rather, therefore, than a century of chaos and stagnancy, the 15th century was a period of adaptation and development of the Frisian legal system.

Although the classical Frisian law texts of the Frisian Land Law were long outdated by the 15th century, attempts were made to update the classical texts to fit the changed reality of the 14th and 15th centuries, as is evident in the addition of a Gloss to the *Freeska Landriucht*. However, classical Frisian law was still consulted and reproduced, and many of its rules reappear in the sources of the 15th century, with Frisian jurists attempting to update the outdated norms to harmonize them with the learned law present in the new legal system. Conse-

 | DOI:10.1163/9789004712706_008

quently, classical Frisian law continued to be applied, and in fact many traditional customs, such as *niarkap* and the judicial oath, survived long after the 15th century.

Overall, this study shows that Frisian law underwent significant changes in the 15th century, with the reception of learned law into the Frisian legal system being a crucial aspect of this change. The study's findings shed light on the nature of these changes and the form that this reception of learned law took.

1 A Reception of Systems, Methods, and Norms

In the introduction, we presented and examined a categorization of the reception of law into three distinct types, namely systematic reception, methodological reception, and normative reception. This study has attempted to evaluate how we could apply this categorization to the reception of learned law that took place in Frisia. While all three types of reception can be found in the Frisian sources, some types were more significant than others. Let us consider each type of reception and what the previous five chapters have revealed about them.

1.1 *A Reception of Systems*

A systematic reception involves not a reception of singular legal elements, but of an internally consistent and systematic approach to law. While we have not observed a complete adoption of the legal system of the *ius commune*, systems and approaches regarding some aspects of law were received in the Frisian legal system. This was observable in two topics in particular: the law of contracts and procedural law.

First, it is evident that Frisian jurists largely adopted the law of contracts of Canon law (Chapter 2). Frisian law of contracts in the 15th century was open and general instead of closed and specific. It required all agreements to be kept (*pacta sunt servanda*), and considered a naked agreement (*pactum nudum*) to be actionable, both of which were central characteristics of Medieval Canon law. The reception of the system of the Canon law of contracts is also evident in the structure of contracts within the text of the *Jurisprudentia Frisica*. Instead of being loosely connected by terminology as in classical Frisian law, all contracts are grouped together, showing that they were approached within the common framework of contracts.

Second, a partially systematic reception is evident regarding procedural law (Chapter 3). Manuals such as the *processus iudicii* indicate that Frisians received the system of procedures from learned law. They conducted their own procedures as Romano-canonical procedures, using evidence and methods of learned law. Consequently, it can be argued that Frisian law received the system of procedural law from the *ius commune*. However, this reception was not fully superseding, and many traditional Frisian elements of procedure, such as the judicial oaths, remained.

1.2 *A Reception of Methods*

Methodological reception refers to the adoption of doctrines, methods and ideas that change the way people think about law. This reception is particularly significant in the sources of the 14th and 15th centuries.

Firstly, consider the application of reasoning and methods on the classical Frisian custom of *niarkap* (Chapter 2). Rather than rejecting *niarkap*, the Frisian texts argued for its validity by incorporating it into learned law, namely as a long-standing and therefore, according to the *ius commune*, valid custom. They argued for women's ability to take over a sale, which they were already allowed to do under classical Frisian law, using arguments from learned law rather than pointing to previous custom. This demonstrates that the Frisians applied reasoning and doctrines to confirm their own customary practices.

Secondly, Frisians clearly adopted the Romano-canonical procedures from learned law, applying them in practice and allowing parties to litigate in this manner (Chapter 3). Simultaneously, they retained the way in which judicial oaths functioned in their society, but received other procedural elements of evidence, such as witness testimony and written instruments.

Thirdly, a methodological reception is evident in the Frisian legal texts' approach to theft (Chapter 4). The new, late-15th-century concept of theft included wrongdoings that were previously classified as something other than theft, such as obstructing a house search and assisting a thief. In this manner, the Roman law approach to theft was adopted, and the way Frisians thought about theft was amended.

Fourthly, the house search as a crucial element of discovery of theft remained, but was aligned with the new rules regarding theft and obligations resulting from theft (Chapter 4).

Fifthly, there was a shift in how Frisians thought about last wills, with these increasingly being viewed as instruments for organizing succession instead of solely for pious purposes (Chapter 5).

Lastly, a methodological reception is evident in the changes in the ways in which women and widows were conceptualized (Chapter 6). The legal status of women and widows increasingly approached the standards of the *ius commune*. Frisians applied the reasoning of learned law to explain why women had to be under guardianship; for example, because of their perceived frailty. They provided reasons for why mothers could be guardians of their children and why they could not if they remarried, with these reasons being derived from learned law. In summary, learned law provided the arguments that were used in Frisian legal sources to provide legitimacy for their legal norms.

1.3 *A Reception of Norms*

Normative reception occurs at the lowest level, where legal elements are found in the provisions and rules of law texts. This study has identified two fundamental types of normative reception: the adoption of new norms and the alteration of existing norms, both of which are intertwined.

First, Frisians adopted additional norms when their own laws lacked them. They integrated new proofs, such as witnesses and instruments, into their legal system (Chapter 3). This normative reception is deeply integrated into the methodological and systematic reception of procedural law in Frisia.

A reception of Roman norms is also evident regarding last wills and testaments in Frisia (Chapter 5). Frisians adopted many requirements of Roman law for drawing up a will, such as the instituting of an heir, the number of witnesses, and the possibility of making codicils, and applied them to varying degrees. These norms were received from Roman law and replaced norms of Canon law, rather than classical Frisian law.

Second, normative reception also included the replacement or alteration of existing norms in Frisia. The obligations resulting from theft, which were both penal and reipersecutory, became entirely penal in the *Jurisprudentia Frisica* (Chapter 4). Similarly, the Roman distinction between a fourfold and a twofold penalty was received.

The equating of Frisian *mundskip* and Roman *tutela* also led to the introduction of new norms for when and how women could be guardians (Chapter 6). A Frisian woman gained considerably more power as a tutor than as a *mund* in classical Frisian law, but she also had to accept new restrictions derived from learned law, such as renouncing an appeal to the SC *Velleianum* and the loss of guardianship if she remarried.

Normative reception in Frisia varied, depending on the field of law, but every subject examined shows some adoption of norms of Canon and Roman law. However, because this study was limited to only five legal concepts from divergent fields of law, no definitive conclusions can be drawn regarding normative reception in all aspects of Frisian law.

2 Motivations for Reception in Medieval Frisia

The central question of this study was the motivation behind Frisians' adoption of foreign legal elements and changes to their legal system. The absence of a central authority, due to the existence of the Frisian freedom, meant that any changes in the 15th century could only have come from the Frisians themselves. Frisian jurists were the principal actors in the dissemination and reception of learned law. They had studied at universities in Europe and brought their knowledge and interests back to Frisia, likely as the authors of the collections and law books examined in this study. Although their names have not been identified, their motivations and goals significantly shaped the reception of learned law in Medieval Frisia.

This is in contrast to the 16th century, when change was imposed through a central authority. The focus of this study has consequently been solely on the period before 1500. The introduction identified two reasons for the reception of foreign legal elements: necessity and prestige. The chapters in this study demonstrate when Frisians adopted foreign legal elements out of necessity or prestige and when they were motivated by other reasons.

2.1 *Motivated by Necessity*

Consider the contemporary saying used at the beginning of this study, "If it ain't broke, don't fix it," and whether Frisians were motivated by a broken legal system to try and remedy it by adopting foreign legal elements. In some respects, the absence of a large quantity of rules facilitated the adopting of new rules, as in the case of contracts, where Canon law provided comprehensive norms (Chapter 2). In other instances, new norms were introduced when classical rules existed only in customs but were not recorded. For example, the *Jurisprudentia Frisica* recorded rules for specific groups of individuals in relation to *niarkap*, such as in-laws and unborn children, who were not explicitly mentioned in classical Frisian law (Chapter 2).

2.2 *Motivated by Prestige*

There is limited direct evidence to suggest that Frisians received learned law out of veneration or prestige. However, it is evident that they believed Roman and Canon law to be applicable in certain situations. At times, Frisian sources and litigants appearing in Frisian courts asserted that Frisian rules contradicting Roman law were invalid. An example of this can be found in the case of *niarkap* in the *Excerpta Legum* (Chapter 2). This indicates that certain Frisians held Roman law in high esteem, even if only as a means of supporting their own position.

Interestingly, prestige is also a possible motivation for the creating of the *Freeska Landriucht* and its publication in the incunabulum *D*. The intention may have been to present the traditional texts detailing the laws that the Frisians had followed for centuries, as well as the privileges, such as the Frisian freedom and the right to litigate (Chapter 3). Consequently, prestige motivated not only a deeper connection with Roman law, but also an inward look at the classical law texts of the Frisians.

2.3 *Motivated by Other Reasons*

While necessity and prestige were motivating factors for the Frisians to adopt foreign legal elements, they alone cannot account for the reception of learned law in the 14th and 15th centuries. The reception of learned law was a conscious choice by many Frisians and reflected in their individual acts. Many Frisians preferred Roman law for testamentary norms because it was better suited for organizing succession than Canon law, with its pious bequests, or classical Frisian law, with its intestate succession (Chapter 5). The changing desires and intentions of Frisian testators drove them to adopt wills drawn up according to Roman law.

Other factors that contributed to the reception of learned law were the existing similarities between classical Frisian law and Roman or Canon law. For instance, the concept of theft in Frisian law was similar to the *furtum* of Roman law, and both were primarily delicts pursued by a private accuser (Chapter 4). This made it easier for Frisians to adopt the methods and norms of Roman law. Similarly, classical Frisian agreements were loosely connected as a law of contracts, making them more amenable to receiving the open and general system of contracts of Canon law, as opposed to the closed and specific Roman law of contracts (Chapter 2).

These general factors all contributed to the reception of learned law in the 15th century. But despite the efforts undertaken in this study, primary sources often provide no definitive answers as to why Frisians and Frisian jurists adopted, adapted or applied extraneous legal elements.

2.4 *Motivations against Reception*

An equally important question as the question of the reasons *for* reception is the question of why Frisians and Frisian jurists did *not* adopt certain elements of foreign law and chose instead to maintain their own legal system unchanged.

Firstly, the relevance of traditional Frisian customs must be considered. The right to take over a sale was a crucial aspect of familial and communal land structures, and those entitled to it had an interest in preserving this custom

(Chapter 2). The judicial oath was also a significant feature of classical procedures and an essential element of a society based on honor (Chapter 3). Therefore, despite the reception of the procedural system of the *ius commune*, the oath continued to serve as an important means of furnishing proof, both in legal practice and in the written sources of the 15th century.

The same can be said for the classical practice of house searches, which, although aligned with the new legal system, remained part of the discovery process of theft (Chapter 4). The emphasis on secrecy as a particularly harmful act also persisted, as seen in the consistency regarding the differences between robbery and theft: theft was always defined by secrecy, and robbery by the public act. These findings demonstrate that some important classical customs and practices were retained, albeit in a new legal system that had incorporated many elements of learned law.

Secondly, in the case of last wills, the decision to impede reception was perhaps motivated more by practicality than by a desire to hold onto tradition (Chapter 5). Wills with fewer than seven witnesses and without a priest present were drawn up and accepted because the practicality of making a testament was more important than following the adopted norms of Roman law.

These reasons against adopting legal elements of foreign law demonstrate that Frisians actively chose when to receive foreign law and when to maintain their own legal customs.

3 The Development of Reception in Frisia

The reception of law is often a process extending over many decades or even centuries. This was evident in Frisia, where significant developments took place in the 14th and 15th centuries. The way the reception occurred changed over time and was influenced by written sources. Despite these changes, it is possible to observe some general developments characterizing the change in Frisian law and how Frisian jurists facilitated the reception of learned law.

3.1 *The Development of Reception in the 14th Century*

The interaction between classical Frisian law and learned law in the 14th century was marked by an attempt at harmonization in primary sources. Concepts that were similar in Frisian law and Roman or Canon law were compared and equated, and Frisian customs were incorporated into the system of learned law. For instance, the burden of proof in learned law was related to the Frisian idea of a right to prove (Chapter 3), while the judicial oath was classified within the procedural law of the *ius commune* as one of the various kinds of proof

(Chapter 3). Furthermore, the Frisian *mundskip* was interpreted in the same way as the Roman *tutela*, leading to the application of norms related to the *tutela* (Chapter 6).

In some cases, the interpretation and harmonization of Frisian and learned law concepts occurred even when fundamental differences existed. For example, the categorization of theft as either manifest or non-manifest in Frisian law was related to the similar but different distinction between *furtum manifestum* and *non-manifestum* (Chapter 4). At times, glosses made by educated Frisian jurists directly contradicted the provisions of learned law they quoted. However, the purpose of these glosses was not always accuracy, but often simply to compare or correct the main Frisian text. Nonetheless, they demonstrate that Frisians were interested in updating their classical Frisian law and contextualizing it with the law of the *ius commune*.

Finally, the examination of Frisian wills shows that there was a tentative intention to create a Frisian testamentary tradition that was secular rather than ecclesiastical (Chapter 5), as demonstrated by the references to Roman law concerning last wills in the *Freeska Landriucht*.

In conclusion, the reception in the 14th century was characterized by comparison, equation and harmonization of Frisian law and learned law. This provided the foundations for the subsequent changes in the 15th century.

3.2 *The Development of Reception in the 15th Century*

The reception of learned law in the 15th century was more significant than in the 14th century. In the first half of the 15th century, many classical Frisian customs were integrated into the systems of learned law, such as *niarkap* into the law of contracts (Chapter 2) and the judicial oath into the Romano-canonical procedure (Chapter 3). Neither of these changes was fundamentally compatible with the *ius commune*. At the same time, we also find the application of Roman norms in the first half of the 15th century, particularly regarding last wills and testaments, where the *Excerpta Legum* specifies that seven witnesses and the instituting of an heir were necessary (Chapter 5).

The second half of the 15th century saw an increased reception of norms and rules. Norms on theft, using the Old Frisian language and its terms, were adapted, including the distinct twofold and fourfold penalties of Roman law (Chapter 4). We also observed the same regarding tutorship of women in Frisian law, and the prohibition on being a guardian after remarrying (Chapter 6). The use of these terms, which resulted from the comparisons and interpretations of the 14th century, allowed for continuity between the old, classical Frisian law and the new, Romanized law.

In conclusion, the majority of the reception occurred in the sources of the 15th century, including the reception of systems, methods and norms. However, the sources of the 14th century, and the Frisians who engaged with learned law during that period created the foundations for the later developments. The reception of learned law was therefore not just a process that began in the 15th century, but one that built upon the works and thought of the preceding centuries.

4 A Canonized Frisian Law?

Finally, returning to Gerbenzon's assertion that Frisian law became "Canonized" in the 14th and 15th centuries, this study has examined whether Frisians received elements of Roman or Canon law. It is evident that Frisian law was not "Romanized", given that later scholars could remark on the strong presence of Roman law in the 16th century; this change had not yet occurred by the end of the 15th century. However, it is also insufficient to state that Frisian law was influenced only by Canon law before 1500.

Regarding the law of contracts, there is evidence of a "Canonization" of Frisian law, as well as partial "Canonization" of procedural law. The latter adopted the system and structure of Canon law but also retained elements of Frisian law, such as the judicial oath. Therefore, it is more accurate to refer to a hybrid Canon-Frisian procedural law.

Interestingly, other aspects of Frisian law, such as theft and testaments, were "Romanized". The subject of theft was heavily influenced by Roman law, possibly due to the similar approaches in both legal traditions regarding theft, including private penalties and distinctions between different forms of theft (manifest, non-manifest). On the topic of testaments, there is also clear evidence of an intentional reception of Roman law rather than a continued application of Canon law. Consequently, the existing tradition of making wills according to Canon law was "Romanized".

In conclusion, this study can partially confirm Gerbenzon's assertion that classical Frisian law was strongly influenced by Canon law, especially in its structure. Methods and approaches to law were adopted from the *ius commune*, but norms were sometimes also received from Roman law. Returning to Van Apeldoorn's assertion that Roman law was valid and had binding power from the 13th century onwards, this is clearly an overstatement. However, Van Apeldoorn is correct in that Roman law was known and had significant authority in the Frisian legal system long before 1500, especially with regard to fields such as theft and testaments.

Therefore, the "Canonization" of Frisian law was merely one aspect, albeit the most significant, in the reception of learned law. It is possible that this development continued in the 16th century, and that the reception of Roman norms in a "Canonized" Frisian legal system led to the exceptional presence noted by Ulrik Huber in the 17th century.

5 Future Considerations

This study and the underlying research aimed to provide a comprehensive overview of reception in Frisia during the 15th century, focusing on five different topics in various fields of law and society. This approach was novel and is the first analysis of its kind for Medieval Frisia. Research on Frisian legal history has been sparse, and this study has shed light on many aspects of Frisian law that were previously unknown. However, the vastness of the subject meant it was not possible to cover every aspect of law. Therefore, future historians of Frisia will have to delve deeper and examine aspects that were not included in this study.

Regarding contract law, specific contracts such as contracts of sale, lease or hire could be further investigated to reveal new information about contract law in Late Medieval Frisia. Furthermore, this study focused on only one particular wrongdoing, theft, but other wrongdoings such as murder, heresy or damage by animals may yield corresponding or different results. The wills that Frisians wrote also warrant further investigation, including the question of whether secular or ecclesiastical courts had jurisdiction over such wills. Additionally, many aspects of the lives of women and widows could be explored, including their roles in business, politics and society, as well as their marriages.

Alternatively, many other fields of law merit consideration. New research could reveal different insights, comparable results or new findings. This study also made only limited use of comparisons with other places and regions in Europe, such as the procedural law of Medieval Norway. Therefore, future research could focus on such comparisons, not only with neighboring regions but also with similar legal systems that underwent similar or different developments regarding the reception of learned law. Such comparisons may provide additional insight into Frisian law or offer new findings for other legal systems.

5.1 *After 1500*

This study concludes at the end of the 15th century. However, the changes in Frisian law until the 17th century, when Huber wrote his famous words, have not been fully accounted for. The legal system in Frisia in 1500 was not one where Roman and Canon law dominated. Therefore, it is likely that more changes occurred in the 16th century. This includes not only a stronger reception of

Roman law in Frisia, as Huber noted, but also a consequent disappearance of Canon law. This latter aspect is particularly interesting in view of the "Canonization" of Frisian law in the period to 1500. Further research is necessary to determine what led to the situation that Huber described.

This book intentionally ends with the loss of the Frisian Freedom and the beginning of foreign rule in Frisia. It is possible that the changes after 1500 were determined more by these new powers than by the Frisians themselves. Whether a hybrid legal system would otherwise have prevailed or whether change would have led to a system that reflected learned law even more remains unknown. Despite this uncertainty, it is evident that the people of Frisia were already actively creating a new legal system.

Bibliography

Primary Sources

Andrea, Giovanni de. *Summula de processu judicii* (A. Wunderlich, ed.), Basel: Sumtibus Schweighauseri, 1840 (originally published in the 13th or 14th century).

Andrea, Giovanni de. *Additiones ad Speculum iudiciale Guillelmi Duranti.* (originally published in the 13th or 14th century).

Andrea, Giovanni de. *In tertium decretalium librum novella commentaria.* Venice, 1612. (originally published in the 13th or 14th century).

Andrea, Giovanni de. *In quintum decretalium librum novella commentaria.* Venice, 1612. (originally published in the 13th or 14th century).

Bartolus de Saxoferrato, *Commentaria. In Primam Digesti Noui Partem.* Venice, 1569. (originally published in the 14th century).

Bos-Van der Heide, Henny S.E. *Het Rudolfsboek.* Leeuwarden: van Gorcum, 1937.

Breuker, Ph.H. *Landrecht der Vriesne.* Leeuwarden: Fryske Akademy, 1996.

Brouwer, Jelle. *Thet autentica riocht met inleiding, glossen, commentaar en woordenlijst.* Assen: Van Gorcum, 1941.

Buma, Wybren Jan, and Wilhelm Ebel. *Das Brokmer Recht.* Göttingen: Vandenhoeck & Ruprecht, 1965.

Buma, Wybren Jan, and Wilhelm Ebel. *Das Emsiger Recht.* Göttingen: Vandenhoeck & Ruprecht, 1967.

Buma, Wybren Jan, W. Ebel. *Das Fivelgoer Recht.* Göttingen: Vandenhoeck & Ruprecht, 1972.

Buma, Wybren Jan, and Wilhelm Ebel. *Das Hunsingoer Recht.* Göttingen: Vandenhoeck & Ruprecht, 1969.

Buma, Wybren Jan, and Wilhelm Ebel. *Das Rüstringer Recht.* Göttingen: Musterschmidt, 1963.

Buma, Wybren Jan, P. Gerbenzon, M. Tragter-Schubert. *Codex Aysma. Die Altfriesischen Texte.* Assen: Van Gorcum, 1993.

Buma, Wybren Jan, W. Ebel. *Das Fivelgoer Recht.* Göttingen: Vandenhoeck & Ruprecht, 1972.

Buma, Wybren Jan, Wilhelm Ebel and Martina Tragter-Schubert. *Westerlauwerssches Recht 1. Jus Municipale Frisonum, Erster Teil.* Göttingen: Vandenhoeck & Ruprecht, 1977.

Buma, Wybren Jan, Wilhelm Ebel and Martina Tragter-Schubert. *Westerlauwerssches Recht 1. Jus Municipale Frisonum, Zweiter Teil.* Göttingen: Vandenhoeck & Ruprecht, 1977.

Craig, Thomas. *Ius Feudale. Tribus Libris Comprehensum.* Edinburgh: Tho. & Walt. Ruddimannos, 1732.

Craig, Thomas. *Ius Feudale. Tribus Libris Comprehensum*. London: Impensis Societatis Stationariorum, 1655.

Durand, Guillaume. *Speculum Iudiciale*. Lib. 2. Turin, 1578. (originally published in the 13th century).

Fairbanks, S. *The Old West Frisian Skeltana Riucht*. Cambridge: Harvard University Press, 1939.

Hettema, Montanus. *Jurisprudentia Frisica, of Friesche regtkennis: Een handschrift uit de vijftiende eeuw. Eerste Stuk*. Leeuwarden: HC Schetsberg, 1834.

Hettema, Montanus. *Jurisprudentia Frisica, of Friesche regtkennis: Een handschrift uit de vijftiende eeuw. Tweede Stuk*. Leeuwarden: HC Schetsberg, 1835.

Hettema, Montanus. *Jurisprudentia Frisica, of Friesche regtkennis: Een handschrift uit de vijftiende eeuw. Derde Stuk*. Leeuwarden: HC Schetsberg, 1835.

Huber, Ulrik. *Heedensdaegse Rechtsgeleertheyt soo elders, als in Friesland gebruikelijk*. Leeuwarden: Hero Nauta, 1686.

Huber, Ulrik. *The Jurisprudence of my Time (Heedendaegse Rechtsgeleertheyt). Translated by Percival Gane*. Durban: Butterworth & Co., 1939.

L.O. (1602): *Statuten, Ordonanntien, ende Costumen van Frieslandt. Ten bevelen van de Heeren Staten des selben Landts*. Franeker: Gillis vanden Rade, 1602.

L.O. (1723): *Statuten, Ordonanntien, Reglementen en Costumen van Rechte van Frieslandt. Volgens Resolutie van de ed. mog. Heeren Staten des selven Landts*. Leeuwarden: Henrik Halma, 1723.

Nijdam Han, Jan Hallebeek and Hylkje de Jong. *Frisian Land Law. A Critical Edition and Translation of the Freeska Landriucht*. Leiden/Boston: Brill, 2023.

Richthofen, Karl Freiherr von. *Friesische Rechtsquellen*. Berlin: Nicolaische Buchhandlung, 1840.

Sandars, Thomas Collett. *Institutes of Justinian*. London: Longmans, Green, 1922.

Spruit, J.E, and J.M.J. Chorus (eds.). *Corpus Iuris Civilis : Tekst En Vertaling. XII Addendum. Libri Feudorum*. Amsterdam: Amsterdam University Press, 2016.

Telting, Albartus. *De Friesche Stadrechten*. 's Gravenhage: Martinus Nijhoff, 1883.

Verhoeven, Gerrit, J.A. Mol. *Friese testamenten tot 1550*. Leeuwarden: Fryske Akademy, 1994.

Vries, Oebele. *Ferdban. Oudfriese Oorkonden en hun Verhaal*. Gorredijk: Noordboek, 2021.

Literature

Aert, Laura. "The legal possibilities of Antwerp widows in the late sixteenth century." *The history of the family* 12.4 (2007): 282–295.

Algra, Nikolaas Egbert. *Ein: enkele rechtshistorische aspecten van de grondeigendom in Westerlauwers Friesland*. Groningen: P. Noordhoff, 1966.

Algra, Nikolaas Egbert. *Oudfries recht 800–1256*. Leeuwarden: Fryske Akademy, 2000.

Andersen, Per. *Legal Procedure and Practice in Medieval Denmark*. Leiden/Boston: Brill, 2011.

Andersson, Theodore M. "The Thief in Beowulf" *Speculum* 59 (1984): 493–508.

Ankum, Johan Albert. "Cessation de la Minorité—Études Sur le Statut Juridique des Enfants Mineurs dans l'Histoire du Droit Privé Néerlandais à Partir du Treizième Siècle" *Tijdschrift voor rechtsgeschiedenis /Revue d'Histoire du Droit/The Legal History Review* 44 (1976): 291–335.

Ankum, Johan Albert. *Elementen van Romeins recht*. Zwolle: W.E.J. Tjeenk Willink, 1976.

Apeldoorn, Lambertus van. "Het Romeinsche Recht in Friesland" *Mededelingen der Nederlandsche Akademie van Wetenschappen, Afdeeling Letterkunde*. Amsterdam: N.V. Noord-Hollandsche Uitgevers Maatschappij, 1940.

Atamer, Yeşim M. "Rezeption und Weiterentwicklung des schweizerischen Zivilgesetzbuches in der Türkei." *Rabels Zeitschrift Für Ausländisches Und Internationales Privatrecht/The Rabel Journal of Comparative and International Private Law* 72 (2008): 723–754.

Atzeri, Lorena. *Roman Law and Reception*. Mainz: Institut für Europäische Geschichte, 2017.

Auer, Anika M. "Konfliktlösung durch Ordalien" in: Mayenburg, David von (ed.). *Konfliktlösung im Mittelalter*. Frankfurt am Main: Springer, 2021: 161–168.

Babusiaux, Ulrike, Christian Baldus, Wolfgang Ernst, Franz-Stefan Meissel, Johannes Platschek and Thomas Rüfner (eds.). *Handbuch des Römischen Privatrechts*. I–III. Tübingen: Mohr Siebeck, 2023.

Baldwin, John W. "The Intellectual Preparation for the Canon of 1215 against the Ordeals." *Speculum* 36 (1961): 613–636.

Bartlett, Robert. *Trial by Fire and Water. The Medieval Judicial Ordeal*. Oxford: Clarendon Press, 1988.

Bary, E.H., and H.D. Meijering. *Het Westerlauwers Zeendrecht volgens de inkunabel van het Friese landrecht*. 1972.

Basedow, Jürgen, Klaus J. Hopt, and Reinhard Zimmermann. *Handwörterbuch des europäischen Privatrechts*. mpipriv.de, 2009, https://hwb-eup2009.mpipriv.de/index.php/Rezeption. Accessed: 19.01.2020.

Bassani, Alessandra. "A Coffer for the Will" in: Di Renzo Villata, M.G. (ed.) *Succession Law, Practice and Society in Europe across the Centuries*. Cham: Springer, 2018: 231–247.

Benham, Jenny. "Law, language and crime in Denmark and England: a comparative approach." In: Salonen, Kirsi (ed.). *How Nordic are the Nordic Medieval Laws? Ten Years After: Proceedings of the tenth Carlsberg Academy Conference on medieval legal history 2013*. Copenhagen: Djøf Forlag, 2014.

Berents, Dirk Arend. *Misdaad in de middeleeuwen: een onderzoek naar de Criminaliteit in het laatmiddeleeuwse Utrecht: proefschrift*. Vol. 2. Haarlem: Gottmer, 1976.

Berger, Adolf. *Encyclopedic Dictionary of Roman law*. Philadelphia: The American Philosophical Society, 1991.

Bezemer, C.H. "Romeins recht vs. sociale rechtvaardigheid. Een voorbeeld uit de Republiek." *Bw-Krant Jaarboek* 22 (2007): 121–132.

Boehm, Christopher. "The Natural History of Blood Revenge" in: Netterstrøm, Jeppe Büchert and Bjørn Poulsen (eds.). *Feud in Medieval and Early Modern Europe*. Aarhus: Aarhus University Press, 2007: 189–203.

Bos-Van der Heide, Henny S.E. *Het Rudolfsboek*. Leeuwarden: van Gorcum, 1937.

Brandt, Ahasver von. "Mittelalterliche Bürgertestamente. Neuerschlossene Quellen zur Geschichte der materiellen und geistigen Kultur." *Sitzungsberichte der Heidelberger Akademie der Wissenschaften, philosophisch-historische Klasse* 75 (1973): 5–32.

Bremmer, Jan, and Lourens Van Den Bosch (eds.). *Between Poverty and the Pyre*. London: Routledge, 1995.

Bremmer, Rolf H. *A Bibliographical Guide to Old Frisian Studies*. Odense: Odense University Press, 1992.

Bremmer, Rolf H. *An Introduction to Old Frisian. History, Grammar, Reader, Glossary*. Amsterdam/Philadelphia: John Benjamins, 2009.

Bremmer Jr, Rolf Hendrik, Geart van der Meer, and Oebele Vries, eds. *Aspects of Old Frisian Philology*. Vol. 31. Rodopi, 2007.

Bremmer, Rolf H. "Codifying the Law: Frisian Legal Manuscripts around 1300." in: Kwakkel, Erik (ed.). Vernacular Manuscript Culture 1000–1500. Leiden: Leiden University Press, 2018.

Bremmer, Rolf H. *Hir is eskriven. Lezen en schrijven in de Friese landen rond 1300*. Hilversum: Verloren, 2004.

Bremmer, Rolf H. "More than Language: Law and Textual Communities in Medieval Frisia." In: Gobbitt, Thom. *Law | Book | Culture in the Middle Ages*. Leiden, Boston: Brill, 2021.

Bremmer, Rolf H. "The orality of Old Frisian law texts." *Amsterdamer Beiträge zur älteren Germanistik* 73.1 (2014): 1–48.

Breuker, Ph.H. *Landrecht der Vriesne*. Leeuwarden: Fryske Akademy, 1996.

Brundage, James. *Medieval canon law*. London: Longman, 1995.

Buijtenen, Maria Petrus. *De grondslag van de Friese vrijheid*. Van Gorcum, 1953.

Buitelaar, Marjo. "Widow's Worlds. Representations and realities." In: Bremmer, Jan, and Lourens Van Den Bosch (eds.). *Between Poverty and the Pyre*. London: Routledge, 1995: 1–18.

Buma, Wybren Jan. *Het Godsoordeel in de Oud-Friese literatuur*. Groningen: JB Wolters, 1949.

Buss, Harm. *Letztwillige Verfügungen nach ostfriesischem Recht*. Aurich: Verlag Ostfriesische Landschaft, 1966.

Caenegem, Raoul-Charles van. *Geschiedenis van het Strafprocesrecht in Vlaanderen van de XIe tot de XIVe Eeuw*. Brussel: Paleis der Academien, 1956.

Caenegem, Raoul-Charles van. *Geschiedenis van het strafrecht in Vlaanderen van de XIe tot de XIVe eeuw*. Brussel: Paleis der Academien, 1954.

Cappon, Cornelius Marinus. "De erfstelling in de Friese testamenten tot 1550. Een plaatsbepaling" in: Mol, J.A. (ed.). *Zorgen voor zekerheid. Studies over Friese testamenten in de vijftiende en zestiende eeuw*. Leeuwarden: Fryske Akademy, 1994: 38–73.

Cappon, Cornelius Marinus. *De Opkomst van het Testament in het Sticht Utrecht*. Deventer: Kluwer, 1992.

Cappon, Cornelius Marinus. "Het notariaat in de late Middeleeuwen (+/-1250–+/-1540)" in: Gehlen, A., and P.L. Neve (eds.). *Het notariaat in de Lage Landen (+/-1250–1842). Opstellen over de geschiedenis van het notariaat in de Lage Landen vanaf de oorsprong tot in de negentiende eeuw*. Deventer: Kluwer, 2005: 3–29.

Cavallo, Sandra, and Lyndan Warner. *Widowhood in medieval and early modern Europe*. London: Routledge, 2014.

Clarke, Peter. "Western Canon Law in the Central and Later Middle Ages." In: Pihlajamäki, Heikki, Markus D. Dubber, and Mark Godfrey (eds.). *The Oxford Handbook of European Legal History*. Oxford: Oxford University Press, 2018: 266–286.

Coing, Helmut. "Die europäische Privatrechtsgeschichte der neueren Zeit als einheitliches Forschungsgebiet" *Ius Commune* 1 (1967).

Conring, Hermann. *De Origine Juris Germanici*. Helmstadt: typis & sumtibus Henningi Mulleri Academiae Typographi, 1665.

Cordes, Albrecht, et al. (eds.). *Handwörterbuch zur deutschen Rechtsgeschichte*. 2. Edition. Online: https://www.hrgdigital.de/inhalt.html, 2004.

Costa, Pietro. "In search of legal texts: which texts for which historian." In: Michelsen, Dag (ed.). *Reading Past Legal Texts*. Oslo: Unipax, 2006: 158–182.

Dackling, Martin. "Traditional or modern peasants? odelsrett and bördsrätt in parliamentary debates, 1810–1860: Traditional or modern peasants?" *Scandinavian Journal of History*, 46(1) (2021): 63–83.

Daniel, Andreas. *Gemeines Recht*. Berlin: Duncker & Humblot, 2003.

De Blécourt, A.S. "Heerlijkheden en Heerlijke Rechten." *Tijdschrift voor rechtsgeschiedenis /Revue d'Histoire du Droit/The Legal History Review* 1 (1918): 489–519.

De Blécourt, A.S. *Kort Begrip van het Oud-Vaderlands Burgerlijk Recht*. Groningen: J.B. Wolters, 1967.

Decock, Wim. *Theologians and Contract Law*. Leiden/Boston: Martinus Nijhoff, 2013.

De Langen, Gilles, and Johannes A. Mol. "Church Foundation and Parish Formation in Frisia in the Tenth and Eleventh Centuries: A Planned Development?" *The Medieval Low Countries* 4 (2017): 1–55.

De Moor, Tine, and Jan Luiten Van Zanden. "Girl power: the European marriage pattern and labour markets in the North Sea region in the late medieval and early modern period." *The Economic History Review* 63.1 (2009): 1–33.

Despars, Nicolaes. *Cronijcke van den lande ende graefscepe van Vlaenderen, gemaect door Jor Nicolaes Despars. Van de jaeren 405 tot 1492. Voor de eerste mael thans in het licht gegeven en met noodige aenteekeningen opgehelderd door J. de Jonghe*. I. Brugge, 1837.

Dirks, Florian. "Der Eid in der Konfliktlösung" in: Mayenburg, David von (ed.). *Konfliktlösung im Mittelalter*. Frankfurt am Main: Springer, 2021: 169–174.

Domingo, Rafael. "The Family in Ancient Roman Law" SSRN *Electronic Journal* 10.2139/ssrn.2955100, 2017.

Domingo, Rafael. "The Roman Law of Contracts. An Overview." ssrn.com, 29.03.2017, https://ssrn.com/abstract=2942873. Accessed 15. March 2022.

Donahue, Charles. "Proof by Witnesses in the Church Courts of Medieval England: An Imperfect Reception of the Learned Law" in: Arnold, Morris S. et al. (eds.). *On the Laws and Customs of England: Essays in Honor of Samuel E. Thorne*. Chapel Hill: University of North Carolina Press, 1981.

Donlan, Sean Patrick, and Dirk Heirbaut. "'A Patchwork of Accommodations': European Legal Hybridity and Jurisdictional Complexity—An Introduction" In: Donlan, Sean Patrick, and Dirk Heirbaut (eds.). *The Laws' Many Bodies*. Berlin: Duncker & Humblot, 2015: 9–34.

Eisenhardt, Ulrich. *Deutsche Rechtsgeschichte*. Verlag CH Beck, 1999.

Ennen, Edith. *Frauen im Mittelalter*. München: CH Beck, 1985.

Epstein, Steven. *Wills and wealth in medieval Genoa, 1150–1250*. Cambridge, Mass.: Harvard University Press, 1984.

Erler, Adalbert, Wolfgang Stammler, and Ekkehard Kaufmann. *Handwörterbuch zur deutschen Rechtsgeschichte*. Berlin: E. Schmidt, 1964.

Feenstra, Robert. "Römisches Recht und Kaiserrecht in den Altfriesischen Rechts quellen" *Philologia Frisica anno 1956* (1957): 26–34.

Feenstra, Robert. *Zur Rezeption in den Niederlanden*. Milan: Giuffrè, 1953.

Flach, Dieter. *Die Gesetze der frühen römischen Republik: Text und Kommentar*. Darmstadt: Wissenschaftliche Buchgesellschaft, 1994.

Floßmann, Ursula. *Die Gleichberechtigung der Geschlechter in der Privatrechts geschichte*. Wien/New York: Springer Vienna, 1977.

Fockema Andreae, S.J. "De onzelfstandigheid der vrouwen." *Bijdragen tot de Nederlandsche rechtsgeschiedenis* I (1888).

Foreville, Raymonde. "Lateran I–IV." In: Dumeige, Gervais and Heinrich Bacht (eds.). *Geschichte der ökumenischen Konzilien*. Mainz: Matthias Grünewald, 1970.

Franklin, Peter. "Peasant Widows' "Liberation" and Remarriage before the Black Death." *Economic history review* (1986): 186–204.

Froide, Amy M. "Marital Status as a Category of Difference: Singlewomen and Widows in Early Modern England." Bennett, Judith M., and Amy M. Froide, eds. *Singlewomen in the European past, 1250–1800*. Philadelphia: University of Pennsylvania Press, 2011: 236–269.

Garlati, Loredana. "Women's Succession from the Middle Ages to the Modern Era." Di Renzo Villata, Maria Gigliola (ed.) *Succession Law, Practice and Society in Europe across the Centuries*. Cham: Springer, 2018. 207–230.

Gelting, Michael H. "Odelsrett—Lovbydelse—Bördsrätt—Retrait Lignager: Kindred and Land in the Nordic Countries in the Twelfth and Thirteenth Centuries." In Hansen, Lars Ivar (ed.). *Family, Marriage and Property Devolution in the Middle Ages*. Tromsø, 2000.

Gerbenzon, Pieter. "Aantekeningen over de Jurisprudentia Frisica-Een Laat-Vijftiende-Eeuwse Westerlauwers-Friese Bewerking Van de Excerpta Legum (Eerste Deel)." *Tijdschrift voor rechtsgeschiedenis/Revue d'Histoire du Droit/The Legal History Review* 57 (1989): 21–67.

Gerbenzon, Pieter. "Aantekeningen over de Jurisprudentia Frisica-Een Laat-Vijftiende-Eeuwse Westerlauwers-Friese Bewerking Van de *Excerpta Legum* (Tweede Deel)." *Tijdschrift voor rechtsgeschiedenis/Revue d'Histoire du Droit/The Legal History Review* 57 (1989): 339–374.

Gerbenzon, Pieter. *Apparaat voor de studie van Oudfries recht*. I. Literatuur. Groningen, 1981.

Gerbenzon, Pieter. *Apparaat voor de studie van Oudfries recht. II. Bronnen*. Groningen, 1981.

Gerbenzon, Pieter. "Der altfriesische *asega*, der altsächsische *eosago* und der althochdeutsche *esago*." *Tijdschrift voor Rechtsgeschiedenis* 41 (1973): 75–91.

Gerbenzon, Pieter. "Canon and Roman Law in the So-Called Codex Parisiensis" in: Bremmer, Rolf H., et al. (eds.). *Aspects of Old Frisian Philology*. Amsterdamer Beiträge zur älteren Germanistik 31–32 (1990): 125–145.

Gerbenzon, Pieter. *Codex Parisiensis*. 's-Gravenhage: Nijhoff, 1954.

Gerbenzon, Pieter. *Emo van Huizinge, een vroege decretalist*. Groningen: J.B. Wolters, 1965.

Gerbenzon, Pieter. "Enkele nieuwe gegevens over de receptie van het Romeinse recht in Friesland" *Tijdschrift voor rechtsgeschiedenis/Revue d'Histoire du Droit/The Legal History Review* 27 (1959): 133–157.

Gerbenzon, Pieter. *Excerpta legum: onderzoekingen betreffende enkele Friese rechtsboeken uit de vijftiende eeuw*. Groningen/Djakarta: Wolters, 1956.

Gerbenzon, Pieter. *Friese Rechtstaal en Vreemd Recht*. Groningen: Wolters, 1958.

Gerbenzon, Pieter. "Kanonisches Recht in den friesischen Rechtsquellen." *Philologia Frisica anno 1956* (1957): 35–43.

Gerrits, Matthijs and Johannes A. Mol. "Macht, geweld en monniken. De escalatie van een vete in de Friese Zuidwesthoek 1482–1495." In: *De Vrije Fries* 93 (2013): 53–97.

Goody, Jack R. "Inheritance, property and women: some comparative considerations." In: Goody, Jack R., Joan Thirsk, and Edward Palmer Thompson. "Family and inheritance." *Past and Present Publications* (*USA*) (1976).

Goody, Jack R., Joan Thirsk, and Edward Palmer Thompson. "Family and inheritance." *Past and Present Publications* (*USA*) (1976).

Goody, Jack, and John Rankine Goody. *The development of the family and marriage in Europe*. Cambridge: Cambridge University Press, 1983.

Gosses, Izaak Hendrik. "De Friesche hoofdeling", in: Izaak Hendrik Gosses (ed.), *Verspreide geschriften*. Groningen: Wolters, 1946: 402–450.

Graziadei, Michele. "Comparative Law, Transplants, and Receptions" In: Pihlajamäki, Heikki, Markus D. Dubber, and Mark Godfrey (eds.). *The Oxford Handbook of European Legal History*. Oxford: Oxford University Press, 2018.

Green, Dennis Howard. *Language and history in the early Germanic world*. Cambridge: Cambridge University Press, 2000.

Grimm, Jakob. *Deutsche Rechts Alterthümer*. Göttingen: Dieterische Buchhandlung, 1828.

Hallebeek, Jan. "Dispositions *ad pias causas* in Gratian's *Decretum*. Should the *portio Christi* be restricted to the child's share?" In: Zimmermann, Reinhard (ed.). *Der Einfluss religiöser Vorstellungen auf die Entwicklung des Erbrechts*. Tübingen: Mohr Siebeck, 2012: 79–102.

Hallebeek, Jan. *Fons et Origo Iuris. Een Historische Inleiding tot het Vermogensrecht*. Amsterdam: VU University Press, 2007.

Hallebeek, Jan. *Layci erant coiudices: Over de rol van leken in de Westerlauwerse seendprocedure*. Amsterdam: Vrije Universiteit Amsterdam, 2019.

Hallebeek, Jan. *Lijf ende Goedt. De juridische bescherming van de menselijke persoon en diens vermogen. Een schets van de continentale rechtsgeschiedenis*. Amsterdam: Vrije Universiteit Amsterdam, 2017.

Hallebeek, Jan. "Structure of Medieval Roman Law: Institutions, Sources and Methods." In: Pihlajamäki, Heikki, Markus D. Dubber, and Mark Godfrey (eds.). *The Oxford Handbook of European Legal History*. Oxford: Oxford University Press, 2018: 287–309.

Hallebeek, Jan. "The Gloss to the Saunteen Kesta (Seventeen Statutes) of the Frisian Land Law." *Tijdschrift voor Rechtsgeschiedenis/Revue d'Histoire du Droit/The Legal History Review* 87.1–2 (2019): 30–64.

Halpérin, Jean-Louis. "The Age of Codification and Legal Modernization in Private Law." In: Pihlajamäki, Heikki, Markus D. Dubber, and Mark Godfrey (eds.). *The Oxford Handbook of European Legal History*. Oxford: Oxford University Press, 2018: 908–928.

Hamerster, Dominicus. *Naukeurige en duidelyke verklaring over de statuten, ordonnantien, reglementen, en costumen van rechte in Frieslandt*. Leeuwarden: Abraham Ferwerda, 1753.

Hannan, Jerome D. "The canon law of wills." *Jurist* 4 (1944): 522–547.

Heirbaut, Dirk. "Reading Past Legal Text" In: Michelsen, Dag (ed.). *Reading Past Legal Texts*. Oslo: Unipax, 2006: 91–112.

Helmholz, Richard H. *The spirit of classical canon law*. Athens, Georgia: University of Georgia Press, 1996.

Henstra, Dirk Jan, and Anne Tjerk Popkema. *Friese graafschappen tussen Zwin en Wezer: een overzicht van de grafelijkheid in middeleeuws Frisia (ca. 700–1200)*. Van Gorcum, 2012.

Hettema, Montanus de Haan. "De Godsoordeelen in Friesland" De Vrije Fries 4 (1846): 269–305.

His, Rudolf. *Das Strafrecht der Friesen im Mittelalter*. Leipzig: Dieterich'sche Verlagsbuchhandlung, 1901.

His, Rudolf. *Das Strafrecht des deutschen Mittelalters. Die Verbrechen und ihre Folgen im allgemeinen*. Vol. 1. Weimar: T. Weicher, 1920.

His, Rudolf. *Das Strafrecht des deutschen Mittelalters. Die einzelnen Verbrechen*. Vol. 2. Weimar: T. Weicher, 1935.

Hoad, T.F. (ed.). *The Concise Oxford Dictionary of English Etymology*. Oxford: Oxford University Press. (2003). Accessed Oxford Reference (www.oxfordreference.com) on 19. April 2022.

Hofmann, Dietrich, and Anne Tjerk Popkema. *Altfriesisches Handwörterbuch*. Heidelberg: Universitätsverlag Winter, 2008.

Hofmann, Gisela. "Gold, Silber, Kleinodien, kostbare Gewänder und Gebrauchsgegenstände aus Edelmetall im mittelalterlichen Friesland." *Us Wurk* 58 (2009): 73–151.

Hooker, Michael Barry. *Legal Pluralism. An Introduction to Colonial and Neo-colonial Laws*. Oxford: Clarendon Press, 1975.

Howell, Martha C. *Women, production, and patriarchy in late medieval cities*. Chicago: University of Chicago Press, 1986.

Huber, Ulrik. *The Jurisprudence of my Time (Heedendaegse Rechtsgeleertheyt). Translated by Percival Gane*. Durban: Butterworth & Co., 1939

Husa, Jaakko. *A new introduction to comparative law*. Oxford: Bloomsbury Publishing, 2015.

Immink, P.W.A. "Getuigen in Het Oude Friese Recht." *Tijdschrift voor Rechtsgeschiedenis* 31 (1963): 427–462.

Janes, Dominic. "Treasure Bequest: Death and Gift in the Early Middle Ages" in: Hill, Joyce and Mary Swan (eds.). *The Community, the Family and the Saint. Patterns of Power in Early Medieval Europe*. Turnhout: Brepols, 1998: 363–377.

Janse, Antheun. "De waarheid van een falsum. Op zoek naar de politieke context van het Karelsprivilege." *De Vrije Fries* 71 (1991): 7–28.

Janse, Antheun. *Grenzen aan de macht. de Friese oorlog van de graven van Holland omstreeks 1400*. Den Haag: Hollandse historische reeks, 1993.

Johnston, Thomas S.B. "Old Frisian Law and the Frisian Freedom Ideology: Text and Manuscript Composition as a Marketing Device." in: Bremmer, Rolf H., Thomas S.B. Johnston and Oebele Vries (eds.) *Approaches to Old Frisian Philology*. Amsterdam: Brill, 1998: 179–214.

Johnston, David, ed. *The Cambridge companion to roman law*. Cambridge: Cambridge University Press, 2015.

Kaller, Paul. *Der Sachsenspiegel. In hochdeutscher Übersetzung*. München: C.H. Beck, 2002.

Kaser, Max. *Das römische Privatrecht: Erster Abschnitt. Das altrömische, das vorklassische und klassische Recht*. München: Beck, 1971.

Kaser, Max. *Das römische Privatrecht: Zweiter Abschnitt. Die nachklassischen Entwicklungen*. München: CH Beck, 1975.

Keefer, Sarah Larratt. "Ut in omnibus honorificetur Deus. The Corsnæd Ordeal in Anglo-Saxon England" in: Hill, Joyce and Mary Swan (eds.). *The Community, the Family and the Saint. Patterns of Power in Early Medieval Europe*. Turnhout: Brepols, 1998: 237–264.

Klaarbergen, Berend Wijbe van. *Das altwestfriesische jüngere Schulzenrecht*. Laverman, 1947.

Köbler, Gerhard. *Deutsche Rechtsgeschichte: ein systematischer Grundriss der geschichtlichen Grundlagen des deutschen Rechts von den Indogermanen bis zur Gegenwart*. München: Vahlen, 1990.

Korpiola, Mia. "High and Late Medieval Scandinavia: Codified Vernacular Law and Learned Legal Influences." In: Pihlajamäki, Heikki, Markus D. Dubber, and Mark Godfrey (eds.). *The Oxford Handbook of European Legal History*. Oxford: Oxford University Press, 2018: 379–404.

Koschaker, Paul. *Europa und das Römische Recht*. Beck, 1947.

Kowaleski, Maryanne. "Singlewomen in Medieval and Early Modern Europe: The Demographic Perspective." Bennett, Judith M., and Amy M. Froide, eds. *Singlewomen in the European past, 1250–1800*. Philadelphia: University of Pennsylvania Press, 2011: 38–81.

Krause, Hermann. *Kaiserrecht und Rezeption*. Heidelberg: Winter Univ. Verlag, 1952.

Küper, Wilfried. "His, Rudolf" in: *Neue Deutsche Biographie* 9 (1972), p. 248f. [Online-Version]. www.deutsche-biographie.de: https://www.deutsche-biographie.de/pnd1194918oX.html#ndbcontent. Accessed: 28. August 2022.

Kunkel, Wolfgang. "Das Wesen der Rezeption des römischen Rechts." *Heidelberger Jahrbücher*. Springer: Berlin, Heidelberg, 1957: 1–12.

Kunkel, Wolfgang. "The Reception of Roman law in Germany: An Interpretation". Strauss, Gerald (ed.). *Pre-Reformation Germany*. London: Macmillan, 1972.

Kuyk, J. van. "Bijdrage tot de Geschiedenis van den Tweekamp" *Tijdschrift voor Strafrecht* 23 (1912): 312–342.

Ledlie, James Crawford. "Gaius" in: Macdonell, John, and Edward Manson (eds.). *Great Jurists of the World*. London: John Murray, 1914.

Lehmann, Karl. *Das Langobardische Lehnrecht*. Göttingen: Dieterich'sche Verlagsbuchhandlung, 1896.

Lengen, Hajo van, Rainer Driever and Wilhelmus Johannes Kuppers (eds.). *Die Friesische Freiheit des Mittelalters: Leben und Legende*. Aurich: Ostfriesische Landschaft, 2003.

Lesaffer, Randall. "Law and History" in: Van Klink, Bart, and Sanne Taekema. *Law and Method*. Tübingen: Mohr Siebeck, 2011.

Lesaffer, Randall. *Inleiding tot de Europese Rechtsgeschiedenis*. Leuven: Universitaire Pers Leuven, 2004.

Litewski, Wiesław. *Der römisch-kanonische Zivilprozeß nach den älteren ordines iudiciarii*. I. Kraków: Wydawnictwo Uniwersytetu Jagiellońskiego, 1999.

Litewski, Wiesław. *Der römisch-kanonische Zivilprozeß nach den älteren ordines iudiciarii*. II. Kraków: Wydawnictwo Uniwersytetu Jagiellońskiego, 1999.

Lokin, Jan H.A., Frits Brandsma and Corjo Jansen. *Roman-Frisian Law of the 17th and 18th Century*. Berlin: Duncker & Humblot, 2003.

Luts, Marju. "Jurisprudential Reception as a Field of Study" *Juridica International* 2 (1997): 2–6.

Mate, Mavis E. *Daughters, Wives, and Widows after the Black Death: Women in Sussex, 1350–1535*. Woodbridge: Boydell & Brewer Ltd, 1998.

Mehringer, Rudolf. "Wörter und Sachen" in: *Indogermanische Forschungen. Zeitschrift für Sprach- und Altertumskunde* 18, Straßburg: Verlag von Karl J. Trübner, 1905/1906: 204–296.

Meijering, Hendrik Derk, and Johannes Adrianus Nijdam. *'Wat is Recht?'. De receptie van Oudfries recht in de Groninger Ommelanden in de 15e en 16e eeuw.: Een editie met vertaling*. Gorredijk: Bornmeer, 2018.

Meijering, Hendrik Derk. *De Willekeuren van de Opstalsboom (1323)*. Groningen: V.R.B.-Offsetdrukkerij, 1974.

Meijers, E.M., Eggens, J. (ed.) *Het Testament*. Arnhem: S. Gouda Quint, 1951.

Meyers, E.M. "Het Friese en het Drentse erfrecht en huwelijksgoederenrecht" *Akademie Dagen* 2, Amsterdam: N.V. Noord-Hollandsche Uitgevers Maatschappij, 1949: 37–71.

Miller, William Ian. *Bloodtaking and peacemaking: Feud, law, and society in Saga Iceland*. Chicago: University of Chicago Press, 2009.

Mol, Johannes A. "Friezen en het hiernamaals. Zieleheilsbeschikkingen ten gunste van kerken, kloosters en armen in testamenten uit Friesland tot 1580" in: Mol, J.A (ed.). *Zorgen voor zekerheid. Studies over Friese testamenten in de vijftiende en zestiende eeuw*. Leeuwarden: Fryske Akademy, 1994: 175–214.

Mol, Johannes A. (ed.). *Zorgen voor zekerheid. Studies over Friese testamenten in de vijftiende en zestiende eeuw*. Leeuwarden: Fryske Akademy, 1994.

Mol, Johannes A., and Justine Smithuis. "De Friezen als uitverkoren volk: religieus-patriottische geschiedschrijving in vijftiende-eeuws Friesland." *Jaarboek voor Middeleeuwse Geschiedenis* 11 (2008): 175–204.

Mol, Johannes A. "Hoofdelingen en huurlingen. Militaire innovatie en de aanloop tot 1498." In: Frieswijk, Johan (ed.). *Fryslân, staat en macht 1450–1650. Bijdragen aan het historisch congres te Leeuwarden van 3 tot 5 juni.* Hilversum/Leeuwarden: Verloren/Fryske Akademy, 1999.

Mousourakis, George. *Fundamentals of Roman private law.* Springer Science & Business Media, 2012.

Müller, Wilhelm, and George Friedrich Benecke. *Mittelhochdeutsches wörterbuch.* II/1. S. Hirzel, 1863.

Munske, Horst Haider. "Angelsächsisch-altfriesische Beziehungen in der Rechtsterminologie für Missetaten." In: Hoekema, Teake, Y. Poortinga and J.J. Spahr van der Hoek (eds.). *Flecht op 'e koai.* Groningen: Wolters-Noordhoff, 1970: 40–52.

Munske, Horst Haider. *Der germanische Rechtswortschatz im Bereich der Missetaten. 1. Die Terminologie der älteren westgermanischen Rechtsquellen.* Berlin/New York: Walter de Gruyter, 1973.

Munske, Horst Haider, et al., eds. *Handbuch des Friesischen/Handbook of Frisian Studies.* Walter de Gruyter, 2013.

Nicholas, David. *The domestic life of a medieval city: women, children, and the family in fourteenth-century Ghent.* Lincoln: University of Nebraska Press, 1985.

Nijdam, Han. "Compensating Body and Honor: The Old Frisian Compensation Tariffs." In: Turner, Wendy and Sara Butler (eds.). *Medicine and the Law in the Middle Ages.* Leiden: Brill, 2014: 23–57.

Nijdam, Han. "Wat was een mensenleven waard? Over weergeld en compensatie, in het bijzonder in middeleeuws Friesland." *Madoc. Ttijdschrift over de Middeleeuwen* 24 (2010): 195–205.

Nijdam, Johannes Adrianus. *Lichaam, eer en recht in middeleeuws Friesland: een studie naar de Oudfriese boeteregisters.* Hilversum: Verloren, 2008.

Noomen, P.N. "Consolidatie van familiebezit en status in middeleeuws Friesland" in: Mol, J.A (ed.). *Zorgen voor zekerheid. Studies over Friese testamenten in de vijftiende en zestiende eeuw.* Leeuwarden: Fryske Akademy 1994: 73–174.

Noomen, Paul N. "De Friese vetemaatschappij: sociale structuur en machtsbases." Frieswijk, Johan (ed.) *Fryslân: staat en macht.* Hilversum: Verloren, 1999.

Noomen, Paul N. *De stinzen in middeleeuws Friesland en hun bewoners.* Hilversum: Verloren, 2009.

Nordby, Ole-Albert Rønning. *The Judicial Oath in Medieval Norway.* Oslo: University of Oslo, 2018.

Nörr, Knut Wolfgang. *Romanisch-kanonisches Prozessrecht.* Heidelberg: Springer, 2012.

Oosten, Meelf Sybens van. "Inleidende beschouwingen over het oudere Friese bewijsrecht" *Tijdschrift voor Rechtsgeschiedenis/Revue d'Histoire du Droit* 18 (1950): 440–476.

Oosten, Meelf Sybens van. *De Ambtshalve Vervolging naar Oud-Friesch Recht.* Leiden: J.J. Groen & Zoon, 1938.

Oosten, Meelf Sybens van. "Vredeban en bezitsbescherming" in: Langemeijer, Gerard. *Speculum Langemeijer.* Zwolle: Tjeenk Willink, 1973.

Oven, J.C. van. "Testamentum" in: Meijers, E.M., Eggens, J. (ed.) *Het Testament.* Arnhem: S. Gouda Quint, 1951.

Pennington, K. "Due Process, Community, and the Prince in the Evolution of the Ordo iudiciarius." *Rivista Internazionale* di *Diritto Comune* 9 (1998): 9–47.

Popkema, Anne Tjerk. "Die altfriesischen Eidesbezeichnungen." *Amsterdamer Beiträge zur älteren Germanistik* 64.1 (2007): 325–355.

Rengers, Petrus Ulbo. *Dissertatio juris publici Frisici inauguralis de innovationibus a Saxoniae ducibus in Frisia factis.* Leiden: Cornelium de Pecker, 1776.

Richthofen, Karl Freiherr von. *Untersuchungen über Friesische Rechtsgeschichte.* 1. Berlin: W. Hertz, 1880.

Richthofen, Karl Freiherr von. *Untersuchungen über Friesische Rechtsgeschichte.* 2.1. Berlin: W. Hertz, 1882: 1–608.

Richthofen, Karl Freiherr von. *Untersuchungen über Friesische Rechtsgeschichte.* 2.2. Berlin: W. Hertz, 1882: 609–1325.

Rijksoverheid. *Gemeenten krijgen meer ruimte om huur- en koopwoningen toe te wijzen aan inwoners met lokale binding.* www.rijksoverheid.nl, 13 September 2022. Accessed: 07.12.2022.

Robijn, Vincent. *Het recht van een vrije Friese stad: de stadboeken van Bolsward (1455–1479).* Utrecht: Uitgeverij Verloren, 2005.

Robinson et al. *European Legal History: Sources and Institutions.* 3rd ed. London: Butterworths, 2000.

Rüfner, Thomas. "Substance of Medieval Roman Law: The Development of Private Law" In: Pihlajamäki, Heikki, Markus D. Dubber, and Mark Godfrey (eds.). *The Oxford Handbook of European Legal History.* Oxford: Oxford University Press, 2018: 310–332.

Rüfner, Thomas. "Testamentary Formalities in Roman Law." In: Reid, Keneth, et al. (ed.). *Comparative Succession Law: Volume I: Testamentary Formalities. Oxford: Oxford University Press,* 2011: 2–27.

Schmidt, Heinrich. "Häuptlingsmacht, Freiheitsideologie und bäuerliche Sozialstruktur im spätmittelalterlichen Friesland." *Vorträge und Forschungen* 53 (2001): 285–309.

Schulte, Friedrich von. *Die Geschichte der Quellen und Literatur des Canonischen Rechts von Gratian bis auf die Gegenwart. II. Von Papst Gregor IX. bis zum Concil von Trient.* Stuttgart: Ferdinand Enke, 1877.

Schuur, Jurrien Rinus Gerrit. "De herkomst van het Karelsprivilege." *It Beaken* 67 (2005): 53–78.

Schuur, Jurrien Rinus Gerrit. "De Middeleeuwse Friese Vrijheid. Een sociaal of politiek verschijnsel?" *It Beaken* 67 (2005): 17–30.

Schwerin, Claudius von. *Die Formen der Haussuchung in indogermanischen Rechten.* Mannheim: Bensheimer, 1924.

Seif, Ulrike. "Römisch-kanonisches Erbrecht in mittelalterlichen deutschen Rechtsaufzeichnungen." *Zeitschrift der Savigny-Stiftung für Rechtsgeschichte: Germanistische Abteilung* 122.1 (2005): 87–112.

Sheehan, Michael McMahon. *The will in medieval England: From the conversion of the Anglo-Saxons to the end of the thirteenth century.* Toronto: PIMS, 1963.

Siems, Harald. *Studien zur Lex Frisionum.* Ebelsbach: Rolf Gremer, 1980.

Snell, Bruno. *Leben und Meinungen der Sieben Weisen.* München: Ernst Heimeran, 1938.

Sordi, Bernardo. "Public Law before 'Public Law'" In: Pihlajamäki, Heikki, Markus D. Dubber, and Mark Godfrey (eds.). *The Oxford Handbook of European Legal History.* Oxford: Oxford University Press, 2018: 706–728.

Spreckelmeyer, Goswin. "Zur rechtlichen Funktion frühmittelalterlicher Testamente." in: Classen, Peter, (ed.) *Recht und Schrift im Mittelalter.* Sigmaringen: Thorbecke, 1977.

Spiekhout, Diana. "De pracht van middeleeuwse Frise dracht." In: *Vrijheid, Vetes, Vagevuur: de middeleeuwen in het Noorden.* Leeuwarden: Noordboek/HL Books i.s.m. Fries Museum, 2022: 45–57.

Stein, Peter. *Roman law in European history.* Cambridge: Cambridge University Press, 1999.

Stein, Peter. "Roman law in Medieval Scotland" In: Stein, Peter. The Character and Influence of the Roman Civil Law. Historical Essays. London: Hambledon Press, 1988: 269–317.

Steinacker, Harold. "'Traditio cartae' und, 'traditio per cartam' ein Kontinuitätsproblem." *Archiv für Diplomatik* 5 (1960): 1–72.

Sterringa, Annemarth. "The most miserable women of all: widows in medieval Frisia", in: *Approaches to Old Frisian Philology* 49, 1998: 285–302.

Tamm, Ditlev and Helle Vogt (eds.). *The Danish Medieval Laws.* London, New York: Routledge, 2016.

Telting, Isaac. "De invoering van het Romeinsche regt in Friesland." *Tijdschrift voor het Nederlandsch regt* 1 (1868): 1–57.

Thorlaksson, Helgi. "Feud and Feuding in the Early and High Middle Ages. Working Description and Continuity" in: Netterstrøm, Jeppe Büchert and Bjørn Poulsen (eds.). *Feud in Medieval and Early Modern Europe.* Aarhus: Aarhus University Press, 2007: 69–94.

Tosh, John. *The pursuit of history.* 3rd edition. Harlow: Longman, 1999.

Tragter-Schubert, Martina. "Zur Totschlagsklage im Altwestfriesischen Jüngeren Skeltarecht." *Tijdschrift voor Rechtsgeschiedenis/Legal History Review* 46.3 (1978): 251–256.

Van Iterson, Willem. "Vrouwenvoogdij," *Tijdschrift voor Rechtsgeschiedenis/Legal History Review* 15, no. 1 (1937): 78–96.

Vellinga, E. "Keysers Orkena." *Bijdragen tot de geschiedenis van het notariaat in de provincie Friesland van de aanvang af (midden 15e eeuw) tot de invoering van de Franse wetgeving (1811)*. Leeuwarden: VNAL, 1995.

Vellinga, Evert. "Keysers Orkena: Notarius Publicus." *It Beaken : Meidielingen Fan De Fryske Akademy* 12 (1950): 184–192.

Verhoeven, Gerrit. "De Beoorkonding van Testamenten in Middeleeuws Friesland" in: Mol, J.A (ed.). *Zorgen voor zekerheid. Studies over Friese testamenten in de vijftiende en zestiende eeuw*. Leeuwarden: Fryske Akademy, 1994: 13–36.

Verwijs, Eelco, Jacob Verdam. *Middelnederlandsch woordenboek*. M. Nijhoff, 1941. [Online Edition]. www.ivdnt.org: http://gtb.inl.nl/iWDB/search?actie=article&wdb=MNW&id=50522&lemmodern=schrijver&Betekenis_id=50522.sense.1. Accessed: 28. August 2022.

Vries, Oebele. "*Also dat wy habbet ferdban kloppet* Die Terminologie des Friedebannes bei der Eigentumsübergabe von Immobilien in der altfriesischen Urkundensprache." In: Vries, Oebele. *De Taal van Recht en Vrijheid*. Gorredijk: Bornmeer, 2012: 243–261.

Vries, Oebele. *Asega, is het dingtijd?: de hoogtepunten van de Oudfriese tekstoverlevering*. Leeuwarden: Sterk, 2007.

Vries, Oebele. "Frisonica libertas: Frisian freedom as an instance of medieval liberty." *Journal of Medieval History* 41.2 (2015): 229–248.

Vries, Oebele. "Geschichte der Friesen im Mittelalter: West- und Ostfriesland." In: Munske, Horst Haider (ed.). *Handbuch des Friesischen*. Tübingen: Max Niemeyer Verlag, 2001.

Vries, Oebele. "In een werheyde dissis meckbrewis Altfriesische Eheverträge, insbesondere ihre Terminologie." *Northern Voices: Essays on Old Germanic and Related Topics, Offered to Professor Tette Hofstra* 6 (2008): 241–264.

Vries, Oebele. *Het Heilige Roomse rijk en de Friese vrijheid*. Leeuwarden: De Tille, 1986.

Vries, Oebele. "Literatuur van recht en vrijheid. Geschreven Fries tot 1540." Oppewal, Taeke et al. *Zolang de wind van de wolken waait. Geschiedenis van de Friese literatuur*. Amsterdam: Uitgeverij Bert Bakker, 2006: 21–29.

Vries, Oebele. "*Nijaer is sijd ende pliga allijnna in Freesland* Die Terminologie bei der Ausübung des Näherrechts im Altfriesischen." In: Vries, Oebele. *De Taal van Recht en Vrijheid*. Gorredijk: Bornmeer, 2012: 262–283.

Vries, Oebele. "Seka mit brande ende mit breke. Oudfriese terminologie met betrekking tot het rechtsinstituut 'woesting'" in: Vries, Oebele. *De Taal van Recht en Vrijheid*. Gorredijk: Bornmeer, 2012: 282–307.

Vries, Oebele. "Thet is ac londriucht. Landrechte und Landrecht im mittelalterlichen Friesland." *Amsterdamer Beiträge zur älteren Germanistik* 73.1 (2014): 571–587.

Watson, Alan. *The Digest of Justinian*. Philadelphia: University of Pennsylvania Press, 1985.

Weimar, Peter. 'Liber feudorum', in: *Lexikon des Mittelalters*, vol. 5. Stuttgart: Metzler, [1977]–1999: 1943–1944.

Whitman, James Q. *The Origins of Reasonable Doubt. Theological Roots of the Criminal Trial*. New Haven/London: Yale University Press, 2008.

Wieacker, Franz. "Zum heutigen Stand der Rezeptionsforschung" in: Fries, Erich. *Festschrift für Joseph Klein*. Göttingen: Vandenhoeck & Ruprecht, 1967.

Wiegand, Marvin. "'As good as possible according to the laws': Testamentary Witnesses in Fifteenth-Century Frisia." In: Vermeer, Mark, Wouter Druwé and Maciej Mikuła (eds.). *Testamentary Freedom, Ius Commune and Particular Law (c. 1400–1620)*. Leuven: Peeters, 2023.

Wiesner, Merry E. *Gender, Church and State in Early Modern Germany: Essays by Merry E. Wiesner*. London: Routledge, 2014.

Wiesner, Merry E. *Working women in renaissance Germany*. New Brunswick: Rutgers University Press, 1986.

Zijlstra, Samme. *Het geleerde Friesland—een mythe. Universiteit en maatschappij in Friesland en Stad en Lande ca. 1380–1650*. Leeuwarden, Fryske Akademy, 1996.

Index

www.ingramcontent.com/pod-product-compliance
Lightning Source LLC
Chambersburg PA
CBHW071334230926
51849CB00002B/396
9789004709928